The Cambridge Companion to Edward Albee

Edward Albee, perhaps best known for his acclaimed and infamous 1960s drama *Who's Afraid of Virginia Woolf?*, is one of America's greatest living playwrights. Now in his seventies, he is still writing challenging, award-winning dramas. This collection of new essays on Albee, which includes contributions from the leading commentators on Albee's work, brings fresh critical insights to bear by exploring the full scope of the playwright's career, from his 1959 breakthrough with *The Zoo Story* to his most recent Broadway success, *The Goat, or Who is Sylvia?* (2002). The contributors include scholars of both theatre and English literature, and the essays thus consider the plays both as literary texts and as performed drama. The collection considers a number of Albee's lesser-known and neglected works, provides a comprehensive introduction and overview, and includes an exclusive, original interview with Mr. Albee, on topics spanning his whole career.

D1128921

THE CAMBRIDGE
COMPANION TO
EDWARD ALBEE

EDITED BY
STEPHEN BOTTOMS

CAMBRIDGE
UNIVERSITY PRESS

CAMBRIDGE UNIVERSITY PRESS
Cambridge, New York, Melbourne, Madrid, Cape Town, Singapore, São Paulo

Cambridge University Press
The Edinburgh Building, Cambridge CB2 2RU, UK

Published in the United States of America by Cambridge University Press, New York

www.cambridge.org
Information on this title: www.cambridge.org/9780521834551

© Cambridge University Press 2005

First published 2005

Printed in the United Kingdom at the University Press, Cambridge

A catalogue record for this book is available from the British Library

ISBN-13 978-0-521-83455-1 hardback
ISBN-10 0-521-83455-4 hardback
ISBN-13 978-0-521-54233-3 paperback
ISBN-10 0-521-54233-2 paperback

58843134

All my plays are about people missing the boat, closing down too young, coming to the end of their lives with regret at things not done, as opposed to things done. I find that most people spend too much time living as if they're never going to die. They skid through their lives. Sleep through them sometimes. Anyway, there are only two things to write about – life and death.

Edward Albee, interviewed in 1991

Don't forget the laughs and slapstick so essential to the success of any of my plays.

Albee to the cast of *A Delicate Balance*, 1967

CONTENTS

CONTENTS

ILLUSTRATIONS

NOTES ON CONTRIBUTORS

THOMAS P. ADLER is Professor of English at Purdue University, where he has taught dramatic literature since receiving his Ph.D. from the University of Illinois at Urbana in 1970. He has published widely in the areas of modern British and modern American drama, with a particular emphasis on Williams and Albee. Among his several books is *American Drama, 1940–1960: A Critical History* (1994). This essay marks his fifth appearance in a Cambridge Companion volume.

LINDA BEN-ZVI is Professor of Theatre Studies at Tel Aviv University, Israel, and Professor Emerita in English and Theatre at Colorado State University. She has published *Samuel Beckett* (1986) and *Susan Glaspell: Her Life and Times* (2004). She has edited *Women in Beckett* (1990), *Susan Glaspell: Essays on her Theater and Fiction* (1995), *Theatre in Israel* (1996), *Drawing on Beckett* (2003), and *The Road to the Temple* (2004), and is co-editing with J. Ellen Gainor *The Complete Plays of Susan Glaspell* (2005).

CHRISTOPHER BIGSBY is Professor of American Studies at the University of East Anglia. He has published more than twenty-five books on British and American culture, including *Albee* (1969), *The Black American Writer* (1977), the three-volume *A Critical Introduction to Twentieth Century American Drama* (1982–85), *David Mamet* (1985), *Modern American Drama 1945–2000* (2000), and *Contemporary American Dramatists* (2000). He is the editor of *Contemporary English Drama* (1981), *Arthur Miller and Company* (1990), *The Portable Arthur Miller* (1995), the three-volume *The Cambridge History of American Theatre* (with Don Wilmeth, 1998–2000), and two volumes titled *Writers in Conversation* (2001). He is also the author of four novels: *Hester* (1994), *Pearl* (1995), *Still Lives* (1996), and *Beautiful Dreamer* (2002). Most recently, he has edited *The Cambridge Companion to David Mamet* (2004) and written *Arthur Miller: A Critical Study* (2004).

STEPHEN BOTTOMS is Professor of Drama and Theatre Studies at the University of Leeds. He is the author of *The Theatre of Sam Shepard: States of Crisis* (1998), *Albee: Who's Afraid of Virginia Woolf?* (2000), and *Playing Underground: A Critical History of the 1960s Off-Off-Broadway Movement* (2004). His articles include work on performance art and performance studies, as well as theatre and drama, and he works regularly as a theatre director.

JOHN M. CLUM is Professor of Theatre Studies and English and Chair of the Department of Theatre Studies at Duke University. He has published essays on Tennessee Williams, Sam Shepard, and Larry Kramer, among others. His books include *Acting Gay: Male Homosexuality in Modern Drama* (1992), *Something for the Boys: Musical Theater and Gay Culture* (2001), and *He's All Man: Learning Masculinity, Gayness and Love from American Movies* (2002). He is also a playwright whose work has been produced in theatres across the United States.

RUBY COHN is Professor Emerita of Comparative Drama at the University of California (Davis). She has written and edited some dozen books and a hundred articles on contemporary drama.

J. ELLEN GAINOR is Professor of Theatre and Associate Dean of the Graduate School at Cornell University. She is the author of *Shaw's Daughters: Dramatic and Narrative Constructions of Gender* (1992) and *Susan Glaspell in Context: American Theater, Culture, and Politics, 1915–48* (2001), both of which received *Choice* awards for outstanding scholarship. She has edited the collections *Imperialism and Theatre* (1995) and *Performing America: Cultural Nationalism in American Theater* (with Jeffrey Mason, 1999), and is currently co-editing with Linda Ben-Zvi *The Complete Plays of Susan Glaspell*. She is also an editor of the forthcoming *Norton Anthology of Drama*.

PHILIP C. KOLIN is Professor of English at the University of Southern Mississippi and the founding co-editor of *Studies in American Drama, 1945 – Present*. He has written extensively on Albee, David Rabe, and Tennessee Williams. He has edited, among many other books, *Critical Essays on Edward Albee* (with J. Madison Davis, 1986), *Conversations with Edward Albee* (1988), *David Rabe: A Stage History and Bibliography* (1988), *Speaking on Stage: Interviews with Contemporary American Playwrights* (with Colby H. Kullman, 1996), and *The Undiscovered Country: The Later Plays of Tennessee Williams* (2002). He wrote *Williams: A Streetcar Named Desire* for the Cambridge Plays in Production Series (2000), and most recently edited *The Tennessee Williams Encyclopedia* for Greenwood (2004). Kolin has also published several books on Shakespeare and is currently the General Editor of the Routledge Shakespeare Criticism Series. With Maureen Curley he has founded a new poetry journal entitled *Lilies: A Journal of Christian Poetry*.

GERRY MCCARTHY was until recently Professor of Theatre Studies at the University of Ulster. He has particular interests in acting and in the critical languages which address processes of acting and other media of performance. He has worked practically as a director and as an acting coach in France, Canada, and the United Kingdom. His published work ranges from Shakespeare and Molière to Beckett and contemporary American dramatists. He is the author of *Edward Albee* (1987) and *The Theatres of Molière* (2002).

BRENDA MURPHY is Professor of English at the University of Connecticut. Among her books are *American Realism and American Drama, 1880–1940* (1987), *Tennessee Williams and Elia Kazan: A Collaboration in the Theatre* (1992), *Miller: Death of a Salesman* (1995), *Congressional Theatre: Dramatizing McCarthyism on Stage, Film, and Television* (1999), *O'Neill: Long Day's Journey Into Night* (2001), and, as editor, *The Cambridge Companion to American Women Playwrights* (1999).

MATTHEW ROUDANÉ is Professor and Chair of the Department of English at Georgia State University in Atlanta. He has written two books on Albee: *Understanding Edward Albee* (1987) and *Who's Afraid of Virginia Woolf?: Necessary Fictions, Terrifying Realities* (1990), and is the editor of both *The Cambridge Companion to Tennessee Williams* (1997) and *The Cambridge Companion to Sam Shepard* (2002). His other books include *Conversations with Arthur Miller* (1987), *Public Issues, Private Tensions: Contemporary American Drama* (1993), and *Approaches to Teaching Miller's Death of a Salesman* (1995). Roudané is editor of the *South Atlantic Review* and served as dramaturge for 7 Stages Theatre in Atlanta, where he worked with Joseph Chaikin, who directed Albee's *A Delicate Balance* in 2002. As a Fulbright scholar, he taught American drama at the Universidad Complutense de Madrid, Spain, in 2004.

RAKESH H. SOLOMON teaches in the Department of Theatre and Drama at Indiana University, Bloomington. He is the author of *Albee in Performance: The Playwright as Director*, forthcoming from Indiana University Press, and is currently completing *Culture, Politics, and Performance in Colonial India, 1753–1947*. He has published numerous journal articles on contemporary American theatre as well as British and Indian theatre, and has contributed essays to *Edward Albee: A Casebook* (2003) as well as

Alan Ayckbourn: A Casebook (1991). Other essays are forthcoming in *Theatre International: Essays on the Theory and Praxis of World Theatre, Popular Theatres of South and Southeast Asia*, and *Re/writing National Theatre Histories*. A past editor of *South Asian Review*, Solomon has received senior fellowships from the National Endowment for the Humanities and the American Institute of Indian Studies.

ACKNOWLEDGMENTS

I would like to express my thanks to all the contributors to this book – for their cooperation in all things, and for their prompt responses to my inquiries. Thanks to them, my first experience of editing a collection has proved a less onerous task than I had imagined it might be. I am especially grateful to Matthew Roudané, for his advice in the early stage of approaching contributors, and to Tom Adler, for graciously consenting to act as "editor" on my own chapter for this collection – and in doing so, offering such useful feedback, and not asking for cuts! I would also like to thank Richard Bapty, at Glasgow University Library, for his advice on all things bibliographic, and Vicki Cooper, my ever-enthusiastic commissioning editor at Cambridge University Press.

Special thanks are due to Edward Albee himself, for consenting to be interviewed for this collection, for his swift approval of the resulting transcript, for permission to consult his closed archive at the Billy Rose Theatre Collection of New York Public Library, and for his kind permission to reproduce brief quotations from the unpublished manuscript of his play *Occupant*, in the essays by Ruby Cohn and Christopher Bigsby. I am also very grateful to Mr. Albee's assistant, Jakob Holder, for his unstinting help in facilitating all this.

NOTES ON THE TEXT

Edward Albee's plays frequently use three-dotted ellipses . . . to suggest brief pauses, or as indications of how an actor is to pace a speech. Since quotations including such ellipses feature throughout the essays in this collection, I have chosen to use square-bracketed ellipses [. . .] as an indicator of those instances where the author of the chapter has abbreviated the quotation itself. Albee's own dots remain unbracketed, and thus clearly distinguishable. To avoid unnecessarily cluttering the text, however, ellipses in quotations from sources *other than* Albee's plays are indicated with dots but not brackets, as is conventional.

Dates attributed to Albee's plays indicate the year of first performance, rather than of composition or publication, unless the text clearly indicates otherwise (for example, in the case of an unperformed play).

CHRONOLOGY

1928　Born March 12 in Washington D.C. to Louise Harvey. Adopted by Reed and Frances Albee at two weeks of age. Raised by this wealthy family, inheritors of fortune made by Keith-Albee chain of vaudeville theatres.

1939　Leaves Rye County day school.

1940　Goes to Lawrenceville boarding school, New Jersey.

1943　Expelled from Lawrenceville. Enrolls at Valley Forge Military Academy, Pennsylvania.

1944　Expelled from Valley Forge. Enrolls at Choate School, Connecticut.

1946　First play, *The Schism*, published in *Choate Literary Magazine*. Graduates from Choate and goes to Trinity College, Hartford, Connecticut. Expelled for failure to attend classes and chapel.

1947　Works for WYNC radio.

1949　Enrolls briefly at Columbia University. Writes three-act drama of familial and sexual tensions, *The City of People* (unpublished, unproduced). Following fight with adoptive mother, Albee leaves home and moves to Greenwich Village, working odd jobs and writing poetry and prose.

1951　Writes *Ye Watchers and Ye Lonely Ones*, a play in three scenes, dealing with struggles of four gay men (unpublished, unproduced).

1952　Moves in with composer William Flanagan, who becomes an important mentor figure.

1953　Meets Thornton Wilder, who encourages Albee to write plays. Writes *The Making of a Saint*, a verse play set in a railroad station, and dedicates it to Wilder (unpublished, unproduced). (Other unpublished plays and play fragments from the 1950s include *The Invalid*, *The Ice Age*, *An End to Summer*, *The Dispossessed*, and others.)

1955　Begins work as telegram delivery boy for Western Union.

1958   Writes *The Zoo Story*. Stops work with Western Union.

1959   September: *The Zoo Story* premieres in German, in translation by Pinkas Braun, at Berlin's Schiller Theater Werkstadt, in double bill with Samuel Beckett's *Krapp's Last Tape*.

1960   January: *The Zoo Story* receives American premiere at the off-Broadway Provincetown Playhouse. Directed by Milton Katselas, it is again paired with *Krapp's Last Tape*. In April *The Death of Bessie Smith* premieres in Berlin at the Schlosspark Theater, and *The Sandbox* at the Jazz Gallery in New York. *FAM and YAM* premieres in Westport, Connecticut, in August.

1961   January: *The American Dream* premieres in New York at the York Playhouse, with Sudie Bond as Grandma. Initially in double bill with Albee's adaptation of Melville's short story *Bartleby* (written as libretto for William Flanagan's operatic score), but *Bartleby* is swiftly closed and replaced in March by American premiere of *The Death of Bessie Smith*. *Dream* and *Bessie* both directed by Alan Schneider.

1962   October: *Who's Afraid of Virginia Woolf?* premieres on Broadway at the Billy Rose Theatre. Directed by Alan Schneider, with Uta Hagen as Martha and Arthur Hill as George. Critical response is mixed, and Albee is controversially denied the Pulitzer Prize for Drama for 1962–63. However, production is an instant box-office hit and runs until 1964, when it transfers to London for British premiere, with stars intact.

1963   October: Albee's adaptation of Carson McCullers's novella *The Ballad of the Sad Café* premieres on Broadway at the Martin Beck Theatre. Directed by Alan Schneider, with Colleen Dewhurst as Miss Amelia. Also that fall, Albee and his producers, Richard Barr and Clinton Wilder, use some of profits from *Virginia Woolf* to establish the Playwrights' Unit at the Village South Theatre, providing a platform for untested new playwrights. Albee also makes first attempt at directing his own work, with a low-profile production of *The Zoo Story* in Pennsylvania.

1964   December: *Tiny Alice* premieres at the Billy Rose Theatre, prompting critical controversy. Directed by Alan Schneider, with John Gielgud as Brother Julian and Irene Worth as Miss Alice.

1965   British premiere of *Tiny Alice* staged in London by Royal Shakespeare Company. Albee is reconciled with adoptive mother after seventeen-year estrangement (father died in 1961, while Albee was incommunicado).

1966   January: Albee's adaptation of James Purdy's novel *Malcolm* premieres on Broadway at the Schubert Theatre. Critically panned, it closes inside a week. In September *A Delicate Balance* opens at the Martin Beck Theatre, starring Jessica Tandy and Hume Cronyn, and goes on to win Pulitzer Prize. Both plays directed by Alan Schneider. Meanwhile, Warner Brothers premieres Mike Nichols's film version of *Who's Afraid of Virginia Woolf?*, starring Elizabeth Taylor and Richard Burton, and Albee is brought in as script doctor on a musical adaptation of Truman Capote's *Breakfast at Tiffany's* (closes in December during out-of-town try-outs).

1967   November: Albee's "Americanization" of Giles Cooper's play *Everything in the Garden* opens on Broadway at the Plymouth Theatre, directed by Peter Glenville, with Barbara Bel Geddes and Barry Nelson.

1968   September: following March premiere at Buffalo's Studio Arena, *Box* and *Quotations from Chairman Mao Tse-Tung* open on Broadway at the Billy Rose Theatre, in repertory with other Albee shorts. Directed by Alan Schneider.

1969   British premiere of *A Delicate Balance* staged in London by Royal Shakespeare Company.

1971   March: *All Over* premieres on Broadway at the Martin Beck Theatre, under John Gielgud's direction, with Jessica Tandy and Colleen Dewhurst as Wife and Mistress. Playwrights' Unit closes. Albee begins life-long relationship with sculptor Jonathan Thomas.

1972   British premiere of *All Over* staged in London by Royal Shakespeare Company.

1973   American Film Theater releases film version of *A Delicate Balance*, directed by Tony Richardson, with Katharine Hepburn and Paul Scofield.

1975   January: *Seascape* premieres on Broadway at the Schubert Theatre. Directed by Albee, starring Deborah Kerr and Barry Nelson. Goes on to win Pulitzer Prize.

1976   March: *Listening* premieres in U.K. as radio play on BBC Radio 3, codirected by Albee and John Tydeman. In December *Counting the Ways* premieres in London at the Royal National Theatre, directed by Bill Bryden. Albee also directs acclaimed Broadway revival of *Who's Afraid of Virginia Woolf?* with Colleen Dewhurst and Ben Gazzara.

1977   January: *Listening* and *Counting the Ways* receive American stage premieres together at the Hartford Stage Company, Connecticut, under Albee's direction. Angela Lansbury and William Prince star.

1980 January: *The Lady from Dubuque* premieres on Broadway at the Morosco Theatre, directed by Alan Schneider. Irene Worth takes the title role. It closes after twelve performances.

1981 March: Albee's adaptation of Vladimir Nabokov's novel *Lolita* premieres on Broadway at the Brooks Atkinson Theatre, with Donald Sutherland as Humbert Humbert. Produced by Jerry Sherlock and directed by Frank Dunlop. Albee disowns the production, which closes swiftly. Also that year, he writes *Another Part of the Zoo*, a variation on the scenario of *The Zoo Story*, for showing at a private benefit function.

1983 April: *The Man Who Had Three Arms* opens on Broadway at Lyceum Theatre, following a try-out run in Chicago the previous fall. Directed by Albee, with Robert Drivas, it closes swiftly. In the following month, *Finding the Sun* premieres under Albee's direction at the University of Northern Colorado, Greeley. Also staged at University of California at Irvine, in double bill with another new piece, *Walking*, which is subsequently abandoned by Albee.

1987 May: *Marriage Play* premieres at the English Theatre in Vienna, Austria, under Albee's direction, with Kathleen Butler and Tom Klunis. American premiere comes five years later in 1992, at the Alley Theatre of Houston, again with Klunis, and with Albee directing.

1988 Named Distinguished Professor of Drama at the University of Houston, where Albee teaches annual playwriting class.

1989 Death of Albee's adoptive mother, Frances Cotter Albee.

1991 June: *Three Tall Women* premieres at Vienna's English Theatre, under Albee's direction, with Myra Carter as A.

1992 April: *The Lorca Play* premieres under Albee's direction at University of Houston but is subsequently withdrawn by the playwright. July: American premiere of *Three Tall Women* at River Arts Repertory, Woodstock, directed by Lawrence Sacharow.

1993 October: *Fragments* premieres at the Ensemble Theatre of Cincinnati, Ohio, under Albee's direction. The same fall, New York's Signature Theatre Company opens season of works by Albee, which includes New York premieres of *Finding the Sun*, *Marriage Play* and *Fragments*.

1994 February: New York City premiere of Sacharow's production of *Three Tall Women* at the off-Broadway Vineyard Theatre, with Myra Carter, Marian Seldes, and Jordan Baker. Transfers to Promenade Theatre, and wins Pulitzer Prize. Meanwhile, British premiere of *Three Tall Women* opens at the Theatre Royal,

Haymarket, before transfer to Wyndham's Theatre in West End. Directed by Anthony Page, with Maggie Smith.

1996 April: Broadway revival of *A Delicate Balance*, directed by Gerald Gutierrez, with George Grizzard, Elaine Stritch, and Rosemary Harris. In the fall, in London, the Almeida Theatre's acclaimed production of *Who's Afraid of Virginia Woolf?*, with Diana Rigg and David Suchet, transfers to West End run at the Aldwych Theatre. Directed by Howard Davies.

1997 October: major British revival of *A Delicate Balance* opens at the Haymarket Theatre. Directed by Anthony Page, with Maggie Smith.

1998 September: *The Play About the Baby* premieres in London at the Almeida Theatre. Directed by Howard Davies, with Frances de la Tour.

2001 February: American premiere of *The Play About the Baby*, at New York's Century Center for the Performing Arts. Directed by David Esbjornson, with Marian Seldes. May: British premieres of *Finding the Sun* and *Marriage Play* at the Royal National Theatre, directed by Anthony Page.

2002 March: *The Goat, or Who is Sylvia?* premieres on Broadway at the Golden Theatre, directed by David Esbjornson, with Bill Pullman and Mercedes Ruehl. Wins Tony award for best new play on Broadway. Meanwhile, projected premiere of *Occupant*, at the Signature Theatre Company, is cancelled owing to illness of its star, Anne Bancroft. (As of 2004, the play remains unproduced and unpublished.)

2004 April: Almeida Theatre's British premiere production of *The Goat* transfers to West End run at the Apollo Theatre. Directed by Anthony Page, with Jonathan Pryce.
May: *Peter and Jerry*, a double bill of *The Zoo Story* and its new companion piece, *Homelife*, premieres at the Hartford Stage Company, Connecticut. Directed by Pam McKinnon.

Figure 1. Edward Albee, circa 1962.

I

STEPHEN BOTTOMS

Introduction:
The man who had three lives

It is now more than forty years since Edward Albee's *Who's Afraid of Virginia Woolf?* – the play for which he is still best known – gave him his first Broadway hit and propelled him into the front rank of American playwrights. Today, he is frequently listed alongside Eugene O'Neill, Tennessee Williams, and Arthur Miller as one of the nation's great (white, male) dramatists of the twentieth century. Other candidates for that shortlist have appeared since (David Mamet, perhaps Sam Shepard, Tony Kushner), but these writers, operating primarily in the decentered, post-1960s world of off-Broadway and regional theatre, have never been Broadway mainstays in the way their predecessors were. Thus Albee, who hit Broadway just before Broadway's preeminence as a launching pad for serious drama began seriously to be questioned, has for many years tended to be seen as "the last of the line," and, consequently, as a figure not only of the establishment, but also of the past. In a fragmented, postmodern theatre culture full of young pretenders and competing, multicultural voices, it is all too easy to forget that the somewhat patrician figure of Edward Albee was himself once a controversial young iconoclast, and indeed that, throughout his long career, he has consistently refused to do what is expected of him – and has the sling and arrow scars to prove it.

Albee's somewhat paradoxical position in American culture was perhaps summed up by the Kennedy Center's honors ceremony of 1996, at which he was lauded by (the perhaps equally paradoxical) President Clinton: "Tonight our nation – born in rebellion – pays tribute to you, Edward Albee. In your rebellion, the American theatre was reborn."[1] Still sufficient of a rebel to become the first playwright to provide a sympathetic treatment of bestiality on the Broadway stage – with 2002's *The Goat, or Who is Sylvia?* – Albee seems to delight, even now, in prodding and unsettling conventional sensibilities, often with a kind of vaudevillian glee. And yet he is also a deeply serious, highly erudite figure, very much a member of the literary establishment. He is, in short, a writer of many faces, many moods, and any

I

assessment of Albee's fascinating, diverse body of plays should, perhaps, be similarly multifaceted. In assembling perspectives from a wide variety of critics, of different ages and scholarly backgrounds, this collection seeks to be open-ended rather than conclusive in its assessments. The views of the contributors, as the old line goes, do not necessarily represent those of the editor – and rightly so.

Nevertheless, in introducing this book, it is perhaps useful to provide a concise mapping of Albee's career, against which to contextualize subsequent chapters. That career, it seems to me, can be divided roughly into three periods – early, middle, and (if he will forgive me) late – much as, in his 1991 play *Three Tall Women*, Albee refracts the depiction of a woman's life into three "ages."

Albee's early career was characterized by a long apprenticeship of trial-and-error experimentation, followed by a sudden, almost meteoric rise to success and notoriety. During his twenties, after having decisively walked out on his wealthy, adoptive parents, he lived inconspicuously among the artists and bohemians of New York's Greenwich Village. He tried his hand at several different genres and styles of playwriting – from the three-act naturalism-cum-melodrama of *The City of People* (1949), to the metaphysical parable format of *The Making of a Saint* (1953–54). Written in rigidly metered rhyming couplets and dedicated to Thornton Wilder (whose *Pullman Car Hiawatha* seems to have been a key influence), the latter depicts a group of passengers waiting at the station for the train of life. Like his other early manuscripts (now held in the Albee archive of New York Public Library's Billy Rose Theatre Collection), *Making of a Saint* seems at once entirely untypical of Albee's later work, and yet haunted by his now familiar existential preoccupations: will one choose to *take* the train of life, or remain seated in the delusory security of the station? Similarly, in *The Invalid* (1952), a young man of twenty-four (Albee's own age, at that point) is faced with the choice between "participating" and "not participating," and opts for the "extraordinary lethargy" of the latter – much as Tobias in *A Delicate Balance* or Charlie in *Seascape* were to do – and so becomes the canceled-out figure of the title (invalid; in-valid). In *The City of People*, the young Alan attempts to make the opposite choice, by accepting the love of a woman, Anna, who might help him to escape the rarefied, intellectual ivory-tower environment in which he has been raised by his professorial father, and to face the daunting yet thrilling urban sprawl of the title – and in doing so, to replace the comfortingly abstract constructions of words and ideas with *real* experience. Alan, though, prefiguring other Albee children, was born "perfect but lame," and – as the cherished, symbolic substitute for his now-dead mother – has always been protected and guarded jealously by his father

George. Their relationship, Anna suggests, has a "delicate balance" that she is afraid to tamper with: will Alan cope with having to confront the world at large?

With the benefit of hindsight, these early manuscripts seem redolent with "Albee-esque" concerns, but they are also – as the playwright himself would be the first to acknowledge – both derivative and unwieldy. It was not until 1958, at age thirty, that Albee finally found his own voice as a dramatist, when he sat down to write *The Zoo Story* – the one-act play that was to make his name. Drawing on the relative poverty of his own life at the time, and on his experiences while working in "the city of people" as a Western Union telegram delivery boy, Albee created the menacing, world-weary, but highly articulate character of Jerry, to give unfettered expression to his sharply critical view of the conventional, bourgeois world embodied by Peter. Albee later described the experience of writing the play as a kind of revelation for him; it was the first time he felt as if the characters' language and rhythms were simply flowing, unforced, from his subconscious. *The Zoo Story* also proved a revelation in the context of the American theatre of the time, embodying onstage the restless, youthful energy of the disenfranchised "Beat" generation, as well as providing a homegrown response to the recent innovations of European "absurdist" playwrights such as Samuel Beckett (whose *Krapp's Last Tape* Albee's play was initially paired with in double bill).

Premiering in Greenwich Village in January 1960, in the same Provincetown Playhouse that had launched Eugene O'Neill's career in the 1910s, *The Zoo Story* single-handedly transformed New York's off-Broadway theatre scene into a viable arena for the discovery and development of new American playwrights. Thanks to a ruling by Actors' Equity, producers at small alternative theatres had been able, since the start of the 1950s, to mount fully professional productions on a lower wage-scale than Broadway, but they had nevertheless tended to "play safe" during that decade. Off-Broadway theatre in the 1950s was largely characterized by revivals of the kind of classic plays that were no longer commercially viable on Broadway itself. *The Zoo Story*, however, with its compelling and controversial dialogue, and its affordably low-budget "two men and a park bench" minimalism, drew the attention of critics, producers, and public alike to the regenerative potential of off-Broadway as a launch-site for new playwriting voices. Albee became chief advocate and poster boy for this new "movement," writing a string of further one-acts over the next couple of years, and declaring in the *New York Times* that the Broadway theatre, driven primarily by commercial concerns, "panders to the public need for self-congratulation and reassurance, and presents a false picture of ourselves to ourselves . . . For it is a lazy public that produces a slothful and irresponsible theatre."[2]

Given such provocations, it is hardly surprising that Albee's own first Broadway production, with his first multi-act play, *Who's Afraid of Virginia Woolf?* (1962), attracted even more interest and controversy than had his previous work. Fusing domestic realism with the cyclical verbal interplay and mysterious uncertainties characteristic of the so-called "theatre of the absurd," this play attracted virulent hostility from some critics, and qualified, rather condescending praise from others. To the surprise of many, it also proved instantly popular with audiences. This brutal, hilarious play – depicting the drunken, late-night confrontation of college professor George and his wife Martha, enacted for the benefit of their unsuspecting guests – ran on Broadway for two years, and later spawned a highly successful movie version. With some of the profits from the show, Albee and his producers Richard Barr and Clinton Wilder established the Albarwild Playwrights' Unit at the Village South Theatre in Greenwich Village, where new one-act plays by promising writers were staged, free of charge, to invited audiences every weekend. Surviving from 1963 to 1971, the Unit brought professional standards to the Village's burgeoning "off-off-Broadway" scene, and provided a testing-ground for a generation of young playwrights whose careers were partially inspired by Albee's example. Writers as diverse as Amiri Baraka, Adrienne Kennedy, Lanford Wilson, John Guare, and Sam Shepard all continue to acknowledge a profound debt to him.

Albee's problem in the mid-1960s, however, was knowing how to sustain and develop his own writing career, now that he had reached the lofty heights of Broadway success. Determined to keep experimenting with form and content, he resisted the temptation to settle into a predictable, easily marketed dramatic style. One option might have been to retreat to the relative safety of smaller-scale, off-Broadway theatre, but Albee, Barr, and Wilder believed that – having established a foothold on the Great White Way – it was their responsibility to keep up the challenge to its complacency; to insist that popular accessibility and aesthetic integrity were not necessarily inimical. The afterglow of *Who's Afraid of Virginia Woolf?* guaranteed them a Broadway honeymoon of sorts. Albee's delicate adaptation of Carson McCullers's novella *The Ballad of the Sad Café* was respectfully received in 1963, running for a healthy (if not rosy) 123 performances, and in the following year his next original play, *Tiny Alice*, became the talking-point of the season. This complex puzzle-box of a play, a meditation on the uncertain relationships between religion, sexuality, and reality itself, might have been ridiculed and dismissed outright had it appeared at a later stage of Albee's career, but post-*Virginia Woolf* it generated sufficient intrigued, infuriated debate among audiences to do decent business.

By January 1966, however, when Albee's second novel adaptation, based on James Purdy's *Malcolm*, closed on Broadway inside a week, after receiving universally dismissive reviews, it was clear that the honeymoon was over. Undramatic and meandering, *Malcolm* was, most agree, a serious miscalculation on Albee's part. With hindsight, it can also be seen as marking the beginning of the long middle period of his career. Over the next decade and a half, Albee's star went into decline with critics and public alike, as show after show closed on Broadway after runs that were modest at best. Part of the problem was that critics tended to compare every new play unfavorably to *Who's Afraid of Virginia Woolf?* (even though the original reviews for that piece had themselves been distinctly mixed). Beyond that, though, Albee was doing what he had always done, following his creative nose wherever it led – which was often into distinctly uncommercial territory. Some of his work proved too formalistic or intellectually oriented to be popularly appealing (as with 1968's *Box-Mao-Box* triptych, in which static, disconnected figures talked at cross-purposes), some of it too bleak or depressing (as with the starkly beautiful *All Over*, from 1971, in which a dying man's family wait for him to expire). As if in prophetic anticipation of troubles to come, Albee wrote in a June 1965 letter to his former lover and mentor William Flanagan that he felt caught

> twixt the devil of compromising for public acceptance (V. Woolfs don't come along every day, with their acceptance coming from only partly the right reasons) and the deep blue sea of writing good plays as one wants to write them, having them done well, *be* good plays, and yet have them rejected, thereby becoming a "failure" because one does not have continuing public and critical "success."[3]

There were, of course, occasional silver linings to the grey cloud that Albee now found himself under – most notably the two Pulitzer Prizes that he won for *A Delicate Balance* (1966) and *Seascape* (1975). Even these plays, however, had closed after disappointing Broadway runs (the latter survived for just sixty-five performances), and endured largely negative reviews. Indeed, when *A Delicate Balance* won the Pulitzer, there were those who suggested that this was merely in belated recognition of *Who's Afraid of Virginia Woolf?*, which had controversially been denied the prize when the award scheme's board of trustees had overturned the recommendation of their drama panel. Others argued, still more cynically, that Albee had created a play that was deliberately similar to *Virginia Woolf*, in a bid to recapture popular and critical attention. This depiction of an alcohol-soaked, upper-middle-class family teetering on the brink of terminal implosion is, in fact, far more muted and restrained in tone than its biting, spitting predecessor – more Chekhovian lament than Strindbergian dance of death. The play's relatively uncommercial status was underlined by Walter Kerr's *New York Times* review, which dismissed it as a "void in which the characters live and have their non-being."[4] Conversely, though, *Village Voice* critic Michael Smith – a champion of off- and off-off-Broadway theatre – regarded *A Delicate Balance*'s box-set naturalism and socially privileged characters as embodying the values of Broadway, "which I despise."[5] Even today, the real worth of *A Delicate Balance* remains hotly disputed: among contributors to this volume, for example, Thomas Adler rates it as "the pivotal American drama of the second half of the twentieth century," while Ruby Cohn sees it as merely "diluted *Virginia Woolf.*"

Among Albee's Pulitzer winners, *Seascape* might more plausibly be accused of being shaped to fit commercial requirements. The first of Albee's plays to undergo "out-of-town try-outs" on its way to Broadway, it was also the first to be substantially revised during rehearsals, as Albee cut his convoluted three-act script drastically down to just two. The resulting play, while playfully linking personal growth to the Darwinian theory of evolution, works primarily as a kind of light comedy of mismatched manners – as two humans and two giant lizards meet on a beach and compare notes on existence. The major surgery to which Albee subjected *Seascape* seems indicative of the pressure he was under at the time: after years of critical hostility, his confidence in his own abilities seems to have been severely dented. His once prolific creativity had also tailed off markedly since the late 1960s. After presenting a new Broadway show every year for seven years (1962 to 1968), he completed only two during the next decade – *Seascape* and *All Over*. From 1968 he also dispensed with the services of his ever-present but much-criticized director, Alan Schneider. Albee elected to direct the premiere of *Seascape* himself.

Throughout the 1970s Albee also struggled with alcoholism, but while his "drying out" toward the end of the decade seems to have facilitated a new burst of creativity – with three new plays appearing in the four years at the start of the 1980s – the critical responses to his work proved more hostile than ever. *The Lady from Dubuque* (1980), *Lolita* (1981, adapted from Nabokov's novel), and *The Man Who Had Three Arms* (1983) were all assaulted with a ferocity out of all proportion to whatever crimes against taste or dramaturgy they may have committed. Albee, it seemed, was now yesterday's man, a remnant of the 1960s completely out of place in the new, Reaganite 1980s. But if Broadway had lost patience with Albee, the same may have been true in reverse. *The Man Who Had Three Arms*, in which a demented circuit lecturer rails against his audience (as "played" by the actual theatre audience), was a brutally scathing, deliberately "tasteless" attack on complacent, middlebrow values. Albee must surely have known that it was never going to run for long on Broadway (even Richard Barr refused to back it as producer), but he defiantly insisted on having *The Man Who* mounted there anyway. Biographer Mel Gussow reports that, on the morning the reviews came out, Albee "bought a copy of the *Times* in Times Square, read the deadly notice, and said to [his partner] Jonathan Thomas, 'Oh well. That's that. Let's go home.'"[6]

It was nearly two decades before another new Albee play premiered on Broadway. The 1980s marked the beginning of Albee's third career phase, during which he had, in effect, to start again from scratch, gradually rebuilding a life and reputation for himself. Regarded as a failed has-been in the New York theatre world, Albee decided to go where he was wanted, and began accepting invitations from colleges and universities to speak, to teach, and to direct plays. He developed, for example, a longstanding relationship with the University of Houston, in Texas, where he still regularly teaches a spring-semester playwriting class – thus continuing his commitment to mentoring new writing talent. Yet Albee's own writing benefited, too, from this period in the theatrical "wilderness." Various new plays were written to commission for small low-profile theatres, including *Finding the Sun* (1983) for the University of Northern Colorado, *Marriage Play* (1987) for the English Theatre in Vienna, Austria, and *Fragments* (1993) for the Ensemble Theatre of Cincinnati. At first glance, these relatively short pieces might also seem fairly insubstantial: indeed, *Fragments* is subtitled "A Sit-Around," in self-deprecating recognition of that fact that the characters simply sit around and talk, without apparent purpose or "through-line." Yet closer examination of these plays reveals all kinds of intriguing undercurrents in mood and characterization, as well as some ingenious formal games with scene structures. Released from the pressure of being a "major American playwright," writing "major plays" for Broadway, Albee seems to have relished the chance to return to writing unassuming "chamber pieces" for more intimate spaces, just as he had with *Listening* and *Counting the Ways* – two companion one-acts that first appeared together in 1977 at the Hartford Stage Company, in Connecticut.

After ten years as *persona non grata* in New York, Albee's reputation among audiences and critics there began to be rehabilitated in 1993, when the nonprofit Signature Theatre Company launched an entire season dedicated to limited-run productions of Albee's shorter, lesser-known plays: a reappraisal was in the offing. The following year, Albee's *Three Tall Women* – first seen in Viennese obscurity in 1991 – opened off-Broadway and won him his most favorable notices in decades, as well as a third Pulitzer Prize. Frequently over the years, Albee's work had been accused of seeming too coldly intellectual or unfeeling, but *Three Tall Women* shattered that stereotype, by providing a strangely affectionate portrait of an elderly, dying woman, modeled directly on Albee's recently deceased mother, at three stages of her life. The play eschews sentimentality, in favor of a warts-and-all depiction of a cantankerous, bigoted old woman, viewed nonjudgmentally but from a certain wryly amused distance. With this moving, accessible character study – written with the same kind of concise, unassuming directness that characterizes much of his later work – Albee deservedly found himself with an unexpected hit on his hands. *Three Tall Women* played at the 400-seat Promenade Theatre for 582 performances – a run exceeded in length by only one previous Albee play, *Who's Afraid of Virginia Woolf?*

Three Tall Women was swiftly followed by acclaimed revivals of *A Delicate Balance*, both on Broadway and in London's West End, thereby completing Albee's rehabilitation. Suddenly he was being showered with awards and honors, and feted as the respected elder statesman of the American theatre. This late career revival was something that had eluded Tennessee Williams, who had died in 1983 after twenty years of critical opprobrium, and even Eugene O'Neill, whose late great works were only fully appreciated after his death. Albee, however, has remained in no doubt as to the fickleness of fashion and popularity, and has continued to do things his own way. Since the mid-1990s he has completed two new plays that are as distinctive and original as anything he had written previously. *The Play About the Baby*, aptly described by *Newsday* as "an exhilarating, wicked, devastating piece of emotional terrorism," depicts the theft and disappearance of a young couple's infant as a kind of savage vaudeville routine.[7] Although its premiere at London's Almeida Theatre in 1998 was received coolly by reviewers, it went on to play a very healthy run off-Broadway in 2001, and – as the commentaries in this volume make clear – is already coming to be regarded as one of his most important plays.

Baby's disorientating combination of bouncing wit and bleakly tragic vision also prefigured *The Goat, or Who is Sylvia?* Opening on Broadway in 2002, this extraordinary piece about a prize-winning architect helplessly smitten with a farmyard animal careers from comedy-of-manners into a titanic marital confrontation bloodier than anything in the Albee canon. Prompting a critical controversy (as opposed to dismissive ridicule) comparable to that accorded to *Tiny Alice* in 1964, *The Goat* ran for a year, won a Tony award, and was shortlisted for yet another Pulitzer Prize. Judging by current form, Albee's "late" career phase may yet turn out to be his richest and most productive, just as was O'Neill's. In 2004, as if to demonstrate his having come full circle, back to the kind of acclaim he received early in his career, Albee completed a new companion piece for *The Zoo Story*, titled

Homelife: yet another marital encounter, this one charts Peter's day with his wife Ann, immediately prior to his fateful meeting with Jerry in Central Park.

* * *

The essays in this collection are arranged in a broadly chronological order, in relation to the plays they discuss. Thus, for example, the first piece, Philip Kolin's essay on Albee's early one-acts, is followed by Matthew Roudané's on *Who's Afraid of Virginia Woolf?* These pieces both provide very persuasive variations on the traditional readings of these plays – with Kolin emphasizing in particular the aspects of social commentary and angry satire apparent in the breakthrough works, and Roudané focusing more on the interpersonal dimensions of *Virginia Woolf*, which of course also border on the metaphysical, thanks to George and Martha's preoccupation with questions of truth and illusion. Albee's unusual ability to fuse social relevance with existential profundity has, of course, been one of the defining features of his work, and these first two essays establish this clearly.

The third essay changes gear somewhat, with John Clum offering a rather more skeptical perspective on Albee's next two original plays, *Tiny Alice* and *A Delicate Balance*. Treating them both as portraits of marriages (an unusual move in the case of the former), Clum emphasizes – like Roudané – the ways in which the leading characters deceive themselves and each other, to avoid confronting the rot in their relationships. Yet where Roudané, in relation to *Who's Afraid of Virginia Woolf?*, sees these bleaker aspects of the work as preparing the way for an essentially affirmative outcome, Clum's reading is somewhat darker, suggesting that Albee's relationships seem ruled more by entropy than renewal. He pursues this, also, through an analysis of the dysfunctional couples portrayed in Albee's later play *Finding the Sun* – which features the playwright's only depiction of a homosexual relationship, alongside heterosexual ones. Clum asks some difficult questions of Albee, but this essay's juxtaposition with the next one, by Thomas Adler, puts yet another spin on the discussion. Adler, also discussing *A Delicate Balance*, but this time in relation to Albee's other, later Pulitzer Prize winners, *Seascape* and *Three Tall Women*, argues that it is precisely in Albee's ability to explore the darker corners of the human heart that his greatness lies. Each of the Pulitzer plays explores the potential for personal growth and evolution, he argues, but it is in *A Delicate Balance*'s depiction of a family *refusing* that dangerous challenge, and insisting on maintaining a numbed equilibrium, that the most painful truths are to be found.

Albee's ongoing concern with that most significant relationship of all – between one's life choices and the inevitability of one's death – is given particular focus in Brenda Murphy's essay on "Albee's Threnodies." Here she charts the evolution of Albee's plays on death and dying – from *All Over* through *The Lady from Dubuque* to, again, *Three Tall Women* – demonstrating a gradual shift of concern from the disturbing impact of a death on those living, to the release and reflection that may be brought to the one about to die. According to this reading, *Box* and *Quotations from Chairman Mao Tse-Tung*, which directly preceded *All Over*, represent Albee's most abstract and coolly distanced treatment of entropy and death – whereas *Three Tall Women* is his most personal and involved. Intriguingly, though, in the next essay, by Gerry McCarthy, *Box* and *Mao* are viewed altogether differently – as the purest expression of Albee's deeply *felt* concern for the ways in which language, in its tones, rhythms, and interplay, as much as its explicit content, can conjure emotional textures akin to those created by music, in the mind of the attentive listener. McCarthy goes on to offer a fascinating argument about Albee's insistence on creating plays which exist primarily in the present, onstage (much as the performance of music does), rather than in some imagined, fictional elsewhere. The "realism" of Albee's plays, he suggests, lies less in the Method-style psychological realism of "believable characters" doing "believable things" (a realism that Albee, early in his career, ridiculed as "really and truly The Theatre of the Absurd"[8]) than in the *reality* of thought and feeling being conjured in the mind of the spectator as the play progresses, with all its immediate, theatrical twists and turns. Albee's recent *The Play About the Baby* is, for McCarthy, an exemplary instance of this approach.

McCarthy's essay also heralds something of a shift of emphasis in the collection as a whole. If the essays in the first half of the book tend to focus on Albee's major themes and concerns, often from a primarily "literary" perspective, most of those in the latter half view him more explicitly as a theatremaker. My own essay on Albee's "monster children" explores his ingenious theatricalization of novels such as *Lolita* and *The Ballad of the Sad Café*, while also focusing attention on *The Man Who Had Three Arms* – arguably his most critically despised play, but one which I see as his most explicit attempt to challenge and shake up the complacency of theatre audiences, by exploiting the very immediacy apprehended by McCarthy. Christopher Bigsby follows this up with a survey of some of the lesser-known plays written by Albee during the 1980s and 1990s, after *The Man Who* had finally put paid to his career as a Broadway playwright. Bigsby echoes the thematic concerns of previous essays by emphasizing Albee's ongoing preoccupation with the need to *live* life, rather than sleep through it, but he also echoes McCarthy in demonstrating that these concerns have, of late, been expressed through insistently reflexive theatrical strategies. Rakesh Solomon then focuses in on one of the pieces analysed by Bigsby – *Marriage Play* – to discuss Albee's approach to directing it in a series of different productions between 1987 and 1992. The revealing interview which he includes, recorded while Albee was in rehearsal with the play, says a great deal about the rigor and clarity of intention which the playwright brings to honing both text and performance.

Linda Ben-Zvi's essay brings another, highly original twist to this emphasis on Albee as theatre-maker, by exploring the traces of vaudevillian showmanship that have manifested themselves in his work ever since *The Zoo Story* and *Who's Afraid of Virginia Woolf?*, and all the way through to *The Play About the Baby*, via *Counting the Ways* – which Albee himself subtitles "A Vaudeville." The playwright might have reservations about Ben-Zvi's attempts to tie this discussion to his family history (his adoptive grandfather having been one of America's leading vaudeville impresarios), but he would surely appreciate her awareness that the anarchic, comedic potential of vaudeville can function as far more than "mere" entertainment – as she demonstrates through her shrewd analyses of the relationships between form and content in these plays.

With Ben-Zvi's essay having recapped Albee's career, at pace, right up to the turn of the millennium, J. Ellen Gainor then rounds up with her fascinating analysis of Albee's most recent major play, *The Goat, or Who is Sylvia?* (Alas, *Homelife* premiered just too late for us to include critical reflection on it in this collection.) Picking up on questions of sexuality also traceable here in the essays by Clum and myself, Gainor argues that Albee does not intend Martin's bestiality as metaphor – that his broaching of this taboo is another, gloves-off attempt to challenge the assumptions of his audiences (in the same combative tradition as *The Zoo Story* and *The Man Who Had Three Arms*). At the same time, Gainor also presents an enlightening analysis of the play's more metaphoric dimensions, tracing its literary and theatrical allusions back to Shakespeare and the Greeks, while also providing first-hand observations on the play's Broadway performances.

The collection closes with two contrasting attempts to "survey" Albee's career as a whole, to date. Albee himself, in conversation late in 2003, talks about his most recent work as well as his oldest – reflecting on the forty-five years between *The Zoo Story* and its partner *Homelife*, and also on a wide range of other topics, from Ibsen's lack of humor through to George Bush's "war on terror." Albee's playful but pithily to-the-point way with words is neatly mirrored in the "Afterword" that precedes this interview, in which Ruby Cohn – whose career as a critic has been roughly contemporaneous with Albee's as a playwright – provides a personal assessment of his plays' astutely self-aware uses of the English language.

* * *

Albee's delight in words is immediately apparent to any reader of his plays, which are always strongly dialogue-driven. What may be less obvious, especially given that all but a handful of his plays are only rarely produced on stage, is that he is also very concerned with the sounds and rhythms created by those words, and with concrete stage images. To write a play, he stresses in this book's concluding interview, is to create something musical and sculptural, as well as literary: verbal and physical presence must intersect.[9] Visually, Albee's stages are often very sparsely furnished, as the playwright adopts a minimalistic approach that brings particularly tight focus to the performers themselves, and to those few, select, iconic elements that are present. (Indeed, he discusses the need for precise balance in such selection in Rakesh Solomon's piece here on *Marriage Play*.) Moreover, even where fully detailed, naturalistic sets are called for, these environments speak as clearly as the characters that inhabit them: in *Who's Afraid of Virginia Woolf?*, George and Martha's New Carthage home needs to be as cluttered as their lives; in *A Delicate Balance*, the plush, upper-middle-class comforts of Tobias and Agnes's house need to be as tastefully, ornamentally arranged as the interpersonal equilibrium of the title.

It is, perhaps, one of Albee's great paradoxes that he remains utterly uninterested in pursuing conventional stage realism for its own sake, and yet utterly insistent on the fact that most of his plays are "realistic." Even *Seascape*, he maintains, is perfectly realistic: this is really what happens when giant talking lizards meet elderly couples on beaches. Such statements are not, it must be stressed, simply a case of Albee playing games. Rather, his notion of what is "real" is quite the opposite of the unthinking realism of so much theatre, film, and television, which seeks slavishly to reproduce the outward appearance of everyday life as we normally perceive it. Our very notions of what is real, his plays repeatedly imply, are themselves the product of habitual assumptions, even fictional constructions. If theatre can serve to remind us of this – to alert us to the unexamined artifice of the everyday – then it may well be, as Albee says in my interview with him, "more real than anything." When Antonin Artaud wrote of "the theatre and its double" (the title of his seminal book of manifestos), he meant that life ought to change to mirror the revelations of the stage, rather than the other way around.[10] It is no coincidence that more than one contributor to this volume sees parallels between Artaud and Albee.

These points are perhaps best illustrated with reference to the Albee play that most directly explores the layered relationship between theatre and life,

Tiny Alice. The central stage element in the play is a giant scale model of the castle-mansion in which the action is ostensibly taking place. This very consciously "sculptural" object was responded to as such by the sculptor Louise Nevelson, who, Albee notes, "was one of the few people instinctively to see to the core of my play."[11] It is also, however, a kind of stage within a stage; artifice within artifice. Thus when Brother Julian (on his first visit to the mansion) peers in the tiny window of the room supposedly replicating the one they are standing in, Butler asks him – only half-jokingly – whether he can see miniatures of the two of them inside. Later, when a mysterious fire *inside* the model seems to prefigure an "actual" fire in the mansion's chapel, the disorientating possibility emerges that it is not the model that replicates the mansion, but the mansion that replicates the model. The mansion may *seem* authentic – its bricks may even, as the Lawyer notes, have been individually numbered and shipped over from England, to be perfectly reconstructed as a genuine piece of the old country. Yet it is nonetheless, Lawyer stresses, a replica.[12] Albee thus presents an idea that anticipates Jean Baudrillard's later suggestion that we read landscapes as representations of our maps, rather than vice versa; that we view the real in terms of the constructions we expect it to be consistent with.

"We must . . . represent, draw pictures, reduce or enlarge to . . . to what we can understand," Miss Alice later remarks (98). And while Lawyer may warn Julian "never to confuse the representative of a . . . thing with the thing itself" (33), the question remains how we can ever *know* the thing itself, when our understanding is always already informed by our maps or representations of it. The point is underlined further when Lawyer describes the corrupt Cardinal as "the representative of an august and revered . . . body" (33). He means the Catholic Church, of course, but his hesitation over the last word emphasizes the status of language itself as approximation, as metaphor: even the body, the physical ground of human being, is implicated as the stand-in for, the representative of, something else – just as it is when used by an actor.

Tiny Alice, in fact, presents the bodies of its actors as multilayered fictions. Butler at one point conducts an entire conversation with Lawyer, in the "role" of the absent Julian (69–70). Miss Alice removes the mask and dress of an old crone to reveal herself as much younger and healthier. Even then, it eventually emerges, she is playing an assigned role, rather than *herself* – as indeed the actual actress is doing, quite literally. (On reflection, the layers of artifice keep on multiplying – just as the model of the mansion may have, within it, a tiny model of the model, and so on.) As for Julian, his role-play is less conscious, but the trajectory of the play traces the gradual breakdown of his own sense of "self" – and of the concept of reality on which it is predicated. Once, in the past, we learn, he spent several years in a mental asylum, because "I could not reconcile myself to the chasm between the nature of God and the use to which men put . . . God" (35). Butler immediately relativizes his statement: "Between your God and others', your view and theirs." Julian reflexively insists, "I said what I intended" (36), yet he eventually has to ask himself whether his God is indeed absolute reality, or an imagined mirror of his own desires; and thus, whether his insistence on living by that God's dictates constitutes faithful humility or grotesque arrogance – or both (77). Again, Butler has a simple solution: "what's happened is you're acting like the man you wish you were" (66). Everyday behavior is an enactment of imagined roles on the stage of life. There is no simple, pure reality or truth to rely on, the play implies, that is not preceded and informed by representation and performance: "We do not know. Anything. End prologue" (98).

Albee thus destabilizes not only epistemology (how can we *know?*), but the very ontology of the stage world we are watching (where *are* we; what world *is* this?). At the very end, there is even the suggestion that Julian and the others are inside a model themselves (and of course they are, quite literally), when a great, dark shadow passes across the stage, as if a giant face is peering in the window, obscuring the light. Through *Tiny Alice*, Albee invites his audiences, too, to question their own concepts of what is real – and, perhaps, to "think outside the box"; outside the containing frame they may have created for their own life-performances. Visually and metaphorically, Albee's plays are full of frames, boxes, confining rooms – coffins. In *Tiny Alice*, even the seemingly powerful Cardinal – trapped within the pomp and pomposity of his role – is aligned with the cardinal birds he keeps in a small cage.

Ultimately, Albee reminds us, we stay alive by staying alert; by continually questioning the traps that we set for ourselves, the roles we box ourselves into. And as his plays from *Zoo Story* onward demonstrate, we may sometimes need to take a risk, a blind leap of faith, to free ourselves, however dangerous or frightening that may seem. (In Julian's case, of course, the shattering of his life-frame results in madness; though Albee plays provocatively on the double meaning of "asylum" as both madhouse and refuge.) Moreover, as Albee stresses in the interview that closes this book, this need to keep challenging ourselves, to resist the allure of conventionalized lies, is a political imperative as much as an existential one – and one that, amid the global "realities" of the early twenty-first century – is as painfully relevant as ever.

NOTES

1. Quoted in Mel Gussow, *Edward Albee: A Singular Journey* (New York: Simon and Schuster, 1999), p. 385.

2. Edward Albee, "Which Theatre is the Absurd One?," in *American Playwrights on Drama*, ed. Horst Frenz (New York: Hill and Wang, 1965), pp. 172–173.
3. Quoted Gussow, *Edward Albee*, p. 226.
4. Quoted ibid., p. 265.
5. Michael Smith, "Theatre Journal," *Village Voice*, September 29, 1966, p. 22.
6. Gussow, *Edward Albee*, p. 327.
7. Cited on the back cover of the acting edition of Albee's *The Play About the Baby* (New York: Dramatists Play Service, 2002).
8. Albee in Frenz, p. 168.
9. The exception to this, perhaps, is his written-for-radio play *Listening* – the one Albee piece which nobody I approached for this volume opted to write about.
10. Antonin Artaud, *The Theatre and Its Double*, trans. Mary C. Richards (New York: Grove, 1958).
11. Albee, in his introduction to the exhibition catalogue *Louise Nevelson: Atmospheres and Environments* (New York: Whitney Museum, 1980), p. 16.
12. Edward Albee, *Tiny Alice, Box and Quotations from Chairman Mao Tse-Tung* (Harmondsworth: Penguin, 1971), p. 58. Further references will be cited parenthetically in the text.

2

PHILIP C. KOLIN

Albee's early one-act plays: "A new American playwright from whom much is to be expected"

Edward Albee launched his career with a series of one-act plays. As he records in the 1960 preface to one of them, *The American Dream*: "I have, in my brief . . . three years, five plays, two of them but fifteen minutes long."[1] With these five plays – *The Zoo Story* (1959), *The American Dream* (1961), and *The Death of Bessie Smith* (1960), plus the shorter *The Sandbox* (1960) and *FAM and YAM* (1960) – Albee is credited with changing the course of American theatre history. Many critics, including Harold Clurman from whose review I take my subtitle, greeted Albee with unbounded enthusiasm.[2] Alan Schneider, acclaimed director of *The American Dream* and *Who's Afraid of Virginia Woolf?* (1962), believed Albee's early plays were the "most original and powerful work I'd come across in years."[3] Martin Esslin honored these breakout one-acts as the "promising and brilliant first examples of an American contribution to the Theatre of the Absurd."[4] Like Tennessee Williams, Albee already had a portfolio bulging with longer, unpublished and unproduced plays before he wrote these one-acts, but like Williams again and Chekhov, he made a major contribution to the genre of the short play at the beginning of his career, and continued to write them, as *Box* (1968), *Listening* (1976), *Counting the Ways* (1976), *Finding the Sun* (1983), and *Marriage Play* (1987) all testify.

In his early one-acts, Albee flew to fame on the angry bird of youth. Thirty years old when he wrote *The Zoo Story*, he came to be seen as the *enfant terrible* of the American theatre, attacking the cherished myths of his own country and theatre. Politically, these early plays, particularly *The Zoo Story* and *The Death of Bessie Smith*, pummeled American conformity with scathing satire and ideological fervor. Albee's targets were materialism, racism, artificial values, complacency, lack of communication, and the debilitating effects of illusions. These early works are diatribes against public, national sins. What Albee said about *Who's Afraid of Virginia Woolf?* in 1976 is retrospectively pertinent to these early one-acts: "The play is an examination of whether or not we, as a society, have lived up to the principles of the American

Revolution."[5] Clearly for Albee, as these one-acts stress, we have not. As social protests, Albee's one-act plays called America to be self-reflexive at the start of a decade in which the Kennedy and Martin Luther King assassinations, the Watts riots in Los Angeles, the Vietnam War, and the Stonewall protests of gays and bisexuals would all force the nation to confront its failings. Like Elmer Rice, Clifford Odets, or Arthur Miller, though far removed from their brand of dramatic polemics, Albee wanted to shake up American complacency.

If Albee rattled American dreams, he also undermined the dramatic realism that dominated the American theatre at the time. Although he incorporated techniques and ideas from the "absurdist" plays of European playwrights such as Beckett, Genet, and Ionesco, Albee's voice was also distinctively American, pressing for social change and reform. His work contrasts starkly with Neil Simon's early comedies of the 1960s and 1970s that enshrined such American values as happy families, profitable businesses, and audience-satisfying resolutions. Among critics and audiences alike, Albee quickly established himself as a master of language, a stylist who was precise and probing. In these one-acts, foreshadowing his later, full-length plays, Albee's dialogue was sharp and devastatingly on target. These early works powerfully influenced the rise of off-Broadway theatre, where they debuted and where, later in the 1960s and 1970s, some of the most productively experimental plays for the American theatre premiered. Many of these new-generation playwrights – such as John Guare, Sam Shepard, Adrienne Kennedy and Lanford Wilson – owed their opportunity for success to Albee's pioneering one-acts. Great things often have small beginnings.

* * *

The Zoo Story was Albee's first produced play, and has been proclaimed by Christopher Bigsby as "the most impressive debut by any American dramatist."[6] Like the work of many prophets, though, Albee's play premiered outside his native land in a workshop production in German at the Schiller Theater in West Germany in 1959, as part of a double bill with Samuel Beckett's *Krapp's Last Tape*. Six months later, *The Zoo Story*, still paired with Beckett's play, came to the off-Broadway Provincetown Playhouse, and it was repeatedly revived in different double bills at various New York theatres over the next six years. It won Albee his first Obie award and has since gone on to become his most frequently staged play. *The Zoo Story* also launched Albee's directing apprenticeship a few years after its American debut. (Ironically, he has noted that the 1963 *The Zoo Story* he directed was "probably the worst production ever."[7]) Mixing earthy naturalism and alienating, absurdist effects, *The Zoo Story* has received a bewildering variety of interpretations ranging from being seen as a homosexual pass, to an

Figure 2. *The Zoo Story*, 1968 Broadway revival. With Donald Davis as Peter and Ben Piazza as Jerry.

admonition not to talk to strangers in Central Park, a Christian allegory about Peter denying Jerry (Christ) three times, and an attack on fragmentation, isolation, or lack of communication.[8] The U.S. Senator Prescott Bush, the father and grandfather of presidents, denounced the play on the Senate floor as "filthy," tainted with communism – thereby reflecting the paranoia of the Cold War era.[9] Yet whatever its message(s), *The Zoo Story* became a central script in American and world theatre, a canonized text.

Like many of Albee's plays to follow, *The Zoo Story* creates a dialectic through the seemingly polar opposites of character, geography, fictionalities, and even props – Jerry versus Peter; the rooming-house versus Central Park; animal versus man; freedom versus imprisonment; conformity versus confrontation. The play runs on paradoxes, especially the lesson Jerry wants to teach Peter – that "neither kindness nor cruelty [. . .] creates any effect beyond themselves [. . .] the two combined together at the same time are the teaching emotion" (35) – and the way in which Peter can learn that "a person has to go a very long distance out of his way to come back a short distance correctly" (21). It seems contradictory, even absurd, to go a long way to arrive at a destination only a short distance away, but that is the ultimate message of Jerry's mission to Peter. Jerry's long monologues reach the pithy conclusion that Peter needs to appreciate himself through others. Through these paradoxes, *The Zoo Story* unravels a parable about the human condition – that is, how seeming opposites can be reconciled only through a synthesis of communication and commitment.

With Jerry's arrival, a new voice came into the American theatre. Albee empowered the disempowered. Living on the margins of society, Jerry is the antiestablishment, counterculture hero. He is the dark stranger, the social outcast, the orphan, the Other. In many ways, Albee scripted a self-portrait. Alan Schneider recalls that Albee was described to him as a "mysterious and reclusive young American," not unlike the older Jerry.[10] Like Jerry, Albee traveled all over New York encountering strangers when he delivered telegrams for Western Union, a job he held for over two years before writing *The Zoo Story*. Albee, like Jerry again, was streetsmart. In appearance, humor, and confrontational chutzpah, Jerry is totally unconventional. Commenting on his antiestablishment attire, the German critic Friedrich Luft observed that Jerry had "a longing for death in blue jeans."[11] He is the opposite of the vacuous, Hollywood-looking American Dream in Albee's play of the same name. Exuding the ethos of the late 1950s and 1960s, Jerry is a part of the new generation of beatniks who frequented coffee houses, lived a bohemian lifestyle in Greenwich Village (as Albee himself did in the 1950s and 1960s), and inhaled the caustic humor of Lenny Bruce, Mort Sahl, and Dick Gregory. Some of Jerry's lines are irreverently funny, such as "Now animals don't take to me like Saint Francis" (30). Above all, though, Jerry is the rebel, the precursor of the radical left, the Hippies, the Vietnam War protesters.

Jerry's aesthetics synchronously coincided with those of the Beat generation. His character can be read through the works of Jack Kerouac, Allen Ginsberg, William Burroughs. Like the Beats, Jerry takes aim at a homogenized America where progress insulates thought, separating people from one another. At times he can be poetic and at others menacing, wild-eyed, filling the stage with shocking outbursts. Emulating the jazzy, disheveled lifestyle of the Beats, Jerry has had sex with men as well as with women, lives on the fringes of respectability, and seeks psychic asylum through flight and travel. From his first line, "I've been to the zoo," Jerry sounds like a Beat poet in his desire to travel, to escape the conventional and to tell about it. Like Jack Kerouac, he is on the road, a picaro on speed. (Ironically, George

Maharis, the first actor to play Jerry, starred in a popular 1950s television series, *Route 66*, chronicling the adventures of two young men who drive across the country in search of adventure.) Advocating the Beat-honored tradition of escaping an oppressive environment, Jerry tries to get out of his own skin and under the skin of others, most chillingly the dog's and Peter's. His goal is to break down barriers, to live his life more fully, an Albee imperative as well as a Beat mantra.[12]

Peter is the opposite. He is passive, inhibited, unwilling to give up his solitude for confrontation. A conformist and isolationist, he is both Jerry's nemesis and his hope, enemy, and heir. Living the credo of the "Organizational Man," Peter is an upper-middle-class drone whose job, family, and lifestyle validate the mainstream rituals of the Eisenhower 1950s, as modeled by Gregory Peck in the film *Man in the Gray Flannel Suit* (1956). Peter lives by a routine that restricts and defines him: he works for a publisher (a safe occupation as an editor, as opposed to being a polemical writer), has a wife who prescribes his pleasures, raises two daughters (no son – which Jerry sees as an indictment of his virility), keeps two parakeets, and allots the same time each Sunday to reading in the park. Symbolically, his preference is for *Time*, a magazine whose title and pithy aphoristic style underscore Peter's allegiance to conformity and deadlines, allowing for little expression of, or danger resulting from, individuality. Satirizing the United States through *Time*, Beat poet Allen Ginsberg asks his personified country in his well-known poem "America" (1956), "Are you going to let your emotional life be run by *Time Magazine*?" America replies: "I am obsessed by *Time Magazine*./ I read it every week. Its cover stares at me every time I slink past the candy store . . . It's always telling me about responsibility."[13] A follower of herd psychology, Peter leads an unexamined life, devoid of risk, challenge, spirit. He is the compliant citizen who, in Jack Kerouac's words, has sold out to the "cop souls" of late 1950s America.

A key to Jerry's relationship with Peter can be found in Jerry's self-portrayal as a "permanent transient" (37), one of the most evocative paradoxes in *The Zoo Story*. Jerry is both trapped prisoner and peripatetic parolee. He belongs to the same group of fugitives as Tennessee Williams's Val Xavier in *Orpheus Descending* (later a film called *The Fugitive Kind*), or Sebastian Venable in *Suddenly Last Summer* – a play which Albee acknowledges as a key influence. Inspired by the storytelling structure of *Suddenly Last Summer* (1958), Albee was also drawn to Williams's unconventional hero types such as Sebastian. (Ironically, Williams used Albee's phrase "permanent transient" to describe another resident of the liminal world, the Gnädiges Fräulein in his 1966 play of the same name.) Jerry is a soul on the run, a fugitive from schedules, family ties, loneliness, and, most of all, time. His dialogue stresses the necessity of his transiency; "I took the subway down to the Village so I could walk all the way up Fifth Avenue to the Zoo" (21). Jerry's goal is to secure "solitary but free passage" (35), but at the same time he advertises the injustices to the self in a world indifferent to individuality and relationships. Most important for Jerry is saving a drone like Peter from a life of sterile stalemate. Yet, paradoxically, as the fugitive-savior he is compared to "a hold-up man" (19), escapes from the boarding-house which he likens to a "jail" (33), and is threatened with the police by Peter. Troped as a criminal, Jerry is made the enemy in a conformist state that would disqualify him as an "un-American" outsider. As Michel Foucault was subsequently to argue in *The History of Sexuality* and *Discipline and Punish*, a capitalist state often brands someone mad or criminally deviant in the name of an expedient status quo. The ritualistic fugitive/transient, Jerry mesmerizes Peter and audiences alike as he takes them on a journey through the various layers of his psychic and physical autobiography.

In Jerry's stories, lives are connected or separated by symbolic geography. Space and the environment play a major part in America's dichotomous cultural landscape that Albee seeks to invade and to expose in *The Zoo Story*. Underscoring Jerry's role as transient and cultural criminal are the enclosures of his rooming-house, a penitentiary of the psyche, "a tormented house" (28). Jerry describes the building, the residents, and his possessions in terms of confining enclosures. Semiotically speaking, *The Zoo Story* is about cages, boxes, frames, bars, encasements, the shrinking territorialities of prison cell or madhouse. In advertising the play, many theatre posters, programs, and playbills have depicted a cage or a row of bars as the commanding symbols of the play. The tight, enclosed space, the box, a containment within the larger containment of the theatre's frame, is a frequent physical trope in Albee, as in his *The Sandbox* and *Box* (1968). Like a prison cell, Jerry's room is "laughably small, and one of my walls is made of beaverboard [which] separates my room from another laughably small room" (22). His fellow inmates he neither knows nor, in some cases, sees. "And in the other front room there's somebody living there, but [. . .] I've never seen who it is. Never. Never ever" (22). She "lives behind closed doors" (35), and cries all the time. Jerry does see the "colored queen who always keeps his door open; well not always, but always when he's plucking his eyebrows" (22). This resident/inmate is socially marginalized twice over because of race and gender.

His lustful landlady, the "gatekeeper" in this prison, tries to "corner" Jerry in the hallway, grabbing him, pushing him, pressing him, "in some foul parody of sexual desire" (28). It is in this narrow passageway, too, that Jerry encounters the dog, another gatekeeper (34). The story of Jerry and the dog is, as Albee and many critics have declared, "a microcosm of the play," and it contains the essence of his zoo experience and fuels the tension that Jerry hypnotically imparts to Peter.[14] Jerry did not need to travel to Central Park to find out about the pain and isolation; he learned these from his experiences with the dog, too. Occupying about one-quarter of the play, the story is highly significant spatially and rhetorically. Structurally, it is the centerpiece of the play, occurring almost at midpoint of the script, encasing Jerry in the same kind of shrinking, existential hall/hell where the dog and landlady are linked through challenging and threatening him. Both the dog and the woman are old, diseased, sexually tainted. The dog, who "almost always has an erection . . . of sorts," is its own walking prison or charnelhouse. "You can see the ribs through his skin," as if he were behind bars. He has "bloodshot eyes," and "tiny, tiny ears and eyes [. . .] infected maybe" (30). Ironically, these are the organs most necessary to make contact with another individual. But the dog, like Jerry's cohabitants, is suspicious of relationships, and grimly guards the entryway to their doleful, individual human cages (the rooms). Jerry's dog story can be seen as a play within a play, a story of Jerry by Jerry, an enclosed script, or fiction, within the larger contours of the play. Jerry performs the story as a piece of metatheatre for Peter to watch. His narrative describes (en)closed encounters of the worst kind, since this parable, buried in Jerry's psyche, is one of communication failure. Both dog and performer "feign indifference" – thus prompting Jerry to teach Peter a new lesson about an old dog: that is, bad animal behavior and bad human behavior are the same. Jerry hopes that, though his tactics of kindness and cruelty did not win the dog over, they may Peter.

Enclosed spaces also shape the size/uses of objects in Jerry's room, again suggesting isolation, the containment of the lost, absent, or imaginary. Among Jerry's fugitive's/narrator's props are "two picture frames, both empty," "a small strongbox without a lock," "a can opener, one that works with a key." These are the emblems of incarceration – "frames," "strongbox," "key." Jerry's life, without meaningful contacts, is framed with nothingness (just as *The Zoo Story*'s proscenium frames a stage empty but for Jerry, Peter, and the bare park benches). Like a prisoner, too, Jerry has "a hot plate that I'm not supposed to have" (23). He also catalogues "letters . . . please letters" seeking human contact, but they are "weighed down" under the rocks, hidden, trapped, imprisoned by stone-hard silence and isolation, just as the people are in the cages/rooms of Jerry's tenement.

Jerry's other relationships are also described in spatial terms, the language of enclosures, cages. As the dog story emblematizes, various other fictions (stories) that Jerry relates are themselves embedded within one another – as if contained in the enclosure of Jerry's play, inside Albee's play. Jerry is lost in the passageways of his life voyage. His aunt "dropped dead on the stairs to her apartment" (24). People escape Jerry by seeking exits to hallways: "I never see the pretty little ladies more than once, and most of them wouldn't be caught in the same room with a camera" (25). Most important, he has been to the zoo where animals, like people, are caged. "Well, all the animals are there, and all the people are there" (40). Near the end of the play, Jerry tells of the "lion keeper com[ing] into the lion cages" (40), reinforcing verbally and spatially his observations on the imprisonment of human/animal relationships. In the zoo, "everyone [is] separated by bars from everyone else" (40).

Cages and confinement are not unique to Jerry's city tenement. Deconstructing the national ecology of America's open spaces – the land of the free and home of the brave – Albee pursues the prison motif of Jerry's narratives into Central Park, though Albee admits it is a "Central Park of the imagination."[15] He positions Central Park against Jerry's rooming-house on the Upper West Side, bucolic versus urban settings. Yet Albee shows how similar these two sites are, because of the social forces that strive to control these landscapes and the people who frequent them. Peter lives in cages no less removed from human contact and communication than do the residents of Jerry's rooming-house. The park setting allows Albee to physicalize the entrapment of individuals from very different backgrounds. In describing one space in the park, Jerry refers to the gay cruising area where men hide in the bushes or in the trees (43), imprisoned by social stigma, while at the other end of the park, and the spectrum of respectability, Peter is equally trapped. Although not of the park, Peter, nonetheless, like the gays, is imprisoned there. Dressed in the uniform of the indentured capitalist, "he wears tweeds [. . .] and carries horn-rimmed glasses," apparel with bars/stripes/enclosure patterns (11). William Daniels, who played Peter in the American premiere of *The Zoo Story*, aptly wore a striped tie mirroring the geometric design of the bars of a zoo cage or prison.

Cages also figure prominently in Peter's conventional family life. His daughter "keeps the two parakeets in a cage" (18). Chastising Peter for his unlived life, Jerry shouts, "This is probably the first time in your life you've had anything more trying to face than changing your cats' toilet box" (45). Peter's world, like Jerry's, is boxed in, packed with garbage. When Jerry tickles – and then punches – Peter (using the paradoxical blend of kindness and cruelty he exercised with the dog), he hits him in his ribcage, reinforcing the image of Peter's solitary confinement in his own skin. At first enjoying the playfulness, Peter revealingly laughs, "I had my own little zoo there for a moment" (39). Albee's minimal set of two park benches also visually suggests bars, caged areas, enclosures, symbols of Peter's retreat from contact and commitment. In its slats and metal the bench resembles a longitudinal cage, imprisoning Peter in solitude and conformity. The bench is both prison and protection, a sign of his status quo, a fixture. Crucial to one of the most explicitly theatrical moments in the play, the fight over the bench and Jerry's death physicalize the themes of imprisonment and isolation Albee has been enunciating. Jerry's insistence on possessing Peter's bench is surely a cruel satire on American society's insistence on compartmentalization. The subtext of the action says: This is your patch; this is mine; we can't share; we must have our own isolated territories.

The story of Jerry at the zoo will ultimately be framed in other small enclosures for later viewing on television screens, as he intentionally stresses to Peter at the beginning of the play, "I've been to the zoo. [. . .] You'll read about it in the papers tomorrow if you don't see it on your TV tonight" (15). But how many viewers will see the meaning and transcendence of Jerry's death that Peter eventually accepts? Jerry's death is intended as a catharsis for the complacent, a wake-up message to get involved in life – ours and others. Ironically, Jerry evicts Peter from his bench and transforms him from the respectable conformist into a "permanent transient." In a 1984 interview, Albee maintained that "Peter is not going to be able to be the same person again."[16] In fact, several critics have pushed for new identities for Peter based upon Jerry's impact on him. Robert Bennett claims that Peter accepts the "brotherhood" Jerry offers.[17] Albee himself confessed that Peter and Jerry were "the two Edwards, the one who lived back in Larchmont [the wealthy New York suburb where he grew up] and the one who lives in New York City."[18] Biographical implications aside, Jerry forces Peter to define and refine himself in light of the radical assault on his established modes of determining identity and evaluating perceptions. Jerry's teaching lesson was more than a walk in the park; it was a profound challenge to boundaries, traditions, and ideologies.

* * *

Serving as a thematic, but not necessarily a strictly chronological, bridge between the premieres of *The Zoo Story* and *The American Dream* (1961) are Albee's shortest one-acts, *The Sandbox* and *FAM and YAM* (1960) – plays that also attack hollow rituals, obstacles to communication, and the theatre of realism. Subtitled "An Imaginary Interview" between FAM, a famous American playwright, and YAM, a young American playwright, *FAM and YAM* premiered in Westport, Connecticut, in August 1960.[19] Although usually glossed over as a slight "play in one scene," *FAM* continues Albee's quarrel with the establishment, extending it to Broadway playhouses and producers. *FAM and YAM*, like *The Zoo Story*, sets up polar opposites but, unlike *The Zoo Story*, has no intention to reconcile them. The young, aggressive, and recently produced dramatist YAM contrasts with the smug, paunchy, and sherry-swilling FAM in whose exclusive apartment the conversation/interview takes place. YAM is clearly Albee himself, "*intense, crew cut in need of a trim, an old issue of* Evergreen Review *under one arm*" (82). (The *Evergreen Review*, an alternative magazine whose title perhaps indicates its disregard for *Time*, published and promoted the Beats: its presence here further establishes Albee's own affinity with these literary and social iconoclasts.)

YAM tells FAM that he wants to do an article, "In search of a Hero," about him, unquestionably mocking FAM. Pretending to put questions to the famous author, YAM assails "everybody" in theatre – the owners are "ignorant, greedy, hit-happy real estate owners," the producers are "opportunistic, out-for-a-buck businessmen," directors are "slick, sleight-of-hand artists," critics set themselves up as "social arbiters," and the playwrights "are nothing better than businessmen themselves" (91–93). Growing tipsy with successive sherries, FAM agrees, cordially responding with trite phrases such as "Oh my," "Oh yes . . . wonderful, wonderful" to YAM's rapid-fire accusations. With his alcohol-induced giggling, vapid responses, and smug attitudes, FAM behaves like Peter.

Albee's satire drips with professional (and personal) venom, piercing to the quick the theatre establishment he and his peers wanted to topple. He singles FAM out, along with Miller, Williams, and Thornton Wilder as the "pros," the survivors of the Broadway establishment. FAM is a satiric portrait of William Inge – "*a slightly rumpled account executive? . . . a faintly foppish Professor of History? Either one will do*" (82). Albee had met and sought counsel from Inge, and had even visited Inge in his exclusive Sutton Place apartment in New York: he carefully records details of its furnishings in *FAM and YAM*. Writing himself into the script, Albee contrasts the Broadway "pros" with the younger generation of playwrights whom FAM mockingly names – "Gelber, Richardson, Kopit . . . (*Shrugs.*) Albee . . . you . . . (*Mock woe.*)" (89). Indeed, YAM's fledgling success off-Broadway – DILEMMA, DERELICTION, AND DEATH – is perhaps an allusion to *The Zoo Story*: its title is printed in capital letters in the script as if written on Jerry's old typewriter, which used only capitals. Condescendingly, FAM remarks, "You youngsters are going to push us out of the way" (89). With "an unintentionally teeth-baring smile," YAM sardonically responds, "Well, maybe there'll be room for all of us" (89).

But after YAM refuses to have a drink, leaves, and calls FAM from the lobby to thank him again for the interview, FAM shouts, "THE INTERVIEW, THE INTERVIEW": "*his face turns ashen . . . his mouth drops open,*" and the expressive paintings "*frown* [. . .] *peel* [. . .] *tilt* [. . .] *crash*" (96). The irony is that he, like Peter, has said practically nothing, but has indicted himself nonetheless. Courtesy of Albee's satire, FAM experiences a triple shock – what he took for pleasantries with YAM was indeed the interview; what he jocularly agreed to with each sherry was his own undoing by criticizing the establishment of which he was a part; and, finally, what credibility he had as an artist vanishes when *"one of the Modiglianis frowns"* (96). Albee, the artist and later curator, has the last laugh as the great art that FAM took for granted abandons him.

The Sandbox was commissioned by, but never performed at, the Spoleto Festival. It premiered instead at the Jazz Gallery in April of 1960, and was subsequently televised in 1961. Like *The American Dream, The Sandbox* centers on the figure of Grandma, and the play is dedicated to Albee's beloved maternal Grandmother Cotter who died in 1959, and with whom he sympathized for being a victim, like him, of her daughter, Albee's adoptive mother Frances Loring Cotter Albee. She and Reed Albee, of the Keith-Albee vaudeville circuit, adopted him when he was an infant, and raised him in wealth and privilege in Larchmont, a suburb about twenty-five miles from New York City.[20] He rebelled against this upbringing, however, satirizing his parents in his portraits of domineering mothers and weak fathers. After he was expelled from the family and penniless, his paternal grandmother left him a trust fund to help him to live and write, reinforcing the kindness Albee received from his grandmothers.

The Sandbox introduces three characters who also appear in *The American Dream*: an emasculated Daddy, a cruel, aggressive Mommy, and a morally honest Grandma. Albee stopped working on *Dream* to write *The Sandbox* for Spoleto, and then returned to the longer play a few months later. *The Sandbox* encapsulates such familiar Albee targets as anti-Momism, hollow rituals, failure to communicate, sterile couplehood, complacency, and hypocrisy. On a brightly lit stage, Mommy and Daddy, presenile and vacuous, deposit Grandma in a child's sandbox to die, and bring in a musician to play a dirge-like flute composition written by Albee's mentor/partner William Flanagan. A typical early Albee couple, Mommy and Daddy cannot communicate because they have nothing meaningful to say. Locked in an emotional stalemate, they resemble Peter and FAM in their inability to make contact with others. The couple's dialogue is filled with banalities, clichés, and deflated words, emptied of real meaning. Mommy, thinking Grandma has died – after the lighting has dipped and risen again – unfeelingly parrots the sacred sincerity of Psalm 30, 11–12: "Our long night is over. We must put away our tears, take off our mourning . . . and face the future" (18). Mommy is an angry cartoon.

Devaluing life, Mommy and Daddy treat Grandma like a dog, making her sleep on an army blanket under a stove. Near death, she is infantilized, shouting nonsense syllables and throwing sand at Mommy and Daddy. Half-buried in the sand, Grandma deserves comparison with Beckett's similarly submerged couple, Winnie and Willie in *Happy Days*.[21] At the conclusion of *The Sandbox*, Grandma is first rallied and then helped to die by an athletic young man who calls himself the Angel of Death. Like Grandma, this would-be Adonis awaits his future, which he hopes will be a call from a studio to give him a Hollywood name. For now he is a vapid abstraction. A seriocomic deathwatch, *The Sandbox* looks forward to longer Albee plays in which far more daunting angels of death summon characters to eternity – *All Over* (1971), *The Lady from Dubuque* (1980), *Three Tall Women* (1991).

In addition to offering these easily accessible satiric types in *The Sandbox*, Albee again confronts a larger, more powerful foe – the conventional, real-istic theatre – and, like the absurdists, dismantles its conventions, deftly, comically. Resisting sentimentality, Grandma undercuts theatrical illusion by demanding, "Don't put the lights up yet . . . I'm not ready" (18), and then deconstructs the fourth wall by addressing the audience directly. Albee's stage effects (sound, lights) also reinforce the artificiality of theatrical conventions, and many social ones as well. Acting like a stage manager, Grandma gives cues to the musician, "Keep it nice and soft." The Young Man, similarly, breaks away from a realistic narrative with a hilarious intrusion: "Uh . . . ma'am . . . I have a line here" (19). In so doing, he calls attention to the artificiality of role-playing in the theatre of realism. *The Sandbox* is a witty performance of a performance.

* * *

The American Dream, Albee's second big success, premiered off-Broadway in January 1961, when he was thirty-two, at the York Playhouse, and sub-sequently ran for more than 360 performances at various New York the-atres. The longest of Albee's one-acts, *Dream* is also the most satirically ferocious, enhancing his reputation as an angry young man. Several crit-ics were outraged by his invective, and a few even refused to review the play. Because of its absurdist techniques, many critics saw *Dream* as an Ionesco take-off, echoing *The Bald Soprano*. Although Albee was hailed as the "American Ionesco," he saw the play as a homage to Ionesco, not an imitation of him.[22] In the tradition of an American jeremiad, *Dream* bris-tles with social outrage while being framed as broad comedy.[23] According to Albee, "The play is an examination of the American Scene, an attack on the substitution of artificial for real values in our society, a condemna-tion of complacency, cruelty, emasculation, and vacuity; it is a stand against the fiction that everything in this slipping land of ours is peachy-keen" (53–54). As the title indicates, Albee satirizes the mythos of the fabled American Dream, the idealized cultural self-image on which America was founded and supposedly flourishes.

At the heart of *The American Dream* is Albee's attack on consumerism, America's insatiable desire for satisfaction, pleasure, wealth. Mommy, the domineering matriarch, voices the chief complaint of a materialistic America, "You just can't get satisfaction these days" (76). (Interestingly enough, Albee's play predated by only a few years the Rolling Stones's most famous song of the 1960s, "(I Can't Get No) Satisfaction.") Convinced by convention that her social position is determined by the color of her hat, Mommy recounts in the play's opening exchange how she went back to the department store to exchange a "beige" hat for a "wheat" one – which, we see, is the same color in the doublespeak of American consumerism. Cupidity, whether acquiring desirable objects, beautiful bodies, or power, becomes the basis for personal and indeed national identity. Little wonder that Albee targets the depraved power of money to set moral standards in America. Mommy tells Daddy, "I have a right to live off you because I married you [. . .] and I have a right to all your money when you die" (67), while the American Dream himself proclaims, "I'll do anything for money" (109). Although far different in characterization and plot from *Death of a Salesman*, *Dream* excoriates the same materialistic demons that Willy Loman battled. In an economy of getting and not giving, every relationship is mired in greed, artificiality, and selfishness.

In *The American Dream*, Albee skewers the same complacent American couple (a familiar Albee dyad) carried over from *The Sandbox*: Mommy and her emasculated husband Daddy plot to send Grandma away. Grandma is the only sincere and compassionate character in *Dream*, speaking out against hypocrisy and violations of human dignity. These three are visited by Mrs. Barker from the Bye-Bye Adoption Service, who twenty years ago brought them a foundling. (Shades of Albee's life story abound here.) The couple murdered this child and are now eager to adopt his more accommodating twin, the vacuous American Dream himself. The action occurs in an artificially lit, middle-class living room (a popular Albee setting – see also *Who's Afraid of Virginia Woolf?*, *A Delicate Balance* (1966), *The Lady from Dubuque*, and *Everything in the Garden* (1967) for similar locations). In this American nuclear family home, Albee explodes his satiric bombs.

Plot, setting, and character – all intentionally minimal – undermine the stability of the comfortable American family epitomized in such television sitcoms of the 1950s and 1960s as *Life with Riley*, *Ozzie and Harriett*, *Father Knows Best*, *The Donna Reed Show*, and *Leave it to Beaver*. As the leading agent promoting the ideology of consumerism, television sold everything from detergents to family values.²⁴ These programs bubbled over with comedic situations validating the American family in a consumer-glorified economy, such as problems with raising children, visits from busybody neighbors, confrontations with in-laws, and perfunctory conjugal spats. But Albee savagely turns these culturally self-congratulatory television programs inside out to bewail the horrors of the American Dream, as David Rabe did in *Sticks and Bones* during the Vietnam War ten years later. In *The American Dream*, which takes the form of a kind of grotesque sitcom, Daddy does not know best; he does not even know how to find his own room (102). His wife is not a giving and loving homemaker but a harridan, a "Mommy dearest" who dismembers her child in her quest for satisfaction. Mrs. Barker, her fellow clubswoman, institutionalizes murder and mediocrity with little recognition of or responsibility for the differences between them.

Focusing on a key component of the Dream, Albee assaults America's sexual purity and potency. Historically, fables about "George Washington slept here" – attached to many farmhouses in Continental America – sexualized and thus empowered the American Dream, and Hollywood glamor continued the process. Albee debunks the artificiality of this mythos by reversing and challenging gender roles and expectations. Daddy is feminized through a series of tropes that emasculate him. He has had an operation in which "the doctors took out something that was there and put in something that wasn't there" (83), replacing his penis with a vagina ("the something that wasn't there" is the female yonic symbol). After surgery, Daddy "has tubes now, where he used to have tracks" (90), giving him a new feminine identity, through Albee's humor suggesting fallopian tubes or tubal ligations. Analogously, Mommy threatens to take Grandma's "television and shake all the tubes loose" (89). Getting "qualms," Daddy is "like an old house," according to Mrs. Barker, who uses a loaded Jungian symbol associated with female nurturing and protection. Confused, Daddy asks, "Was I really masculine?" (74). When his sexuality is aroused, it is again expressed in female terms. Seeing Mrs. Barker removing her dress, Daddy acts like a schoolgirl – "I just blushed and giggled and went sticky wet" (79) – defusing the power of the male gaze. Daddy's sexual dysfunctions are also metaphorically linked to the American body politic. Mommy sarcastically observes, "All his life Daddy has wanted to be a United States Senator, but now [. . .] he's going to want to be Governor" (83). Another sexually charged word, a "governor" controls a state as well as how fast a car runs, but Daddy's incomplete sexuality ironically disqualifies him for political or home rule. Meanwhile, if Daddy is feminized, Mommy has neither feminine nurturing nor sexual desire but instead adopts a cruel, paternalistic air with Daddy. In her caustic barbs,

Mommy is a likely precursor of the witch/earthmother roles that George accuses Martha of playing in *Who's Afraid of Virginia Woolf?*

Albee's satiric techniques interrogate the relationship between this dysfunctional society and its (ab)use of language. Grandma's declaration that "we live in the age of deformity" (86) expresses this reciprocal stigma. In America conformity leads to deformity and deformity substitutes for conformity. *The American Dream* is riddled with clichés, advertising slogans, non sequiturs, the dead language of consumerism. In the upside-down world of Albee's America, language is dangerously empty, unreliable, and contradictory. When Esslin in *The Theatre of the Absurd* first advanced the idea of "devaluation of language" in Albee's plays, critics applauded.[25] But language in *Dream* is more than devalued; it is performatively destructive. When it is abused, so is the family, sex, history, even theatre. Although superficially comic, the malapropisms in *Dream* strip human beings of their dignity and identity. Calling their son a "bumble of joy," Mommy and Daddy dehumanize him as an offending object, reducing the child to a bungling mistake, a social *faux pas*. Referring to him as an "it" allows them to justify mutilation. Because the bumble did not provide satisfaction, it was expendable. "So they called up the lady who sold them the bumble [. . .] They wanted satisfaction; they wanted their money back" (101). Institutionalizing bumbling, Mrs. Barker agrees with them. Defending the sacredness of life and counseling about the repercussions of child killing, Philip Nye and Anna Peters maintain that women who have an abortion want to avoid the pang of grief by refusing to consider the fetus a human being. As Nye and Peters argue, "to grieve you have to humanize the baby, name the baby."[26] Clearly, Mommy and Daddy neither grieve nor name their bumble, thus debasing life with one key word.

Old people are just as vulnerable as children because of the travesties of language in *The American Dream*. Grandma is reduced to an unwanted possession to be carted off. Mommy, her daughter, asks Daddy, "Why don't you call a van and have her taken away?" (87). By thus dehumanizing Grandma, Albee anticipated 1990s allegations that nursing homes are human warehouses where seniors are transformed into lifeless parcels. Albee physicalizes such an indignity when Grandma comes on stage "*loaded down with boxes, large and small, neatly wrapped and tied*" (63), a metonymy for her wear-dated existence in Mommy and Daddy's eyes. Inside the boxes are the symbols of Grandma's discarded life: "some old letters, a couple of regrets . . . Pekinese . . . blind at that . . . the television . . . my Sunday teeth" (120). Hers are the possessions of loss, similar to the empty, broken, and framed objects in Jerry's room in *The Zoo Story*, as well as evocative reminders of what Albee possibly remembered seeing in Grandma Cotter's room/prison in Larchmont.[27]

Because of the deformity of language, what is private is made embarrassingly public in America. In a parody of the conventional hospitality ritual, Mommy asks Mrs. Barker, "Would you like a cigarette, a drink and would you like to cross your legs?" (77), and a little later inquires, "Are you sure you're comfortable? Won't you take off your dress?" Mrs. Barker replies, "I don't mind if I do," and undresses to her slip (79). In a similarly public exposure of private matters, we are told that Daddy "cried and smiled" when he first saw the bumble, and "said some more intimate things, which were totally irrelevant but which were pretty hot stuff" (48). Most damningly, though, the mutilation of the child is disclosed in righteous and matter-of-fact language as if Mommy and Daddy were the aggrieved parties whom the child/bumble offended. This ritualistic slaughtering is debased into a comic nightmare through the very act of telling about it. Building a play around a lost, imaginary, or deceased child is a staple of Albee's dramatics from *Virginia Woolf* to *A Delicate Balance* to *The Play About the Baby*. In what amounts to a parodic (in)version of *Medea*, *Thyestes*, or Shakespeare's *Titus Andronicus*, it is revealed that Mommy and Daddy tore the child apart, limb by limb, organ by organ, appeasing the false gods of American consumerism. Grandma calmly relates how when the bumble cried, Mommy "gouged those eyes right out of its head" (99) and when they caught it "interested in its sex parts," they "cut its hands off at the wrists" (100). Lopping off its penis and tongue, Mommy and Daddy finally kill the child. During this reportage, Mrs. Barker supplies running commentary, condoning Mommy and Daddy's behavior in the name of social propriety. She turns ritualistic butchery, the subject of horrific tragedy in an earlier theatre, into a topic of polite, social discourse, supplying yet another indictment on Albee's part of the depravity of consumerism.

Critically, the dismemberment is symbolic on many levels. As if performing a vivisection on the emotions, Mommy and Daddy amputate those body parts central to giving and receiving love – "eyes to see, sexual organs [with] which to love, hands to touch, and tongues to speak."[28] Moreover, below the surface of Albee's savagely comic prose lies the capitalist belief that parents can regard their child as property. Swiftian in expressing their economic rights, Mommy, Daddy, and Mrs. Barker advance the commodification of human flesh (the child) for the parents' financial justification or satisfaction. Ironically, though, the couple reap a market of loss with the dimunition, body part by body part, of the child. The mutilated body becomes the site where Albee's script meets national identity and accountability.

PHILIP C. KOLIN

Which brings us to the American Dream himself, the Young Man for whom the play is named, as well as the leading symbol of why things in America are not "peachy-keen." Representing the bleak ideal in the American economy of identity, he rings the doorbell looking for work and is immediately welcomed by Grandma. This Young Man, the lost twin of the bumble whom Mommy and Daddy mutilated, is all surface and no substance, the artificial man. Describing himself as "Clean-cut, Midwest farm boy type, almost insultingly good looking in a typically American way. Good profile, straight nose, honest eyes, wonderful smile," he has Hollywood inscribed all over. He resembles that other pop-cultural idol, Elvis Presley, who also had a twin who died in childbirth, and who was groomed for stardom by Colonel Tom Parker – taught to remove from his image any perceived threat to wholesome American values. Albee may not have had Elvis in mind, but *The American Dream* does tweak the glamor of showbiz in a homogenized America. After exchanging banalities with Mrs. Barker and Grandma, the Young Man leaves the stage, only to reappear for the benefit of Mommy and Daddy. Showcasing him as if he were the winner of a beauty pageant, Mrs. Barker goes to the front door and "*the Young Man is found therein. Lights fill up again as he steps into the room*" (112). His second entrance is a faux epiphany, a mélange of burlesque, vaudeville, and photo op. Visual, clichéd, mercenary, and shallow, the Young Man is a cartoon-like character in an antimimetic performance.

This second twin reinforces the dangers of the American Dream even more caustically than does the first. Through the story of the Young Man's life, Albee gives us a rerun of the past as well as a doomsday look at the present and future. The first twin at least had feelings – he "cried [his] heart out," "had eyes for Daddy," and "called Mommy dirty names" (100). His arriviste brother has none. Since they were "torn apart at birth," though, the Young Man has "suffered losses," cannot "love anyone with his body," and has "been drained, torn asunder" (115), replicating emotionally what his twin went through physically. Naturally, Mommy is immediately attracted to the Young Man, poking him in immodest awe of his physique, and gleefully hires him. Through the biographies of these two boys, Albee unpacks the speciously ameliorative ideology of consumerism. True to the familiar promises of a consumer-pleasing economy, Mommy and Daddy end up buying one twin and getting another free – thereby getting their money's worth from the Bye-Bye Adoption Agency (a pun on Buy/Buy, according to Ruby Cohn).[29] By destroying the first twin and, at Mrs. Barker's suggestion, adopting the second, Mommy and Daddy finally appear to receive (temporary) satisfaction. Yet as Grandma says at the conclusion of *The American Dream*: "I guess that just about wraps it up. I mean, for better or worse, this is a comedy, and I don't think we'd better go any further. No, definitely not. So let's leave [. . .] while everybody's happy . . . while everybody's got what he wants . . . or everybody's got what he thinks he wants" (127). Here is the goal and the fear of the materialistic, consumer-driven America that Albee exposes, as well as an indictment of a theatre mired in conventional, comedic endings.

* * *

Albee explores yet another dimension of the American Dream-turned-nightmare in *The Death of Bessie Smith* (1960) – the seditious clichés of racism and color within an absurd world of violence. Once again, he attacks the institutionalization of hate and hypocrisy, indifference and prejudice. *Bessie* is a terrifying work about the legendary blues singer who died after an automobile accident in 1937 because a white hospital in Memphis reportedly refused to admit her. The play becomes even more chilling because of the nightmare feel and meaninglessness surrounding her death and its impact on the other characters – a bigoted white nurse, a light-skinned African-American orderly, and an ineffective and callow white intern who wants to fight in the Spanish Civil War. Bessie, the black diva, has been mythologized in Langston Hughes's poetry, James Baldwin's novel *Another Country*, Tennessee Williams's *Orpheus Descending*, and Sherley Anne Williams's cycle of poems *Some One Sweet Chile* (1982). Albee's play, which Mel Gussow labels as "the most overtly political of all his works" (132), contributes to the myth.[30]

Unfortunately, *Bessie* has also been one of Albee's most neglected works. It premiered, like *The Zoo Story* the previous September, in Berlin, on April 21, 1960, but without the accompanying enthusiasm generated by the earlier play. *Bessie* received a better reception off-Broadway, when paired with *The American Dream* in March 1961, but still critics complained about its melodrama, loose structure, lack of resolution, and diffuseness. Ever the experimenter, Albee chose in *Bessie* a more fluid form to accommodate the rapid flux of terror – of abandonment (as in *A Delicate Balance*), of false promises (as in *Seascape*), and the folly of pretense (as in *Virginia Woolf*). *Bessie* unfolds rapidly with scenes alternating between the Nurse's house and the hospital, and with the offstage events of Bessie's traveling and death reported by Jack, her companion. *Bessie* is one of Albee's most cinematic works. There are places in the script ideally suited for flashbacks, close-ups, monologues, cinematic dissolves, fade-outs, split screens, and shots of the Nurse intercut with those describing Bessie. Albee did write a screen-play version of *Bessie*, but it was never produced. Essentially, the very strengths of Albee's play assured that it would not work as a film: this is a dialogue-dominated script premised on the theatrical device of an unseen,

PHILIP C. KOLIN

off-stage character. Moviegoers might insist on seeing Bessie larger than life.

Yet Bessie, like Albee's other unseen characters (such as the bumble in *The American Dream* or Tobias's son in *A Delicate Balance*), exerts a powerful force in the play, especially through association with the music heard at crucial times. We hear it at the beginning of the play when the Nurse's father shouts, "You play those [. . .] nigger records full blast . . . me with a headache" (30). We hear it in Scene 3 as Jack awakens Bessie for their trip north, and at the very end of the play, when Jack reports that she is bleeding to death. Like a piece of the blues that Bessie herself might have sung, Albee's play scores the deceptions of life and the heartbreaks of love. His initial stage direction synergistically alludes to the blues: "*At the curtain, let the entire stage be dark against the sky which is hot blue*" (25). Possibly Albee had in mind the famous opening stage direction of another play that is saturated with the blues and "Blue piano" – *A Streetcar Named Desire*: "The sky that shows around the dim white building is a peculiarly tender blue" reflecting "the atmosphere of decay."

Albee, many of whose best friends at the time were composers, has frequently compared playwriting to writing music, and in *Bessie Smith* he demonstrates how to put this belief into practice. Providing a contrapuntal effect, Albee juxtaposes two couples – one white (Nurse and Intern) and the other black (Bessie and Jack) – throughout the play to establish parallels and tensions between the Nurse and Bessie. Ultimately, the Nurse is trapped emotionally just as Bessie is physically when her arm is imperiled in the car accident. Aptly in charge of "admissions," the Nurse confesses, "I am sick of the smell of Lysol . . . I could die of it . . . I am sick of going to bed and I am sick of waking up. [. . .] I am tired of the truth . . . and I am tired of lying about the truth . . . I am tired of my skin . . . I WANT OUT" (70–71). She seems completely imprisoned in her own self-hatred and concomitant contempt of others. Yet Albee's first scene with her father provides some psychological grounding for the Nurse's existential dilemma. She is not just a monster or misogynist caricature, but, rather, the creation of a loveless and cruel society. She debases herself by attacking the blackness – the marginalized Other – within herself. Unfortunately, there is no Jerry to push her into greater awareness and appreciation of self and other. Albee thus decries the way racial segregation warps and traps black people and white people alike. The black music we hear in *Bessie* comments on the Nurse's heartbreaks as well as the singer's.

Both women are further characterized through a series of parallels involving automobiles, travel, and doomed attempts to escape.[31] The Nurse's love affair with the Intern, a cloying and sordid ritual in his "beat up" car, contrasts with the honest intensity and love that Jack shows for Bessie, alive and dead. Similarly, in an ironic reversal of the usual order of racial privilege, the Nurse craves the freedom and acclaim that the black woman has already attained. Tragically though, Bessie's death does not bring change or insight into the other characters' lives: they interpret it only in terms of their own narrow, self-protective interests. The Orderly wonders why a dead person has been brought to the hospital, the Intern furiously justifies his inability to save her, and the Nurse hysterically attacks the Intern for failing to be the "great white doctor" (80). In a letter to Albee before the German premiere, Pinkas Braun – who was instrumental in getting both *The Zoo Story* and *Bessie* performed in Germany – insightfully observed that the "arrival . . . of a dead Negro . . . beyond help [is] a gesture of hope beyond hope."[32] This may be why Bessie is unseen in Albee's play.

The Death of Bessie Smith is very much a drama about racial bigotry, but it also shares much in common with *The Zoo Story* and *The American Dream*. On the surface, *Bessie* may appear to be filled with naturalism, but like *The Zoo Story* or *Dream*, it has a hypnotic, surrealistic undercoating. Like them, *Bessie* attacks social rituals, the illusions of power, and a callous society that robs the individual of dignity, identity, and life. Albee's satire is no less bitter, just bloodier, in *Bessie*. Despite the fact that she dies offstage and Jerry dies in front of an audience, Bessie's death is described in much more gruesome detail. Some of Jerry's techniques spill over into *Bessie*. Comparable to Jerry's story of the dog and his loveless background are Jack's two speeches – the first on Bessie having to go north to sustain her career, and the second, scattered over several pages, on her "emergency" and his futile pleas for help. Moreover, as in *The Zoo Story*, *Bessie* focuses on the pain and suffering of the outcast-fugitive as well as the artist's plight in a hostile society. Like Mommy in *Dream*, the Nurse cannot get satisfaction sexually, socially, or professionally. Although she is a much more human portrait than Mommy (and some critics even consider that the Nurse is the center of Albee's play), both women are nonetheless part of a system that abandons civic responsibility and spreads psychic chaos instead.

As in *The Zoo Story* and *The American Dream*, too, *Bessie* pricks the illusions of identity. Peter's smugness, Mrs. Barker's officiousness, FAM's hypocrisy – all surface, though more violently, in *Bessie*. Albee strips the *poseur*-players in all these breakout one-acts of their masks. In *Bessie*, the Orderly is accused by the Nurse of bleaching his skin to look white; in like measure, the Intern attacks the Nurse for her sexual hypocrisy, claiming that (since her self-hatred is even greater than her inculcated race hatred) she would be subconsciously willing to marry a black man. Further self-deceit is seen in the belief of the Nurse's Klan-loving father that he is a friend of the mayor (he is not), and in the white hospital's pretense that it treats the wounded with mercy, while taking pride in refusing Bessie help. Dreams are not so much deferred in *Bessie* as they are destroyed. Only the looming mythos of the unseen diva remains: "No one has exclusive rights on Bessie" (37). In his early, revolutionary one-acts, Edward Albee showed his family, his country, and the American theatre that they did not have exclusive rights to the way in which he could voice his art.

NOTES

1. Edward Albee, *The American Dream and The Zoo Story* (New York: Signet, 1961), p. 53. Further references to these plays will be cited parenthetically in the text.
2. Harold Clurman, "Theatre," *The Nation*, February 11, 1961, p. 125.
3. Alan Schneider, *Entrances: An American Director's Journey* (New York: Viking, 1986), p. 271.
4. Martin Esslin, *The Theatre of the Absurd* (New York: Doubleday, 1961), p. 268.
5. Quoted in Gerry McCarthy, *Edward Albee* (New York: St. Martin's Press, 1987), p. 15.
6. Christopher Bigsby, *Modern American Drama: 1945–2000* (Cambridge: Cambridge University Press, 2000), p. 129.
7. Sylvie Drake, "Few Tears on this 'Virginia Woolf,' " *Los Angeles Times*, October 10, 1989, Calendar section, p. 4.
8. The first three interpretations were advanced by the following respectively: Richard Kostelanetz, "The Art of Total No," *Contact* (Oct/Nov 1963), pp. 62–70; Tom Driver, *Christian Century* (February 17, 1960), p. 193; Rose Zimbardo, "Symbolism and Naturalism in Edward Albee's *The Zoo Story*," *Twentieth-Century Literature* 8 (April 1962), pp. 10–17; the other themes have been discussed by a variety of critics, including Esslin; Anne Paolucci, *From Tension to Tonic: The Plays of Edward Albee* (Carbondale: Southern Illinois University Press, 1972); Gilbert Debusscher, *Edward Albee: Tradition and Renewal* (Brussels: Center for American Studies, 1969); C. W. E. Bigsby, *Confrontation and Commitment: A Study of Contemporary Drama* (Columbia: University of Missouri Press, 1968); and Michael E. Rutenberg, *Edward Albee: Playwright in Protest* (New York: Avon Books, 1970).
9. Mel Gussow, *Edward Albee: A Singular Journey* (New York: Simon and Schuster, 1999), p. 146.
10. Schneider, *Entrances*, p. 270.
11. Friedrich Luft, "Die Zoo-Geschichte," *Die Welt*, October 1, 1959.
12. For an elucidation of Beat principles, see Gregory Stephenson (ed.), *The Daybreak Boys: Essays on the Literature of the Beat Generation* (Carbondale: Southern Illinois University Press, 1990); Edward Halsey Foster, *Understanding the Beats* (Columbia: University of South Carolina Press, 1992); and Ann Charters, *Jack Kerouac: A Biography* (New York: St. Martin's Press, 1994).
13. Allen Ginsberg, *Collected Poems, 1947–1980* (New York: Harper Collins, 1988).
14. Philip C. Kolin (ed.), *Conversations with Edward Albee* (Jackson and London: University Press of Mississippi, 1988), p. 84.

15. Kolin, *Conversations*, p. 81.
16. Ibid., p. 187.
17. Robert Bennett, "Tragic Vision in *The Zoo Story*," *Modern Drama* 20 (March 1977), pp. 55–66.
18. Gussow, *Edward Albee*, p. 93.
19. Edward Albee, *The Sandbox, The Death of Bessie Smith* (with *FAM and YAM*) (New York: Signet, 1963). Further references to these three plays will be cited parenthetically in the text.
20. Bigsby, *Modern American Drama*, p. 129.
21. See Ruby Cohn, *Dialogue in American Drama* (Bloomington: Indiana University Press, 1971), p. 137. Cohn also connects Grandma's cruel fate with Beckett's *Endgame*, in which Hamm puts his decrepit parents in an ashbin.
22. Steven Drukman, "Won't You Come Home, Edward Albee?" *American Theatre* 15.10 (December 1998), p. 17.
23. See Lincoln Konkle, "American Jeremiah: Edward Albee as Judgment Day Prophet in *The Lady from Dubuque*," *American Drama* 7 (Fall 1997), pp. 30–49.
24. See Lawrence R. Samuel, *Brought to You By: Postwar TV Advertising and the American Dream* (Austin: University of Texas Press, 2001).
25. Esslin, *The Theatre of the Absurd*, p. 267.
26. Philip Nye and Anna Peters, *Ending the Cycle of Abuse: The Stories of Women Abused as Children and the Group Therapy Techniques That Helped Them Heal* (New York: Brunner/Mazel Trade, 1995).
27. Gussow, *Edward Albee*, p. 33.
28. Brian Way, "Albee and the Absurd: *The American Dream* and *The Zoo Story*," *Stratford-Upon-Avon Studies* 10 (London: Edward Arnold, 1967), p. 191.
29. Cohn, *Dialogue*, p. 137.
30. Gussow, *Edward Albee*, p. 132.
31. See Philip C. Kolin, "Cars and Traveling in Edward Albee's *The Death of Bessie Smith*," *College Language Association Journal* 30 (June 1987), pp. 472–480.
32. Quoted in Gussow, *Edward Albee*, p. 134.

Figure 3. *Who's Afraid of Virginia Woolf?*, Broadway premiere, 1962. With George Grizzard as Nick, Uta Hagen as Martha, and Arthur Hill as George. Set by William Ritman.

3

MATTHEW ROUDANÉ

Who's Afraid of Virginia Woolf?: Toward the marrow

Love had a thousand shapes. There might be lovers whose gift it was to choose out the elements of things and place them together and so, giving them a wholeness not theirs in life, make some scene, or meeting of people (all now gone and separate), one of those globed compacted things over which thoughts linger, and love plays.

Virginia Woolf, *To the Lighthouse*

Before they slept, they must fight; after they had fought, they would embrace. From that embrace, another life might be born. But first they must fight, as the dog fights with the vixen, in the heart of darkness, in fields of night.

Virginia Woolf, *Between the Acts*

Who's Afraid of Virginia Woolf? (1962) is Edward Albee's most affirmative play. Given the accusatorial narrative animating the play, calling this his most affirmative work may seem a bit curious. After all, George and Martha, and Nick and Honey, are characters who take delight in attacking others, in belittling those whose self-interests differ from their own, and in betraying those whose conceptions of reality differ from their own. Irony and sarcasm are born from characters who increasingly obey compulsions they seek to resist. And those compulsions have become so suffused within their language and action that these characters have devolved, in the Beckettian sense, into habit, their routines anesthetizing their responses to the self, the other, and the culture they inhabit. Moreover, after some three and a half hours of bloodletting, many in the audience point to the verbal and psychological assaults as evidence that this is a drama whose negativity and ambiguity confirm the playwright's essentially pessimistic stance. By the end of so many Albee plays, and especially *Who's Afraid of Virginia Woolf?*, these critics argue, a kind of nihilism infiltrates the stage. Indeed, for many, an ungovernable Darwinianism pushes George and Martha as well as Nick and Honey onward, their shared lack of clear purpose in their respective lives the only discernible certainty in a play filled with uncertainty.

On the surface, such a reading is understandable. George, a less than successful associate professor of history at a small New England college, and Martha, his wife, "seem to be having *some* sort of a" marital meltdown.[1]

The daughter of the college's president, Martha is an angry, frustrated – and remarkably strong woman. George, a humanist whose private life and professional career have foundered, has become so preoccupied with history that he has, in effect, abrogated claims to self-reliance and has withdrawn from any real commitment to the self and the other. After a faculty party, Martha has invited Nick and Honey over for a nightcap. Nick, a young biologist new to the college, emerges as a smug opportunist, a patronizing scientist who married, we discover, for money, not love. His wife Honey is on the one hand a comedic airhead who provides much humor, and who also appears subjugated by her husband and endures his trivializing remarks throughout the evening. On the other hand, Honey, like Martha, harbors much frustration and, beyond that, is plagued by a sense of dread and terror. What first seems to be merely an obligatory brief, late-night visit turns into an all-night party in which George and Martha, and, in their own way, Nick and Honey, come to terms with their own troubled lives. And coming to terms, in this play, involves verbal insults, physical attacks, and, finally, a series of epiphanic moments in which their own fundamental conditions are laid bare. So it is not surprising that many regard this play as a quintessentially negative work.

Such a bleak assessment, however, does not really capture the spirit and resolutions that ultimately reveal themselves in *Who's Afraid of Virginia Woolf?* Such spirit and resolutions may be best located in the final moments of the play. For here Albee shifts the texture of the action in the drama's denouement. After the intense exorcism scene in Act 3, and after Nick and Honey make their final exit, Albee fills the last four pages of the script with thirteen brief questions ("MARTHA: It was . . . ? You had to? / GEORGE: (*Pause.*) Yes." [240]). The questions are first tactical, then personal, and finally metaphysical. Unmasked by their own actions, shorn of the fictional and dramatic world they have constructed this evening, George and Martha, and perhaps Nick and Honey, have just experienced a cathartic, purging moment – what Albee calls "the cleansing consciousness of death"[2] – and now recognize the importance of facing their lives without illusions. Faced with the alternative (abandonment, aloneness, loss, rejection, anger, and so on), George and Martha reformulate their own minimal but important society among themselves. The fragility of their sanity, of their marriage, of their very existences acknowledged, this couple reunites. Forgiveness is brokered. Mixing self-disclosure with self-awareness, George and Martha recognize their sins of the past and are, perhaps, ready to live their lives without the illusions that have deformed their world for the past two decades. They will, Albee implies, work within their own freshly understood emotional speed limits to restore order, loyalty, and perhaps even love to their world. In brief, their language at the play's end, I believe, privileges a grammar of new beginnings, however uncertain such new beginnings may prove to be.

Who's Afraid of Virginia Woolf? also signaled a new beginning for its author. Until this point, Albee had staged his work abroad, in Germany, and in small off-Broadway venues in New York City. However, Albee, Alan Schneider, the director, and Richard Barr and Clinton Wilder, the producers, decided to stage the play at Broadway's Billy Rose Theatre.[3] Starring Arthur Hill and Uta Hagen as George and Martha, and George Grizzard and Melinda Dillon as Nick and Honey, the play, which premiered on October 13, 1962, became an instant hit, bringing the still relatively underappreciated Albee from the margins to the very epicenter of the American stage. The play ran for some 664 shows before packed houses. Whether in praise or scorn, theatregoers responded. It was, many hoped, a play that demonstrated that Broadway – ever on the verge of financial collapse and increasingly becoming a showcase theatre – could still be an initiating theatre, where daring, fresh work could be staged before mainstream audiences. What was true, the critics felt, for O'Neill, Williams, and Miller, might be true for this new, iconoclastic playwright.

Although Broadway, it turned out, would never return to the glory days of the earlier twentieth century – when it was the site for staging the best in new American drama – Albee succeeded with *Who's Afraid of Virginia Woolf?* in rekindling an excitement about the American theatre. Suddenly the theatre mattered again. When Albee published a slightly irreverent piece in the *New York Times* nine months before *Virginia Woolf* premiered, in which he called Broadway the true theatre of the absurd because of its cultural production of and its preference for superficial work; when Albee found himself on the cover of *Time* magazine and traveling at the height of the Cold War to the Soviet Union with John Steinbeck and others; when the play was controversially denied the Pulitzer Prize it so clearly deserved; and when he championed such unknown playwrights as Sam Shepard and Adrienne Kennedy, Albee was seen as the new anger artist, one whose moral seriousness and acerbic wit made him the one who surely would help to revive the American stage.

And, to a degree, *Who's Afraid of Virginia Woolf?* did just that. It went on to win numerous awards and was widely taught at universities throughout the country. When the play was subsequently staged in various cities across America and abroad, it was sometimes censored – sometimes it was even banned. Some psychologists used the play as a perfect "case study" for their patients undergoing marriage counseling. The movie version, starring

Elizabeth Taylor and Richard Burton, became one of the most lucrative films of 1966 for Warner Brothers and garnered thirteen Oscar nominations that year. The play has remained enormously popular, and if cultural tastes have shifted since its 1962 premiere, so that its once-shocking language no longer seems nearly so, it still is regarded as one of the key works in American dramatic history. Albee's language opened the Broadway stage to a riposte that was as refreshing to 1962 audiences as were Williams's lyrical dialogues in *The Glass Menagerie* seventeen years earlier and Mamet's streetwise dialogues in *American Buffalo* thirteen years after. It is hardly surprising that some of the contemporary era's most talented actors and actresses – Richard Burton, Paul Eddington, Uta Hagen, Diana Rigg, Colleen Dewhurst, and Billie Whitelaw, to name a few – have poured themselves into *Who's Afraid of Virginia Woolf?*

While most see the play as a heated domestic drama, *Virginia Woolf* is not without its political textures. Indeed, the play has a purchase on the public's consciousness, too, because it captures selected public issues of the nation as those issues are registered through the private anxieties of the individual. The anger of the play reflects Albee's rebellion against a culture whose identity greatly transformed during his youth. In the late 1940s and through the 1950s, Albee took measure of and became disenchanted with the rapidly shifting industrial, social, and historical climate of America. A young man in his teens and twenties during this period, Albee felt as perplexed with American culture as would Jerry, his first antihero in *The Zoo Story* (1959). An emerging civil rights movement, the frigidity of the Cold War, the building tensions in Southeast Asia that soon saw America involved in the Vietnam debacle, the assassination of a president and other important leaders in the country, and many other transnational events all created a sense of civic unease, as Americans struggled to maintain some moral balance between public virtue and private desire. In the months before Albee premiered *Who's Afraid of Virginia Woolf?*, U.S.-Soviet relations headlined world news. For six days in October 1962, as the cast went through final rehearsals; Khrushchev and Kennedy brought us to the brink of nuclear war. The Soviets had shipped missiles to Cuba; America threatened military intervention, and Khrushchev blinked. The crisis was diffused when the missiles were ordered back to the Soviet Union. After the Korean War in the earlier 1950s, and the Soviet Union's successful launching of Sputnik in 1957, the resolution of the Cuban missile crisis was seen as both a triumphant moment for America and a terrifying warning about the very precariousness of existence, given the nuclear threat that nearly became Apocalypse Now. And yet, as new-frontier optimism swept the land and *Virginia Woolf* dazzled Broadway, Kennedy also authorized sending American troops to Vietnam.

America was becoming more aware of its faults – no minor point for a country which saw itself and its supposed perfections as some kind of proof of its lack of imperfection – but still seemed energized by a naive ebullience and unwavering faith in the myth of the American Dream. The pot of gold at the end of the rainbow surely loomed just beyond the horizon, many Americans felt, even as Albee lamented in 1960 that too many people in America had substituted "artificial for real values in our society," and insisted that his theatre was "a stand against the fiction that everything in this slipping land of ours is peachy-keen."[4] Until November 22, 1963 at noontime – when an assassin's bullets shattered Camelot – America reveled in its post-World War II idealism, though with *The Zoo Story*, *The Death of Bessie Smith* (1960), *The American Dream* (1961), and *Who's Afraid of Virginia Woolf?* Albee altered the aesthetic battleground of defining nationhood with a dissenting voice of genuine theatrical and cultural power. So beyond the clever naming of his characters – George and Martha supposedly being named after George and Martha Washington, the country's first First Family, and Nick being named after Nikita Khrushchev – lies a politicized cultural critique of a country that, for Albee, was in moral decline. It was, Albee also felt in 1962, a decline fueled in part by the refusal of a large number of Americans to look beyond the surface platitudes of the day, and by the resulting banalization of national ideals and of Western civilization itself. And this is why, when reflecting on the script, it is important to consider George's telling "marrow" allusion.

Near the play's end, George explains to a baffled Honey, "When you get down to bone, you haven't got all the way, yet. There's something inside the bone . . . the marrow . . . and that's what you gotta get at" (155). The marrow allusion is significant, for it provides a key moment in the action, a controlled emotional highpoint for George, a revelatory emotional still point for the audience. Here George finally realizes what is necessary to save not his marriage, but his and Martha's very existence: the son-myth deforming their world must be confronted and, against unfavorable odds, purged from their psyche. The marrow allusion signifies George's awareness that stripping away the illusion governing their lives is essential for their very being in the world. Such knowledge prepares the audience for the ambivalent resolutions established after three long acts. Beneath the play's playfully devastating gamesmanship and animosity lies the animating principle of genuine love which – sometimes unspeakably, sometimes ironically, always paradoxically – unites George and Martha. George realizes that, to excise the incubi haunting their psyches, he must first emotionally prepare Martha for "total war" (159), by externalizing the child-myth, which symbolically places us in the "marrow" or the essence of their relationship. Catharsis precedes spiritual regeneration.

The very exorcizing process that liberates George and Martha prompts many critics to fault the play. Too sentimental, too indeterminate, the play's resolution for many produces hollow resonances. The exorcizing of the son-myth is hardly believable psychologically, and the tenuous reunion of George and Martha seems unearned. The emotional tension that Albee constructs, other critics feel, collapses miserably from its own weight: the killing of the child and the denouement simply do not account for all the evening's dizzying events. "Coming after two acts of cascading turbulence," writes one reviewer, "this plot resolution is woefully inadequate and incongruous, rather like tracing the source of Niagara to a water pistol."[5] Shorn of their private fantasy, George and Martha emerge more as two infantile adults recovering from an evening of self-generated hysteria than as caring or conscious individuals. They survive, for Harold Bloom, "only to endure the endless repetition of drowning their breaths, in this harsh world, in order to go on telling their story." Bloom consigns George and Martha to shallow caricature figures whose histrionics reduce the play to little more than "a drama of impaling, of love gone rancid because of a metaphysical lack." After the exorcism, Bloom argues, George and Martha reduce themselves to near-nothingness. "George talks, ineffectually; Martha brays, ineffectually; that is their initial reality, when we come upon them. Martha barely talks, or is silent; George is almost equally monosyllabic, when we leave them. A silent or monosyllabic ineffectuality has replaced chattering and braying, both ineffectual. Nothing has happened, because nothing has changed, and so this couple will be rubbed down to rubbish in the end."[6]

Rather than appearing oversimplified or emotionally unearned, however, the ending of Who's Afraid of Virginia Woolf? appears more convincing in both performance and text when we see that it stages the revisioning process that Albee implies is necessary for his characters' spiritual aliveness. The play stages a battle between the sexes, but Albee's real interest lies in presenting love as a unifying presence. Albee supplants the lack of compassion in The Death of Bessie Smith and the apathy in The American Dream with George and Martha's care and love. Love's opposite – indifference – is nowhere in evidence in Virginia Woolf. His dialogue mixes kindness and cruelty, what Jerry in The Zoo Story calls the "teaching emotion," making George and Martha's verbal clashes, for better or for worse, a felt element of their relationship. Thus George can describe his wife as a "spoiled, self-indulgent, dirty-minded, liquor-ridden" woman (157), and Martha may counter with the fact that, "You see, George didn't have much . . . push . . . he wasn't particularly . . . aggressive. In fact he was sort of a . . . *(Spits the word at GEORGE's back.)* . . . A FLOP! A great . . . big . . . fat . . . FLOP!" (84). They are duelists who thrive off individual and collective wizardry, shrewdness, and cleverness. Their wittily devastating repartee is born out of a deep love for the other, a point they lose sight of but regain in Act 3. Here the tensions and asymmetries between George and Martha give way to rapprochement, rapprochement to relationship, and relationship to love. The threat of anomie yields to the hope of authentic engagement.

At the very end of the play, Albee presents a revelatory minimalist scene. After the tensions of the exorcism ease, he deploys a different kind of language. Structurally, the scene parallels the opening moments of the play with Martha's repeated question-asking. Whereas the opening questions were laced with sarcasm, gamesmanship, and anger, however, the closing inquiries are free from such nervous tensions. Earlier, George and Martha reveled in questions that maimed. They are now more willing to ask difficult questions tenderly, questions geared toward restoring order and marriage. The rhetorical gallantries and linguistic attacks are nowhere in evidence. These two connoisseurs of verbal dueling now communicate simply, directly, with no wasted emotion. Once so ennobled by their lexical inventiveness, by the very performativity of their performance, which conferred upon an illusion the status of objective reality, George and Martha are brought to earth, not merely by sacrificing their son, but also by sacrificing the kind of language that so animates this evening's actions. The game-playing, for now, is over: the scene signifies the end of their shared fantasy, the compression of words underscoring their newfound perception. In place of embellished repartee we hear a disjointed, splintered exchange, a duologue whose tonal quality emphasizes their reentry into the here and now – and into the Real. Anxiety and fear remain; but relationship replaces hatred, love overrides indifference. Where once the vacant spaces between them were masked with a marvelously devastating language-war, now those vacancies are granted their presence, as insecurities are no longer concealed within linguistic ambushes. The tenderness apparent in this halting, closing exchange suggests their willingness, not to return to "sanity" or "happiness," but to begin the complex process of confronting their essential selves honestly.

The play's closure affirms what Jerry in *The Zoo Story* discovered: "sometimes a person has to go a very long distance out of his way to come back a short distance correctly."[7] The ending of *Who's Afraid of Virginia Woolf?* heralds in muted tones the first steps in living, in Jerry's words, "correctly." Albee resists oversentimentalizing the ending by providing no guarantee of order, comprehension, or survival. Ambivalence prevails. And this is precisely why the play's resolution succeeds in theatrical terms: Albee concedes that the ever-real presence of human fallibility, mutability, and the potency of self-annihilating myths lurk as destructive temptations. This explains, in part, the playwright's comment on O'Neill. *Virginia Woolf*, Albee has said for nearly a half a century, stands as a response to *The Iceman Cometh* (1940), a response acknowledging that the abrogation of the self, of the will to being, is but a drink or fiction away. For O'Neill's heroes, illusions help. For Albee's, they destroy. Within *Virginia Woolf*, as repressed desires give way to honest admissions, so denial gives way to acceptance.

An important feature of the play's ending, then, concerns the resilient ability of George and Martha's collective imagination to reconstruct reality by subordinating illusion to truth. Theirs is a recognition of the regenerative powers implicit in facing existence without what Henrik Ibsen in *The Wild Duck* calls "life-lies." Albee enjoys referring to the affirmative textures of his play, a play that challenges the sorts of illusions paralyzing the figures in *The Iceman Cometh*. "It's about going against the 'pipe-dreams.' After all, *Who's Afraid of Virginia Woolf?* just says have your pipe-dreams if you want to but realize you are kidding yourself."[8]

Before reaching any such insight, however, Albee leads his characters through a three-act structure that chronicles George and Martha's slow realization that their pipe-dream, their imaginary son, is "kidding" as well as killing them. Such recognition, though, comes only after two decades of fabricating and nurturing their child-illusion. Private mythology turns to public issue, however, early in Act 1, as Martha's offstage remarks to Honey about her son signal an ominous shift in the marriage relationship and the psychodynamics of the games they play. The impact of Martha's revelation is immediately apparent not only in the dialogue but in the nonverbal language as well:

> HONEY: (*To GEORGE, brightly.*) I didn't know until just a minute ago that you had a *son*.
> GEORGE: (*Wheeling, as if struck from behind.*) WHAT? (44)

Private game now jars with public façade, for this revelation, whether deliberately or inadvertently delivered by Martha, violates the rules of the game established a lifetime ago by this couple: to keep their son-myth discreet, private. Their secret history thus exposed, the "Fun and Games" of Act 1 turn more threatening, confusing, and problematic.

Albee decenters the audience. He deliberately leads them into a series of unknowns. What are we to make of George's story about "bergin" (bourbon)? Is George the real subject of his (non?)fiction novel that Martha's father censors? Do George and Martha have a child? Indeed, Albee particularly generates a sense of mystery regarding the son, for George and Martha allude to him throughout the performance, obliquely at first, with greater specificity later, and often with a nervous tension. Not until the exorcism will the audience, with Nick and Honey, realize that the son is a fiction, a lie of the mind. What originally began as mere game-playing, the lovers' fanciful construction of a symbolic child to substitute for a real child that they, for reasons never articulated in the play, could never have, has grown into a bizarre relationship on the verge of imploding from its own neuroses. When Martha confides to Honey, unwittingly perhaps, that they have a child, she breaks the unwritten codes of the game, forcing a confrontation regarding their grasp on objective reality. More than a social embarrassment – after all, what's so unusual about mentioning one's child? – Martha's announcing their son's existence signals, George realizes, that their private life has disintegrated into an unreal make-believe world. Distinctions between truth and illusion, and that relatively narrow space between the real and the imaginary, become blurred, not by the continual drinking, but by a psychotic reliance on (when it's convenient, at least) fiction as truth. George's haunting monody – "Truth and illusion. Who knows the difference, eh, toots? Eh?" (201) – is more than a witty, sarcastic, or even ironic comment.

His many truth and illusion references shape some of the deeper epistemological dimensions of the play. Such dimensions became increasingly pronounced in subsequent Albee plays, especially *Tiny Alice* (1964), *Box* and *Quotations from Chairman Mao Tse-Tung* (1968), and *Three Tall Women* (1994). The truth and illusion refrain also testifies to George's awareness of and commitment to sorting through the real and the imaginary (even though George, himself, cannot always do so clearly), and places his verbal attacks in a broader context. George confirms the point when the comic outburst shifts into a more tragic insight: "But you've taken a new tack, Martha, over the past couple of centuries . . . I don't mind your dirty underthings in public . . . well, I *do* mind . . . but you've moved bag and baggage into your own fantasy world now, and you've started playing variations on your own distortions, and, as a result . . . " (155). This moment crystallizes the dangers of their games and is as revealing to George as it is vital to Martha. As if coming out of a years-long drunken stupor, George gradually realizes, as booze, compromise, and passivity give way to sober insight, thought, and action, that he must shock Martha into some definitive awareness of her (and his) deteriorating state. George, like Albee himself, must become the anger artist. His lines taper off in the passage above, but the implication is clear: Martha and George will descend deeper into their own form of madness if they do not relinquish their dependency on such "distortions." So while it is helpful to view *Who's Afraid of Virginia Woolf?* through the truth and illusion binary, perhaps it is even more accurate to acknowledge the fluidity of the truth-illusion matrix; or, as Stephen Bottoms suggests, this is a play that "does not so much invert O'Neill's dichotomy [between truth and illusion] as dissolve it."[9]

Such fluidity, in part, comes from Albee's ongoing interest in presenting characters who are "imbalance[d]," who are "out of kilter." He feels his task as a playwright is to "represent what those imbalances are."[10] Hence Jerry raves throughout *The Zoo Story* (1959), Julian confesses that he was once institutionalized in *Tiny Alice* (1964), and Agnes in *A Delicate Balance* (1966) openly worries about being possessed by demons. Imbalances, even forms of madness, reveal themselves in selected later plays as well: the disturbed young woman in *Listening* (1976) slits her wrists, Himself in *The Man Who Had Three Arms* (1983) appears nearly insane throughout the play, and the "imbalances" infiltrate the action of *The Play About the Baby* (1998) and, in surprising ways, in *The Goat, or Who is Sylvia?* (2002).

Albee inscribes the imbalances within the ostensible realism of the play's action and language, resulting in a gradual stripping away of structures of order, the façade of rationality. By Act 2 we have a sense of the characters' anger; but only in Act 3 do we comprehend the extent of George and Martha's psychic dislocations and share in the shock of recognition. What originally seems closer to anger and frustration shifts into a broader, more disarming range of human emotions. On one level, their madness preserves their supposed sense of coherence and lucidity. Madness, for George and Martha, sanctions the birth and growth of the child, and provides the appropriate rationalizations needed to sustain the myth. Indeed, for years the child has fulfilled the couple. "He walked evenly between us," Martha says, "a hand out to each of us for what we could offer by way of support, affection, teaching, even love" (221). Illusions, denials, and self-betrayals are the things used to reconstitute their previously arid world. However, the severity of their "imbalances" intensifies. Each act reflects the shift, the play's structure mirroring a disconcerting intensity: the "Fun and Games" of Act 1 build to the "Walpurgisnacht" of Act 2, and reach a crescendo and coda in the "Exorcism" of Act 3. As the pressure of their myth reaches its critical mass, as rational analysis sparks additional marital skirmishes, George knows that they are at a crux moment in which the past, recollected in hostility, forces a calling of the question. George and Martha are at not only a turning point but a breaking point. They begin to realize the collusion, the disintegration of the self, the abrogation of responsibility, and the surrender of the spirit that have pushed them too far.

George, at least, recognizes that, as he moves closer to self-awareness, another set of possibilities reveal themselves. He is not only a player-in-the-games but the author of the very rules of those games. "We are going on," he declares as an engaged performer, "and I'm going to have at you, and it's going to make your performance tonight look like an Easter pageant" (208). Viewed as a metatheatrical character, George is simultaneously the consummate player of roles and the scripter of such roles, the director of the action, the producer of spectacle. He calls attention to the theatricality of his own theater: the parasol as gun scene; the games he orchestrates ("Hump the Hostess," "Get the Guests," and "Bringing Up Baby"). Above all, George *performs*. He first appears as the external observer of Martha's condition and then suddenly becomes an internal participant, a co-conspirator with Martha in their shared fantasies. *Who's Afraid of Virginia Woolf?* can thus be viewed as a Pirandellian work, a play whose words, gestures, absurdist moments, and epistemological questions transform much of the action – despite its surface realism – into an essentially metatheatrical experience.

Like Pirandello, Genet, and Beckett before him, Albee embellishes selected scenes with a deliberate self-consciousness. At times the play calls attention to its own language while at the same time exposing the pure gamesman-ship of that language, deliberately making the spectator aware of the sheer theatricality involved. George and Martha know that they are, at times, entertaining, acting, even using their guests for their own theatrical pur-poses. To paraphrase Martha, they rise to the occasion. They are performers performing before an audience within an audience – Nick and Honey as well as the actual theatregoer and reader. Part of the sheer playfulness of the play comes from the notion that, in certain scenes, the characters almost become different people.

Albee's Pirandellian textures function on at least two important levels. First, such textures invite the audience to question the nature of the Real. By calling attention to the very nature of theatricality, Albee experiments with the illusion of dramatic mimesis, challenging traditional responses to the the-atre. This is a play that suggests that, with his first foray into Broadway, Albee was eager to take aesthetic risks, to bedevil more conservative audiences with a bold language and experimentalism whose textures and models were more European than American. Soon after the play opened, Albee charged that "Broadway audiences are such placid cows," though his play succeeded in arousing even the more conservative members of the audience.[11] Second, like Pirandello's *Six Characters in Search of an Author* (1922), *Who's Afraid of Virginia Woolf?* invites the audience to break down, or at least minimize, the barrier between itself and the actors, thus creating a more intimate, and dangerous, theatre experience. As Albee observed, "What really happened in *Virginia Woolf?* All the action took place in the *spectator.*"[12] Despite the proscenium arch, and despite what emerges as the play's blatant theatricalism, Albee's voracious and clever script, and the play's claustrophobic set, generate an uneasy intimacy between actor and spectator. This is a play about those seeing and those seen. Albee does not direct George and Martha to confront or argue with the actual audience, as Julian Beck and Judith Malina had members of the Living Theatre do in *Paradise Now* (1968). Still, Albee scripts an aggressive text, testing the emotional limits of the actors and actresses, and expanding the boundaries of theatre as collective, communal spectacle. Albee discussed this point two decades after *Virginia Woolf* appeared, observing the important interactions of the actors and the audiences within his theory of drama:

> In nine or ten of my plays, you'll notice, actors talk directly to the audience. In my mind, this is a way of involving the audience; of embarrassing, if need be, the audience into participation. It may have the reverse effect: some audiences don't like this; they get upset by it quite often; it may alienate them. But I am trying very hard to *involve* them. I don't like the audience as voyeur, the audience as passive spectator. I want the audience as participant. In that sense, I agree with Artaud: that sometimes we should draw blood. I am very fond of doing that because voyeurism in the theater lets people off the hook.[13]

With its relentless verbal dueling, *Virginia Woolf* "draws blood," directly involving the audience in its calculated violence. Albee subverts the authority of his script by casting the seers (the audience) into what is being seen (the performance). In rejecting the spectator's traditional role as voyeur, he wishes to engage the audience as concretely and as emotionally as possible. Perhaps the relevance of Antonin Artaud's theories to Albee's plays becomes more discernible when we consider their relationship to the audience. Albee may be regarded as a leading proponent of using cruelty as a method of purging oneself of demons, of effecting a sense of catharsis, factors which seem germane to Artaud's "theatre of cruelty."

In 1938 Artaud published *The Theatre and Its Double*, a provocative study concerning the art of drama – a study that was, incidentally, first published in English translation in 1958, just as Albee was about to emerge as a new, demonic voice in American theatre. Artaud tackles many issues in the book, including the civic function of the theatre, and the ways in which the theatre can exteriorize metaphysical concerns. The dramatic experience should "disturb the senses' repose," should "unleash the repressed unconscious," and should precipitate nothing short of "a virtual revolt."[14] Cruelty, for Artaud, is the key alchemical element that could generate a revolt within the audience, an audience Artaud views as the bourgeois theatregoers who expected realistic performances. Yet his theories extolling aggression and violence are grounded more in the cerebral and metaphysical than the merely physical, and his theories address religious and mythic experiences that emanate from what he sees as the magical quality of live performance. Artaud was fascinated by the talismanic and transcendent potential of the theatre: by probing into primal, archetypal realities, he theorized, the actor and playwright could release suppressed desires buried within the subconscious by outward societal norms and mores. The implicit miraculism of live theatre could liberate, he felt, and these ideas clearly have a purchase on Albee's dramaturgy.

Ultimately, Albee does not stage the kind of theatre Artaud envisioned: Albee would seem too conventional, too reliant on language for Artaud. Still, Artaud casts an important shadow for Albee. Referring to Artaud's influence on his own work, he emphasizes the value of staging militant performances:

> All drama goes for blood in one way or another . . . Sometimes the act of aggression is direct or indirect, but it is always an act of aggression. And this is why I try very hard to involve the audience. As I've mentioned to you before, I want the audience to participate in the dramatic experience . . . If the drama succeeds, the audience is *bloodied*.[15]

This is precisely the case with *Who's Afraid of Virginia Woolf?* As Nick and Honey soon become participants in George and Martha's metatheatrical performances within the performance, so, too, may the audience become participants "in the dramatic experience." Audience participation, for Albee, contributes to the ritualized forms of confrontation and expiation that are central to this play. And this is why Albee sees Artaudian violence and death as, paradoxically, life-giving:

> If audiences approach the theatre . . . and are willing to participate; if they are willing to have the status quo assaulted; if they are willing to understand that the theatre is a live and dangerous experience – and therefore a *life-giving force* – then perhaps they are approaching the theatre in an ideal state and that's the audience I wish I were writing for.[16]

Albee's desire for mixing violence, danger, and understanding prepares the audience for a life-giving force in Act 3 of *Virginia Woolf*.

In Act 3, "The Exorcism," Albee explores the interstice generated by the truth and illusion matrix. Here the fictive son assumes a most real place within Martha's consciousness during the exorcism. She has become psychologically dependent on this fantasy – a fantasy conceived out of her fearful need, twenty-one years before, to fill a void in her marriage and her own existence. Since then, she has crossed a threshold, so that her child does not merely occupy her thoughts – he possesses her, like some demon spirit. George knows this and, especially in the final act, sets his sights on banishing the son-myth – precipitating a ritualized form of expiation through the performance of an exorcism. Through this stylized process of expunging what was once an innocuous game, but which has now mutated into a pathological obsession, the play invites associations with the mythological history of past rites for the cleansing of evil spirits inhabiting individuals. An exorcism is a ceremony that attempts to dispel or frighten away demonic forces. Structurally, then, Act 3 plays counterpoint to the Walpurgisnacht of Act 2. In old German lore, St. Walburga, a British missionary, worked in an eighth-century convent that became one of the centers of civilization in Germany. Her name was given to Walpurgisnacht, the May Day festival in which witches reveled in an orgiastic, ritualized Sabbath on Brocken, the tallest peak in the Harz Mountains. These are rugged mountains that in St. Walburga's day were thickly forested. During "Walpurga's Night," the witches' Sabbath, demon spirits were exorcized from villages and villagers by a rite in which incense, holy water, and a cacophony of loud noises were used to achieve purgation. By invoking the rite of exorcism, Albee broadens the scope of his domestic drama: its mysterious religious and cultural connotations become part of the iconography of the play. The sacredness of the unknown, the inscrutability of an existential terror become the mystical stage upon which George and Martha enact their fears. In Act 3 demon spirits are first confronted, then externalized through "Bringing Up Baby," and are finally frightened away by the exorcism itself.

In his influential study of myth and ritual, René Girard theorizes that sacrifice is essential if community order and harmony are to be restored. "Violence," Girard writes in *Violence and the Sacred*, "is the heart and the secret soul of the sacred."[17] Sacred violence in the form of a ritual sacrifice, Girard suggests, ultimately cleanses the community of violence. He develops a fascinating account concerning the relatedness of anthropology, classical tragedy, and Freud; and his ideas about the roles of violence, sacrifice, and the ways in which these forces influence community and spiritual vitality place the violence and exorcism we see in *Who's Afraid of Virginia Woolf?* in a positive context. George, by the third act, must come to terms with the sacred violence he must unleash. Thus, as conductor of the exorcism, George first must discover "some way to really get at" his wife (156), a point that critics often take as proof of the couple's viciousness and hatred for the other. But just the opposite is the case. To orchestrate the exorcism, George necessarily begins with an invocation to the inner demons released in Walpurgisnacht by enraging Martha to a psychological breaking point. He can thereby bring up the demons for an essentially religious reckoning. Hence

"Total war" (159). The viciousness of their arguments is a key ingredient, as Girard might suggest, a method of exteriorizing the unconscious fear, the demons lurking within Martha's psyche.

George constructs a set of fictions to reorder reality. Confiding to Honey news that his son is dead, he initiates the exorcizing process. He discusses the need to "peel labels" (212), a reference to stripping away the emotional attachments blocking Martha from accepting the death of their son. While he seems unsure of his exact procedure, he knows how far the peeling process must go: through the skin, bones, and to "the marrow" (213). As George probes from the skin toward the marrow, so, Albee suggests, the aware individual must explore the various levels of perception, from the surface to the deeper levels of consciousness and experience. As part of the exorcism, George involves Nick and Honey in this performance within the performance, and throughout Albee balances the heaviness of the occasion with humorous moments – his method of blending wit and witchcraft, of defamiliarizing the gazing spectator. So it is that a disoriented Honey, while in the throes of her own awakening, can back up George's outrageous story about his son's death: Yes, she lies, George devoured the Western Union telegram that "crazy Billy" delivered, which bore the terrible news (234–235). The directing force of the whole exorcism is a passionate involvement in the process itself: to get at the marrow means to bring up the baby, demystify the child, excise the illusion, and, perhaps, restore spiritual health. Playing the game by his rules, George guides Martha through the ritual, providing the objective corrective when needed, the loving assurance when necessary. The dramatic focus is on the depth and power of Martha's attachment to their myth, a child whose presence counterbalanced the absence within their marriage, whose very being was created out of a fear of unfulfillment, an existential experience of nothingness.

This last act, "The Exorcism," is to Albee's play what the final section, "The Lighthouse," is to Virginia Woolf's *To the Lighthouse*: the turning point as well as an overall image of resolution and unity. Just as George's actions force Martha to begin to confront and come to terms with her dependence on the child-myth, so the ending of Woolf's novel focuses on Lily's coming to terms with her past as she embarks on a new life in her present world, a world that, despite death, reflects for Lily harmony and wholeness. It is also telling that *To the Lighthouse* was, for Woolf herself, an exorcism, a way for her to reckon with the anxieties she experienced in her personal dealings with her parents. Toward the end of the novel, Lily dwells on the kinds of questions which Albee seems also to invite in *Who's Afraid of Virginia Woolf?*: "Was there no safety? No learning by heart the ways of the world? No guide, no shelter, but all was miracle, and leaping from the pinnacle of a tower into the air? Could it be, even for elderly people, that this was life? – startling, unexpected, unknown?"[18] Perhaps these are the kinds of questions Martha will ask herself, the kinds of inquiries born of an awareness Albee would like to instill within the spectator as well. George and Martha will learn that there is no "safety," but in their journey to their own lighthouse, they may learn, as Lily did, to accept their lives without the past deforming their present.

Invoking the name of one of the exemplary modernists of the twentieth century, the very title of Albee's drama invites all sorts of speculations, though Albee downplays the significance of her presence. Originally entitled *The Exorcism*, the play became *Who's Afraid of Virginia Woolf?* when, as Albee was working on a draft of the play months before its premiere, he remembered seeing, in the earlier 1950s, in a bar in Greenwich Village, some graffiti scrawled on the mirror: "Who's Afraid of Virginia Woolf?" He liked it and had his new title. However, beyond the supposed randomness of selecting his play's title looms the specter of Virginia Woolf. In her diaries, essays, and novels, as in her personal life, Woolf explored the gulf between the ideal and the real, and the attendant anxieties inscribed within the long shadow between. Albee did not compose his play with Virginia Woolf per se on his mind, and yet there is that conspicuous title. To dismiss the Virginia Woolf allusion is to risk not appreciating some of the deeper symbolic resonances within the play. Beyond the nursery rhyme tune of the "Mulberry Bush," whose words Albee replaces with the title of the play, remains Virginia Woolf.[19] For Albee's is a play about those reckoning with a lifelong struggle against one's inner demons. It is equally a play about a Martha who can finally answer the question posed by the play's title by admitting, "I . . . am . . . George . . . I . . . am . . . " (242). Like her own fictionalized child, Martha fears being alone, abandoned, and, indeed, fears life itself to such an extent that she has constructed, with her husband, a complicated set of false illusions. Perhaps this is why the playwright has said, "And, of course, who's afraid of Virginia Woolf means who's afraid of the *big bad* wolf . . . who's afraid of living life without false illusions[?]."[20] The differences between Albee's and Woolf's works – in terms of language, subtlety, genre, identity politics, and psychology, are vast, yet certain links reveal themselves.

What is seen and how the real is knowable; the impending decline of civilization; the intermingling of lucidity and forms of madness; the fusion of traditional forms with new imaginative inventions; death and sexuality: these are just some of the issues to which both writers seem drawn. Perhaps the most compelling link between Woolf and Albee concerns their preoccupation with fear. Woolf's public art mirrored her private anxieties, and in *To the*

Lighthouse, as elsewhere, she drew on such tensions while sculpting her narratives. As a child, she was fearful that the fire in her nursery might flame high enough to touch the walls in her room; in *To the Lighthouse*, Cam fears the dancing shadows on the nursery wall; in *Who's Afraid of Virginia Woolf?* we are told that the fictional son, as a child, kept a toy bow and arrow under his bed, "For fear. Just that: for fear" (219). In her autobiographical work, *Moments of Being*, Woolf reported that, to allay her child's fears at night, her mother would tell Woolf to think of beautiful distractions to get her mind off the fire; in *To the Lighthouse*, Mrs. Ramsay, the mother, does the same thing for Cam, the child. In *Who's Afraid of Virginia Woolf?*, Martha recalls how she comforted her "beautiful, beautiful boy" from similar types of fear (220). Fear of the unknown, of psychic dark spaces, of living without psychological crutches – these fears paralyze George and Martha, though their ultimate awareness of such ubiquitous fear enables them to rise above its coercive influence.

Albee's awareness of and sensitivity to fear informs the exorcism of the play. Whether in praise or scorn, the exorcism that brings the play to a climax has been the source of much debate. It is also the source of the play's theatrical largeness. Throughout the play, Albee challenges the audience's sense of logic and the nature of the Real. This subversion of audience perception reaches its apogee through the exorcism of the son-myth. Although, after seeing the play, the audience realizes that Albee has worked carefully to orchestrate what turns out to be the murdering of the son-myth, the audience has little or no clue that the child is anything but real.[21] Until Nick's epiphanic moment of comprehension minutes before the play ends – "JESUS CHRIST I THINK I UNDERSTAND THIS!" (236) – we are led to believe that the son lives. Although there is undoubtedly something ambiguous about the status of the son throughout the play, he is mentioned moments into the play and will be referred to with growing frequency as each act develops. In the midst of the exorcism, Albee draws upon that very illusion to highlight the mixture of appearances and realities, and to keep the audience's sense of what is verifiable ambiguous, even mysterious.

If the audience harbors doubts about the son's existence, such misgivings are seemingly laid to rest in Act 3. The meticulous recalling of his childhood confirms his very being-in-the-world. Even a reluctant George concedes that "the one thing in this whole sinking world" that he is sure of is his "chromosomological partnership in the . . . creation of our . . . blond-eyed, blue-haired . . . son" (72). While surely some in the audience begin to suspect that the son cannot be real, others believe that the frequency with which George and Martha refer to their child reinforces the perception that the child lives. In effect, Albee sets us up: he prepares us for an even greater emotional shock by emphasizing the presence of the illusion that, through the unexpected reversal and subsequent recognition, will explode before our gaze.

As George recites the Mass of the Dead, to confirm his son's enforced demise, the polyphonic quality of Albee's layered use of language fills the theatre. The contrapuntal structure of Martha's English side by side with George's Latin gives the performance a musical texture. "I like the sound of the two languages working together. I like the counterpoint of the Latin and the English working together," Albee notes.[22] This stands as the emotional highpoint of the play, all the verbal assaults leading to this moment of expiation, a cleansing intensified by George's religious plea for mercy evoked by his *Dies irae* allusion, the portion of the Requiem Mass that describes the judgment and is a prayer to Jesus for divine mercy. Apocalyptic in nature, at once a mixture of a penitential rite and a secular plea, the exorcism ushers forth a host of mythical-religious associations. No wonder that, within the exorcism scenes, Albee's stage direction reads that there is a *"hint of communion"* in George and Martha's tender exchanges at the play's end (238). Albee, at least, feels that the exorcism is a cleansing, positive way to end his drama: "George and Martha end the play having exorcized some self-created demons and cut a way through all the nonsense to try to make a relationship based on absolute reality. Strikes me as being a fairly affirmative conclusion to apply."[23]

The denouement of *Who's Afraid of Virginia Woolf?* suggests that the son-myth, for now, is nowhere in evidence. The "hint of communion" underpinning George and Martha's verbal and nonverbal communication implies the start of a loving armistice, a definitive change in their relationship to the self and the other. Albee's ending implies more than the reconciliation of husband and wife. It also implies that they can accept life, its ambiguity and flux included, without illusion. It signifies the vital shift from performance to being. In their resolution, they, and perhaps Nick and Honey, acknowledge the value of living authentically. The inconclusiveness of the play's closure, then, minimizes sentimentality while outlining some of Albee's larger concerns: the playwright provides no promise that their marriage will be redeemed, that the illusion is inexorably purged from their world. It remains to be seen if Nick will grow to be something other than a selfish opportunist who married for money and who patronizes his wife. It remains to be seen if Honey, who finally acknowledges her fear of childbirth, will be able to mature into a more independent woman. There seems to be more hope for George and Martha: their new-tempered union will be measured in terms of their willingness to keep their illusions at bay. But uncertainties linger. Questions remain. Self-doubt continues.

There is in Albee's characters' often irreverent and hostile debates a fractured poetry; there is a nervous energy and a passion to the lives of those whose demons he stages. There is, toward the end of the drama, an intensity, a resonance, and a power which lift at least George and Martha (and, perhaps, Nick and Honey) above the illusions that have wreaked havoc in their personal lives. George and Martha are consummate performers, accomplished storytellers, masters of deceit who implicitly challenge the nature of the Real and hence the elaborate structures erected upon it. George and Martha clearly do not always agree with each other within the alienated environment they inhabit, but they make important contact with the self and the other through the fictions which they deploy with such evident relish during this long evening. Ultimately though, their over-play-acting, their performances within performances, yield to an acceptance of something less "dramatic," and more real. Despite their intense fighting, George and Martha forgive, and in forgiving create the possibility for a sense of love to reassert itself.

In *Who's Afraid of Virginia Woolf?*, Albee allows his characters to confront their lives shorn of the bizarre fictions they have nursed for so long. They face a problematic reality. Such realities, however, allow George and Martha to accept and, with acceptance, to love and, with love, to repair the ruins of their past. Through their long night's journey into day, they have gone a very long distance out of their way to come back a short distance correctly. Again, they progress from performance to being. This is why Albee is a mythmaker who deconstructs myths, a storyteller aware of the coercive power of story. He is, like Tennessee Williams before him and Sam Shepard after, a poet of the theatre who himself discovers poetry in the broken lives which are the subjects of his plays, and in the broken society which they inhabit. This is also why *Who's Afraid of Virginia Woolf?* is Albee's valediction forbidding mourning.

NOTES

1. Edward Albee, *Who's Afraid of Virginia Woolf?* (New York: Atheneum, 1962), p. 33. Further references are to this edition and will be cited parenthetically in the text.
2. Edward Albee, *The Plays, Volume 1* (New York: Coward, McCann, and Geohegan, 1981), p. 10.
3. For excellent accounts of the rehearsal process and the choice to stage the play on Broadway, see Mel Gussow, *Edward Albee: A Singular Journey* (New York: Simon and Schuster, 1999), pp. 151–193, and Stephen Bottoms, *Albee: Who's Afraid of Virginia Woolf?* (Cambridge: Cambridge University Press, 2000), pp. 15–33.

4. Edward Albee, *The American Dream and The Zoo Story* (New York: Signet, 1961), pp. 53–54.
5. "Blood Sport," *Time*, October 26, 1962, p. 84.
6. Harold Bloom (ed.), *Edward Albee: Modern Critical Views* (New Haven: Chelsea House, 1987), pp. 6, 8.
7. Albee, *The American Dream and The Zoo Story*, p. 21.
8. Personal interview with the author.
9. Bottoms, *Albee*, p. 13.
10. Personal interview with the author.
11. Philip C. Kolin (ed.), *Conversations with Edward Albee* (Jackson and London: University Press of Mississippi, 1988), p. 22.
12. Ibid., p. 104.
13. Personal interview with the author.
14. Antonin Artaud, *The Theatre and Its Double*, trans. Mary C. Richards (New York: Grove, 1958), p. 41.
15. Personal interview with the author.
16. Ibid.
17. René Girard, *Violence and the Sacred*, trans. Patrick Gregory (Baltimore: Johns Hopkins University Press, 1977), p. 31.
18. Virginia Woolf, *To the Lighthouse* (New York and London: Harcourt Brace Jovanovich, 1955), p. 268.
19. The tune to "Here We Go Round the Mulberry Bush" has traditionally been used for the song "Who's Afraid of Virginia Woolf?" in productions of the play, in order to avoid infringing Disney's copyright on the more obvious tune, "Who's Afraid of the Big Bad Wolf?"
20. Kolin, *Conversations*, p. 52.
21. Since the play is now so well known, today many in the audience know when going into the theatre that the kid is but an illusion – in much the way they know, now, that Godot will never come, when seeing *Waiting for Godot*. However, in October 1962, when theatregoers were experiencing the play for the first time (and when the first scholarly book on Albee still lay five years in the future), there was, for many, a kind of surprise when discovering that the child is but a lie of the mind. It's not unlike the surprise felt when one first realizes that the three women inhabiting the stage simultaneously in *Three Tall Women* (1991) are really one woman at three differing times of her life.
22. Ibid., p. 59.
23. Ibid., pp. 152–153.

4

JOHN M. CLUM

"Withered age and stale custom": Marriage, diminution, and sex in *Tiny Alice, A Delicate Balance,* and *Finding the Sun*

> "I don't want to kiss you, Martha."
>
> George, in *Who's Afraid of Virginia Woolf?*
>
> "Marriage is a confusing business."
>
> Butler, in *Tiny Alice*

For all the controversy stirred by the shock value of the language in Edward Albee's early work, his plays are surprisingly chaste – more about lack of, or loss of, desire than sex. There is an erotic component missing from his plays, sometimes replaced by madcap performativity, as in the games in *Who's Afraid of Virginia Woolf?* or Claire's dipsomaniacal antics in *A Delicate Balance,* and sometimes replaced by explosions of language, as in *The Zoo Story* (1959). Loneliness and alienation seem more important than sexual desire, which is usually more memory than present reality. Albee's *The Zoo Story* can be seen as a Central Park homosexual pick-up, but it ends in penetration by knife, not penis. Jerry may remember fondly his one homosexual affair, but he has forsaken homosexuality for joyless heterosexuality. Indeed, the rejection of the possibility of homosexual love for a compromised heterosexuality on the part of Albee's characters and the playwright himself, in his work, is a particular problem for critics of Albee's plays and may be responsible for some of their chilliness. Albee seems unable to read his own sexual desires and experiences into his heterosexual characters, which creates a nonerotic coolness. It is no wonder that frustration, not desire, is the compelling emotion in Albee's work.

While some critics have attacked Albee's misogyny, he actually sympathizes with his strong women who are failed by the men they married. The language may be blasphemous or obscene, but its target is literal and metaphorical impotence. Albee's women rail against, or triumph over, men who seem unable or unwilling to "get it up." Yet the sexual frustration in his work is a figure for the emotional and spiritual frustration experienced by his husbands and wives; for marriage – frustrated, unsatisfying marriage – is a central theme of Albee's work. Wives catalogue with revulsion details of their spouses' or lovers' bodies and sexual behavior. Husbands rebuff their wives' sexual overtures. The reason is often despair rather than impotence or lack of desire. Even in his youth, Albee focused on the sexual and spiritual malaise of middle-aged men who have lost the potency, illusions, and certainty of youth.

"I am the Earth Mother, and you're all flops," Martha drunkenly declares in Act 3 of *Who's Afraid of Virginia Woolf?* after young, handsome, studly Nick has failed to "get it up" for Martha.[1] Nick is another version of Albee's American Dream, physically beautiful, intelligent, ruthlessly ambitious, but missing some basic human qualities. Throughout *Virginia Woolf*, Nick is in conflict with Martha's husband George, a middle-aged intellectual lacking Nick's ambition and, perhaps, potency: Nick has sired the child Honey aborts, while sterile George and Martha can only destroy an imaginary child. Neither George nor Nick can measure up to Daddy, Martha's ambitious, successful progenitor who is, for Martha, the measure of a man. But Daddy, the icon of masculine power, is dead. Men never "measure up" in Albee's plays. They are either castrated by monstrous women, as in *The American Dream* (1961), where the ineffectual father's organs have been replaced by tubes and the son's appendages have been cut off, or they wither away of their own will. Impotence, involuntary or perversely willed, seems to be the universal condition for Albee's men. At the end of *Virginia Woolf*, George's intellect and sense of history win over Nick's pragmatism, as they also defeat Martha's illusions of power and fertility. But what is left, after all the brilliant wordplay and the theatrically vital, if destructive, gamesmanship have ended, are aridity and fear, which are all George has to offer. George has triumphed, but it is the victory of negativity. In the plays after *Virginia Woolf*, Albee's men have more in common with the impotent Daddy of *The American Dream* or henpecked Peter of *The Zoo Story* than they have in common with George. His later husbands have given up any active role in their marriage or in their nondomestic lives. In *Marriage Play* (1987), a middle-aged husband wants to leave his wife of thirty years. "What I have discovered is this," he proclaims, "nothing is enough!"[2] "Nothing" becomes a major force in all these plays.

In this essay, I want to explore the ramifications of impotence and marriage in three plays: *Tiny Alice* (1964), *A Delicate Balance* (1966), and a short play that I think is central to understanding Albee's work, *Finding the Sun* (1983). As we shall see, Albee can conceive even less possibility of fulfilling relationships for his gay characters than he does for his middle-aged straight couples.

* * *

Figure 4. *Tiny Alice*, Broadway premiere, 1964. With John Gielgud as Brother Julian and Irene Worth as Miss Alice. Set by William Ritman.

"A union whose spiritual values shall be uppermost"

In his biography of Albee, Mel Gussow writes of *Tiny Alice*: "Depending on one's point of view, it is either a tantalizing intellectual exercise, a deeply probing study of religious martyrdom, a work with a severely schizoid personality, or simply a flagrant act of hubris."3 While most critics have focused on the metaphysical trappings of *Tiny Alice*, a play whose central action can be seen as a kind of existential passion or nihilistic parody of the Christian myth, it is more productive to read the play as a companion piece to Albee's other plays about marriage. After all, though the trappings are pseudo-Christian, the philosophical underpinning of *Tiny Alice* is basically Existentialism 101, familiar to any university student at the time. Julian's cry of discovery – "Consciousness, then, is pain"4 – was hardly original to anyone who had read Sartre or Camus or J. D. Salinger; and who had not in 1964, except, perhaps, the reviewers for New York newspapers who seemed particularly baffled by the play?

Tiny Alice, then, is best understood in the context of Albee's other marriage plays. Indeed, considered sequentially among Albee's original plays, it stands between his two most celebrated dissections of marriage, *Who's Afraid of Virginia Woolf?* (1962) and *A Delicate Balance* (1966). In this play filled with homosexual innuendo and heterosexual banter, a virginal male who is a lay brother (a double entendre?), is seduced into marriage only to find out that he has married something incorporeal, if his bride exists at all. In a parody of the marriage of nuns to Christ, Julian marries an idea of divinity, or the void that people replace with mythic divinity. His wedding feast is also the moment of his death, but I would suggest that though he is betrayed by his nominal wife and her companions, he is incapable of being a husband.

How old is Julian? In the original production, the part was played by a decidedly middle-aged John Gielgud, partnered by a mature Irene Worth as Miss Alice. Gielgud's age and old-fashioned classical acting style – as well as his much-documented bafflement with the role – exacerbated the confusion many felt while watching the first production of *Tiny Alice*.[5] However, Julian could as easily be thirty as fifty. Indeed, *Tiny Alice* would make more sense and fit more neatly into the pattern of Albee's other works (despairing middle age destroying youth) if Julian were a younger, potentially potent man surrounded by cynical, middle-aged antagonists. Would not the Cardinal be more likely to hire a younger, more attractive assistant?

Julian carefully protects his innocence, which he conflates with his faith. Religion – the God men create and the institutions established to maintain the mythology surrounding that God – is for him both insufficient and blasphemous. He has voluntarily spent six years in an asylum to escape spiritual compromise. In the process, he also escaped any real human social or sexual intercourse. Twice in the play, Julian recounts sexual experiences in erotically charged language. The first is his description of a sexual experience – possibly hallucinated – with a fellow inmate who thought she was the Virgin Mary. Julian finds the young woman lying on the ground, raising her arms to him in supplication: "Help me, help me, oh God, God, help me . . . oh, help, help" (62). Julian, who, above all, longs "to be of great service" (118), cannot resist the cry for help. The real or hallucinated event is for him highly erotic: "I came closer, and the sounds, her sounds, her words, the roaring in my ears, the gossamer and the milk film, I . . . a ROAR, AND OCEAN! Saliva, perfume, sweat, the taste of blood and rich earth in the mouth, sweet sweaty slipping . . . ejaculation" (62). The roaring in Julian's ears and the milky film over everything could be read as sexual imagery, but they recur in the play as manifestations of his mental illness. His sexual intimacy with the young woman is probably as fantastic as her subsequent belief that she had been impregnated by Jesus Christ. This Virgin Mary does not bear divinity: she dies of cancer of the womb. As in *Who's Afraid of Virginia Woolf?* with its talk of hysterical pregnancies, abortion, and infertility, there is only barrenness and disease in traditional sites of sexuality and fertility. Julian's description of his sexual experience with the delusional young woman does not present a moment of intimacy, a union of flesh or spirit. It is a solipsistic description of the sensations he experienced, more masturbatory fantasy than intercourse.

The other, even more erotically charged experience of sexual contact he describes is his childhood fantasy of martyrdom: "I could entrance myself and see the gladiator on me, his trident fork against my neck, and hear, even hear, as much as feel, the prongs as they entered me; the . . . beast's saliva dripping from the yellow teeth, the slack sides of the mouth, the . . . sweet, warm breath of the lion; great paws on my spread arms" (124). Julian's vision of martyrdom is as much a description of passive sexual surrender as a description of a gruesome death. The gladiator is "on" him, the prongs of the trident "enter" him, and the lion pins him down before his fangs penetrate his head and the blood from his wounds "bathed . . . my groin" (125). Julian's most vivid sexual fantasy, then, is homosexual, passive, and masochistic, merging sexual ecstasy with oblivion. In many ways, Julian is typical of Albee's men (Peter, Daddy, George, Tobias), who are passive, potentially masochistic personalities – men who have to be seduced by more powerful, more active women. In *Tiny Alice*, we also have a man whose primary sexual fantasy is homosexual finding himself trapped in a barren heterosexual marriage which could never be fulfilling for him. Foster Hirsch sees *Tiny Alice* as a "flamboyant fable in which the scared lay brother is tricked into heterosexuality," but the play also posits that heterosexuality is an impossible choice for Julian.[6] Since John Gielgud's homosexuality was known to many theatre cognoscenti as a result of his arrest under Britain's then draconian antihomosexual laws, it was difficult not to read Julian as at least potentially gay.

As Julian recounts his childhood fantasies of martyrdom, Miss Alice puts her arms around his neck, across his chest, and proposes marriage to him. As she opens her gown and appears nude in front of him, Julian tries to resist by reiterating his wish to sacrifice himself "on the altar of . . . the . . . Lord . . . God . . . in . . . Heaven" (116–117). When Julian finally moves to Miss Alice and is embraced by her, both speak of sacrifice. "You will be hers; you will sacrifice yourself to her," Miss Alice cries, while Julian still speaks of his sacrifice to God. This temptation is one in which Julian remains passive, emotionally and spiritually separate from Miss Alice. We are to believe that the end of Act 2 leads to an unseen sexual union, but it is difficult to imagine Julian being anything but passive and compliant in such an activity. Is his kneeling before Miss Alice the prelude to oral sex with her or merely a form of subservience and worship? Julian is not tempted away from the life of the spirit to the life of the flesh. He is "tempted" away from one vision of sacrificial worship to another.

What tempts him? Is it truly a sexual temptation? Is it the sight of Miss Alice's naked body that lures Julian away from the Church and into marriage, or the combination of Miss Alice's words and Julian's own fantasy of submission and sacrifice? Here Albee is playing with traditional notions of the relationship of spiritual and physical ecstasy – the sort we see in the great paintings of Saint Sebastian, in which a beautiful, feminized man is depicted in a posture of passive surrender while his flesh is being penetrated. What does actual sex have to do with this moment of exaltation? If there has been sex, it is only because Miss Alice has been able to join her words and body to Julian's queer fantasies.

In the third act, when Julian speaks of his marriage, he never mentions the person to whom he is married, never uses the word "love," but rather waxes poetical again about his feelings, his sensations: "I can't tell you the . . . radiance, humming, and the witchcraft, I think it must be, the ecstasy of this light, as God's exactly; the transport the same, the lifting, the . . . the sense of service, and the EXPANSION" (140). While Julian's solipsism and narcissism seem linked primarily to his spiritual journey (if it can be called that), it is also typical of all Albee's isolated characters. It is, after all, by placing his characters in the context of marriage, ideally a lifelong sharing, that Albee dramatizes what makes the ideal impossible. The question here, as in so many of Albee's plays, is what does marriage mean in a world in which we no longer believe in the ideals and religious structures that support the institution? What does marriage mean for people who cannot breach their own isolation? At the end of Tiny Alice, Julian is forced to accept the isolation he has always experienced but has made bearable through his religious fantasies. Julian, shot and dying, is left to create another moment of ecstasy.

Julian marries nothing, or a miniature simulacrum of the woman he thought he married, but what is Miss Alice? In his brutal, homophobic attack on Tiny Alice, Philip Roth catalogues the themes of the play: "male weakness, female strength, and the limits of human knowledge."[7] But "male weakness" and "female strength" do not begin to explain the gender dynamics of Tiny Alice. The play begins in an all-male world, the homosocial, celibate world of the Catholic Church which Julian has chosen to serve. It begins with a dialogue, laden with vitriol and homosexual innuendo, between two men, a Cardinal and a Lawyer, former fellow students at a boys' school. The only harmonious companionship we see in the scene, and perhaps in the play, is that between the two caged birds. "They are a comfort to each other," the Cardinal notes (5), but later, when alone, asks the birds if that is true: "Do . . . do you . . . have much to say to one another, my dears? Do you? You find it comforting?" (22). The caged birds are one physical image of marriage.

Miss Alice is a creature of the men around her. While they seem to serve her, as their functional identities (Lawyer, Butler) suggest, she actually serves them. There is no strong woman here, only a woman rebelling against the position imposed on her by men. Her only revenge is to demean the signs of masculinity on their bodies: "Is it the hair? Is it the hair on your back that I loathe most? Where the fat lies on your shoulderblades, the hair on your back . . . black, ugly? [. . .] Is it your . . . what is the polite word for it . . . your sex? [. . .] ugly coarse uncut ragged . . . PUSH!" (75). In such a relationship, love can only mean momentary lust or possession. As the Lawyer tells Miss Alice: "To love is to possess, and since I desire to possess you, that must mean conversely that I love you, must it not?" (72). In Albee's plays, the struggle between masculine assertion of power and feminine rebellion can never be resolved without anger or regret.

Yet there is another dimension to the deadly marriage ceremony in *Tiny Alice*. In one sense, Philip Roth, for all his cruel heterosexism, was right in his analysis of the play. It is possible to read *Tiny Alice* as a queer vision of heterosexual marriage. Julian faces what many gay men faced in 1964: the choice of an isolated life or the compromise of a loveless heterosexual marriage which could lead to even greater feelings of isolation and entrapment. Marriage could be seen as a sacrifice to the way of the world, supported by the Church and the law. As we shall see in *Finding the Sun*, as late as 1983 Albee could not envisage the possibility of gay men living happily together in a relationship; he could only see them placing themselves unhappily in unfulfilling heterosexual marriages.

One of my professors once said that tragedy is watching a character get what he wants. In getting Alice, Julian gets what he wants: complete surrender to an abstraction and complete solipsism, which in the play is also death. Is this a marriage? In the sense that marriage in Albee is never truly a merging, but always conquest or surrender, never a loving union but always mutual isolation, Julian is married. That this marriage is also asexual, a union of a feminized male with a disembodied idea, is of a piece with Albee's other chaste marriages.

* * *

It's sad to know you've gone through it all, or most of it, without . . . that
the one body you've wrapped your arms around . . . the only skin you've ever
known . . . is your own – and that it's dry . . . and not warm.

A Delicate Balance

In many ways, *Tiny Alice* and Albee's next original play, *A Delicate Balance*
(1966), are companion pieces. Both center on the implications of the discovery of the void, the "nothing" at the heart of human experience, and
assume that human love is the only counter to the existential terror that
nothing causes, while presenting examples of the failure of that potentially
healing love. The move from *Tiny Alice* to *A Delicate Balance* is the move
from an ostensibly metaphysical drama that centers on a marriage to a play
about marriage with realistic trappings but metaphysical implications. In *A
Delicate Balance*, the failed relationships are signified by a failure to relate
sexually. That sexual failure represents a spiritual exhaustion.

A Delicate Balance gives us a weekend in an affluent suburban living room.
Its owners, Tobias and Agnes, have been married for more than thirty-six
years. Their first child was a daughter, Julia, who comes back home after
the failure of her fourth marriage and demands the rights of a child – her
childhood room and the care and devotion of her parents. Their son, Teddy,
died in childhood, after which Tobias ceased to have sexual relations with his
wife. "We *could* have had another son; we could have tried," Agnes says, but
for a year after Teddy's death Tobias, racked with guilt, "spilled his seed" on
Agnes's belly, which was for her a form of desertion: "'Don't leave me then,
like that,'" he remembers her pleading. "'Not again Tobias. Please? I can take
care of it: we *won't* have another child, but please don't . . . leave me like
that.' Such . . . silent . . . sad, disgusted . . . love."[8] However, Agnes did not
voice those pleas when they might have restored their sexual relationship,
and Tobias, fearful of the responsibility and potential loss of another child,
moved into a separate bedroom. Agnes lived with this sudden diminution of
their marriage, which left her bitter and cold. Tobias made a series of passive
choices – literal withdrawal during the sex act and, eventually, withdrawal
into another bedroom – turning their marriage into a chaste one.

"We *could* have had another son" (137), Agnes claims thirty-odd years
later. Not another daughter – another Julia who seems to seek in men
something she is missing or, given her passive father, missing in her own
upbringing – but a son. So at the heart of this marriage, as in so many Albee
marriages, is a dead or missing son. The parents in *The American Dream*
dismember their son, then seek a replacement who will be physically perfect,
but passive. The new son is as spiritually damaged as his twin was physically
maimed. The son in *Who's Afraid of Virginia Woolf?* is nonexistent, which
is a blessing since George and Martha no doubt would psychically destroy

him long before his twenty-first birthday. This imaginary son is killed off, destroyed in the battle between his parents. He began as a game and ended as the stake in a crueller game. A mother's rejection of her gay son is the crucial action in *Three Tall Women*. Would Teddy – a son – have kept Agnes and Tobias's marriage alive? Is he named Teddy after the traditional infant's companion, the teddy bear, comforting and cuddly but not human? More important, why is Tobias riddled with guilt over Teddy's death? In what way is he responsible for his son's premature death?

Julia says that she loved her gay former husband, Charlie, because "he seemed so like what Teddy would have been" (65). "Your brother would not have grown up to be a fag" (65), Toby declares, but popular psychology of the 1960s would claim that the chilly domineering mother and passive father combination made homosexual boys. Having been raised in an extreme version of such a family, Albee seems to have believed that myth. Why is it so important for Tobias to believe his son would be heterosexual, other than that homosexuality would bring shame on Teddy's parents in their conservative, circumscribed, country club world?

Tobias, then, has only one surviving child, daughter Julia, and chooses to live in a house of battling women. Agnes and her Delphic, dipsomaniacal sister, Claire, are constantly at each others' throats, though neither can exist without the other. Julia seems to resent her parents, but she returns home every time a marriage breaks up. Here we have three tall women reminding Tobias of his refusal to be decisive, of the consequences of his shrinking from responsibility and love. In *The Zoo Story*, Jerry mocks Peter for living in a family with three females, a wife and two daughters. According to Jerry, a "real man" would live in a more masculine environment or be more dominating in a house full of women. Yet men like Tobias renounce their position in their households. They choose passivity, the line of least resistance, leaving the women to maintain order. "We let our . . . men decide the moral issues" (132), Agnes tells Tobias, with a telling pause before "men" – but in doing so, the women have also abrogated their responsibility, have allowed their marriages and lives to dwindle.

On the second night of the weekend on which the play takes place, a house full of family and guests forces Tobias back into bed with Agnes, but there is no sex, no talk. Agnes remarks, "There was a stranger in my room last night" (123), and in many ways her husband has become a stranger to her. She knows that only a return to her bed will bring the marriage to life once again. On the same night, their friends Harry and Edna – who have moved in with Agnes and Tobias to stave off the fear of "nothing" which drove them out of their own home – have a failed attempt at reigniting sexual intimacy. Harry tells Tobias, "I got out of bed and I . . . crawled in with Edna. *She* held me. She let me stay awhile, then I could see she wanted to, and I didn't . . . so I went back. It was funny" (156). Edna has a very different version of the same event: "He . . . came to my bed last night, got in with me, I . . . let him stay and talk. I let him think I . . . wanted to make love, he . . . it pleases him, I think – to know he would be wanted, if he . . ." (163). Both versions recount an event in which the woman seems to initiate a sexual act and the man, while taking pleasure in his wife's desire, has no interest in sex and withdraws. Harry and Tobias are indeed the same in their disinclination to have sex with their wives – their willful impotence. However, the loss of sex is part of a larger separation. Harry describes the current state of his marriage to his supposed best friend, Tobias: "Edna and I . . . there's . . . so much . . . over the dam, so many disappointments, evasions, I guess, lies maybe . . . so much we remember we wanted, once . . . so little that we've . . . settled for . . . we talk, sometimes, but mostly . . . no. We don't . . . 'like.' Oh, sure, we *like* . . . but I've always been a little shy – gruff, you know, and . . . shy. And Edna isn't . . . happy" (159). A failed marriage is the end result of too many compromises, too many evasions and lies.

Agnes begins and ends *A Delicate Balance* with her fear, perhaps desire, that she might someday go mad. Her idea of madness is far from violent – indecorous insanity simply would not do in the affluent country club world that Tobias and Agnes inhabit. Her madness, rather, would be a withdrawal: "becoming a stranger in the world, quite . . . uninvolved" (3). This form of madness is what many of the characters in the play seek – a calm detachment like that of Tobias; indifference, irresponsibility. The diminution of their marriages into sexless, regret-filled companionship is a figure for their emotional and spiritual lives. In each moment of the play, there is a potential for change, for actions that would turn marriages, families, and friendships into something meaningful, and each opportunity is lost. Is Albee saying, as Agnes does, that everything is "too late, finally" – that the moment of possible redemption that would come from active involvement in the human community has passed these people by? In Albee's later dissection of a failed marriage, *Marriage Play*, the husband says, "We stare into the dark and know that nothing is enough, *has* been enough, *could* be enough, that there is *no way* not to have . . . wasted the light; that the failure is built into us, that the greatest awareness gives to the greatest dark" (38). *A Delicate Balance* may represent this kind of resignation.

As the married couples accept the bare bones of a marriage, so Albee seems to say that his characters have crossed a point of no return and that they are now incapable of change. As the playwright put it in a 1982 interview, "I thought it [*A Delicate Balance*] was basically about the fact that we become rigid through disuse and that the opportunity for making choices vanishes ultimately."⁹ However, the play also suggests the opposite, that change is possible but too frightening to allow. Claire says to Tobias, "Just think, Tobias, what would happen if the patterns changed: you wouldn't know where you stood and the world would be full of strangers; that would never do" (145). Claire's description of a new order, of change and renewal, sounds very much like Agnes's description of insanity, "becoming a stranger in the world." So even beneficial change is resisted or ignored. Agnes points out what is left when there is no real love, or even "like," among the characters: "Blood holds us together when we've no more . . . deep affection for ourselves than others" (152). The lack of feeling extends to one's self, but family coherence will at least stave off the realization of loss and emptiness.

What is the emptiness that drives Harry and Edna from their home into the household of their best friends? The "nothing" that frightens them sounds like the existential nothing Julian is forced to marry in *Tiny Alice*, the existential void. However, there is something else going on here. As Christopher Bigsby points out, Albee is more a social critic than philosopher.¹⁰ The "nothing" that terrifies Harry and Edna is in great part their marriage, the spiritually empty household, the result of their failed marriage. They claim not so much a hiding place as a family – a loving human community. When Julia asks Claire what Harry and Edna want, she responds, "Succor . . . . Comfort . . . . Warmth" (91–92), those things one claims from a loving family and which Julia demands as her birthright. Tobias has failed to provide those for Agnes, Agnes for her sister, Tobias and Agnes for their daughter and for their best friends. Like the dwindling of Harry and Edna's marriage, this is the result of a series of decisions and failures, not a necessary state. Whatever past possibilities existed, now there are the forms of relationships without the emotions to support them. Tobias says to Harry, "The fact I like you well enough but not enough . . . that best friend in the world should be something else – more – well, that's my poverty" (161), and poverty is the operative term here – a state of want, of lack. The same could be said of all the relationships in the play.

The most hostile conflict in *A Delicate Balance* is that between Agnes and her sister, Claire, who seems like the agency of misrule in the play. Claire will not allow the household to settle into the sterile orderliness that Agnes wants. Her primary objective seems to be to irritate her coldly composed sister and to rouse people into honest discussion and, perhaps, action. Yet Claire is also the most able to understand the behavior of the other characters, offering wry, but compassionate, commentary. "I'm still alive, I think" (152), she claims, but even her liveliness is at the cost of being at an emotional distance from all the characters.

Marriage, then, is both an ideal and a measure of failure of the most basic human emotions. At the end of *Marriage Play*, Gillian, the wife, claims: "Passion in a marriage never dies; it changes. When the passion of passion wanes there are all the others to rush in – the passion of loss, of hatred, the passion of indifference; the ultimate, the finally satisfying passion of nothing" (37). If "a good marriage – a useful marriage – makes individuals" (39), she goes on to say of their marriage, "With any luck, we've not compensated, we've complemented. Well, at least that's how it is supposed to go" (40). Gillian and her husband disagree over "nothing." Gillian has accepted "the passion of nothing" as what her marriage now offers, while her husband's acceptance of the maxim, "nothing is enough," means giving up his marriage as well. Gillian tells him, "You put in a garden every year; you always have; it's hopeless every year – everything: the garden, going on, everything" (40). The important thing is maintaining the form – the garden and marriage. Otherwise everything falls apart. None of the characters in *A Delicate Balance* is ready to accept "the passion of nothing," which they still fear.

* * *

"And I have to be married to a fairy!"
Finding the Sun

Finding the Sun is like a ballet or a Mozart opera: a round of couplings, recouplings, solos, and separations. The themes are marriage and mortality. Here Albee has moved his action out of the affluent, hermetic interiors of his full-length works and, as in *The Zoo Story*, has provided an outdoor setting that is both realistic and symbolic. On one hand, the setting is a New England beach – Nantucket or Martha's Vineyard, perhaps – occupied by a prosperous group of residents and visitors. On the other hand, the beach contains its traditional symbolism of the shore between life and death, and its inhabitants long to find the sun, "the source of all life."[11] Finding the sun would be finding happiness, love, a reason to live – yet a death wish seems more prevalent among the eight characters assembled on this beach: three married couples and a widowed mother with her adolescent son.

Each of the marriages is a recoupling. For the oldest couple, it is a remarriage for companionship. Gertrude, who is sixty, has been married twice before to older men whom she has lost, "not through carelessness, but time" (8). Henden, Gertrude's current husband, is ten years older than her. His wife of forty-six years died of a brain tumor and Henden married again "to be *married* as much as anything, a continuity" (11). Henden claims to like Gertrude "very much," but that is far from a claim of love. Marriage for them is custom, socially ingrained and unquestioned. Yet it is enough, perhaps, for people of their age, though marriage does not assuage their sense of isolation, particularly at the thought of death.

The problematic marriages in the play are those of Henden's son, Daniel, and Gertrude's daughter, Cordelia, and of Benjamin and Abigail. As Gertrude puts it, "They travel in a pack; they are not happy" (35). Daniel and Benjamin were lovers before they married their wives and, while both men are attempting to be good husbands, they are still in love with each other and cannot stand being apart. When we view the play through the perspective of domestic realism, Daniel and Benjamin's decision to marry does not seem credible or necessary in the early 1980s, when the play was written: it is more part of the experience of men of Albee's generation. Why is it that Albee, who has had serious, long-term relationships, cannot imagine one in his plays? Daniel says to his father Henden, "There is my *nature* and *Benjamin's* nature and we are doing what we *can* about it, though I think we're *idiots*. We've fallen between stools, Father; we were better perched on our specialness . . . our disgrace, perhaps . . . But we are *trying*. Jesus, we're trying!!" (30–31). In other words, according to Daniel, his and Benjamin's marriages are contrary to their nature, but in their case, nature must be counteracted through appropriate heterosexual marriage. Homosexuality is both "specialness" and "disgrace," a term of shame, and abjection, though it is really their failed attempts at heterosexuality, their betrayal of their wives, that can be seen as disgraceful. We are given no reason for the break-up of Daniel and Benjamin's relationship beyond Daniel's shame and wish to marry. Daniel, who may be bisexual, decides to marry Cordelia, after which Benjamin finds a wife out of loneliness, desperation, or retaliation.

The marriages lead to varying degrees of unhappiness for all four members of this sad marital network. Benjamin is falling apart emotionally without Daniel and within an unsatisfying marriage. His wife, Abigail, tries to drown herself. Cordelia, however, has a clear sense of the limitations of her marriage. She likes the fact that "Daniel is more interested in our friendship than our marriage" (24), so that when one day he realizes how silly their marriage is, they will still be friends. The problem is not a lack of sex in their marriage. They claim to love each other, but Daniel cannot offer exclusivity: "I've got a very roomy heart," he tells Cordelia when she asks if he has male lovers (15). Cordelia knows that if he were straight, there would be other women instead of other men: "I *like* being his only woman" (24). Yet however rational the basis for their marriage is, they are both frustrated.

One of the issues Albee raises repeatedly in his critiques of marriage is the impossibility of monogamy. In *A Delicate Balance*, both Tobias and Harry have cheated on their wives with the same woman (Claire?). Martha is far from being a faithful wife in *Who's Afraid of Virginia Woolf?* In *Marriage Play*, Jack tells his wife, "Instinct tells us when the mind and appetite get together it's then time to do it, and with or to whatever is nearby and to be fancied . . . Why does 'I love you' mean 'I vow not to put this into that?'" (35). Is Daniel's "very roomy heart" and lively sexual appetite a violation of the spirit of marriage? If the basis for marriage is friendship, then sexual exclusivity does not necessarily enter in. Daniel loves Cordelia and Benjamin. Daniel has sex with Cordelia, Benjamin, and other men. What does his marriage mean in any traditional sense? His frustration is the result of the irrelevance of monogamous marriage to his sexual and emotional circumstances. Still, he chose to be married, and his wife chose to be married to a man she knew was gay.

Benjamin and Abigail's marriage has even less rationale. There is no physical expression of affection, even holding, and Abigail is consumed with frustration and jealousy. She would like to believe that Benjamin has changed but clearly does not trust him: "I never let him out of my sight" (9), and seeing him with Daniel is a reminder of how tangential she is to him. Benjamin, on the other hand, would settle for sharing Daniel with Cordelia rather than continue in a miserably unhappy marriage. At the end, Daniel cannot go to his wife, who has just been saved from drowning, because he does not know what to say to her.

Perhaps the trio of Daniel-Cordelia-Benjamin is the ideal solution to their desire to be connected and their inability to love by the moral and social imperatives of marriage. Henden and Gertrude can be content with their marriage because they expect so little out of it. The four younger people want comfort, solace, love. Benjamin cries out that he needs the comfort of a physical embrace – "*Hold me!? Someone!?*" (39) – and ironically it is Cordelia who holds him. The comfort of an embrace is the momentary assurance that one is not alone, that one's pain is not felt in isolation.

Edmee, the widowed mother, has chosen a life outside marriage. After the death of her husband, she has shared her bed with a variety of men and one woman, but her primary relationship is the extremely close one she has with her adolescent son, Fergus, who has become the only man in her life (other than her sexual partners, who seem to be no more than that). Edmee realizes that Fergus may be "too much" to her, though she would like to believe that the Oedipal feelings are all his: "I have birthed him, I have held him, rocked him, comforted him, bathed him, scolded him, dressed him, guided him . . . why on earth should I want to fuck him?" (15). Despite her protestations, desire seems to be a part of her feelings for her son, as it is for other Albee mothers. Given the sexless or sexually frustrating marriages in the play, is Edmee's relationship with Fergus any less of a marriage? Edmee tells Gertrude that her fear is that her beautiful, bright boy "will turn out to be less than he promises. I don't want to be around when his hair recedes or his body starts its way to fat; I don't want to see the expression in his eyes when he looks at this life and sees it's not going to be quite what it might have been. Tarnish! That's what I don't want to see . . . tarnish" (29). Does maturity have to lead to disappointment? Can Fergus opt out of the compromises the other characters have settled for?

While the other characters are enduring the consequences of the decisions they have made, young Fergus is aware that he has not yet made any major decisions. He spends the play questioning the other characters and confronting them with the truth of their relationships; then, at the end of the play, he disappears. Since he has told the audience that he has no intention of killing himself, he may have symbolically disappeared into maturity, which would entail a separation from his mother and a rejection of the compromised straight and gay relationships he has seen on the beach. Or perhaps, like his father, he has met with a terrible accident in the water. Chance death is always a possibility in the world of this play: Fergus's father's fatal accident, Abigail's parents' death in a freak hot-air balloon accident, and Henden's sudden passing into eternal sleep at the play's end. If Fergus has died, he and Edmee have been spared what she most feared for him – disillusionment caused by too many of the compromises that pass for maturity. She may also be spared having to accept a gay son, as Fergus seems intensely curious about Daniel and Benjamin's relationship.

At the end of the play, the sun goes behind a cloud, leaving the beach a desolate gray. The last sounds are cries of loss from characters who realize that they are ultimately inconsolable and alone – Gertrude's for Henden, Edmee's for Fergus, Benjamin's cry for Daniel, and Daniel's cry for God as he discovers the death of his beloved father: loss of spouse, son, lover, father; the familial ties that bind. No one cries for poor Abigail, who survives her suicide attempt but seems to have killed her unsatisfactory marriage. Marriage ideally is seen as a cure for isolation but the action of *Finding the Sun* shows characters who are lonely and who die alone. Loveless marriage does not cure loneliness or one's awareness and fear of "nothing," but love takes more courage than most of these characters can muster.

* * *

"Oh, God!"

Nathaniel Hawthorne once said of Herman Melville, "He can neither believe nor be happy in his unbelief." These plays suggest that the same is true of Edward Albee. God is invoked but does not seem to offer any solace. In each play, characters look for a moment of spiritual conversion that is never experienced. Marriage, which should offer emotional, sexual, and spiritual union, and which might be a replacement for the consolations of religion in a godless world, offers instead discontent and disappointment. Is the form of marriage itself an impossibility because humans cannot possibly live according to its restrictions and its necessary foundation in love, or do people simply fail out of their own weakness and lack of will? Albee would like to believe in the ideal of marriage, but he seems to find no pragmatic basis for such a belief. Nor does he see a true loving union being possible for his gay characters, who place themselves in miserable marriages.

NOTES

1. Edward Albee, *Who's Afraid of Virginia Woolf?* (New York: Atheneum, 1962), p. 189.
2. Edward Albee, *Marriage Play* (New York: Dramatists Play Service, 1995), p. 38. Further references to the play are to this edition and will be cited parenthetically in the text.
3. Mel Gussow, *Edward Albee: A Singular Journey: A Biography* (New York: Simon and Schuster, 1999), p. 213.
4. Edward Albee, *Tiny Alice* (New York: Atheneum, 1965), p. 181. Further references to the play are to this edition and will be cited parenthetically in the text.
5. Albee clearly admired Gielgud. He and his producers hired the veteran actor to direct *All Over* in 1971.
6. Foster Hirsch, "Evasions of Sex: The Closet Dramas," in *Critical Essays on Edward Albee*, ed. Philip C. Kolin and J. Madison Davis (Boston: G. K. Hall, 1986), p. 127.
7. Philip Roth, "The Play That Dare Not Speak Its Name," in *Edward Albee: A Collection of Critical Essays*, ed. C. W. E. Bigsby (Englewood Cliffs, NJ: Prentice-Hall, 1975), p. 109.
8. Edward Albee, *A Delicate Balance* (New York: Atheneum, 1966), pp. 137–138. Further references to the play are to this edition and will be cited parenthetically in the text.
9. David Richards, "Albee After the Plunge," in *Conversations with Edward Albee*, ed. Philip C. Kolin (Jackson and London: University of Mississippi Press, 1988), p. 180.
10. C. W. E. Bigsby, *A Critical Introduction to Twentieth Century American Drama, Volume Two: Williams, Miller, Albee* (Cambridge: Cambridge University Press, 1984), p. 260.
11. *Finding the Sun* (New York: Dramatists Play Service, 1994), p. 7. Further references to the play are to this edition and will be cited parenthetically in the text.

5

THOMAS P. ADLER

Albee's 3 $^{1}/_{2}$:
The Pulitzer plays

At the end of *Who's Afraid of Virginia Woolf?* (1962), after George has intoned the Mass of the Dead for the imaginary child who has been exorcised, and after Honey and Nick have been educated out of selfishness into mutuality and sent home to bed, George and Martha are left alone to live on without any comforting illusion. It is early Sunday morning, but the mood is one of doubt and uncertainty. Although, as George insists, "It was . . . time" for them to alter the foundation that has kept their marriage working, he can only offer a tentative assurance that "maybe" now "It will be better"; and even though Martha asserts that she is "cold" and "afraid," there can be no turning back – though she will be able to depend upon his strength and support (as he "puts his hand gently on her shoulder") to help see them through whatever new terrors might come.[1] For in Albee, embracing change, while essential for growth, is always frightening because it means facing the unknown.

The drama jury voted to award Albee what would have been his first Pulitzer Prize for *Virginia Woolf*, but, apparently because of what they considered shockingly coarse language, the Pulitzer board at Columbia University refused to endorse their recommendation; so no prize was given that year, and in protest, the two members of the jury (John Mason Brown and John Gassner) declined further service. Albee, however, would go on to win the award three times: for *A Delicate Balance* (1966), for *Seascape* (1975), and for *Three Tall Women* (1991). (In 2003 he would be one of three finalists for the prize for *The Goat, or Who is Sylvia?* (2002), his play about "the limits of tolerance" and the mysterious ways of the human heart in choosing its objects of desire.[2]) When the award was announced for *A Delicate Balance*, which had received a mixed critical and popular reception, many journalists concluded it was a consolation prize for *Virginia Woolf*, and thought Albee might refuse to accept it, but he responded that "an honor in decline is still an honor, a considerable one," and that he did not wish to dishonor others who received the prize by rejecting it.[3]

Albee's three Pulitzer winners all continue his exploration, begun in *Virginia Woolf*, of change and the unknown. If one arranges them not in chronological order of composition but rather in order of the relative age of their protagonists, then they offer three different perspectives on this topic. For Nancy and Charlie in *Seascape*, around the same age as, or just slightly older than, George and Martha, change is still a possibility, whereas for Agnes and Tobias in *A Delicate Balance*, a decade older, it is too late for change. For the ninety-something A, in *Three Tall Women*, change is no longer even at issue or desired – she simply awaits the stoppage of death. Each of these works is characterized by moments or periods of sexual dissonance that threaten to alter relationships in a decisive way, and each looks at how one responds to difference and the Other. All three are marked as well by brilliant coup de théâtres on Albee's part. Finally, the three plays demand to be read as one would long poems, with the same attention to detail, especially in choice and repetition of words.

Given its emphasis on the opportunity for change, the generally optimistic *Seascape* – a parable-like play that Albee originally conceived as the *Life* half of a diptych with *All Over* (1971), the *Death* panel – ends with the challenge "All right. Begin."[4] As Matthew Roudané notices, however, the question of whether things will be "for the better" appears to replicate the "tentativeness" and "precariousness" that sound at the close of *Virginia Woolf*.[5] The comfortably middle-aged Nancy and Charlie, children safely grown and gone, have been picnicking on the beach, undisturbed but for the sound of a jet plane overhead, "growing, becoming deafeningly loud, diminishing" (3), which periodically breaks the peace and threatens to pollute the pristine landscape should it fall. As in Albee's other "seascape" plays, *The Sandbox* (1960) and *Finding the Sun* (1983), the archetypal setting here keeps in equipoise birth and death, beginning and ending. Nancy muses, in an increasingly piquant manner, about her and Charlie's differing outlooks over what to do with the time remaining to them. Filled with a kind of Wilderian "wonder" at experience and adventuresomeness over what lies ahead, she urges that they must "do *something*," whereas the complacent Charlie, with "we'll see" serving as a kind of motto, is content to "put off," "settle in," and vegetate, to "do nothing" in what Nancy terms a condition of "purgatory *before* purgatory" (10–11) that she finds abhorrent and unalterably rejects. She believes that man must create his own happiness by making a Kierkegaardian leap of faith and discovering some positive value in life. Simply by having lived as long as they have, they have "earned a life" and the time to "*try* something new" (43–44). Whereas Charlie, fearful of change, desires stasis, Nancy accepts flux as a part of life – as, indeed, the necessary precondition for progress and growth. If her language is poetic, his is flat and without interest in "imagery"; if she is oriented toward the future, he speaks of the past, of having "had a good *life*" and "been a good husband" and "a good lover" (35). Although he possessed a spirit of inquisitiveness and adventure in adolescence, shedding his clothes and diving down under the sea, he resists her entreaties that he do that again, for he has put away such childish things. Charlie opts for refusing to seek out anything beyond his narrow ken, and for continuing in his placid existence devoid of "the glaciers and the crags" (43), until the release of death after a life well lived. Nancy, on the other hand, eventually entertains the disconcerting thought that she has perhaps "been married to [Charlie] far too smoothly for far too long" (103), and that there can develop a loneliness or a premonition of death not just after, but even during, sexual intimacy.

Recalling a painful time when Charlie underwent some vaguely under-stood emotional crisis and, for seven months, was overtaken by "inertia," Nancy admits she was worried that he might have been having an affair and that passion might have gone from their lives altogether. This, she explains, plunged her into a realization that her own life had a gaping emptiness – she had, for example, until then "never thought of another man, another pair of arms, harsh cheek, hard buttocks, pleasure, never at all" (25) – and might have been neither as full nor as fulfilling as she once imagined. When she lit-erally saw his back turned toward her in bed, she thought she might divorce him and try to turn "back" time to when she was eighteen and experience what she had missed, until she found that he "came back . . . eventually" (26) by pulling out of his despondency and returning his attentions to her. Albee has always intimated what he expresses emphatically in *Seascape*, that one of the chief characteristics distinguishing mankind from the animals, along with an awareness of one's own "mortality" and the ability to "make art" (147), is the logos, the power of language and the ability to flesh out the word metaphorically, symbolically, and anagogically, so that things reverberate on several different levels at once – as with Nancy's permutations of the word "back," about which she remarks, metacritically, "nice, isn't it, when the real and the figurative come together" (26).

Albee himself brings the literal and symbolic together in *Seascape* when Leslie and Sarah, the two lizard-like creatures, come up out of the sea to con-front Nancy and Charlie. Sarah will even expand upon the connotations of the word "back" when, fearful of what she sees on land among the humans – and with those terrifying jets flying overhead – she momentarily wants to return to the sea and descend back down the evolutionary ladder. She and Leslie, as allegorical figures, are what Nancy and Charlie's ancestors once were, and the older couple are what the younger saurian pair can become. Sarah and Leslie came up out of their habitat in the sea because, as she explains, they suddenly had a feeling of dis-ease and discomfort, of having outgrown what was down there and sensing that they no longer "*belonged* there any more" (136). They experienced, as Nancy would put it, the disillusionment that can be redirected in either a positive or a negative way. So Leslie and Sarah's predicament – faced as they are with the attractive temptation of "making do down there" (137), of taking comfort in passively settling in and thus settling for less than a full existence – exactly parallels Charlie's. Nancy responds to their temptation with a "once-upon-a-time" story whose moral is that only dissatisfaction with how things are can give one the will to change and usher in evolutionary advance (of a nonthreatening Lamarckian rather than a violent Darwinian sort).

Challenged by the unexpected appearance of Leslie and Sarah, Charlie begins to reveal his own vulnerability and admits to being frightened by what he does not "*know*": "by deep space? Mortality? Nancy . . . not being with me" (85). Like George and Martha before them, Charlie and Nancy become teachers of Leslie and Sarah, giving them lessons in communication and anatomy, in sexual reproduction and childrearing. Recognizing that what separates man from beast is precisely the human's "aware[ness that] it's *alive*, [and] that it's going to die" (149), Charlie sees that to complete the transformation from animal to human that the younger couple embarked upon with their sense of uneasiness in their old life in the sea, he must make them experience truly human emotions. But when it comes to tutoring them to think about feelings, another of those attributes about which only human beings can be self-conscious, Charlie discovers that words by themselves do not always suffice. Nor, as Jerry realized in *The Zoo Story* (1959), is "kindness" by itself always sufficient, so that "cruelty," too, may need to be part of the equation: "the two combined together, at the same time, are the teaching emotion" that may be necessary in order "to reach each other."[6] Charlie, recently content to ease himself painlessly out of the picture by withdrawing from all purposive activity and reluctant to act, to put himself out for anything or anyone, now understands (as George did, also) that he must actually hurt someone in order to help. By playing on Sarah's fear that Leslie might leave her and not come back, Charlie causes Sarah to break down in tears; because of this hurt, an angry and defensive Leslie pummels and chokes Charlie – though he ultimately will come to thank him (as Nick wordlessly does George), because, as Liam Purdon notes, "as Albee indicates in the conclusion . . . it is through the examination of the emotions, difficult as it may be, that one attains the totality of being."[7]

Having tasted these dark human emotions of sorrow and wrath, Leslie and Sarah want more than ever to return to the security of the womblike sea. What convinces them not to retreat is Nancy and Charlie's insistence

Figure 5. *A Delicate Balance*, Broadway premiere, 1966. With Jessica Tandy as Agnes and Hume Cronyn as Tobias.

that they "come back up" and stay, and the assurance that they "could *help*" by "*tak[ing* them] by the hand" (157–158) – in a gesture reminiscent of the one that closes Mike Nichols's film version of *Virginia Woolf* – in order to assuage their fear and doubt. The unexpected encounter has been a salvific test that Charlie, a representative middle-aged Everyman who had fallen prey to a potentially debilitating ennui and boredom, has passed, thereby repeating one of the recurrent patterns in Albee's plays: helping Leslie and Sarah to begin the mythic journey out of their pre-moral condition into one that is more fully human has meant that Charlie himself has undergone a regenerative epiphany in coming to realize that he, like all of humankind, must either "mutate or perish" (145). In saving others, he has saved himself.

* * *

At first glance, it might appear that the curtain line of *A Delicate Balance*, Agnes's "Come now; we can begin the day," is a precursor of the end of *Seascape*.[8] As Gerry McCarthy notices, the Friday night through Sunday morning action of *A Delicate Balance*, if read symbolically, would seem to indicate a movement from Passion, through waiting or "Descent into Hell," to Resurrection, and from this he concludes that the play ends on a guardedly positive note of "the new clarity with which the household faces life," and a restored "acceptance of community" after the interlopers have left.[9] Yet a close examination of the play's pattern of conflict reveals that Agnes's concluding line must be read ironically. *Seascape* may reuse the word "begin," but (as was true with the positively and negatively charged meanings of "back" in that play) the meaning is totally opposite from in the earlier work. Unlike Nancy and Charlie's visitors who stay to begin a great journey, though admittedly one fraught with uncertainties, Agnes and Tobias's guests, Harry and Edna, go away with their needs unmet. Rather than a bright play with open vistas, *A Delicate Balance* is decidedly autumnal in mood; a "gradual ... demise of intensity" and "the dark sadness" (86, 134) have overtaken the lives of the upper-crust family inhabiting this Eliotian metaphysical drawing-room drama.

Although Agnes's syntactically complex musings at the start about losing her sanity evoke images of "drifting" and "gentle loosening of the moorings" (3), theirs is a world of carefully constructed, self-imposed stasis, so long in place that they have blocked out an awareness of any other way of life. Agnes is elegant, steely, steady; she sees herself as the essential "fulcrum" that keeps the balance from tottering, the one who "maintain[s]" the status quo and "keep[s the family] in shape" (84). Even the artificialities of her mannered and meticulously wrought language, the haughty diction and brittle surface, indicate a protective veneer that keeps things that would be in any way unsettling from breaking through; as Foster Hirsch comments, "language is used as a means of protection and concealment; words keep feelings in check."[10] Tobias suffers from a more advanced and chronic case of Charlie's initial ennui; he typically moves out of the heat, avoiding whatever might question the settled pattern of their lives. But their grown daughter, Julia, a "quadruple amputee" home from a fourth failed marriage and wanting only a warm place where she can belong, provides the negative spin on what they refuse to hold up to examination, calling her mother "drill sergeant," "nanny," and "pope," and accusing her father of having become a "cipher," a "very nice but ineffectual, essential, but not-really-thought-of, gray . . . noneminence" (66).

Agnes might be aghast at the notion that the sexes are becoming too similar and decry the way that this upends traditional male/female roles, yet she remains convinced, like Martha in *Virginia Woolf*, that someone needs to be "stronger," and she is prepared to undertake that role if necessary. If Tobias – who espouses the motto "We do what we can" (9) as a rationalization for taking the easy way out and not attempting more – has retreated from a position of authority, it is partly because, as he reveals in the story about his cat (analogous to Jerry's of the dog in *The Zoo Story*), he does not want to lay himself open to criticism or face accusations of failure for being neglectful and not returning love. His life is no longer one of grand gestures, if it ever was, but of no gestures at all, since to act is to risk "being judged" and found wanting. Yet Agnes has judged him for leaving her bed after the death of their son Teddy, and never coming back. While he excused practicing coitus interruptus as a way to protect Agnes from further hurt and loss, she found his withdrawing and coming on her belly only "sad," and thought that Tobias was out of love with her.

The sudden arrival of Harry and Edna on their doorstep, come to move in and stay, may not be as visually striking as that of Leslie and Sarah approaching over the dunes – after all, these best friends from the suburbs are, as Albee's stage directions specify, "*Very much like Agnes and Tobias*" (vi). However, the threat they bring with them is potentially much more devastating because it calls into question the very basis of a life free from "mountains" or "chasms" (later to reverberate in Charlie's desire for no "glaciers" and "crags") that Agnes and Tobias have so assiduously sculpted for themselves. Quite simply, Harry and Edna were sitting at home, and suddenly (again, like Sarah's sense of discomfort, though magnified) "WE WERE FRIGHTENED – AND THERE WAS NOTHING" (49). Virginia Perry comments perceptively on the inarticulateness and lack of specificity in naming the source of their terror, proposing that "Albee thus suggests that man's deepest fears are ineffable, unable to be assuaged by words . . . creating an inconsolable sense of isolation." She continues, "Harry and Edna find themselves face-to-face with the pre-Logos nothingness – the emptiness before the order of language, before identity, before existence."[11] This "nothing," of course, is qualitatively different from Charlie's desire to while away the rest of his time doing nothing. Here it connotes an existential anguish, the utter absence of absolutely everything upon which one has come to depend, leaving one with a sense of incomprehensible meaninglessness, terrified because facing the void.

The disease they carry with them is infectious and one from which others may not be "immune," as Agnes's sister Claire, who resides in their home, perceives. "Not named [Claire] for nothing" (108), she is a seer or a kind of wise fool, related, as Anne Paolucci notes, to "the ancient Sibyl, who spares no one in her flashes of insight – not even herself."[12] Clearsighted about her own life – she refuses to excuse her behavior under the guise of alcoholism, insisting that she is a willful drunk – she will (somewhat like Larry Slade in O'Neill's *The Iceman Cometh*) prod others from the sidelines, announcing her presence with an appealingly brazen panache: lying on the floor with a drink balanced on her forehead, or breaking into a room with an accordion chord, or yodeling amid her precisely targeted verbal barbs. Claire understands that Harry and Edna, by asking to be taken in, are testing the limits or boundaries of love and friendship, and that Tobias and Agnes are undergoing a "BI-OP-SEE" that will reveal whether they are infected by a kind of insidious disease.

Agnes puts the responsibility to "take in" or "throw out" clearly on the shoulders of Tobias, claiming that it has always been only his "illusion" that she "rules," so that he would not feel guilty for having ceded his authority. She may "hold" the reins, but he, she claims, has always "decide[d] the route" (136) by making the moral decisions, after which she has merely steered them accordingly. Realizing that if he rejects Harry and Edna and sends them away it will be tantamount to admitting that their whole lives have been empty, Tobias – in one of Albee's wonderful verbal arias – begs the intruders to remain. But if Charlie's "stay" uttered to Leslie and Sarah is a calm invitation, Tobias's "Please? Stay?" to Harry and Edna (who have already decided to leave) is a desperate plea, uttered more for themselves than for the others. As Albee himself puts it, this is Tobias's "last opportunity to do something worthwhile in [his] life," and he flubs it.[13] His weak "I tried" is too little; it is knowledge gained "too late" to effect any change, and it comes with the awareness that the time for any really significant change is forever gone. But then, Tobias was aware all along, as George warned in *Who's Afraid of Virginia Woolf?*, that tolerating descent down the evolutionary ladder means reaching a point where it is impossible ever to "really [come] back again" (25). The nothingness is no longer just exterior, but is now interior to them and can only be lived with.

"Too late," in fact, has been a recurrent refrain in *A Delicate Balance*, appearing a third and final time in Agnes's magisterial, but no less moving for that, summation about how choice diminishes with the passage of time, so that the fabric of one's life becomes unalterably set and change becomes impossible: "Time happens, I suppose. To people. Everything becomes . . . too late, finally. You know it's going on . . . up on the hill; you can see the dust, and hear the cries, and the steel . . . but you wait; and time happens. When you *do* go, sword, shield . . . finally . . . there's nothing there . . . save rust; bones; and the wind" (171). Or, as Albee himself expresses it in his Introduction, "The play concerns . . . the rigidity and ultimate paralysis which afflicts those who settle in too easily, waking up one day to discover that all the choices they have avoided no longer give them any freedom of choice, and that what choices they do have left are beside the point" (ii). This intuition of the way that one's decisions reduce the options available for all future decisions, halving them over and again at every step along the way, seems a peculiarly American formulation of the interplay between free choice and determinism, helping to support an interpretation of Agnes's closing line as heavily ironic. The demons released in the dark night have been sent on their way, but the order that Agnes reimposes will close the drapes against the daylight and block out anything that might further threaten the status quo, thus ensuring the continuation of their death-in-life existence.

* * *

If, as we have seen, *Seascape* and *A Delicate Balance* both have the word "begin" in their final line – the first as an imperative, the second in an ironic mode – the expressionistic *Three Tall Women* ends with the word "stop," signifying the finality of death, which, from the perspective of the play's central figure A, is a consummation devoutly to be wished for. There are, of course, two versions of A on stage in Act 2: the one speaking as her present self, ninety-one or ninety-two, but also split into – likely only in memory – her two former selves, B (herself at age fifty-two) and C (herself at age twenty-six); and the other a mannikin with a face mask of A, as she lay dying upstage, apparently from a stroke. As Robert Brustein and Mel Gussow both note, Albee may have had the Beckett of *Krapp's Last Tape* in mind as a model for a memory play staging multiple selves.[14] Albee's skill at deploying fluid pronoun shifts in the dialogue – "you" becoming "me," "we" becoming "I" – confirms the two younger selves as projections in the mind of the older self. Their differing recollections of the same event – for example, their loss of virginity, which B remembers as "wonderful," to which A counters, "It hurt" – show the way that memory under the pressure of time can hold contradictions in balance. There exist, however, pointed differences from Beckett, since Krapp considers his earlier selves well lost and thus chooses to leave the self fragmented and deconstructed, whereas A welcomes her earlier selves as timely found, ultimately reincorporating and reassembling those fragments into a unified whole, arriving at a level of acceptance that seems foreign to Beckett's central figure.

An equally fruitful inspiration for Albee's dramaturgical strategies in *Three Tall Women* may be found in the visual arts, as John Lahr provocatively suggested when he wrote of the play that "What we get is a kind of Cubist stage picture, where the characters are fragments of a single self."[15] As is well known, Albee is a great connoisseur and collector of primitive and modern art and was, in fact, a devotee and close friend of the sculptor Louise Nevelson. Not only has he written a play about her, *Occupant* (2002), but in 1980 he wrote the introduction to the exhibition catalogue for a retrospective of her works, including the Cubist-inspired sculptures *Dawn's Wedding Feast* (1959) and *Mrs. N's Palace* (1954–77). In a later article on Nevelson, he comments on the way in which the architectonics of her sculptural assemblages are related to musical forms, and praises her art for being "an act of aggression against the familiar and the 'easy,'" while "transform[ing the viewer] from spectator to participant."[16]

In Act 1 of *Three Tall Women*, the three personae, while the same ages as in Act 2, are separate individuals, B being A's paid caregiver/companion and C her law firm's representative. For the play begins as a potent and unsentimental dramatization of aging and its diminishments – the confinement, the demeaning loss of bowel and bladder control, the inability to remember, all the little humiliations and frustrations that taken together enrage A and oftentimes reduce her to tears – and a discussion of the fact of death. Early on, the brusque and no-nonsense B (though, at the same time, kindly and solicitous toward A) bluntly tells C, "You start . . . and then you stop."[17] She then goes on to shock C even more by proposing that, by age six, everyone should be made conscious of the fact that they are dying and "know what it means."

Albee himself has recalled the moment when he came to full consciousness that he, personally, would someday die ("I had an awareness of death when I was 15, but when I turned 36 or 37 I became aware that I, Edward Albee, was going to die"[18]); and just before the end of the play he gives to A a summative speech – every bit as central as Agnes's about time and change – in which she addresses the audience, in a sense tutoring them just as George does Honey and Nick, and Charlie does Sarah and Leslie: "There's a difference between knowing you're going to *die*, and *knowing* you're going to die. The second is better; it moves away from the theoretical" (109). Separated from her dying self, she can see things from a distanced, more objective perspective. Whereas C, naive and romantic and unwilling even to think about her own mortality, insists that her "happiest" moment – a phrase that is a direct verbal echo of Krapp in Beckett's play – has not "happened yet" and so must be to come; and whereas B, believing that she has reached a kind of equilibrium, a plateau with pleasant vistas after having lived and suffered, thinks that that moment must be "now; now . . . always," for A, the present moment, "coming to the end of it," is the "happiest" moment (108–109).

The final visual stage image of her linking hands with B and C, reintegrating the fragmentary, postmodern subjectivities and healing the polyvocality of the previously nonunified subject, becomes a metatheatrical moment, a kind of Beckettian close of play that might be equated with death, as she looks toward that moment "When it's all done. When we stop. When we can stop" (110). The stoppage of memory, together with the loss of possibility for change, signals death. In order to face death with a measure of equanimity, A must ultimately refuse to excuse, and indeed must even express regret for having done those things she should not have done, and for having left undone those things she should have brought to completion. To arrive at the more expansive perspective implied by the play's ending, she must acknowledge the deficiencies and limitations of herself at earlier ages. By staging multiple identities, by splitting or tripling the single consciousness in much the same way as did such Cubist painters as Marcel Duchamp in *Nude Descending a Staircase* or Robert Delauney in *The City of Paris* (both 1912), Albee can show how C changed into B and B into A, how A is the sum of C and B. At her young age, it is unimaginable to C that she will change, and when she looks at A she refuses to accept that she will "become" her: "I deny *you*" (107) – though thanks to B (in a pattern familiar from the effect Charlie had upon Leslie), she becomes more open to thinking about the future. There is much about A that C finds hard to tolerate, especially the ingrown prejudices against Jews and blacks of such longstanding that A is no longer even particularly aware of them. Yet in many ways, it is understandable that A has become hard and defiant, since, like many other Albee women, she had to be "strong" in order to face her sister's alcoholism, her mother's dementia, her husband's long decline from prostate cancer.

Once again, as in *A Delicate Balance* and *Seascape*, the most decisive choices are linked to expressions of the women's physical sexuality, or with their response to the sexuality of others. A's calculated relationships with men have usually eventuated in a betrayal of some sort, for they have been built upon a confusion of the material and the immaterial, as if some object could ever be the measure of love; as C comes to confess, what is desired is the "big diamond" that "glitter[s]" because "It's tangible proof . . . that we're valuable . . . that we're valued" (103). A's penguin-like husband – she was his third wife – short and with one glass eye but a wonderful dancer, was rich and gave her lots of jewelry and "pretty things," partly it seems in return for sexual favors, so that there was always an element of commodity exchange about their relationship. If there is physical shrinkage with age (A is upset that she is becoming shorter), there is also, because of bad choices and accommodations and compromises, a kind of moral shrinkage as well, a spiritual death before the physical one. She recounts an apparently decisive time when she was sitting nude, except for her jewelry, at her dessing table after a party, and her husband entered naked, with a diamond bracelet on his erect penis, wanting her to fellate him; but she "could *never* do that, and I said, No! I can't do that!" He loses his erection, and the bracelet falls "deep into [her] lap. Keep it, he said, and he turned and walked out" (56).

After the recollection of this fracture in their marriage, A "weeps, slowly, inconclusively" and needs B to comfort her. Earlier, when she was the younger B, she had been unfaithful to her husband, committing adultery with the groom in the stable, a betrayal her son came upon by chance and will use against her. If the affair began in "self-pity" and "revenge" for her husband's infidelities, it "turned into pleasure for its own sake," though she fired the groom rather than risk losing the "good deal [she had] with the penguin, a long-term deal" (94). The self-pity arose in part from B's realization of the lack of permanence in human relationships that no longer measure up to earlier expectations, but also from the knowledge that "parents, teachers, all the others" deliberately "*lie* to you," rather than risk hurt by destroying illusions: "You're growing up and they go out of their way to hedge, to qualify, to . . . to evade; to avoid – to *lie*. Never tell it how it is – how it's *going* to be – when a half-truth can be got in there" (93).

As striking as is the coup de théâtre when A enters elegantly dressed downstage while the mannikin lies in bed upstage, it is matched by another entrance late in the play. When A suddenly admits for the first time, "I have a son," he materializes on stage, dressed in the same preppy clothes he was wearing at age twenty-three when B demanded that he "Get out of my house!" (89), when she discovered he was gay. Even Albee himself confesses to being "complete[ly] surprise[d]" at the boy's sudden appearance: "I remember stopping and saying, 'Well, isn't that interesting? How did you ever figure *that out.*'"[19] So if *Three Tall Women* is admittedly biographical, a portrait of the playwright's adoptive mother with whom he remained unreconciled, it is also openly autobiographical in fashioning himself into a stage character. Albee has staged gay characters before, most notably in his short play *Finding the Sun* (1983). Moreover, in *A Delicate Balance*, Tobias bristles at Julia's suggestion that her younger brother, had he lived, might have grown up gay, as if this is something he would never have tolerated. The dead son, Teddy, though he remains unseen, is (as Gussow and McCarthy both note) given a diminutive of the name Edward – though Albee himself has always resisted being called by any nickname.

Here in *Three Tall Women*, A relates that the son had visited her before in hospital, and that he never fails to bring her favorite freesias and candied orange rind, even though she assumes from this that he must want something in exchange. She even claims that, in a premonition of her death, she observed him kissing her "on the forehead" in the hospital room, but nevertheless concludes that he did this devoid of any feeling, purely to comply with what is acceptable form, for she has never forgiven him for being gay: "They were there and they were watching and you kissed me for *them*!" (106). Yet immediately after she recounts that accusatory vision and demands that he face the coldness of her hand in death, the son – who otherwise remains totally silent and without voice, just as he had been silenced and made absent through rejection those many decades before – "shudders, weeps" in a genuine outpouring that recalls A's after she told of turning her husband away. The mother's death is an experience *before* the experience, as close as he (or anyone) can come to knowing what death is until he comes face to face with his own. The son remains absolutely speechless, without words, yet because he is human the feeling and emotion cannot be denied him or suppressed – as Leslie and Sarah came to understand in *Seascape*.

Three Tall Women, with its postmodernist emphasis on intersubjectivity and a multiplicity of viewpoints to demonstrate how perspective can skew perception, and with its disruption of a strictly linear narrative, is – alongside *Box* and *Quotations from Chairman Mao Tse-Tung* (1968) and *Listening* and *Counting the Ways* (1976) – certainly the most formally experimental of Albee's dramas. As August Staub astutely writes, "In its structure, it is . . . so contemporary, in fact, that it might well be called one of the great summation moments of 20th century theatre. [It is] a completely original work . . . of the theatre of its times and a work of seeing and public art."[20] In the Introduction to *Box*, Albee comments on the dual obligation of any playwright to "attempt change" by "mak[ing] some statement about the condition of 'man'" and by "mak[ing] some statement about the nature of the art form with which he is working"; in order to accomplish the second aim and keep art from "wither[ing]," "the playwright must try to alter the forms within which his precursors have had to work."[21] So the challenge that Albee has always set for himself has never been very different from the one he poses for his characters: to change and always venture into unknown territory. His stylistic experimentation has assumed many different forms: from the surrealism of

The Sandbox to the absurdism of *The American Dream* (1961) to the allegory of *Tiny Alice* (1964); from the picaresque journey of *Malcolm* (1966) to the vaudeville of *Counting the Ways* to the dramatized lecture of *The Man Who Had Three Arms* (1983); from the monodrama for a disembodied voice of *Box* to the Pirandellian enigmas of *The Lady from Dubuque* (1980), *Lolita* (1981), and *The Play About the Baby* (1998).

Yet if, from a conceptual and dramaturgical point of view, Albee is continually beginning again, there is a thematic coherence from play to play that imparts to his body of work a unity of purpose and perspective as he explores the isolation that results from lack of communication and rejection because of difference – oftentimes sexual in nature; the complacency and stasis that result from settling in and settling for less rather than challenging moral norms and the status quo; the angst and ennui that accompany one's sense of lost possibilities and diminishing opportunities for change with the passage of time; the retreat into illusion as a comfort against facing the abyss and the fact of mortality; the need for a love that is critical and unafraid to hurt, and for contact and communion with the other to provide strength against the terror of existence. These are all thematic motifs that occur in the Pulitzer plays, and perhaps nowhere as forcefully as in *A Delicate Balance*, which may seem, from a stylistic point of view, among the least adventuresome of Albee's works. As John von Szeliski argues, however, in that play Albee has accomplished what may be among the most difficult and impressive achievements of all, by making "one of the incredibly few major advances in the use of language in the contemporary theatre"; and so, for him it is "a brilliant and highly significant play," "Albee's best play" and "a truly major drama."[22] Unquestionably, *A Delicate Balance* ranks with such classics as *The Iceman Cometh* and *A Long Day's Journey Into Night*, with *A Streetcar Named Desire* and *Death of a Salesman*, and it may yet come to be regarded as the pivotal American drama of the second half of the twentieth century. Albee once expressed his own criterion that "a good play" (echoing what he claimed was true of Nevelson's art) must be "an act of aggression against the status quo – the psychological, philosophical, moral, or political status quo. A play is there to shake us up a little bit, to make us consider the possibility of thinking differently about things."[23] Albee's three Pulitzer Prize plays, along with many of his other works, succeed in doing just that.

NOTES

1. Edward Albee, *Who's Afraid of Virginia Woolf?* (New York: Atheneum, 1962), pp. 240–241.

2. Quoted in Mel Gussow, "Albee Takes His Disappearing Baby to Houston," *New York Times*, April 12, 2000, p. B2.
3. Quoted in Mel Gussow, *Edward Albee: A Singular Journey* (New York: Simon and Schuster, 1999), p. 268. For a discussion of the controversy over the refusal to give the award to *Virginia Woolf*, see Gussow, pp. 188–189, and John Hohenberg, *The Pulitzer Prizes: A History of the Awards in Books, Drama, Music, and Journalism, Based on the Private Files over Six Decades* (New York: Columbia University Press, 1974), pp. 266–269.
4. Edward Albee, *Seascape* (New York: Atheneum, 1975), p. 158. Further references will be cited parenthetically in the text.
5. Matthew C. Roudané, *Understanding Edward Albee* (Columbia, S.C.: University of South Carolina Press, 1987), pp. 149–150.
6. Edward Albee, *The American Dream and The Zoo Story: Two Plays* (New York: Signet, 1961), pp. 35–36.
7. Liam O. Purdon, "The Limits of Reason: *Seascape* as Psychic Metaphor," reprinted in *Edward Albee*, ed. Harold Bloom (New York: Chelsea House, 1987), p. 129.
8. Edward Albee, *A Delicate Balance* (New York, Plume, 1997), p. 178. Further references will be cited parenthetically in the text.
9. Gerry McCarthy, *Edward Albee* (New York: St. Martin's Press, 1987), pp. 82, 97.
10. Foster Hirsch, *Who's Afraid of Edward Albee?* (Berkeley: Creative Arts Books, 1978), p. 48.
11. Virginia I. Perry, "Disturbing our Sense of Well-Being: The 'Uninvited' in *A Delicate Balance*," in *Edward Albee: An Interview and Essays*, ed. Julian N. Wasserman (Houston: University of St. Thomas, 1983), pp. 59–60.
12. Anne Paolucci, "A Vision of Baal: *A Delicate Balance*," reprinted in *Edward Albee: A Collection of Critical Essays*, ed. C. W. E. Bigsby (Englewood Cliffs, NJ: Prentice-Hall, 1975), p. 142.
13. Quoted in Gussow, *Edward Albee*, p. 257.
14. Robert Brustein, "The Rehabilitation of Edward Albee," *The New Republic*, April 4, 1994, p. 26, and Gussow, *Edward Albee*, p. 368.
15. John Lahr, "Sons and Mothers," *The New Yorker*, May 16, 1994, p. 104.
16. Edward Albee, "The World is Beginning to Resemble Her Art," *Art News* 79.5 (May 1994), pp. 100–101. For a more extended discussion of the memory structure, of the Cubist influence, and of the play as a deathwatch like several others in the playwright's canon, see my essay "A's Last Memory: Contextualizing Albee's *Three Tall Women*," in *The Playwright's Muse*, ed. Joan Herrington (New York: Routledge, 2002), pp. 159–174.
17. Edward Albee, *Three Tall Women* (New York: Plume, 1995), p. 13. Further references will be cited parenthetically in the text.
18. Philip C. Kolin, *Conversations with Edward Albee* (Jackson and London: University Press of Mississippi, 1988), p. 105.
19. Edward Albee, "Yes is Better than No," *American Theatre*, September 1994, p. 38.
20. August W. Staub, "Public and Private Thought: The Enthymeme of Death in Edward Albee's *Three Tall Women*," *Journal of Dramatic Theory and Criticism* 12.1 (Fall 1997), p. 153.

21. Edward Albee, *Box and Quotations from Chairman Mao Tse-Tung* (New York: Pocket Books, 1970), p. 9.
22. John J. von Szeliski, "Albee: A Rare *Balance*," *Twentieth Century Literature* 16.2 (April 1970), pp. 124, 130, 123.
23. Edward Albee interviewed by Lester Strong, in "Aggression Against the Status Quo," *Harvard Gay and Lesbian Review* 4.1 (1997), p. 9.

6

BRENDA MURPHY

Albee's threnodies: *Box-Mao-Box, All Over, The Lady from Dubuque*, and *Three Tall Women*

Since the beginning of Albee's career, his plays have been pervaded by arresting and memorable images of death. Grandma scoops sand over herself with a toy shovel as she succumbs to the smiling angel of death in *The Sandbox* (1960). The nurse complains that "the nigger brought a dead woman here" in *The Death of Bessie Smith* (1960). George makes the "flores para los muertos" allusion and reads the Catholic Requiem liturgy after the death of the imaginary son in *Who's Afraid of Virginia Woolf?* (1962). During the late 1960s and 1970s, Albee's interest in death and dying intensified, and he produced a series of plays that explored the process of dying, and the experience of the survivors who witness it, in *Box* and *Quotations from Chairman Mao Tse-Tung* (1968), *All Over* (1971), and *The Lady from Dubuque* (1980). Of these plays, *All Over* and *The Lady from Dubuque* are rare twentieth-century dramas in the mode of the threnody, the funeral dirge or song of lamentation. Another decade later, in *Three Tall Women* (1991), Albee returned to the threnody in a very different frame of mind.

In *All Over*, the family, the doctor, and the best friend and lawyer of a wealthy and famous man gather at his deathbed. Albee's staging suggests that the dying man be hidden from the audience's view by a screen, while the doctor and nurse who attend him and the watchers who have gathered to witness his death are always in view. Henry Schvey has pointed out the significance of this staging in relation to twentieth-century paintings of deathbed scenes, following Edvard Munch's *Death in the Sickroom*, which foregrounds the watchers in attitudes of detached and self-involved suffering, while the dying person sits isolated in the corner. As Schvey notes, "the shocking effect of *Death in the Sickroom* rests in the displacement of focus away from the process of dying and on to the mourners' responses to death . . . What Munch's work captures is not death as it takes possession of the dying, but as the living take possession of death; death is not a supernatural event, but something terrifyingly personal." What's more, Schvey suggests, the painting "emphasizes the dissolution of familial bonds and the awakening of personal fears

91

at the spectacle of another's passing."[1] Like Munch's, Albee's work reflects the attitudes of a society that focuses neither on death, nor on the dying, but on the way in which the potential mourners experience the process of dying. As the wife of the dying man sums up the action of *All Over*: "All we've done . . . is think about ourselves. [. . .] What will become of *me* . . . and *me* . . . and *me*."[2]

The underlying process of the play is what Christopher Bigsby suggests is Albee's fundamental worldview: "The world which Albee observes is entropic. Its basic impulse is disintegrative."[3] As James Neil Harris has suggested, *All Over* is an extension and a particularization of the general theme of entropy that Albee had developed three years earlier in *Box* and *Quotations from Chairman Mao Tse-Tung*.[4] These two one-act plays were intended to be played together. In *Box*, a single, offstage Voice delivers a monologue as the audience looks at a stage set consisting of an enormous cube. *Mao* is meant to follow immediately, with its stage set, the deck of an ocean liner, placed within the cube. It consists of three interlocking monologues: Chairman Mao quotes his own words; Old Woman reads from the sentimental poem "Over the Hill to the Poor House" by the popular nineteenth-century American poet Will Carleton; and the Long-Winded Lady talks to a silent Minister about her husband's death, her own fall from the ship into the ocean, and her daughter. Together, *Box* and *Mao* develop Albee's theme of dissolution on four parallel planes: in *Box*, that of the universal condition; in *Mao*, that of the geopolitical realm in Mao's monologue, that of the family in the Old Woman's rendition of the poem about her children's abandoning her one after the other, and that of the body in the Long-Winded Lady's monologue about her husband's death and her own possible suicide attempt. Albee establishes the major entropic symbolism in *Box* with his allusion to the killing of children through the willful destruction of milk for political reasons: "spilling and spilling and killing all those children to make a point. A penny or two, and a symbol at that, and I suppose the children were symbolic, too, though they died, and couldn't stop. Once it starts – gets to a certain point – the momentum is too much."[5] Of course, Albee, too, is exploiting milk and children to make an artistic point – part of the paradox of art in *Box*.[6]

In *Quotations from Chairman Mao Tse-Tung*, the presentation of a world that is winding down is more straightforward. The quotations from Mao begin with his reformulation of a Chinese folk tale that has the Chinese people working together to remove the two mountains of imperialism and feudalism that oppress them. The image of Communism that he uses is apocalyptic, however, as the "communist ideological and social system" is presented as "sweeping the world with the momentum of an avalanche and the force of a thunderbolt" (20), a statement that Albee juxtaposes with the Long-Winded Lady's onomatopoeic word for a body's dropping into the ocean: "plut!"

This contradictory juxtaposition of hope for the world and apocalyptic destruction foreshadows the treatment of Mao's pronouncements overall. Mao begins with an assertion of the inevitable collapse of imperialism and the triumph of the revolution: "the enemy is nearing extinction while [the revolutionaries] are approaching victory" (23). Mao asserts the goal of a peaceful world: "to achieve a lasting world peace, we must further develop our friendship and cooperation with the fraternal countries in the socialist camp and strengthen our solidarity with all peace-loving countries" (28). Almost in the same breath, however, he asserts the need to "give active support to the national independence and liberation movement in Asia, Africa, and Latin America" and "to just struggles in all the countries of the world" (28). Mao's statements become increasingly bellicose throughout the play, as he asserts that "only with guns can the whole world be transformed" (58) and that it is necessary to "oppose war with war, to oppose counter-revolutionary war with revolutionary war, to oppose national counter-revolutionary war with national revolutionary war, and to oppose counter-revolutionary class war with revolutionary class war" (62). Finally, he states that "without armed struggle neither the proletariat, nor the people, nor the Communist Party would have any standing at all in China" (64–65), and with a rhetorical flourish reminiscent of the George W. Bush administration's justification of the invasion of Iraq, he proclaims, "we are advocates of the abolition of war; we do not want war; but war can only be abolished through war, and in order to get rid of the gun it is necessary to take up the gun. [. . .] Every communist must grasp the truth, 'Political power grows out of the barrel of a gun'" (66). This degeneration from the claim to value peace to the active pursuit of war reflects geopolitical conditions in the twentieth century.

In counterpoint to the bombastic political rhetoric of Chairman Mao is the Old Woman's rendition of Will Carleton's sentimental doggerel about a hardworking, devoted mother who is rejected by her six children, one by one, after her husband's death until finally her son "went to the poormaster, an' put me on the town" (67). This clear and simple depiction of the degeneration of the family and of "family values" is juxtaposed with the monologue of the Long-Winded Lady, the only words in the play that were actually written by Albee. A good portion of it is focused on the death of the Lady's husband from cancer, a "dreadful death – all that he was not: large, random, inaccurate" (36). The Lady recalls her husband saying that "you stop about death, finally, seriously, when you're on to *dying* [. . .] Death is nothing; there . . . there *is* no death. There is only life and dying (47–48).

The difference between dying and death would become a central theme of *All Over*, as would the wife's response to the fact that her husband is dying: "But what about *me*! Think about *me*! [. . .] ME! WHAT ABOUT ME!" (50). The Lady insists that, though her response might give the impression of selfishness, this is "not how I intended it, nor how it is . . . at all. I . . . am *left*. (*Helpless shrug.*) He isn't" (50). She insists that her own suffering is as worthy of note as her dead husband's. "His dying is all over; all gone, but his death stays [. . .] *he* only had his dying. I have both" (51). *All Over* develops the full implications of this theme. It is, in a sense, a threnody for the survivors, the lamentation of those left behind, but it also explores the general theme of entropy or "winding down," and presents a dramatized synecdoche for the existential condition depicted by Munch and by Albee's admired precursor Samuel Beckett – that of waiting. Like *Waiting for Godot*'s, *All Over*'s action consists entirely of waiting, with the important difference that the waiting does finally come to an end with the man's death.

Albee makes the distinction between dying and death clear at the beginning of the play when the dying man's mistress objects to his wife's question – "Is he dead?" – on the grounds of its semantic form. She says that the dying man had once pointed out to her that the verb "to be" was not appropriate for a state of nonbeing, that "one could be dying, or have died . . . but could not . . . be . . . Dead" (*All Over* 4). In one sense, the action of the play is the man's dying, but it is the impact of that dying on the group that exists only in relation to him that is Albee's focus. The whole play is, in a sense, the development of the Long-Winded Lady's question, "what about *me?*"

Albee offers only the most rudimentary information about the dying man. He is wealthy and famous, powerful enough to have freed himself from the hospital when the end was near and to have insisted on being brought home to die. As the family keeps its deathwatch, the house is besieged by reporters, a "final test of fame" according to the nurse, "the degree of it: which is newsworthy, the act of dying itself, or merely the death" (41). As far as the dying man is concerned, the only action of the play is literally entropy, or "winding down." The doctor says that he has cut off the intravenous feeding, and "we're letting him . . . starve, if you will" (21). The man "seems to have diminished every time I turn my head away and come back" (21). Asked if there is any change in the dying man, the nurse responds, "No; none. Well, of course, some. Procession, but nothing, really" (72). This "procession" is the man's only activity, dying. Two moments of excitement occur when his body hemorrhages, and when his heart stops for three beats and then starts again, but the doctor and the nurse tell the watchers this means nothing. The only meaningful event for the man now is death, the end of the process of dying.

The action of the play consists not of the man's dying, but of the ritual of waiting.[7] As the man's best friend and lawyer reminds his daughter, who does not know that she wants to be there, "It's not required that you *do* know. It is more or less required that you *be* . . . I think: here. Family. Isn't it one of our customs? That if a man has not outlived his wife and children – will not outlive them . . . they gather?" (6). Later, the daughter announces her intention to "sit it out" (17) and the wife says she is "waiting out a marriage of fifty years. I am waiting for my *hus*band to *die*" (18). The ritual of waiting has created an artificial social community, a group of people who are defined only by their relation to the dying man, and thus are named only by their relation to him: The Wife, The Mistress, The Best Friend, The Daughter, The Son. A social reflection of the physical process of dying, the entropy in the play is the dissolution (or "winding down") of the social group that is established in relation to him. It becomes clear in the course of the play that the central focus of the group is not The Mistress, as it first appears, but The Wife. As the man dies, the ties of each group member to The Wife are severed until only the primary bond is left, that between her and her husband.

The first breach The Wife makes is between her and The Best Friend, who has also been her lover at some time in the past. She makes it clear that she will not marry him, though this may be the expected action for the two of them, at ages seventy-three and seventy-one, to take (103). More shocking is the mother's casting off of her two children. Of The Daughter, who neither loves anyone nor is loved by anyone, The Wife says, "I don't think I shall speak to her again" (78). To The Son, she says, "I hope you never marry . . . *either* of you! [. . .] Let the line end where it is . . . at its zenith" (81). The Son leaves, conceding that he is "not up to you, mother; never was" (82). Meanwhile, in a sort of minor key, The Daughter is expressing her loathing for The Mistress and her contempt for The Son; The Mistress is expressing her dislike of The Daughter; and The Son finds out that The Best Friend, who is also his employer, has no particular affection for him.

Of all the people in the group, The Wife and The Mistress, who profess to like and admire each other, have the strongest bond. The Wife reprimands her daughter for saying that The Mistress has come and taken her father away, saying "this woman loves my husband – as *I* do – and she has made him happy; as I have. She is good, and decent [. . .] She *loves* us. And we love *her*" (50). But beneath her civilized and reasoned approach to The Mistress is a struggle for a claim to the dying man that emerges as a right to decide what happens to his remains, whether they should go to the "flames," as The Mistress asserts was his last wish, or to the "worms," as The Wife desires.

At the beginning of the play, The Wife acknowledges The Mistress's claim to superior knowledge about the dying man, as when she arranged to have him moved out of the hospital: "Has she arranged it already? [. . .] Well; good. If it is done, splendid [. . .] I no longer feel possessive" (11). Later, however, The Wife declares her intention to have her way about her husband's remains. She tells The Mistress: "I *will* do battle with you there, no matter what you tell me, no matter what an envelope may say, I will have my way. Not a question of faith, or a repugnance; merely an act of will" (79). She comes to see his death as a way of getting him back again: "You may lose your husband while he is alive, but when he is not, then he is yours again" (92). She retreats temporarily, asserting the bond she feels with The Mistress and The Best Friend, saying "cast him in bronze if you like. I won't do battle with you: I like you both too much" (94), but in the end it is her claim on her husband that emerges. She says to The Mistress "*I* don't love *you* [. . .] *I* don't love *anyone. (Pause)* Any more,*" and then says to The Daughter and The Son, "I don't love *you*" and to The Best Friend, her former lover, "And you know I don't love *you*" (108).

What she comes to in the end is an "*enraged shout*," "I LOVE MY HUSBAND!!" (108). As The Wife asserts her primary connection to her husband, she simultaneously completes the dissolution of the community that is created by its relation to him. There is no reason for the mourners to love each other. Like Munch's mourners, they are each isolated in their grief and loss, their particular bond to the dying man in which none of the others really shares, and which none of them can, or wants to, understand. In the end, as The Wife says, "All we've done . . . is think about ourselves" (109), and her final line is a cry that releases the stored up "*self-pitying and self-loathing; pain, and relief*" (110) of thirty years as she says she is crying because she is unhappy and the Doctor says gently that it is "all over" (111). While the Doctor can make an empirical observation that the process of dying has reached its completion, the only fully knowable experience of death, Albee suggests, is its impact on the observer. The Wife loves her husband. She is unhappy in *her* loss. As the Long-Winded Lady says, his dying is all over, but his death stays.

While *All Over* concentrates on the situation of waiting, revealing The Wife's attachment to the dying man only in the last moments, *The Lady from Dubuque* is an intense treatment of the experience of the loving survivor. As Mel Gussow notes in his biography, Albee's "inspiration" for the play was his reading of Elizabeth Kübler-Ross's book *On Death and Dying* (1969), and it is "perhaps no coincidence that the title character was named Elizabeth."[8] As a threnody, the play dramatizes a particular element of Kübler-Ross's now well-known description of the stages of dying – Denial and Isolation, Anger, Bargaining, Depression, and Acceptance – in the context of her chapter on "The Patient's Family." Kübler-Ross notes that "the most heart-breaking time, perhaps, for the family is the final phase, when the patient is slowly detaching himself from his world including his family. They do not understand that a dying man who has found peace and acceptance in his death will have to separate himself, step by step, from his environment, including his most loved ones."[9] This separation, or decathexis, is "often misinterpreted by the immediate family as a rejection," and husbands and wives often react "dramatically to this normal and healthy detachment." It is during this time, she says, "that the family needs the most support, the patient perhaps the least" (Kübler-Ross 170).

The situation that Albee sets up in *The Lady from Dubuque* dramatizes this condition. Jo, who is dying of what is apparently cancer, spends a final evening in the company of her husband Sam and their group of friends, who engage in an evening of parlor games, psychological assault, and biting verbal repartee that is typical of such groups in Albee's plays. Addressing the audience as a witness to the action, Jo asks, "don't you just hate party games? Don't you just hate them?"[10] When the game of Twenty Questions is finally over, she says, "wasn't it boring? Wasn't it all . . . empty ultimately? Didn't we waste our time? [. . .] Especially if you're dying, as I am" (*The Lady from Dubuque* 21). Jo has no patience either for the formal games this group uses to endure the waiting or for the more complicated psychological games that underlie their social interaction. Despite their attempts to evade it, she insists on the fact of her dying, as she confronts her husband: "Your name is Sam, and this is your house, and I am your wife, and I am dying" (7). In a direct reference to Kübler-Ross, she counters Sam's caution that she may one day need the friend she has just insulted with the remark that "I dare say the day will come I'll need you all. Then, of course, the day will come I won't need a soul. And then, of course the day won't come" (47). When Sam responds with mild reproof, "Oh, Jo," she addresses the audience: "That's what they tell us, isn't it – that growing pile of books on how to die? That somewhere along the line you stop needing those you . . . need the most? You loose your ties? God, what do you need then?" (47).

In *On Death and Dying*, Kübler-Ross gives the case study of a Mrs. W. who had reached the point of wanting to be left alone to die in peace. She said that the only thing keeping her alive was "her husband's inability to accept the fact that she had to die," and was angry with him for "not facing it and for so desperately clinging on to something that she was willing and ready to give up." The husband, unable to understand the decathexis that his wife was experiencing, interpreted her need for detachment as "a rejection which was beyond his comprehension" (Kübler-Ross 116). Desperate to hold onto his wife, he insisted on a life-prolonging operation that was so dreaded by the wife that its prospect induced a psychotic reaction in the operating room. When the operation was put off, the wife returned to rationality, and the husband was persuaded to let her face her death as she chose to. In *The Lady from Dubuque*, Jo's husband Sam is an embodiment of the loved one who is unable to face the fact of his wife's dying. Each time she forthrightly refers to her dying, he evades it, acting as though she had made a remark in bad taste: "(*So sad and weary.*) Come on, Jo. Please? [. . .] Please, Jo?" (21). He complains to his friend Edgar that, as Jo "diminishes. She moves away from me in ways I . . . The thing we must do about loss is, hold on to the object we're losing" (61). He responds to Jo's entropic metaphor for her condition – "you're winding down, so . . . wind it up" – with the glumly dogmatic phrase "everything is reversible," and finally explodes: "DON'T GIVE ME YOUR FACTS! YOU'RE SO PROUD OF YOUR FUCKING FACTS!!" (65–66).

Albee suggests that Sam's problem is deeper than the situational inability to recognize his wife's dying and the desire to hold onto her at all costs. As he suggests in an interview with Matthew Roudané, the play is "all about identity."[11] The game that the group is playing in Act 1 is Twenty Questions, and Sam is insistent on their playing one more round, though they are clearly tired of the game and ready to stop. He keeps repeating "Who am I?" until they attend to him and respond. The answer – that he is both of the twins, Romulus and Remus – carries symbolic freight in several ways. Much is made of the central fact of their story, their having been suckled by wolves, when Jo insists on sharing the fact that Sam nibbles and sucks at her breast, still symbolically looking to her for both sexual gratification and maternal nurture and comfort despite her dying condition. He is also both of the twins, Romulus who built the fortifications of Rome, and Remus whom Romulus killed, according to Jo, for saying "Wow! Are those ever lousy fortifications" (16).

Twinning becomes central to the issue of Sam's sense of self in Act 2, as it becomes a fundamental subtext for the play. The most obvious instance of twinning is with Jo's mother. In Act 1 Jo expresses anger at having been deserted by her mother: "Where is she? Where the hell is she? [. . .] IN THE HOUR OF MY GODDAMN NEED!" (18). Sam, on the other hand, insists that Jo has a "perfectly good mother," though he admits that "The lady leaves something to be desired. She's tiny, thin as a rail, blue eyes – darting furtive blue eyes [. . .] pale hair, tinted pink, balding a little; you know; the way women do, when they do. We don't see her much. We don't like her;

I don't like her" (20). In Act 2 Elizabeth appears, looking nothing like this and claiming to be Jo's mother, while Sam insists that she is not. Her friend Oscar, who looks nothing like Sam, appears with her and eventually dresses in Sam's nightshirt, saying, "Don't you think I make a splendid Sam? [. . .] (*Arms wide; beatific*) Am I not . . . am I, indeed, not Sam? (*To the audience.*) Am I not Sam?" (152–153).

The inescapable allusion to the character Sam-I-Am in the Dr. Seuss children's book *Green Eggs and Ham* casts an even more absurd light on Oscar's appearance as a beatific Sam in a nightshirt, and indeed, the whole second act has a hallucinatory quality. In an interview, Albee responded to the suggestion that Elizabeth is believable on a symbolic but not on a realistic level by saying that he was trying to make "the real and symbolic moment identical."[12] Although Albee said that some productions have succeeded at this, most audiences and readers have found the second act more meaningful on the symbolic level. Ronald Rapin has offered a suggestion that Act 2 may be meaningfully read as "Sam's subconscious reaction, his nightmare response, if you will, to the previous night's soirée," and this is a useful context for examining his response to Jo's decathexis.[13] In the context of hallucination or nightmare, the twinning or split that Sam is feeling between Romulus the builder of inadequate fortifications and Remus the doomed truthteller is played out in various ways. Jo's real mother, who ignores her dying, is replaced by Elizabeth, who has come to help her with it (thus Albee's original title for the play, *The Substitute Speaker*). "I have come home for my daughter's dying," she says to Sam. "Get out of my way" (93). She becomes a mythic nurturing figure as she urges Jo:

> Come to me, now. It's time to hold you close, to rock you in my arms. [. . .] (*Soothing.*) Hold you, rock you, take you to my breast [. . .] (*A litany.*) Come, let me stroke your forehead, comb your hair, wash you, lay you down and tell you stories [. . .] protect you from the dark and from the thunder [. . .] (*So tender, gentle.*) Make it better? What have I come for? Come to me.
>
> (117–18)

This gentle, nurturing, undemanding presence which is there simply to ease Jo into death is opposed in the text by Sam's constant demand for Elizabeth to stay away from Jo, and his begging Jo to "tell her we don't know her" (117). Elizabeth's comforting invitation to Jo to rest and finally die in her arms is punctuated by Sam's desperate cries of "NO!" and finally "(*A howl of pain*) NOOOOOooooooOOOOOO!" (118), as he insists that Elizabeth is not Jo's mother.

Elizabeth represents a challenge to Sam to give up his desperate hold on Jo, to surrender his need for her, so that he can do what she needs, and help her to die. Sam asks Elizabeth and Oscar over and over again who they are, until Elizabeth finally responds, "who are *you*?" echoing his own question from the first act. Sam responds, "I'm Jo's husband; this is my house," but Elizabeth and Oscar remind him that it is they who have sat up and "watched the night die" (83). She challenges him, "Did *you* sit up? We heard the cries, and then the silence. Did you sit up, and hold her hand until the drugs had done their work? Did you lie down beside her then, put off the light, and stare up into the dark? Where did you fall asleep? Where did you wake up? Hm?" (83).

In the context of a dream or hallucination, Sam is negotiating the terms of his identity and of his relationship to the dying Jo. Will he continue to be the needy child, Sam-I-Am, or will he become the nurturer, easing his loved one into death, the loving mother Elizabeth and the beatific angel Oscar? When he says to them, "You aren't really here, are you?" Elizabeth responds, "Oh, *we* exist. Worry about your*self*" (96). Finally, Elizabeth presents him with the proposition that all values are relative save one, "'Who am I?' All the rest is semantics – liberty, dignity, possession" (152). When Sam responds, "I don't *know* who I am," she says, "Then how can you possibly know who I am?" (152).

Sam cannot become the strong nurturing presence that Elizabeth represents because his identity is essentially an infantile attachment to Jo. As Jo becomes increasingly detached throughout Act 2 – described as comatose, vague, faint, far-away – Sam becomes more and more desperate about his own loss of identity. He insists, "I have my *own* rights! My own personal rights!" demanding of his dying wife, "Jo! Pay attention to me!" (145). He complains, "my wife is dying; I am invaded" (149). Finally, shaking her, he cries, "if this is what you want, I'm not any part of it; you've locked me out. I . . . don't exist. I . . . I don't exist" (156).

At this point, Jo simply says, "Please . . . just let me die?" (156), a plea that ends in a scream of pain, and with Oscar scooping Jo up in his arms and taking her upstairs to lie her down, "(*soothing, crooning*.) I'll take care of you now; I'll make you better; you'll see; I'll put you right to bed; I'll make you better" (157). This is an almost exact reprise of Sam's action at the end of Act 1, as he carries Jo upstairs after the party, "(*soothing, crooning*.) I'll take care of you now; I'll make you better; you'll see; I'll put you right to bed, and take a cold cloth to your . . ." (72). The difference is that Sam was still insisting that "everything is reversible" (65), while Oscar means to make Jo's dying as comfortable as he can.

Whether Sam can accept his role as Oscar, the angel of death, depends on his ability to accept Elizabeth's offer of comfort to him. When he responds to Elizabeth's reminder that Jo is dying with the cry, "*I'm* dying," she says,

"Oh, no; not yet. You don't know what it *is*" (157). Unlike Jo, Sam has no real understanding of the experience of dying. To help him understand, Elizabeth gives him an image of the end of the world, as bombs go off at such a distance that there is only a flash of light and a beautiful silence. She comforts him with the assurance that there is "no time to be afraid" and that "everything [is] done before you know it" (158–159). Albee offers a poetic image of the stage of acceptance, which, as Kübler-Ross writes, "is almost void of feelings. It is as if the pain had gone, the struggle is over, and there comes a time for the final rest 'before the long journey' as one patient phrased it" (Kübler-Ross 113). As Elizabeth points out, Sam cannot reach that stage for himself until he actually experiences the process of dying, but perhaps he has come to understand it better in Jo. If Act 2 is seen as a dream or hallucination, his subconscious may have worked out the terms of his acceptance of Jo's death – though, as Oscar (Remus to Elizabeth's Romulus) says to the audience, "nothing is retained; nothing" (161). The play's most positive implication is for the audience, an implied character throughout the play, which must come away with a greater awareness of the needs of the dying and their survivors.

In recent years, Albee has moved beyond the survivor's experience to attempt to enter directly into the experience of the dying person through an act of the imagination. *Box, Quotations from Chairman Mao Tse-Tung*, and *All Over* may dramatize what he imagined to be his mother's response to his father's death from cancer in 1961, an event that occurred while Albee was estranged from his adoptive parents, having broken with them and moved out of the house when he was twenty. The strangled emotional response of The Son in *All Over* may be a reflection of the distance he felt from that event, which he has chosen to represent through the eyes of his mother. His mother's death in 1989, however, seems to have given him "the freedom to write about her," as Mel Gussow has put it.[14] It also provided the completion that was necessary to the story of him and his adoptive parents that began with *The Sandbox* and *The American Dream* (1961). He told Gussow, "I don't think it would have occurred to me to do it until 'the subject' was complete" (Gussow 353). According to Gussow, Albee was devastated when he found that his mother's will had been changed without his knowledge in 1986, removing him as executor and principal heir, a gesture he saw as "a parting act of disloyalty" and a "rejection, the final closing down of mother against son" (342). This occurred twenty years after their reconciliation, a period during which Albee says he was "a very dutiful and good son"[15] – spending time with his mother, taking her out, inviting her for visits (during which his partner had to absent himself because of Frances

Albee's homophobia), and attending to her problems. According to his friend Joanna Steichen, there was a great deal more of will than of feeling in this relationship:

> It was a great charade – absolutely charming, mildly affectionate, pleasant reminiscences. None of the bad stuff, none of the scrapes or difficulties. This was for public consumption; other people were present. But I doubt if they spoke any differently when they were alone. I didn't know about Frankie, but Edward is a very affectionate, loyal person, and I think he wanted to have a caring relationship with his mother. He put tremendous effort into it. (337)

In the Introduction to *Three Tall Women*, Albee dismisses the notion that the play could be a form of revenge: "I felt no need for revenge. We had managed to make each other very unhappy over the years, but I was past all that, though I think she was not."[16] As if on second thought, however, he admits that "it is true I did not like her much, could not abide her prejudices, her loathings, her paranoias," but also insists that he admired her pride, her sense of self, and her knack for survival. Albee further insists, in this Introduction, that he did not write the play as a way of coming to terms with his own feelings toward his mother, which he characterized as a "grudging respect I'd slowly developed for her." Instead, he wanted to "write as objective a play as I could about a fictional character who resembled in every way, in every event, someone I had known very, very well." He suggests that his "schizophrenic ability" to both participate in his life and at the same time observe himself participating, allowed him to write the play "without prejudice, if you will."

Three Tall Women consists of two acts in two different styles. In Act 1, which is written realistically – except that the characters are called only A, B, and C – an elderly woman interacts with her middle-aged caregiver and a young woman who has been sent from her lawyer's office to clear up some financial problems, problems that have arisen because of her failing memory and her refusal to relinquish control of her affairs to anyone because of her mistrust and fear of being cheated. Act 1 ends with A having a stroke. In Act 2 Albee shifts to expressionism, as he places a dummy in the bed to represent A in stage present, and transforms the characters into representations of her at ages twenty-six, fifty-two and ninety-two. As a threnody, the play is a response to death that reinterprets the old truism about the dying person's life flashing before her eyes, by trying to create understanding, and perhaps forgiveness, of the dying person through an act of imaginative empathy that allows the playwright to explore and dramatize his mother's frame of mind at three different stages in her life.

Act 1 is an important preparation for the process that occurs in Act 2 because it provides an external and ostensibly objective view of the mother from the point of view of "neutral" observers – the caregiver B, who is fairly sympathetic and even admiring, and the younger C, who is appalled by the physical deterioration and the antiquated prejudices and attitudes she is encountering in A. Realism creates the impression of a stance of objectivity toward A at the same time that, through the dialogue, it allows for the gradual construction of a portrait of A as a mother and an elderly woman. B and C are important mainly as indexes of attitudes toward her that are available to the audience, though they are mainly divided by age and experience, and their responses remain at the level of cliché.

The portrait of A is not a particularly attractive one, though she is clearly shaped by Albee's view of his mother as she entered her nineties: "I was touched by the survivor, the figure clinging to the wreckage only partly of her own making, refusing to go under" (*Three Tall Women* Introduction). A is described in the opening stage directions as "*a very old woman; thin, autocratic, proud, as together as the ravages of time will allow.*" The audience is first introduced to her insisting to C that her age is ninety-one and not ninety-two, as C knows it to be from her "papers." "Vanity is amazing," C observes (3). A speaks to both of the younger women in an imperious way, makes a number of remarks that exhibit her ethnic prejudices, engages in self-pitying crying jags, and purposely breaks a glass, crowing delightedly, "I broke the glass! I took the glass and I threw it down in the sink! I broke the glass and now she has to clean it up!" (28). B gives a detailed description of A's loss of bowel and sphincter control, and of the trouble she has in keeping her clean. The fact that A "won't have" a diaper put on and has to be taken to the bathroom many times a day suggests both the degree of her stubbornness and an admirable sense of dignity. Similarly, the fact that she refuses to have her painful arm, which will not heal from a break because of osteoporosis, amputated, is a measure of her endurance and tenacity as well as her vanity and stubbornness.

Act 1 provides the exposition that is needed for the meaningful encounter with death that occurs in Act 2. Through A's reminiscences to the younger women, the audience becomes aware of her girlhood with her "strict but fair" parents and her mother's ambitions for her to marry wealth; her "wild" youth that consisted of sexual initiation by a young man she loved, followed by her marriage to a soon-to-be-wealthy man she describes as a one-eyed penguin; her passion for riding and her affair with a groom; and through the "bracelet story," one that Albee's mother told to him, an image of her sexual loathing for her husband and of the crass exchange of sex for money that formed the basis of their marriage. Act 1 also provides a few tantalizing allusions to A's contradictory attitude toward her son, whom she refers to only as "he." She looks forward to his visit eagerly – "Will he come today? Is today the day he comes?" (19) – and she complains that he never comes to see her. She talks about the flowers and the candy that he brings her, but she insists "he doesn't love me. [. . .] he loves his boys [. . .] he doesn't love me and I don't know if I love him. I can't *remember!*" (59).

In Act 1 the treatment of death is characterized by an objectivity that reflects the realistic style. B, who tends to the dying A, responds to the younger C's recoiling from the fact of death with a matter-of-fact statement that is also an allusion to Beckett's *Waiting for Godot*:[17]

> Haven't you figured it out yet? (*Demonstrates.*) You take the breath in . . . you let it out. The first one you take in you're upside down and they slap you into it. The last one . . . well, the last one you let it all out . . . and that's it. You start . . . and then you stop. Don't be so soft. I'd like to see children learn it – have a six-year-old say, I'm dying and know what it means. [. . .] Start in young; make 'em aware they've got only a little time. Make 'em aware they're dying from the minute they're alive. (13–14)

Act 1 ends with a monologue by A that is reminiscent of Blanche DuBois's monologue on death.[18] As she sees it, the burden of sustaining the people in her life was left to her, and it was she who suffered through the deaths of her husband and mother: "There's so much: holding on; fighting for everything; *he* wouldn't do it; *I* had to do *every*thing; tell him how handsome he was, clean up his blood. Everything came on *me*" (60). Her mother stank of death at the end and screamed at her that she hated her. She says "they all hated me, because I was strong, because I *had* to be" (60). This includes not only her husband and her mother, but her alcoholic sister, and her son who "left home; he ran away" (60). After the monologue, a stroke sends A into a comatose state, setting up the expressionist subjectivity of Act 2.

As the mannikin representing A's body lies motionless on the bed, the actors transform into the three versions of A at twenty-six, fifty-two, and ninety-two. Through them, Albee presents the audience with three responses to the reality of death. As is expected at this point, C's response is essentially denial: "I don't want to *talk* about it; I don't want to *think* about it. Let me alone" (65). At fifty-two, B is facing death with a grim sense of reality: "It's got to be *some* way . . . stroke, cancer, or, as the lady said, heading into a mountain with a jet" (65–66). She fantasizes about her death coming by a violent accident or by having her throat slit by burglars as she sits at home alone going over invitations or bills. Unlike C, B has some experience with death, as she has witnessed her father's fatal heart attack: "God, the terror in the eyes!" (86). A, however, has advanced to the stage Kübler-Ross calls

Acceptance. She has had the experience of watching not only her father's, but her mother's death, and the six-year process of her husband's dying from cancer: "It's all right at first – except for the depression, *and* the fear – it's all right at first, but then the pain comes, slowly growing, and then the day he screams in the bathroom [. . .] It's terrible! And there's nothing you can do to prepare yourself" (105). Her response to her own death could come from one of Kübler-Ross's case studies: "I wonder how long *this'll* go on. I hope it's quick" (68). As B and C argue about whether youth or middle age is the happier time in life, A trumps them with her superior experience: "You're both such children. The happiest moment of all? Really? [. . .] Coming to the end of it, I think, when all the waves cause the greatest woes to subside, leaving breathing space, time to concentrate on the greatest woe of all – that blessed one – the end of it. [. . .] When it's all done. When we stop. When we can stop" (109–110).

The discussion is not complete, however, until the response of the survivor is accounted for. Unlike *All Over* and *The Lady from Dubuque*, *Three Tall Women* places the survivor's reaction decidedly at the periphery. Although the son appears in Act 2, and performs some actions, such as trying to comfort his mother as she lies in her coma, he has no lines. In a reversal of *All Over*, which characterized the dying man completely through the subjective perception of the survivors, *Three Tall Women* characterizes the survivor through the eyes of the dying woman. While the middle-aged B rages against her son, saying "he packed up his attitudes and he *left*! And I never want to see him again," and that "he *never* belonged" (92), A talks about their reconciliation, superficial and inadequate as it is: "He comes; we look at each other and we both hold in whatever we've been holding in since that day he went away [. . .] We're strangers; we're curious about each other; we leave it at that" (91). A is adamant that she never forgives her son, but "we play the game" (91).

The son's reaction is given in a "premonition" that A has of her death, in which she dies, as Frances Albee did, alone in a hospital room except for her maid and her chauffeur. When her son comes, an hour after her death, with the bouquet of freesia he always brings, she says:

> You stopped at the door of the room, and you knew right away, and you stopped and you . . . *thought!* (*Loathing.*) I *watched* you *think!* And your face didn't change. (*Wistful.*) Why didn't your face ever change? And there you were, and you thought, and you decided, and you walked over to the bed, and you touched my hand, and you bent down, and you kissed me on the forehead . . . for them! They were there and they were watching and you kissed me for *them!*" (106)

This scene presents a view from the grave, as it were, of the survivor's reaction to the death. And the son's reaction is identical to the reaction Albee describes at his mother's funeral:

> I remember I had to go up and touch the coffin. I was expected to stand there for a moment. I didn't feel any emotion whatever. I remember it as a theatrical performance. People were watching. I had to stay there with my hands on the coffin, and I had to sigh. I remember watching myself do it. But I'm not making the comment that it was phony and I was doing it for them.   (Gussow 341)

What Albee hopes to depict is an honest response to death under these circumstances. There is no love between these two people, who have taken refuge in social forms in order to have a relationship during her lifetime, and in the rituals of death afterward. As Albee indicates about the funeral, the ritual is for the living, to help them to accept the death that, in the case of A, has long been not only accepted but welcomed. It is a difficult attitude to dramatize, and indeed some of the early reviewers found the son a useless or extraneous element of the play. Albee's description of the funeral may be seen as an attempt to justify a false or inauthentic response to his mother's death. But there is no doubt that the play itself is scrupulously honest. As he says in his Introduction to the play, there is no doubt that writing it "got her out of my system" at last, though he did not intend it as "self-catharsis" or as a "revenge piece." As a contemporary example of the literature of death, it has served its purpose, and as *The Lady from Dubuque* may bring understanding for those who face the death of a loved one, *Three Tall Women* sheds a revealing, sympathetic light on a death where there should be love but is not. Much to Albee's apparent surprise, the latter play also serves some of the traditional purposes of the threnody, in praising the dead. As his Introduction notes, "very few people who met my adoptive mother in the last twenty years of her life could abide her, while many people who have seen my play find her fascinating. Heavens, what have I done?!"

NOTES

1. Henry I. Schvey, "At the Deathbed: Edward Albee's *All Over*," *Modern Drama* 30 (1987), p. 354.
2. Edward Albee, *All Over* (New York: Atheneum, 1971), p. 109. Further references will be cited parenthetically in the text.
3. C. W. E. Bigsby, *A Critical Introduction to Twentieth-Century American Drama, Volume 2* (Cambridge: Cambridge University Press, 1984), p. 292.
4. James Neil Harris, "Edward Albee and Maurice Maeterlinck: *All Over* as Symbolism," *Theatre Research International* 3 (1978), p. 200.
5. Edward Albee, *Box and Quotations from Chairman Mao Tse-Tung* (New York: Atheneum, 1969), p. 6. Further references will be cited parenthetically in the text.

6. For further discussion of the milk imagery, see Anthony Hopkins, "Conventional Albee: *Box* and *Chairman Mao*," *Modern Drama* 16 (1973), p. 143, and Robert Mayberry, "Dissonance in a Chinese Box: Edward Albee's *Box* and *Quotations from Chairman Mao Tse-Tung*," in *Edward Albee: Planned Wilderness*, ed. Patricia De La Fuente et al. (Edinburgh, TX: Pan American University, 1980), p. 72.

7. David Richard Jones argues that the action of the play is not waiting, but "what they do *while* waiting," the characters' "destruction of an earlier, tentative emotional unity." See his "Albee's *All Over*," in De La Fuente, *Edward Albee: Planned Wilderness*, p. 87. I would suggest that the tentative emotional unity is a function of the ritual of waiting, as is its dissolution.

8. Mel Gussow, *Edward Albee: A Singular Journey* (New York: Simon and Schuster, 1999), p. 310. For other suggestions of the ways in which Kübler-Ross informs the play thematically, see Gabriel Miller, "Albee on Death and Dying: *Seascape* and *The Lady from Dubuque*," *Modern Language Studies* 16.3 (1986), p. 156, and Matthew Roudané, "On Death, Dying, and the Manner of Living: Waste as Theme in Edward Albee's *The Lady from Dubuque*," in *Edward Albee: An Interview and Essays*, ed. Julian N. Wasserman et al. (Houston: University of St. Thomas, 1983), p. 77.

9. Elizabeth Kübler-Ross, *On Death and Dying* (New York: Macmillan, 1969), p. 170. Further references will be cited parenthetically in the text.

10. Edward Albee, *The Lady from Dubuque* (New York: Atheneum, 1980), p. 6. Further references will be cited parenthetically in the text.

11. Matthew Roudané, "An Interview with Edward Albee," *Southern Humanities Review* 16 (1982), pp. 39–40.

12. Philip C. Kolin (ed.), *Conversations with Edward Albee* (Jackson and London: University Press of Mississippi, 1988), p. 188.

13. Ronald F. Rapin, "*The Lady from Dubuque*: Into the Labyrinth," in *Edward Albee: A Casebook*, ed. Bruce J. Mann (New York: Routledge, 2003), p. 104.

14. Gussow, *Edward Albee*, p. 343. Further references will be cited parenthetically in the text.

15. See Bruce J. Mann, "*Three Tall Women*: Return to the Muses," in his *Edward Albee: A Casebook*, p. 8.

16. Edward Albee, *Three Tall Women* (New York: Dutton, 1994). Introduction unpaginated. Further references are to this edition and will be cited parenthetically in the text.

17. "They give birth astride of a grave, the light gleams an instant, then it's night once more." Samuel Beckett, *Waiting for Godot* (New York: Grove, 1954), p. 57.

18. "I, I, *I* took the blows in my face and my body! All of those deaths! The long parade to the graveyard! Father, mother! Margaret, that dreadful way! . . . there was the struggle for breath and bleeding. You didn't dream, but I saw! *Saw! Saw!*" Tennessee Williams, *A Streetcar Named Desire*, in *The Theatre of Tennessee Williams, Volume 1* (New York: New Directions, 1971), pp. 261–262.

7

GERRY McCARTHY

Minding the play:
Thought and feeling in Albee's
"hermetic" works

Edward Albee has noted in his work a shift from greater to less trans-parency (or vice versa) from one play to the next. He has, he observes, a tendency to write from time to time in a "hermetic" fashion. Looking, as we now may, at a lifetime's work, the hermetic Albee stands out against the obviously engaged and accessible dramatist of *Who's Afraid of Virginia Woolf?* (1962) or *Seascape* (1975), as any playgoer or reader will easily rec-ognize. If the distinction has latterly become less radical than it appeared with *Box* and *Quotations from Chairman Mao Tse-Tung* (1968) or, to a somewhat different degree of obscurity, *Tiny Alice* (1964), the hermetic tendency underlies some of the most interesting characteristics of Albee's dramaturgy.

There can be no doubting Albee's deep critical involvement in both the understanding of his own work and also with wider issues concerning new writing and the contemporary American stage. This was most evident in the aftermath of the huge success of *Who's Afraid of Virginia Woolf?* (1962). Albee, lately the Young American Playwright, now the Famous American Playwright, lacked no opportunity to convey his views in numerous inter-views, one notable press conference, and also the contextual writings accom-panying editions of his work. This was also a period in which he came to know personally some seminal figures in playwriting – notably Pinter and Beckett. The latter has remained a significant point of reference in Albee's thinking and, it may be hazarded, in his work.

With the publication of the texts of *Box* and *Quotations from Chairman Mao Tse-Tung*, Albee announced his experimental approach, and explained the responsibility of the dramatist:

A playwright – unless he is creating escapist romances (an honorable occupa-tion, of course) – has two obligations: first, to make some statement about the condition of "man" (as it is put) and, second, to make some statement about the nature of the art form with which he is working. [. . .] And I believe that an audience has an obligation to be interested in and sympathetic to these aims – certainly to the second of them [and] to be willing to experience a work on its own terms.[1]

Perhaps it is as well to interpret "statement" as less oracular than one might fear. The term was current at the time and rather too close to newspaper criticism for the comfort of a writer and thinker who has never rated that profession highly. The making of "statements" is, appropriately enough for Albee, the creation of works for the theatre, as in *Box* and *Mao*, and their "understanding" is the fruit of an audience's experience of the play. He proposes an experience and an entertainment, and not an argument, still less a bald opinion. He goes on to add a *caveat*:

> I may as well insist right now that these two plays are quite simple. By that I mean that while they are fairly complex and they do demand from an audience quite close attention, their content can be apprehended without much difficulty. All that one need do is – quite simply – relax and let the plays happen. (123)

A controlled style and a certain astringency of imagination are the hallmark of a series of plays from *Tiny Alice* onward, and this has always caused the dramatist difficulty with an audience and with critics who looked back to the hectic encounters of Martha and George in *Who's Afraid of Virginia Woolf?* With Albee's double bill the new difficulty lay in a composition for theatrical presentation that departed from accepted understandings of the "play" – a work predominantly in the dramatic medium. The attempt is radical, to Albee's mind, and, in his comments on *Box* and *Mao*, he initially turns to directors, who are asked to respect the accuracy of writing that seemingly translates the drama into another medium of composition and performance: "Alteration from the patterns I have set may be interesting but I fear they will destroy the attempt of the experiment: musical structure – form and counterpoint" (137).

If one is to accept "musical structure" as a key to Albee's experiments in his own medium, then one may consider the analogy of the listener to the musical work; let us say the Debussy prelude. The harmonies created by Debussy, or his use of the whole-tone scale, need not concern any listener who is willing to enter his sound world, accepting its novelty or strangeness. The complexity of the composer's organization of sound is not problematic. It is pleasing or displeasing, and providing there is perception and attention enough in the audience, there is an integrated response based on the initial direct excitement of the nervous system. Now in this example, the mind may be aware of simple generalized states, feelings consistent with possible objects or locations in the world (the equivalent we might suggest of Albee's "simple content"), but these sensations are realized by *specific* experiences derived from *specific* musical events, and may be, in Albee's term "complex."

The relationship of specific and generalized modes of response might explain Debussy's idiosyncratic placing of the titles of his piano *Preludes* at the end of each number. The title is consistent with a *secondary* generalized aspect of experience (or inspiration in the composer). The title ". . . pas dans la neige" ("footsteps in the snow"), affixed to the final bars of that prelude, indicates a generalized reference, a simple "content" consistent with a generalized feeling of space. The aural experience, which is given precedence over the title, or "content," is grounded in specifics of rhythm, pitch, and harmony.

Albee's method in *Quotations from Chairman Mao Tse-Tung* is characterized by such precise structures. "Musical counterpoint" can be distinguished in the parallel development of three lines: Mao's prophetic political vision, the social observation of the Old Woman's folk ballad, "Over the Hill to the Poor House", and the hypercorrection of the Long-Winded Lady's egotistical meditations. The "counterpoint" reveals the potential for confrontation and development that lies between these strands, but which arises only in the mind of the spectator, not in the minds of the performers, who are directed to pursue their accounts without a particular response one to another. Musical structure is being adapted to produce a deliberate disengagement of different elements, which are potentially in (even dramatic) opposition.

The parallel meditations and accounts of the roles engage the spectator in different narratives, *stories that are told*, creating thereby a virtual memory experience. This begs the question of the place of *drama* in a play such as this. Should we see Albee's "musical experiment" as a disengagement from drama, as much as an engagement with the methods and aesthetics of any other performance medium? Plays habitually incorporate narratives as part of present action, and create thereby a structure of past and present experience.[2] Albee, however, is unusual in concentrating here exclusively on monologue-based narratives with no context of dramatic action. There would be in this a certain reflection of musical experience with its illusions of space, memory, and location.

The philosopher Susanne Langer proposes a key definition of the *primary illusion* generated in the mind by different arts and media of performance. The primary illusion of music, she argues, is *time*:

> Musical duration is an image of what might be termed "lived" or "experienced" time – the passage of life that we feel as expectations become "now", and "now" turns into unalterable fact. Such passage is measurable only in terms of sensibilities, tensions, and emotions; and it has not merely a different

measure, but an altogether different structure from practical or scientific time. The semblance of this vital, experiential time is the primary illusion of music. All music creates an order of virtual time, in which its sonorous forms move in relation to one another – always and only to each other, for nothing exists there. Virtual time is as separate from the sequence of actual happenings as virtual space from actual space.[3]

As Langer looks to the virtual experiences that we find in different media, her thinking encompasses the overall integrated *systemic* response to a virtual world, based ultimately on organic processes:

The essence of all composition – tonal or atonal, vocal or instrumental, even purely percussive, if you will – is the semblance of *organic* movement, the illusion of an indivisible whole. Vital organization is the frame of all feeling, because feeling exists only in living organisms; and the logic of all symbols that can express feeling is the logic of organic processes.[4]

The illusion is notably one of "*organic* movement, of an indivisible whole." This predicates an inevitable overlap between different performance media, which each similarly address (through lyric, choreographic, or dramatic means) experience of the "indivisible whole." As if to underline our dramatist's intuitions, Langer's nomenclature allows the organic process to generate a *secondary illusion*, which arises naturally within the ordering of the organic response. That illusion in music is one of *space*, and its quality is derived from its dependence on the primary experience of time in which the organic forms of the auditory experience are apprehended by the human mind:

The frequent references to "musical space" in the technical literature are not purely metaphorical; there are definitely spatial illusions created in music, quite apart from the phenomenon of volume, which is literally spatial, and the fact that movement logically involves space, which may be taking movement too literally. "Tonal space" is a different thing, a genuine semblance of distance and scope. It derives from harmony rather than from either movement or fullness of tone. The reason is, I believe, that harmonic structure gives our hearing an orientation in the tonal *system*, from which we perceive musical elements as holding in *places* an ideal range. But the space of music is never made wholly perceptible, as the fabric of virtual time is; it is really an attribute of musical time, an appearance that serves to develop the temporal realm in more than one dimension. Space, in music, is a *secondary illusion*.[5]

Approached in this way, Albee's interest in using "musical structure" appears to be an experiment in the way in which the sonic and rhythmic score can be adapted to another score which is *fundamentally* not musical at all, but where *the overlapping secondary illusion* can be appropriated. To observe this is not to belittle the imaginative search of the playwright. Implicitly, his concentration on "form" and "structure" should be understood as a pursuit of an outcome that is quite other than even the quasi-musical effects that are sometimes alleged for the euphony of the well-written text. In the case of Beckett, such "musicality" is indeed frequently (and dangerously) cited as a means of explaining the *je ne sais quoi* of his deceptively bare compositions.

Albee's statements about "form" and "counterpoint" are substantiated in the practice of *Quotations from Chairman Mao Tse-Tung*, where material events are structured in time, but where the possibility of dramatic interaction is almost suppressed in his stage directions. There is the merest permission for the Old Woman to note the events on stage: "*She might nod in agreement with MAO now and again, or shake her head over the plight of the LONG-WINDED LADY*" (136). Similarly, the attention of the unspeaking Minister is exclusively on the Long-Winded Lady: "*He must try to pay close attention to the LONG-WINDED LADY, though – nod, shake his head, cluck, put an arm tentatively out, etc.*" (136).

The playing delivers three accounts in "counterpoint." The Long-Winded Lady's are personal memories: private, indirect, and insecure. Chairman Mao's are historical, a scientific narrative predicting the victory of the proletariat. Meanwhile, the Old Woman recites a ballad recollecting suffering and abandonment. While true polyphony depends on consonant and dissonant effects as different voices interact in harmony, such simultaneity is problematic in a medium based on a text articulating thought, purpose, and action. On the other hand, memory – the capacity of mind which experiences music in time – applies equally as speeches recording events are intercut rather than overlaid one on another. In addressing rhythm and tempo, Albee specifically demands performances that respect the *discontinuity* of time effects:

> No one rushes in on the end of anyone's speech; no one waits too long. [. . .] I have indicated, quite precisely, within the speeches of the LONG-WINDED LADY, by means of commas, periods, semi-colons, dashes and dots (as well as parenthetical stage directions), the speech rhythms. Please observe them carefully, for they were not thrown in, like herbs in a salad, to be mixed about. (137)

Conversely, stage directions are permissive. Albee says candidly of his character: "*I care very little about how she looks so long as she looks very average and upper middle-class.*" In keeping with a play which sets out to develop structures akin to music, Albee uses a conventionality of dress which would befit a string quartet.

The values of *theatre* are to the fore in *Box* and *Quotations from Chairman Mao Tse-Tung*: first Albee presents a great box structure for the framing play, then "the deck of an ocean liner," brilliantly lit, emerges from within the outline of the cube. This reflects the events which are examined in the narrative of the Long-Winded Lady, though it scarcely locates the actors in a unified space. The effect is strangely disintegrated (comparable with *The Sandbox*), and awaits the attention of the human mind to discover the lattice of cross-reference, transcending the disparate lines of the performances.

The structuring of the piece occurs, as in music, in time and not in space, and in this it suggests most strongly the nature of the mental exercise that Albee aims to procure. As the texts are all essentially narrative (including the analytical predictions of the materialist Chairman Mao), the mind is stretched across memory. The audience will naturally construct the "polyphonal" effect of the progressive statements made by the theorist and leader of the most alien and un-American of revolutions, the tale of poverty, and the self-indulgent examination of a suicide attempt on board a cruise liner. Mao himself is direct, and his affirmations are secure but impersonal:

> Today two big mountains lie like a dead weight on the Chinese people. One is imperialism, the other is feudalism. The Chinese Communist Party has made up its mind to dig them up. We must persevere and work unceasingly, and we, too, will touch God's heart. Our God is none other than the masses of the Chinese people. If they stand up and dig together with us, why can't these two mountains be cleared away? (138)

Yet from the clarity of Mao, we move to pettifogging detail:

> LONG-WINDED LADY: [. . .] So long ago! So much since. But there it was: Splash!
> OLD WOMAN: 'Over the Hill to the Poorhouse.'
> LONG-WINDED LADY: Well, not splash, exactly, more sound than that, more of a . . . (*little laugh*) no, I can't do that – imitate it; for I only *imagine* . . . what it must have sounded like to . . . an onlooker. An overseer. Not to *me*; Lord knows! Being *in* it. Or doing it, rather.
> CHAIRMAN MAO: In drawing up plans, handling affairs or thinking over problems, we must proceed from the fact that China has six hundred million people, and we must never forget this fact.
> OLD WOMAN: By Will Carleton. (139)

Albee's "counterpoint" requires attention in the audience and a sustained mental focus in the actors. As the field of concern and attention shrinks from the global-political to the personal and incidental, the Long-Winded Lady attends progressively to mind and perception. She moves from the impression that might have been made on a *hypothetical onlooker* as she fell from the ship's deck, to her recollection of witnessing a taxi mount the sidewalk as she emerged from a bakery with a bag of (particularly noted) crullers:

The bag of crullers, and a smile on my face for everyone liked them so, and there it was! Careen . . . and dying . . . and all that glass. And I remember thinking: it's a movie! They're shooting some scenes right here on the street. (*Pause.*) They weren't, of course. It was real death, and real glass, and the fire, and the . . . people crying, and the crowds, and the smoke. Oh, it was real enough, but it took me time to know it. The mind does that.   (144)

The predisposition of the mind to construe its perceptions as so many "drafts" between which it then discriminates is manifest in the face of the shocks of everyday existence and is prey to the delusions of a culture that has industrialized fantasy through the movie screen. But this drafting in the mind of versions of experience is, whatever the "content" (and surely Albee is critical of the human inability to face "reality"), a systemic function, not a failure, of the mind. As the narratives of the Long-Winded Lady return to her falling from the ship, the rambling recollections resume questions of cause: was she pushed? The questions continue: "is there any chance, do you think, well, I don't know how to put it . . . do you think . . . do you think you may have done it on purpose? [. . .] Well; yes; I'm sorry. Thrown myself off? [. . .] (*A sad little half-laugh.*) Good heavens, no; *I* have nothing to die for" (170–171).

As it draws to a close, the play seems to have advanced to the threshold of dramatic composition in the "minding" of the interactions between a speaker and her rescuers. Is this the play that Albee might have written on the scrutiny of a case of possible suicide? Is this *playing* of the account, with its organization of mind, not a *proto-drama*, awaiting a resolution into the multiple minds of dramatic performance?

The question of the *musicality* of these procedures is central to Albee's framing play, *Box*. His recurrent theme of loss is likened to a nervous response associated with tonicity and key structure. These notions are strikingly articulate and well targeted:

It's the *little* things, the *small* cracks. Oh, for every pound of milk they spill you can send a check to someone, but that does not unspill. That it *can* be *done* is the crack. And if you go back to a partita . . . ahhhhh, what when it makes you cry!? Not from the beauty of it, but from solely that you cry from loss . . . so precious. When art begins to hurt . . . when art begins to hurt, it's time to look around. Yes it is. (*Three-second silence.*) Yes it is.   (129)

This allusive discussion links aesthetic states to notions of *loss*: waste, corruption, and neglect in the everyday world. The voice ("*Schoolmarmish*") lectures us on tension and release procured by the experience of a performance:

The release of tension is the return to consonance; no matter how far traveled, one comes back, not circular, not to the starting point, but a . . . setting down again, and the beauty of art is order – not what is familiar, necessarily, but order . . . on its own terms. (*Two-second silence. Sigh.*) So much . . . flies. A billion birds at once, black net skimming the ocean, or the Monarchs that time, that island, blown by the wind, but going straight . . . in a di*rec*tion. Order! (130)

The mingling of the narrative image with what is frankly an aesthetic discussion (of the nature of lyric response) is subtly done. The punctuation of the speeches sets a tempo, as Albee believed it would, and the internal phrasing of the language is strongly directed toward a sustained rhythm consistent with the calculations of thought in the argument.

The most remarkable aspect of this meditation on art is the theoretical basis that it posits for aesthetic experience. The discussion of the tension involved in aural experience and the shift away from the home key is perceptive, and its generalization to other artistic experience is carefully stated. The notion of "setting down" and the resolution of tensions is applicable to other sorts of distancing in other media, and comes quite close to Susanne Langer's discussion of duration and aural movement in music.

Albee works into the expression of an anxiety born of distance a term, "morality," which may be much closer to the experience of drama than of music: "It is not a matter of garden, or straight lines, or even . . . morality. It's only when you can't come back; when you get in some distant key; that when you say, the tonic! the tonic! and they say, what is *that*? It's *then*" (131). This is the moment when "art hurts" and consecrates the moment of "loss", but Albee seems as elsewhere in this work to be rather more concerned with the creation of generalized states than with the pursuit of a specific effect. The narrative image is entertained in mind, and affords the primary illusion of virtual memory, the "spilling of milk." A secondary effect of spatial arrangement – the mass of birds and the counterdynamic of the single bird "moving fast in the opposite way" – depends on memory but evokes also in the integrated system a physical response to space and direction. This it would have in common with music.

* * *

One senses that this *feeling* of space and absence, the "hurt" of art, is intimately linked to Albee's theme of the "lost child" – which he develops with close attention to the shaping of the audience's mental response. We may recall here the difficulty that some found in the use of the "imaginary" child in *Who's Afraid of Virginia Woolf?* and Albee's comments on the naive realism of actors trying to play grief for a "real" child. The approach of a performer seeking an exact correlative in everyday existence is only conceivable in drama, where the purposes generating the action suggest Langer's "indivisible whole." To the realist actor there must be a "necessary narrative" to explain causation in the play's events.

In *Who's Afraid of Virginia Woolf?*, Albee's "loss" arises from playing the forms of his writing and not the imagined lives of his characters. The motif of the lost child is, true, important for the resonance of the dramatist's own life, but his handling of it is characterized by a determined abstraction, almost a need to separate his effects from any naturalistic construction which can be based on the events of the play. It comes as a shock to discover that the play, which can be approached through the folk psychology of lives on a New England college campus, is primarily a score of actions to be played within parameters elastic enough to include the generalized "need" for a child, and not any particular instance. On reflection, that elasticity is felt throughout the work, and the same indeterminate status of the child can attach to, say, the daddy figures, or the mousy pregnancy that haunt the active symbolic figures played before us on the stage. The accessible Albee is ghosted here by the more hermetic and abstract Albee.

His concern is for the mental phenomenon of "representation" rather than with the everyday realism of what could be said to be "represented." The life of the play is found in the immediate processes of performance, and not in a telling of its events – what I am calling the actor's "necessary narrative." Albee here encounters the realist fallacy in Western theatre that obscures much thinking about the nature of acting and about the status of the character. Particularly in the post-Stanislavsky traditions of the American stage, characters are deemed to inhabit and *comprehend* worlds which escape the bounds of the play text. Thus, exercises may be contemplated in which knowledge of the character is gained through exploration of its life in imagined times and circumstances other than those of the stage. The least radical example of this would be the Stanislavsky-inspired adaptation exercise in which the circumstances of the scene are altered so that a better comprehension of its playing may result from the improved knowledge and understanding of more familiar circumstances.

The search for a *truer* performance is founded on an epistemological dilemma. How does the actor "represent" something that is manifest only through his or her playing? How may he or she play something that is as yet unknown, unrealized? The temptation is then to seek the knowledge that is lacking by the suggestion of intelligent possibilities that are felt to be reasonable approximations to the "represented" world of the play. "How would my character feel under these circumstances?" is a familiar question when the rehearsal process is beset by the realist fallacy. The dilemma may be resolved only if the fallacy is exposed. The dilemma was possibly the source of the problem that Albee encountered with Colleen Dewhurst and Ben Gazzara as they rehearsed the final scenes of *Who's Afraid of Virginia Woolf?* The actors played the account of what they could see would be the narrative potential of the scene of bereavement: "When George and Martha lost the child, they were grief-stricken." The consequence was, in Albee's words, the playing of a state of emotion (interestingly expressed in musical terms): "What we were getting was a kind of dirge-like quality . . . mourning. It was heavy and yet not really intense. After I explained the child as a kind of metaphoric game-playing, the dirge-like quality was gone and they were playing more."[6]

The problem arises from what the actor has *in mind* – a "knowledge that," of narrative, as opposed to the embodied "knowledge how," of acting.[7] The actors' mental preoccupation with a narrative past was the source of this unwanted emotion. "Knowledge that" is appropriate to telling the tale, and the recall of actual or virtual memories, but it is also dangerous in the work of the dramatic artist, called to realize the embodied experience of present action. Susanne Langer makes a useful distinction when she discusses the primary illusion of drama as being "virtual history."[8] The virtuality of the stage is lived events tending toward consequences and outcomes in the future. Where the primary mode of narrative is memory, she claims, that of drama is *destiny*. The common notion of the play "telling a story" is only a loose approximation to the witnessing of hypothetical events proposed by the playing of actions on a stage.

Albee requires the actors playing George and Martha to embrace a conception, and to realize it in actions and narratives that arise from one moment to the next. They must listen to one another and interact in the dramatic exchange. Albee governs the interplay of *mind* in his text: he preordains the "how," the actor's knowledge of how to perform. Here we are able to recall Albee's concept of the "musicality" of his dramatic texts. The dramatic interactions set alternative "memories" one against the other, but also explanations, claims, and counterclaims. The player has *in mind* the claim and the prayer, and virtual memories (of the life of the "child") arise naturally from this dramatic objective. Albee, like other dramatists, brings us close to a play on cognition: how are these memories virtual? We know their hypothetical origins, but once these are accepted, memories arise as would the equally hypothetical memories of the actor who insists on treating the child as "real." Yet, again, we know that memory itself is unreliable, and its very nature seems to be constructive, assembling its trace of past experience out of a variety of sources verifiable or not.[9]

It is common to interpret moments of indeterminacy in plays as occasions of deception or denial between the characters. This is attempted in the case of Pinter or Beckett and the attempt is futile, as each of these dramatists has pointed out when accused of obscurity. The plays are, as Beckett would put it: "as stated." In these dramatists, and in Albee, the drama depends on characters and actions that are "as stated" and not as might be even intelligently interpreted. The play is a composition which puts us in mind of virtual events, and which triggers experience to be suffered. The play is a thing of our minds and their responses and not a record of the world. In this Albee is an artist unusually sensitive to drama, and an intelligent and instinctive explorer of the inherent effects of a medium that is built out of purposive action. He understands representation as a function of mind, not, as is frequently the assumption, a process which views the world from particular angles. Mental representations create the phenomenon itself, and Albee's statements are so many essays in the manipulation of mind.

Lest it be thought that what we see here is a characteristic of the postmodern, the example of Shakespeare in his comedies is instructive. There is no "necessary narrative" to the events that prefigure *Twelfth Night*, and which explain Viola's father's child who "pined in thought." Is this child Viola? Or her sister? When Orsino asks, "But died thy sister of her love, my boy?" is the reply a lie, for the "sister" is Viola herself (who manifestly lives, as the boy Cesario), or is it the account of the hypothetical sister and of the nature of the mental representation?

> I am all the sisters of my father's house,
> And all the brothers too, and yet I know not.
> (II.iv)

Even more tellingly, Shakespeare's hypothetical propositions are the very heart of his *As You Like It,* where Rosalind as Ganymede proposes that Orlando woo in her a hypothetical girl, a Rosalind:

> ROSALIND: [. . .] Am I not your Rosalind?
> ORLANDO: I take some joy to say you are, because I would be talking of her.
> ROSALIND: Well, in her person, I say I will not have you.
> ORLANDO: Then, in mine own person, I die.
> ROSALIND: No, faith, die by attorney. (IV.i)

This is, surely, the sort of "metaphorical game-playing" that Albee explained to Dewhurst and Gazzara. For Shakespeare's hypothetical lover we may read Albee's hypothetical child. Similarly, the absurdism of *The American Dream* (1961) signals the status of the "bumble of joy" whose mutilation is narrated by Grandma:

Well, it was very sweet. The woman, who was very much like
Mommy, said that she and the man who was very like Daddy had never been
blessed with anything very much like a bumble of joy.
MRS. BARKER: A what?
GRANDMA: A bumble; a bumble of joy.[10]

The "likeness" to Mommy and Daddy is a construct that tests (or torments)
the mind's capacity to discriminate between propositions. As in Ionesco, the
connections of the "necessary narrative" are joyfully distorted to the point
of absurdity. "Once upon a time," and the clichéd metaphors of everyday
language create the mental image of both the baby, the "bumble of joy"
and the mutilation of the child who cannot satisfy the monstrous parents:
"it cried its heart out," and "only had eyes for its Daddy." Mrs. Barker
generalizes the reaction to these instances: "For its Daddy! Why, any self-
respecting woman would have gouged those eyes right out of its head."
"Well, she did," Grandma replies: "That's exactly what she did" (47).

The style and the technical verve of the writing make clear Albee's delight
in the creative potential of abstraction. The references to adoption and to the
possessive fury of the parents are close enough to his own life experience for
there not to be any doubt about the seriousness of his play, but the playful
nature of the creative hypothesis shared with the audience is evident. The
Grandma role bridges the gap between concern for the world and the joy
of playing. The role also allows Albee to engage overtly in an address to his
audience in which the nature of the experience is revealed as the sequence of
mental representations that it is:

GRANDMA: (Interrupting . . . to audience.) Well, I guess that just about wraps
it up. I mean, for better or for worse, this is a comedy, and I don't think
we should go any further. No, definitely not. So, let's leave things as they
are right now . . . while everybody's happy . . . while everybody's got what
he wants . . . or everybody's got what he thinks he wants. Good night,
dears.   (60)

Albee repeatedly adopts this stance, whether it is an aspect of "insight" in
Jerry in *The Zoo Story*, or Claire in *A Delicate Balance*, or the strangely
indeterminate roles that begin with Elizabeth and Oscar in *The Lady from
Dubuque*, who arrive to be in time for the "dying." Those roles function
in the *metatheatrical* zone where the dramatic composition is engineered to
comment of itself.

* * *

We have a critical term – *metatheatre* – for what was once "the play within
the play," but less obviously do we have an account of the phenomenon that
it denotes. Albee is both fascinated by it and seems to be driven to explore

it, it might be argued as an aspect of the "destabilizing of meaning" in his postmodern context. Yet, again, we may see that Albee's impetus derives from an awareness of the problem of mind and meaning in the theatre *per se*. He has an instinct for the way the mind constructs its multiple representations of the world as so many parallel drafts, between which it discriminates and ultimately selects, and he exercises this very capacity in his shifting, constantly changing and reordered world of play.[11] So we may find a peculiarly phenomenological level in his composition, accompanied by, here and there, expression of concern for the inhabitants of his virtual world.

In *Counting the Ways* (1976), we find this self-conscious theatrical presentation, with the various scenes of marital anxiety played out as short vaudeville numbers. The two actors comment on the timing of exits and entrances, and at one stage are instructed to "identify themselves" and make a more or less improvised declaration to the audience about themselves and their own private or professional lives. In Scenes 16 and 17 we find a telling juxtaposition. The woman entertains a doubt (about how many children they have):

SHE: (*Smiles; cheerful.*) Three.
　　(*HE just stands there. She pantomimes the figure.*)
　　Three! (*He just stands there. Not believing it she pantomimes the figure.*)
　　Four? (*He just stands there. Reassuring herself she pantomimes the figure.*)
　　Three! (*He just stands there. Quite incredulous.*)
　　Four!? (*She exits. He just stands there.*)
　　　　BLACKOUT [12]

In the next scene, which begins "as at the end of Scene 16," He meditates upon feelings that are somehow connected to the strange "loss" of the "fourth" hypothetical child:

HE: (*Standing; smiles.*) Which brings us, then, to a discussion of this thing
　　called . . . "premature grief." (*Imitates her tone, but softer.*)
　　"Not yet!
　　Not yet!"
　　(*His own voice again; nods.*)
　　Yes; yet. 　　　　　　　　　　　　　　　　　　　　　　　　(26)

He makes reference to Auden, and to a not unfamiliar mental habit, that of entertaining the image of the death of oneself or of a lover. Albee seizes on this as he pursues his theme of loss, but does so in terms of the human capacity to feel loss before its onset, or in purely hypothetical terms. As the "discussion" continues, Auden is tentatively approved for the way in which he is "in touch with the mind":

> Auden used to say – you see? I come back to him – Auden is *reputed* to have said that he would imagine a lover's death, to see how it felt – for the sake of poetry, I wager. (*Shrugs.*) Maybe he didn't deeply care; I imagine he did. It's good to get in touch with the mind now and again. No harm. (*Begins to exit; reconsiders.*) Do you believe . . . do you believe the mind and the brain are separate entities? Some scientists are beginning to come back to that view. Scientists! (*Pause.*) Really! (*Exits.*) (26)

More important for the present discussion is probably the much later *The Play About the Baby* (1998), which is set in a symmetrical world of human relationships, with a quartet. The older Man and Woman observe the young Boy and Girl, their instinctive relationship and their sense of future manifested in the baby. The scenes are played with much of the artifice that characterized *Counting the Ways*, so that Man and Woman appear to assist at a ritual game through which the young lovers move to a point of loss, and emerge from their Eden. At the same time, the playing is grounded on notions of mind and the processes of mental representation. The play resumes the common manifestations of love, both as a physical and a moral experience, but as a composition it plays pitilessly with the creative life of the abstraction (the baby). There is more than a hint of Chekhov's melancholy clown Charlotte, in *The Cherry Orchard*, with her desolate game at the conclusion of the play:

> (*LOPAKHIN comes in. CHARLOTTE quietly hums a tune.*)
> GAYEV: Charlotte's happy, she's singing.
> CHARLOTTE: (*picking up a bundle which looks like a swaddled baby.*) Rock-a-bye baby. (*A baby's cry is heard.*) Hush, my darling, my dear little boy. (*The cry is heard again.*) You poor little thing! (*Throws the bundle down.*) And will you please find me another job? I can't go on like this.[13]

The dramatist plays with the means of theatre to secure a response: the "inventions" of a Charlotte lie within the invention of a Chekhov. And so it is with Albee who also uses the blanket trick in his play:

> MAN: (*Gentler.*) Time's up. (*WOMAN hands him the bundle. Out; a barker.*) Ladies and Gentlemen! See what we have here! The baby bundle! The old bundle of baby! (*Throws it up in the air, catches it; GIRL screams.*)[14]

Where we might expect a framework of circumstances to facilitate the progress and comprehension of an action, we encounter speculation on the nature of mind and memory, particularly as perceived by an actor:

MAN: [. . .] All fades, all dissolves, and we are left with . . . invention;
reinvention. I wonder how I'll remember (*Gestures about him.*) all of *this*?
But, since I'm not *there* yet – so to speak – have not, haven't remembered
it . . . (*Brisk.*) well, first we *invent*, and then we *reinvent*. As with the past,
so with the future – reality, as they laughingly call it?   (15)

The passages of narrative, of virtual memory, invention or reinvention,
are criss-crossed with the physical moves of the Boy and Girl, coming and
going to the offstage baby, gamboling naked as they run from making love
and return to it, and fearing for the future. What of the Gypsy who told
her fortune, but might – "as gypsies are *purported* to do" – wish to steal
their baby? Are these strangers here to steal the baby; to hurt them; "to
injure them beyond salvation?" As Girl runs to feed the baby, Boy confronts
this amorphous threat, addressing himself – Albee specifies – "*to 'theoretical
people.' The audience is not to be addressed directly, nor is anyone else*":

Beyond salvation? Injure us beyond salvation? Hurt us to the point that . . . ?
(*To GIRL, off.*) I'm standing guard. (*She doesn't hear, of course. More to
himself now.*) I'll guard you; I'll guard the baby. (*Gentle.*) If there's anybody
out there wants to do this to us – to hurt us so – ask *why?* Ask what we've
done? I can take pain and loss and all the rest *later* – I *think* I can, when it
comes as natural as . . . sleep? But . . . now?   (38–39)

Albee's stage directions would be understood by an actor familiar with the
classical technique of the soliloquy. His term reveals the conception he has
of performance: the actor plays within a creative hypothesis that "out there"
are people who wish to harm you. Albee works to create an action where the
social and personal dimension of a proposition, a threat, can be embodied,
while the mental functions that construct and harbor the proposition are
presented and accepted. The integration of these two levels of mentality is
the problem of the dramatist, and Albee, it can be said, triumphs in this
regard.

The complexity will develop as Albee gives these figures, Boy and Girl,
minimal circumstances – as much parameters for the playing as what might
conventionally be termed "character background." When the newcomers
intervene, they threaten the idyll, but they question it as a mental representation. They exist at the cusp between the play as a mimicry of social
interactions, and the play as a purely abstract vehicle of thought:

BOY: Why are you here? What do you want?
MAN: (*Cheerless smile.*) What do we *want*. Well, it's really very simple. We've
    come to take the baby.
(*Silence.*) [. . .]
MAN: (*Demonstrates.*) We've come to take it.

BOY: I don't . . .
MAN: (*Very explicit.*) A-way; a-way.
GIRL: (*Re-enters from left; hysterical.*) WHERE'S THE BABY?! WHAT HAVE
YOU DONE WITH THE BABY?! (*Silence.*)
MAN: *What* baby? (*Silence.*)
WOMAN: Yes; *what* baby? (53–54)

The play puts us *in mind of* the baby (in the familiar expression) and yet
it raises the question of the very existence of a child. Albee follows here his
instinct to explore drama, theatre, and the inherent value of the integrated
human experience of theatrical play. He is also faithful to the forms and tradition of the dramatic medium. Man is given a speech to open the second act
in which he addresses the audience – even the "stragglers," if there are any –
and promises them "the exposition" ("You'd think they would have it in the
first act!"). With a "shift of tone," he then digresses to the "mindedness" of
popular drama:

> I must tell you something here: I have a troubling sense of what should be –
> rather than what *is*. It chokes me up at simpleminded movies – where good
> things happen to good people? My throat clots, and I think I'm going to cry.
> Because I know that it can never happen in what they call "real life"? (49–50)

There follows the destruction, or aesthetically the deconstruction, of that
simple-minded movie drama. The idea of good things and good people is a
trigger to a parallel knowledge of the abyss. The capacity of the mind stirred
by Albee's play engenders the "hurt" that actors and audience must "get
through."

The systematic cruelty of the reduction of the idea of the baby to a hypothetical "baby" is achieved in a set of careful distortions of material that has
been used in the first act. One might well expect Albee to have commented
on the "musicality" of his technique. Themes are directly repeated, with
modulations of tone: the events in the lives of the young couple (motifs?),
are claimed by their tormenters for themselves as they suggest one or other
of them was in a relationship with the Boy, and that the Woman bore the
child. We find inversions of themes: the gypsies who might have threatened
to steal the baby are identified as the young couple, who do not have a baby
but have stolen it. The impact of all this depends on the structuring and the
playing of the elements of the composition, and not in what, at the time
of *Box* and *Quotations from Chairman Mao Tse-Tung*, Albee would have
termed "content."

We are able to see in this process of development and recapitulation of
themes (not claimed by Albee to be a consciously "musical" aspect of his
form) the way in which the dramatist has always favored and experimented

with the processes and degrees of abstraction that are possible in the medium of drama, circumscribed as it is in its theatrical presentation by the question of semblance and the social occasion which attends its very creation. Men and women upon the stage are difficult to identify as mere performers, for their least action generates a possible context through a figure-ground relationship. Thus Albee's imagination both builds identifying coordinates, and then systematically questions, challenges, or destroys them. This is of course the very antithesis of the "realism" of much contemporary acting, whereby the presence of connected given circumstances permits "secure" decisions on the actor's experiences in the role.

Albee's compositional technique, which so often refuses the continuity of given circumstances, reveals their essentially secondary importance. Parameters are set for playing, but like a key change in music, they may shift and redefine the value of what is done. In *The Play About the Baby*, we know the baby as a mental construct, a suggestion, happily accepted by the mind as the spectator conceives the purposes of Boy and Girl as they tend the child. Progressively, the mind has to conceive that the baby may be taken from Boy and Girl, that the baby has been stolen by *them* from elsewhere, and then that it is not the Girl's at all, but the Woman's. Finally, the indeterminate status of the baby is almost tangible as the play concludes:

> BOY: (*Still in tears.*) No baby?
> GIRL: (*Still in tears.*) No.
> BOY: (*More a wish than anything.*) I hear it crying!
> GIRL: (*Please.*) No; no, you don't.
> BOY: (*Defeat.*) No baby.
> GIRL: (*Begging.*) No. Maybe later? When we're older . . . when we can take . . .
>   terrible things happening? Not now.
> BOY: (*Pause.*) I hear it crying.
> GIRL: (*Pause; same tone as Boy.*) I hear it too. I hear it crying too.
> (*Lights fade.*)   (94)

This is so highly structured as to seem completely abstract. Where is the resolution? Where is the causality of these events? For all that this is far from the meditations of the voice in *Box*, it incorporates an essential element of discrimination, of the splitting of experience into possibilities that exist in counterpoint. This is the effect that Beckett pointed to, in an essay on the work of O'Casey, as "dramatic dehiscence."[15] Resolution would be like the return to the tonic, and at the conclusion of this play one is left with an overwhelming sense of the fragility of that outcome. Most importantly, we find that Albee's structures bring thought and feeling together.

It can often seem that Albee is caught between his longing for the emotional landscape of music, and the fact of his highly developed rationalism. In a recent review by a London critic he is warmly praised for his dramatic gifts, but earns the uncomfortable qualification of "grammarian."[16] The cut and thrust of his dialogue cannot go far, it seems, without the correction of a phrase, even of the appropriateness of a word. The observation is just, but surely Albee is far from being a pedant. The structures of which he speaks are not the clockwork mouse that one winds up and sets in motion. They are the routines and strategies that allow the outputs of the mind to be continuously checked, questioned, even verified. They are the means of goading and stimulating the organism into the experience of its wholeness. As a dramatist, Albee's compositions must shape and structure thought, particularly in the interactions of minds. At the same time, the moral quality of which he speaks himself, and without which any drama is unimaginable, is a powerful motor of Albee's particular genius. The feeling in the world that is so characteristic of the individualized experience of music is parallel to the care and concern for the world that is felt through Albee's work. That *feeling* is remote from the emotionalism of much performance, and is closer to thought than once would have seemed arguable. We may consider, however, the possibility that the instincts of the creative mind, provoking the states of enhanced activity that are the business of art, may reveal something of the interconnected nature of mind itself, of thought and feeling.

NOTES

1. Edward Albee, *Box and Quotations from Chairman Mao Tse-Tung* (London: Penguin, 1971), p. 124. Further references will be cited parenthetically in the text.
2. Interestingly, one of Albee's playwriting students notes his teacher's advice to "Beware Tom Wingfield. He can narrate away things that would make good dramatic action." See online commentary at <http://members.aol.com/david10567/albeenotes.html>
3. Susanne Langer, *Feeling and Form* (London: Routledge and Kegan Paul, 1953), p. 109.
4. Ibid., p. 126.
5. Ibid., p. 117.
6. Daniel Stern, "Albee: 'I Want My Intent Clear,'" *New York Times*, March 28, 1976, Section 2, p. 1.
7. For an account of this problem, see G. Ryle, *The Concept of Mind* (London: Peregrine Books, 1963), particularly Chapter 2.
8. Langer, *Feeling and Form*, pp. 307ff.
9. See Israel Rosenberg, *The Invention of Memory* (New York: Basic Books, 1988).

10. Edward Albee, *The American Dream*, in *New American Playwrights*, ed. Charles Marowitz (London: Penguin, 1966), p. 46. Further references will be cited parenthetically in the text.

11. For a useful discussion of "multiple drafts" in a theory of the mind, see D. Dennet, *Explaining Consciousness* (London: Penguin, 1993), pp. 101ff.

12. *Counting the Ways and Listening* (New York: Dramatists Play Service, 1978), pp. 25–26. Further references will be cited parenthetically in the text.

13. Anton Chekhov, *The Cherry Orchard*, trans. R. Hingley (World's Classics: Oxford, 1980), p. 289.

14. *The Play About the Baby* (New York: Overlook, 2003), p. 88. Further references will be cited parenthetically in the text.

15. See Samuel Beckett, *Disjecta* (London: Calder, 1983), p. 82.

16. Michael Billington's review of *The Goat, or Who is Sylvia?*, *The Guardian*, February 2, 2004.

8

STEPHEN BOTTOMS

Albee's monster children: Adaptations and confrontations

Over the course of his long career, Edward Albee has experienced many ups and downs in terms of the critical reception his plays have received, but the lowest period was surely the early 1980s. Between 1980 and 1983, three new Albee plays opened on Broadway – a notable fact in itself given that he had produced only four new pieces (two of them one-acts) in the whole of the previous decade. Yet if Albee, apparently in recovery from alcoholism, was once again displaying a prolific creativity, the Broadway critics proved, for the most part, utterly unwilling to listen. Having seemingly made up their minds in advance that Albee was merely a shadow of his former self, they tore these plays to shreds as if to punish him for having the temerity to continue writing at all. *The Lady from Dubuque* (1980) was dismissed as "a hopeless stiff" by *Variety*, "really quite awful" by the *New Republic*, and "one of the worst plays about anything, ever," by *New York* magazine.[1] The following year, Albee's adaptation of *Lolita* was angrily condemned as a "deplorable desecration" of Vladimir Nabokov's novel (*Saturday Review*), as "a leering Broadway sex comedy" (*Women's Wear Daily*), and as "a monstrous bore" (*Daily News*).[2] Two years later, *The Man Who Had Three Arms* was met with weary contempt: this "temper tantrum in two acts" (*New York Times*) was "an intolerable audience ordeal" (*Variety*), and "as abject as it is vile" (*New York*).[3] Thanks to their reception, all three plays closed with humiliating speed, and the triple failure left Albee in effective exile from the New York theatre world for the next decade.

The Lady from Dubuque has subsequently been rescued somewhat from its initial drubbing, thanks to some thoughtful scholarly analyses (such as Brenda Murphy's, elsewhere in this volume), but the other two plays continue to be largely disregarded and dismissed. This is, in my own view, quite unjust. *The Lady* may indeed be the most obviously "Albee-esque" of the three, when considered in relation to his other work (with its drunken games-playing in a middle-class living room, it bears obvious comparison to *Who's Afraid of Virginia Woolf?* [1962] or *A Delicate Balance* [1966]), but it also bears the all-too-visible signs of having spent over a decade in rewrites. The initially sprightly cocktail-party chitchat quickly gives way to an often rather turgid display of angst and shouting, and by the second act the emotional thread of the piece gets lost in a jungle of self-conscious symbolism. *The Lady*, I would argue, represents the butt-end of Albee's "difficult" 1970s, whereas by contrast, both *Lolita* and *The Man Who Had Three Arms* were bold new departures for him – strikingly ambitious in their uses of theatricality, and playfully ingenious in their manipulation of the relationship between form and content. In this chapter, I hope to make the case for a reconsideration of these neglected works. In the case of *Lolita*, though, this first requires some attention to its status as one of four published plays adapted by Albee from preexisting sources.[4]

* * *

Albee is unusual among major American dramatists for his consistent interest in the process of adaptation. Yet like *Lolita*, his other adapted plays – *The Ballad of the Sad Café* (1963), *Malcolm* (1966), and *Everything in the Garden* (1967) – have tended to be neglected by commentators, on the usually unexamined grounds that they are not "original" writing.[5] Certainly it is true that in all his adaptations, Albee – a writer honoring his fellow writers – is scrupulously faithful to his source material. Yet the act of adaptation need not be regarded as any less "creative" than that of composition: as poststructuralist thinkers such as Roland Barthes have persuasively argued, no text is truly "original" anyway; each is, in its own way, "a tissue of quotations drawn from the innumerable centres of culture . . . a multi-dimensional space in which a variety of writings . . . blend and clash."[6] More significant than the question of whether an adaptation qualifies as original work are the questions of *which* texts Albee has chosen to adopt and adapt, and *what* he has done with them. For it is notable that, while each of his source texts has been radically different in tone and content, they are linked by certain common tropes. Primary among these are, first, the "adoption" of one character by others, as a kind of surrogate child, and second, the deviation of certain characters from the socially sanctioned sexual "norm." These elements fuse together most intriguingly in *The Ballad of the Sad Café* and *Lolita*.

Ironically enough, the adaptation that most obviously resembles other Albee plays, *Everything in the Garden*, is the one into which he seems to have invested the least of himself. He reworked Giles Cooper's English play, of the same title, for the Broadway stage, at the behest of his producing partner Clinton Wilder. Set in another middle-class living room, and depicting another vehemently feuding husband-and-wife couple, this is a satire on bourgeois values and hypocrisies in which family stability is threatened by sexual misconduct. Jenny, a suburban housewife, turns to prostitution in order to earn extra income with which to "keep up appearances" in front of her seemingly better-off neighbors (who have also, it emerges, been pursuing the same strategy). After much fighting with her husband Richard, Jenny eventually gains his tacit approval of her lucrative labor, provided it is kept suitably quiet.

Albee's adaptation transplants the play's setting from London's suburbs to New York's, and the stiff-upper-lip Englishness of Cooper's characters gives way to some sharper, more aggressive mood swings. Albee also lends the sitcom-style realism a more heightened edge of theatricality. For example, a prying neighbor (eventually murdered by the others) repeatedly addresses the audience directly, as if they are old friends and fellow voyeurs – a strategy Albee was to develop further in both *Lolita* and *The Man Who*. Albee, more than Cooper, seems concerned to remind his (privileged, Broadway) audience that this is not just a kooky comedy, but a play about people like them. Nonetheless, Cooper's basic scene structure, plot events, and thematics remain intact in Albee's version of *Everything in the Garden*, which is best regarded as a transatlantic "translation," rather than an Albee play as such.[7]

Conversely, Albee's three attempts at adapting novels have required him to bring far more of his own creative vision to bear, in order to find a compelling dramatic shape for them. The charges of "unoriginality" seem particularly misdirected in these instances, since when translating a text from one medium into another, the distinctive properties of the source medium are inevitably lost, and must somehow be compensated for through an "original" use of the receiving medium. Albee seems to have relished this challenge: "I've never seen an adaptation of anything that was any good," he noted in 1961, prior to embarking on his first experiment in dramatizing a novel – Carson McCullers's *The Ballad of the Sad Café*; "I'm curious to find out if it's possible [to avoid a] lessening and coarsening of the material."[8] Albee has spoken of trying to inhabit the originating artist's "voice" in order to make his adaptations faithful – "I must indeed become Carson McCullers" – but he has also, necessarily, had to bring his own concerns into play: "I had to be both Nabokov and myself."[9] Gilles Deleuze, a philosopher who had much to say about processes of "becoming," vividly summed up the needs of the adaptation process, when describing his own attempts to articulate the ideas of other thinkers as "a kind of buggery":

> I imagined myself getting onto the back of an author, and giving him a child, which would be his and which would at the same time be a monster. It is very important that it should be his child, because the author actually had to say everything that I made him say. But it also had to be a monster because it was necessary to go through all kinds of decenterings, slips, break-ins, secret emissions, which I really enjoyed.[10]

Albee's stage version of McCullers's *The Ballad of the Sad Café* (1963), like *Lolita* some two decades later, reveals just such an approach: the adaptation represents both a faithful rendering of McCullers's story (often reproducing verbatim passages of the original), and a deft refocusing of its concern with hidden, unspeakable passions.

Set in a town "that is far off and estranged from all other places in the world," McCullers's Southern-gothic novella relies on and revels in the creation, through prose, of an eerily mysterious atmosphere.[11] The central characters are all viewed from a distance, as fundamentally peculiar figures, and the narrative teases the reader with veiled allusions to their queerly unnatural desires. Miss Amelia, a six-foot two-inch, "mannish" woman, falls in love with her cousin Lymon, a hunch-backed dwarf, and swiftly goes from stern self-containment to lovestruck lunacy, showering him with gifts to win his affections. Lymon, however, becomes similarly smitten with Amelia's former husband, Marvin Macy, who in turn views Amelia with an infatuated love that has turned to hate, after her refusal to consummate their marriage. The novella thus treats romantic love in terms of sexual desires that are so obsessive and possessive as to border on the sadomasochistic: "the beloved fears and hates the lover, and with the best of reasons. For the lover is forever trying to strip bare his beloved. The lover craves any possible relation with the beloved, even if this experience can cause him only pain" (34).

In translating this material to the stage, Albee proved himself astutely aware that, where the reader of the novella aligns herself with McCullers's narrative voice – looking on, intrigued, from a distance – the spectator of a play normally needs to find some point of emotional contact with the characters themselves. Setting the play in a single location, the eponymous café which is also the main room of her home, Albee's broadly realistic adaptation places Miss Amelia at the center of the action. McCullers's narrative voice is maintained as a presence, but pushed to the margins – in the form of a narrator figure who appears only between scenes, to provide links and fill in information. As such, the narrator often appears curiously detached from the play as a whole, and these passages are the least satisfying component of an otherwise accomplished adaptation. Yet the strategy nonetheless succeeds in making Amelia seem more immediate as a character; less *mediated* by the voice of another.

Albee also makes her seem less freakish and more sympathetic than in the novella by inventing, for example, a scene in which she movingly describes her daughterly devotion to her father, who died just as she reached adulthood. She has been very much alone ever since, so the arrival of Cousin Lymon is treated by Albee as a chance for her to create a surrogate family unit. Where McCullers indicates that Amelia's interest in Lymon is erotic – "her eyes were fastened lonesomely on the hunchback . . . Her look that night was the lonesome look of the lover" (29–30), Albee instead suggests, through his narrator, that "Miss Amelia loved Cousin Lymon, for he was kin to her."[12] He creates scenes between them in which Amelia's treatment of her newfound, and initially very vulnerable, relative is unmistakably maternal: she welcomes him, in effect, as an adopted son. All the play's characters, moreover, tend to refer to Lymon as "Cousin Lymon" – thereby emphasizing family and the familiar – in notable contrast to McCullers's insistent description of him as "the hunchback," the freak-creature. When Lymon repays Amelia's hospitality by becoming increasingly smug, self-confident, and demanding, she seems to be less a victim of her own strange desires (as implied by McCullers), than a compassionate parent suddenly finding a cuckoo in her nest. Albee thus provides a striking inversion of the dysfunctional parent-child relationship in *The American Dream*, in which the innocent, adopted "bumble" is mutilated by its dissatisfied buyers.

Lymon's infatuation with Marvin Macy is also treated in less sexual terms than those implied in the novella. Lymon is not so much the doubly othered "homosexual dwarf" described by Christopher Bigsby, as an understandably insecure figure who sees himself as a "half man," and longs to be accepted and befriended by the idealized, powerfully masculine figure of Macy.[13] "What you expectin' me to do," Macy asks him at one point, "*adopt* you?" Lymon replies, "(*With exaggerated longing.*) Oh, Marvin Macy . . . *would* you?" (56). Thus, in Lymon's case as in Amelia's, Albee's adaptation actively *expands* the terms of McCullers's central interest in love: "there are many kinds of love," his narrator points out (25), and in the play the desire for belonging is treated as a basic human drive. At the same time, though, Albee leaves enough unspoken and ambiguous that erotic desire cannot altogether be ruled out as a factor in these relationships: as *The Goat* was to make explicit almost four decades later, he views the desires for family, companionship, and sexual contact as being far more confusingly intertwined than conventional wisdom would allow.

Significantly, Albee's most intriguing developments of McCullers's material lie in his treatment of the most overtly sexual passion in the story – Marvin Macy's desire for Amelia. As Bigsby points out, the history of their courting and marriage, "which is given little space or emphasis in Mrs. McCullers' version, becomes virtually one third of [Albee's play]."[14] This allows their early relationship to be comprehensibly developed, in fluidly handled flashbacks, from initial hostility and suspicion, through grudging mutual respect, to uneasy accommodation. Macy becomes fascinated with the tall, cool Amelia, seeing her as "a real grown-up woman" (36) – as distinct from the girls he has reportedly "up-ended" all over the county. He thus makes a sincere, even touching effort to reform himself and win her love.

For her part, the young Amelia, not yet the efficiently self-contained, masculine figure she will become (she wears a dress in the flashback scenes), seems flattered by Marvin's interest in her. She eventually consents to his *"will you marry me?"* with a *"very off-hand"* response of "Sure," after *"an interminable pause, during which she scratches her head"* (39). Her exact thoughts and motives here are left unspoken, but the implication is perhaps that, since marriage is expected of her, Macy seems as good a bet as anyone. Her later refusal to consummate their marriage can thus be read as her realization that she does not desire sex with any man. "Miss Amelia cared nothing for the love of men," McCullers tells us early in the novella (9), and her masculine appearance clearly alludes to the stereotyped image of the "butch" lesbian. Yet while Amelia's infatuation with Lymon subsequently seems to heterosexualize her in McCullers's version, Albee's less sexualized depiction paradoxically leaves open alternative possibilities. Certainly Amelia's initial acceptance and then outright rejection of Macy seems more understandable if one reads these events as forcing her to confront her basic lack of interest in men. Moreover, Albee makes clear that Amelia's transformation into the cold, hardened figure she is later known as *begins* at the point she rejects Macy: it is as if she begins to close down emotionally upon realizing that she will never be able to find a love that is socially permissible.

Meanwhile, the villains of the piece in Albee's treatment are those who create and maintain the prejudices dictating which forms of love are and are not permitted. The novella makes repeated reference to the destructive gossiping of the townspeople, but Albee's play extends this much further by placing all of the more negative characterizations of Miss Amelia – the references to her acquisitiveness, her litigiousness, her vindictiveness – into the mouths of small-minded busybodies, rather than lending them the omniscient truthfulness of the narrator's voice. Onstage, the dozen or so townspeople who frequent Amelia's café collectively become a giggling, chattering chorus of conjecture and disapproval, and their presence in her space becomes increasingly invasive over the course of the play. When Amelia and Macy finally confront each other in a brutal wrestling match (which has unmistakable overtones of sexual assault), these observers even take bets on the outcome, finding entertainment and profit in others' pain. Having lost the unfair fight, though, Amelia finds a way – in Albee's version – to speak back to these cruel spectators. Overcharging a customer for a drink, she explains that it is "five cents for the coke, and a dollar for seein' me. A dollar for lookin' at the freak" (69). There is also an implicit question here for the theatre audience itself, which anticipates more explicit equivalents in plays such as *Lolita* and

The Man Who: have they come to peer voyeuristically at deviants, or to empathize with human beings? In humanizing the outcasts, Albee's *Ballad* also suggests that the group face of the majority may be the more truly freakish.

In a sense, then, Albee reverses the dynamics of McCullers's narrative, even while remaining faithful to its basic outline: rather than portraying Amelia as a gothic grotesque, he makes the "other" comprehensible, while rendering alien the prying, judgmental eyes of the mainstream community. Similar concerns are apparent in Albee's next adaptation – of James Purdy's *Malcolm* (1966). The title character is a latter-day Candide figure, a young man whose father has vanished without explanation, leaving him all alone in the world. Malcolm, however, is so innocent, beautiful, and otherworldly that the story's other characters – grotesque cartoon figures representing contemporary society at large – all want to befriend and adopt him (much as Mommy and Daddy covet the Young Man in *The American Dream*). It seems that everyone wants to "own" a piece of the purity which they, in their various forms of worldly compromise, corruption, and mendacity, have long since lost – but Malcolm's journey from suitor to suitor eventually corrupts and destroys *him*.

Perhaps mindful of the criticisms of his use, in *Ballad*, of a narrator external to the dramatic action, Albee took an alternative approach with *Malcolm*, by seeking to let the characters carry their own story. The results, however, seem miscalculated, since the figures in Purdy's novel exist more as ciphers in a picaresque allegory than as plausible beings in their own right. By mimicking the minimalistic, often monosyllabic dialogue style of the novel, Albee allowed his own gift for more playfully complex dialogic interaction little room to breathe. Moreover, Purdy's meandering, episodic narrative lacks the kind of unifying arc that might lend itself to dramatic adaptation, and Albee found no convincing solution to this problem: the play succeeds only in replacing the novel's dream-like fluidity with awkward, often unexplained transitions between short, seemingly inconsequential scenes.

Perhaps the biggest problem with this adaptation, however, is that Albee also failed to find any theatrical equivalent for the arch, campy wit that sustains and buoys up Purdy's narrative. Indeed, while a stage direction shortly before the play's climax specifies that "*all camp is gone from here to the end of the play*" – presumably to ensure that more serious overtones are emphasized – it is very difficult to see much camp potential in his text even before this statement.[15] Purdy's novel is, on one level, a gay fantasy (with Malcolm as the ephebe being "picked up" by a series of older men and masculine women), and his scene descriptions frequently feature such peripheral images as musclebound, half-naked men working as domestic servants to the main characters.[16] Writing for Broadway in the mid-1960s, however, Albee was obliged to expunge the more obviously homoerotic imagery, and he seems to have left to the director the task of creating – through performance – a texture and style that might echo Purdy's novel. As an interested follower of New York's alternative, downtown arts scene, it is possible that he was influenced, in this respect, by the acclaimed, high-camp spectacles then being produced off-off-Broadway by the Judson Poets' Theatre, such as Rosalyn Drexler's *Home Movies* (1964), and Maria Irene Fornes's *Promenade* (another picaresque for modern-day Candides, 1965), whose success depended in large part on the extravagantly choreographic style of director Lawrence Kornfeld.[17] However, Albee's regular director Alan Schneider, known for his faithful, unadorned productions of dialogue-driven plays, was not noted for either wit or visual inventiveness, and proved ill-suited to the task of bringing stage life to *Malcolm*. His production was panned from all sides, and closed within a week.

* * *

Adapting *Lolita* some fifteen years later, Albee ran into production problems of a very different sort. Since Nabokov's novel is considerably longer than either McCullers's or Purdy's, Albee decided that, to do it justice, his adaptation also needed to be lengthy, and to be staged over two evenings. He still regards his unpublished, two-part version as the definitive play, but this proved unacceptable to the commissioning producer, Jerry Sherlock, who obliged Albee to cut it down to the one-night version now available in print. The problems did not stop there, however: ignoring the subtleties of Albee's text, Sherlock's production aimed squarely for the potential titillation value of this story of a middle-aged academic obsessed with young girls. As Albee himself observes, "directorial vulgarity" and a "salacious short-changing of the production *by* the production" led to "a disgusting misrepresentation of a faithful adaptation of a book I cherish."[18] He confesses to being relieved that the production closed as quickly as it did – even though the critics instrumental in that closure had mostly jumped to the conclusion that *he* was to blame for the vulgarity.

Albee's *Lolita*, then, still awaits a major production to do it justice. Yet even in its truncated, published form, this is a remarkable piece of stage writing, which suggests that Albee had learned some significant lessons from the drawbacks of his previous novel adaptations. The two-act play, which only loosely follows the novel's two-part structure, is comprised not of a string of picaresque incidents but of nine extended, episodic scenes, each of which takes a particular sequence or idea from the book and builds it into a cohesive, self-contained theatrical statement. In the opening scene of Act 2, for example, Albee responds ingeniously to the task of dramatizing the long, disorientating road trip across America on which Humbert Humbert takes his twelve-year-old paramour, Lolita. Unable to create a sense of this "road movie" journey spatially, as Kubrick's 1962 film version does, he instead draws attention to the *temporal* dimension of the trip, by building on Nabokov's implication that this seemingly endless tour represents Humbert's futile attempt to suspend time itself. By detaching Lolita from the real-time progress of school and community, and disappearing into the suspended animation of cyclical journeying, Humbert hopes vainly to keep her from growing up and so losing her childish charms. Albee demonstrates this through the use of a single, motel-room set, into which a maid repeatedly enters to change not only bedsheets but also paintings and windows. The maid always looks the same to Humbert and Lolita, but she keeps insisting that both her name and their location are different from before. Her presence thus creates a sense that disorientating jump-cuts are occurring in time and space: the couple are constantly moving and yet remain imprisoned in a limbo of interchangeable motels.

In the same scene, Humbert's increasingly paranoid sense that they are being followed from place to place is neatly dramatized through the repeated reappearance of his nemesis and fellow pedophile, Clare Quilty, always dressed in different outfits and playing a series of other, minor roles from the novel. A similarly deft interweaving of source materials is also achieved in the next scene. After Quilty has stolen Lolita from him, Humbert finds himself waking up in yet another motel room with a casual girlfriend and an amnesiac young man; no one can remember who the latter is, or how he got there. Albee cleverly adopts this young man, an incidental figure in Nabokov's book, as a dramatic mirror for Humbert's own overpowering sense of loss and dislocation.

Through strategies such as this, Albee creates a densely layered and theatrically cohesive adaptation of Nabokov's novel. Indeed, the imaginative unity of the play as a whole is underlined in the stage directions by the suggestion – ignored in the 1981 production – that a turntable stage might be used to make the transitions between scene settings appear seamlessly fluid. A turntable, properly used, would have further reinforced the play's sense of remaining on the spot while traveling in circles; of revisiting familiar set elements in alternative, unfamiliar configurations. The resulting impressions of slipping time and déjà vu are also insistently apparent in other aspects of the play. For example, Humbert's first, childhood love, Annabel, appears onstage as a physical *echo* of the previously introduced Lolita, rather than standing simply as a precursor to her.

These temporal swings and roundabouts are facilitated in large part by Albee's decision to retain the novel's narrative voice as the foundational layer on which the rest of the play is built. Thus, a simple turn of phrase can immediately propel the stage action forward or back in time. However, unlike Albee's *The Ballad of the Sad Café*, with its detached, omniscient balladeer, *Lolita* knits this narrative voice into the fabric of the action, by splitting it into *two* voices, and placing them in rivalry and conflict with each other. Humbert may suspend the action of a scene to talk directly to the audience about his thoughts and feelings, just as he does in the first person narrative of Nabokov's novel, but he may also be interrupted and even interrogated by "A Certain Gentleman." This additional narrator figure is in fact the one who first welcomes the audience to the play, but Albee leaves us appropriately *un*certain as to who exactly he is. He echoes, perhaps, the presence of "John Ray" in Nabokov's novel – the psychologist whose prefatory note provides an initial framing device for Humbert's memoir – but this Gentleman also presents himself as a "writer, novelist, playwright," and as the author of this story.[19] He seems to be a hybrid of both Nabokov and Albee himself, and as such, one might expect this Gentleman to maintain an aloof, god-like distance on the play's events. Instead, though, he plays an arguably more "realistic" role for a writer – by following his protagonist about and engaging in a critical dialogue with him about his actions and motives (though the other characters only occasionally become aware of his presence). In Pirandellian mode, the Gentleman notes that Humbert "has all the vigor and self-possession we authors are so pleased to find our characters sometimes achieve," but that as a result, he sometimes goes off in "directions I am not altogether certain I care to deal with" (5–6).

Thus, as Thomas Adler has persuasively demonstrated, Albee's is a "meta-*Lolita*" – "foregrounding the making of fictions and the artificialities involved in the making of fictions."[20] In this respect, Albee's dramatization is again very much in the spirit of Nabokov's book: an overtly self-reflexive novel, chock-full of puns and allusions, is rendered as an overtly self-reflexive play. Whether the characters are pointing out the cheap artifice of the set – "plastic ivy!" (15) – or underlining contrivances in the narrative – "plots must turn on something" (30) – the play constantly, playfully reminds the spectator of its own status as fragile stage illusion. Predictably enough, though, several reviewers of the play's 1981 premiere complained that this reflexivity indicated Albee's self-indulgence and irreverence toward Nabokov (one wonders if they had actually read Nabokov's joyously irreverent novel). The dual narrator device was subjected to particular criticism, on the grounds that Humbert spent too much time talking to the Gentleman, and not enough acting out "proper" scenes with other characters. This complaint ignored not only Albee's faithfulness to the form of the novel (in which Humbert's narrative persistently presents the other characters merely as sketched-in satellites to his own dominating consciousness), but also the dramatic dynamics inherent in the developing, triangular relationship between Humbert, A Certain Gentleman, and the theatre audience they both appeal to for support. Albee also repeatedly uses his two narrators to *confront* spectators with their own voyeuristic curiosity. For example, while literally drawing a veil across in front of Lolita's and Humbert's first sexual encounter, the Gentleman addresses his watchers in mock surprise, as if they have voiced a complaint: "You don't really want to *see* it do you? You can imagine it. You all *have* imagined it" (44).

If the audience at Albee's *Lolita* is never allowed to watch in complacent comfort, this, too, is consistent with the original novel. In reading the Nabokov, it is difficult to avoid the constantly unsettling awareness that this is a tale told from the point of view of a self-confessed "pervert," an obsessive pedophile who, as he finally acknowledges, is responsible for ruining Lolita's young life, depriving her of her childhood innocence (regardless of how sexually playful that innocence may have been before his arrival). Nabokov's reader is insistently pulled between an inevitable sympathy for the witty, intelligent man whose thoughts s/he is ostensibly reading, and horror at his inclinations and actions. That tension is further complicated by Humbert's own ongoing ambivalence about his behavior – he seems by turns defiant, apologetic, and appalled. In his adaptation, Albee dramatizes this tension by using A Certain Gentleman to give voice to the more skeptical, uneasy elements of Nabokov's narrative, while leaving the character of Humbert to enunciate his lusts more directly – whether in elaborately self-justifying speeches such as his disquisition on the nature of "nymphets" (they are the lustful ones, more so than him), or in gloves-off admissions of his own rampant appetite: "How am I to get at her!? HOW AM I TO GET AT HER!? TELL ME!! PLEASE!!" (21).

At first glance, this treatment of the protagonist might seem to represent a "lessening and coarsening" of Nabokov's characterization, since by giving Humbert's "conscience" to another character, Albee effectively robs him of much of his complexity. Yet if the play makes Humbert more overtly monstrous than the novel, I would argue that this is no simple failure of craft and sublety on Albee's part. If, in *The Ballad of the Sad Café*, he had succeeded in rendering the central character as more sympathetic, and less grotesque, than she appears in the source text, then it seems fair to assume that his decision to adopt the opposite strategy in *Lolita* was also very carefully taken. By depriving Humbert of the dominant narrative voice, and its seductive subjectivity, and by objectifying him onstage as the obsessive stalker of children that he clearly is, Albee creates an *antisympathetic* dramatization of the character, which effectively prevents spectators from reaching the rather appalling conclusions that some readers of Nabokov have reached. "One cannot help but identify with Humbert's passion," J. Madison Davis writes of the novel, because his "desire for the girl is always couched in terms of the most passionate romantic love." Davis criticizes Albee for failing to emulate "Nabokov's great achievement" of "making the narrator Humbert likable despite his pathetic pedophilia."[21] Clearly, though, any attempt to make a theatre audience "identify with Humbert's passion" would involve rendering the ostensibly prepubescent figure of the actress playing Lolita as a fetishised sex object. (In fact, Jerry Sherlock's production of Albee's *Lolita* attempted precisely this: the publicity relied heavily on images of the actress Blanche Baker, dressed in "baby doll" mini-nightdress, gazing smokily into camera.)

Certainly Albee's Humbert would like us to see things his way, and even pleads that the audience do their "very best to ignore" the Certain Gentleman's insistent undermining of his perspective: "He is parenthetical. *I. I* am in love; and love is the subject here" (8). The Gentleman, however, repeatedly substitutes Humbert's self-image as a "lover" with the clinical term "pedophile" – a word Nabokov's Humbert never uses, and which Albee's refuses to hear: "You cannot *call* it that!!" (63). Thus, far from presenting the play as an apologia for Humbert's passions, Albee uses the dual-narrator device to excavate and emphasize Nabokov's subtextual critique of his destructive delusions. Just as one might expect, given the key concerns of so many of his plays, Albee underlines Humbert's unforgivable abuse of his "parental" responsibility as Lolita's stepfather. Like a sexually exploitative version of *The American Dream*'s Mommy and Daddy, Humbert holds in his mind from the outset an image of the ideal nymphet – a fantasy represented onstage by the life-size doll that he clutches to himself in the opening scene (and periodically thereafter). Lolita, also known as "Dolly," enables Humbert to "get satisfaction" because she matches his prescription so perfectly: to get hold of her, he needs only to "marry the appalling Haze woman, kill her, and then – having become my treasure's stepfather, her legal guardian – do with my Lolita whatever I [will]" (21). The most chilling demonstration of his agenda is provided, however, in the climactic image of Act 1. Having brought Lolita to their first motel room, Humbert reports to her the facts of her mother's accidental death: "*We hear a wailing*," Albee specifies in stage directions, "*the sound of a child desperately crying*" (47). Even as he comforts her in his arms, though – "Hush, my darling; hush Lolita; it's all right" – Humbert gradually guides her head ever nearer to his crotch. "And time stopped," declares A Certain Gentleman, as the action blacks out.

This Humbert, then, is more monster than misguided romantic. Yet having established the basic outlines of the character, Albee does not simply leave him on the level of repellent cartoon inhabited by Mommy and Daddy. A monster he may be, but human also, and Albee goes on to make Humbert's depraved passions seem uncomfortably familiar to the spectator. For while his conquest of Lolita may not attract audience empathy, his subsequent, gradual *loss* of the desired object, once obtained, makes him only too easy to identify with. From the start of Act 2, Humbert and Lolita are depicted less as incestuous father and daughter than as a bickering, dysfunctional couple – "I tell you, they behave like grown-ups," the Gentleman observes (53). Lolita grows increasingly estranged from Humbert, and increasingly willing to remind him, bitterly, of the innocence he has stolen from her. He, though, remains blindly determined to arrest time, to preserve his illusion of their perfect love. "Then pity poor Humbert," the Gentleman instructs the audience: "he still believes that we may tread twice the same path" (60).

On one level, the scale of Humbert's denial of reality makes him laughably pitiful. He believes, for example, that his own passions far exceed anything knowable by others, and even after he has lost Lolita, he maintains that Quilty could not have stolen her from him had he understood the *grand amour* he was wrecking: "he cannot have imagined . . . the breadth of my passion. [. . .] It is unimaginable; it can be guessed at, no more." "*I* imagined it," the Gentleman points out dryly (67). Yet however comical Humbert's "obsession; delusion; enthrallment" (56), the laughter drawn is that of recognition. When he eventually points out that, through his fixation on Lolita, he has "known despair and unbearable joy – loss and possession" (70), it is hard not to concede to him that romantic obsession can indeed make one's life seem more filled with color, event, and intensity. Moreover, Albee suggests, even the most misplaced of loves can perhaps acquire a redemptive force. When Humbert is finally reunited with Lolita, three years on, she is pregnant, exhausted, and has long outgrown the childish looks he was originally fixated with. It is in this moment, in the play as in the book, that Humbert realizes with astonishment that he still loves her – the reality of her, rather than the fantasy. Yet Albee dramatizes this through a poignant twist all his own, showing Humbert attempting to set Lolita free from any continuing emotional hold he has on her, by insisting that he "never wanted your love. [. . .] It was pure, simple lust. [. . .] You were a good lay" (79). In this scene, as he shies away from all physical contact with her, his feelings for her seem more selflessly genuine than at any previous moment. "Pure . . . pure love," he notes to the audience, with surprise: "And now . . . on to murder" (82).

This is the final, deadly irony, and one that Albee makes more explicitly apparent than Nabokov: deprived forever of his grand passion, Humbert's only way to find an appropriately dramatic conclusion to his story is to exact murderous revenge on Quilty. "There's nothing to live for now – except this," he explains to the incredulous Gentleman, before pointing out the other, lifelessly banal options available to him (82). It matters not to him that Lolita herself has raised serious questions about whether Quilty is the man he wants, by hinting heavily that Humbert's paranoia over the existence of a rival might always have been merely that. Humbert requires a big finish to his story, and "Quilty will do!" (78). In true Pirandellian fashion, Quilty thus becomes the character required by the story – a moustache-twirling Hollywood villain whom Humbert can mercilessly shoot multiple holes in. In this final, blackly comic scene, Quilty's endlessly disbelieving protests at his assassination are lifted almost verbatim from the book. Yet Humbert himself, rather than being the narrator of the scene, becomes a silent, implacable executioner, blankly playing out the only action that still has meaning for him. It is as if he knows that he has only to complete this task, and then the author will step in to end the story, his life, and those of all the other characters. Sure enough, the Gentleman wraps it all up, moments later, with a bleakly ironic monologue. The existential overtones are wryly underlined in an oblique allusion to Beckett, as he informs us that Humbert will eventually die during orgasm: "Come and go" (91). "How dare they not list you among the Absurdists," Humbert has earlier remarked to the Gentleman (45), in a line which is at once an admiring nod by Albee to Nabokov, and a bitter acknowledgment of the creator by his creation.

* * *

Lolita was still haunting Albee when he came to write *The Man Who Had Three Arms*, as is evident from its several textual references to Nabokov and his nymphet. His immersion in Nabokov seems also to have been an important factor in freeing Albee from the self-conscious straining for significance that had marred recent plays such as *Seascape* (1975) and *The Lady from Dubuque*, and in helping him to rediscover the daringly free-flowing playfulness of his earlier work. "For me the work of fiction exists only insofar as it affords me what I shall bluntly call aesthetic bliss," Nabokov wrote in retort to those who challenged him to justify *Lolita* by explaining its moral or message, adding wryly that "nothing is more exhilarating than pristine vulgarity."[22] Albee, as if in response to those who had declared his *Lolita* a vulgar desecration of the novel, now sat down to write his most blissfully vulgar and exhilarating play since, I would argue, *Virginia Woolf*.

With *The Man Who Had Three Arms*, Albee seems also to have taken on two unresolved challenges from his work on *Lolita*. One was to create some kind of theatrical equivalent for Nabokov's brilliant evocation of the soulless monotony and banality of the American cultural landscape. Albee's mutating motel conceit had cleverly captured the state of existential suspension which Humbert and Lolita's long road trip induces, but it had not been able to emulate the critical eye that Nabokov casts on the country itself during the observational tangents that frequently spin off from the book's central narrative. By contrast, *The Man Who* focuses squarely on the evocation of contemporary America as a numbing cultural wasteland. The play's basic conceit is that the theatre is really an uninviting lecture hall in some comfortably bourgeois, Middle-American community. (In the original production, the stage was decked out with flagpoles and potted plants, and backed with walls of dark wood paneling.) The theatre audience is thus collectively cast as the assembled subscribers to a long-running and unfortunately titled series of human-interest talks, "Man on Man." The evening begins with circuitous, long-winded welcomes from a chairman and chairwoman, whose attention to the trivial details of notices and housekeeping matters is gleefully caricatured by Albee. The mood quickly turns much edgier, however, after their guest speaker – a last-minute stand-in for the last-minute stand-in – is welcomed to the stage. Himself, formerly a media sensation when he grew a third arm on his back (now withered and gone), launches into a scathing attack on the very lecture circuit that continues to offer him exposure and payment. He rails, for example, at the endless, identical pretalk dinners he has had to suffer all over the country, peopled by embittered nonentities, opening their plastic-wrapped saltines to dip in their stodgy split-pea soup, in function rooms containing spongy sofas with a "purple plastic sheen – a kind of iridescence – the sort of sofa that gives one second thoughts about the West" (449). Within a few paragraphs, Albee vividly conjures up a Sartrean hell of sold souls and cold-meat platters.

Himself clearly despises all this, but his hatefulness encompasses every sense of the word – and suggests a second baton taken up from Albee's work on *Lolita*. In bifurcating Nabokov-Humbert's narrative voice into two characters whose perspectives exist in tension with one another, he had come up with an ingeniously theatrical equivalent for the novel's literary complexity, but he had also somewhat sidestepped the challenge of forcing the reader-spectator to respond to the challenge of being addressed, direct and unmediated, by a protagonist whose perspective on the world is deeply discomfiting, rather than easily identified with. This is precisely what Albee now attempted, through a play composed almost entirely as a rambling verbal assault on its audience. Himself's illustrative use of slides occasionally provides visual variation and comic accent, and the chairman and chairwoman occasionally mutate into characters from his anecdotes, but at these points they function simply to echo and counterpoint his narrative rather than engage him in sustained dramatic scenes. The central dramatic confrontation is always between lecturer and listeners, with the former seeming to treat the latter as a kind of distorted mirror: Himself's loathing of himself, for collaborating in his transformation into a media freakshow, is matched only by his revulsion for the culture and individuals that built him up in this way, whom he finds embodied in front of him. "I find it hard sometimes to distinguish between my self-disgust and my disgust with others" (448), he acknowledges, and his extended monologue is so loaded with bitterness and bile that he seems at times to be completely out of control.

It is worth noting here that Albee had recently attempted a comparable experiment in implicating the audience directly in a critique of contemporary culture. In *The Lady from Dubuque*, the guests at Jo and Sam's party routinely address the audience, not in asides, but openly, as if we, too, are intimates in their conversation. The device seems to interpolate the audience directly into the frequently malicious exchanges, and thus to implicate them, also, as participants in the cancerous cultural condition to which the play repeatedly alludes. Jo's terminal illness, though treated as the very real cause of her imminent death, also implicitly stands as a metaphor for a moral decadence whose symptoms are apparent in the viciously complacent, self-regarding attitudes of this circle of supposed friends. The play's numerous references to the fall of Rome, to the corruption of Richard Nixon, and to the ongoing threat of nuclear annihilation all suggest the outline of a Jeremiah-like condemnation of the terminal decline of American culture: "Perhaps we were already dead," the eponymous lady notes at the play's climax, as she envisages the H-bomb being dropped; "perhaps that was why there was no sound."[23]

The Lady from Dubuque, however, possesses rather too much sound and fury to make its diagnosis stick. There is little here to lure the spectator into an uneasily personal engagement with the proceedings: despite being addressed directly from the stage, few audience members would be likely to feel anything other than revulsion at being implicated as "akin" to these characters. The same danger exists, obviously, with *The Man Who Had Three Arms*, but the later play makes far more unsettling use of its self-reflexive, anti-fourth-wall premise – by confronting spectators more directly (the threat of making direct eye contact with the speaker is ever present), but also by presenting them with a rant that is often as appallingly *funny* as it is assaultive. By contrast with its predecessor, this play-in-the-form-of-a-lecture was apparently written very quickly, in a sustained and focused outpouring of feeling, and its "freefall of writing" (as the *New York Post*'s Clive Barnes described it) is marked by such dazzling wordplay and stinging wit, and by such mercurial gear-shifts between the roles of provocateur, raconteur, rambling drunk and autobiographer, that even some of the reviewers who trashed the play's premiere had to concede that "the talk . . . does hold our interest throughout" (*Daily News*).[24] With Albee's words providing the springboard for "a brilliant, edgy performance" from actor Robert Drivas (under Albee's own direction), the evening was for Barnes both "highly convincing [and] virtuosic in its sustained intensity."[25]

In the absence of any guiding moral voice or dramatic superstructure above and beyond the lecture format itself, spectators at the premiere found themselves in the uncomfortable position of having to navigate their own uneasy responses to Himself's virulently entertaining tirade. Indeed, *The Man Who Had Three Arms* is perhaps most usefully seen as a later counterpart to *The Zoo Story* – the obvious distinction being that where Jerry addresses Peter as the cipher-like embodiment of all things repressed and bourgeois, Himself places the audience in this hapless role (and, it seems, fully expects them to knife him). Significantly though, far from possessing Jerry's impassioned outsider perspective on American life, Himself rails against the hypocrisies of a world in which he is fully implicated. That difference is surely indicative of the changes in Albee's own circumstances: the penniless Western Union delivery boy, whose brief glimpses behind the closed doors of the compartmentalized city had provided him with inspiration for *The Zoo Story*, had become the established playwright who had apparently been to one too many sycophantic functions held in his honor.

Albee had also, like Himself, recently experienced a distinct loss of public interest in his existence, and press reviewers seized on this link as proof that – far from extending the stage world into the auditorium, by casting audience as antagonist – the dramatist had simply sacrificed dramatic fiction altogether. According to this reading, Himself was merely a stand-in for Albee (himself), a thin pretext for him to express his own disgust at an unappreciative world. Those who leaped to this conclusion blithely ignored the glaring question of why any writer would voluntarily depict himself as a repellent, talentless nobody. Yet they also unwittingly underlined the challenge Albee had set for his audiences, in obliging them to find their own responses to the character's discomfiting verbal onslaught: in the case of many reviewers, the response was simply to *avoid* the play by misrepresenting the playwright.

To dismiss *The Man Who Had Three Arms* as mere autobiographical spite is also to overlook the fact that Himself is carefully constructed as an American archetype, as an Everyman figure who has lived the American Dream – or "the Anglo-Saxon, *Protestant* American Dream, at any rate" – to its logical conclusion.[26] The story he tells of his life, complete with illustrative slides, paints him as the boy from Smallville, "a town like any other town" (436), who grows up, acquires wholesome wife and wholesome kids, and moves to Metropolis, where he works his way diligently up the corporate ladder to become an advertising executive. The world of all-American hype and rhetoric implied by that profession then takes over his life in a very immediate way when he grows that third arm, and becomes a media sensation, complete with his own, Colonel Parker-style huckster-manager. What he cannot fathom, therefore, is the culture's insistence on perceiving him as the abnormal Other: "stop treating me like a freak!" he finally demands of his listeners, in a flailing variant on Miss Amelia's dignified rejection of the prying townsfolk at the end of *Ballad*, "I am *not* a freak! I am *you*! I have always *been* you!" (469). He is a nobody watched by nobodies, senselessly celebrated and now equally senselessly destroyed by them, and yet he perversely continues to crave the public eye. Emptiness begets emptiness, but proves as addictive as it is repellent: "Who says we're not a healthy land!" (449).

The social-satirical dimensions of *The Man Who Had Three Arms* are clear, but, as always with Albee, they are set within and against the context of broader, existential questions. The emergence of the third arm can be read as a kind of all-American variant on Kafka's *Metamorphosis* – an extreme physical reaction to, and rebellion against, the meaningless, unthinking conformity of Himself's life choices. Indeed, he unwillingly acknowledges the possibility that, having gained himself "a lovely wife, some decent kids, a fine home, a rewarding and well-paying career," he then "willed my martyrdom – my monsterdom – drew it out of myself . . . from the pericardial unconscious" (459). The new consciousness that the arm lends him, however, is not that of authentic revelation – of the divine light outside Plato's cave – but of pathetic delusion. His wife, he tells us, left him because she could not stand "the blinding light" of media exposure (463), and his own vision has clearly been warped in the glare: "what happens *within* the awareness of *self*" that comes with great fame, he informs us, is "the knowledge that one is larger than life, at least larger than others; the fact that one can change whole areas of public perception" (463). Elsewhere, however, he gloomily confesses that, when such narcissistic convictions fade, "the awareness comes, that low is all, that endless hopeless drudge and grind and scuff and tatter is the end. [. . .] There is not a life, not one – name it if you can! – not a life hasn't seen futility at the end, up ahead, like a highway turning into sand" (432).

The spectator, however, is no more obliged to take such nihilistic negativity at face value, as "truth," than s/he is the pronouncements on the insights afforded by fame. Indeed, it seems that Himself now wallows in cosmic misanthropy as he had once reveled in the spotlight: in a further twist of hubris, he appears now to think of himself as being akin to those "holy men in India [who] gaze into the sun from rise to set. . . . They have gone blind of course, years back, their eyes burned out by the glory, but every day they sit, the eyes burned out, blind eyes staring at the burning . . . staring into the blinding dark" (433). Unlike Humbert then, Himself gains no potentially redemptive insights by the end of the play: as a monster warped by an entire culture rather than by individual lusts, he remains wrapped up in his own sense of resentment, of entitlement, and of self-importance, unable to see beyond them to any deeper self-knowledge.

Perhaps the most disturbing feature of this portrait, however, is the virulent misogyny that appears to go hand in hand with Himself's misanthropy. This is apparent throughout, and most particularly in his various references to a female journalist, supposedly present in the audience, whom he insists on repeatedly, defiantly referring to as a "cunt," and whom he fantasizes about "fucking" in hateful rage. (He claims, instead, to have settled for "goosing" her backstage.) Despite its clearly heterosexual orientation, Himself's misogyny has – predictably enough – been read by some critics as Albee's own. Certainly the fact that there is no other voice in the play to challenge or contextualize it makes it especially unsettling for the spectator, and it is in these passages that the text seems, as Clive Barnes put it in his largely sympathetic review, "dangerously unedited." Yet it may be precisely our instinct to edit or to censor that which we find unsettling, to police the boundaries of the acceptable, that Albee is seeking to challenge here. Certainly nobody could fairly argue that such misogyny is not a plausible part of a character's make-up (perhaps even an American Everyman's make-up?), nor that, as individual spectators, we are incapable of responding with revulsion – just as we are to Humbert's pedophilia. What may be most disturbing here, in fact, is being so forcibly confronted with the *reality* of such attitudes. There is a parallel to be drawn here, perhaps, with the Wooster Group's roughly contemporaneous performance, *Route 1 & 9* (1981), which was initially widely condemned as appallingly racist for its use of grotesque, blackface caricatures unmediated by contextualizing explanations, but which – with the Group's growing renown – came subsequently to be seen as a forceful challenge to the ingrained racism that may lurk at the back of even the most socially progressive minds.[27]

It is tempting to wonder, with hindsight, whether *The Man Who Had Three Arms* might have achieved a more understanding response from critics and audiences had it been presented off-Broadway – perhaps in the downtown area that was home to the Wooster Group and other radical theatremakers. Certainly the relative intimacy of an off-Broadway venue, by comparison with the large Broadway houses, might have served the play's confrontational dynamics better. Moreover, given the emergence downtown, during the 1980s, of an entire culture of monologue-based solo performance work, one can perhaps see Albee as being – once again – ahead of his time. The performances of Eric Bogosian, Karen Finley, and others frequently featured deeply repellent or egomaniacal characters, to whom spectators were obliged to find their own, uneasy responses. Like the work of these alternative artists, *The Man Who* is, by Albee's own admission, a gloves-off challenge to the cosily self-congratulatory standards of bourgeois good taste. For just that reason, though, he maintains that the Broadway audience was the audience that most needed to see it in 1983 – even though the Broadway press pack, in particular, proved itself too determinedly middlebrow to appreciate the ironies involved.

Albee has continued to believe that this play ought to be presented to precisely those it is calculated to upset most. To date, the only publication of *The Man Who Had Three Arms* has been in a self-selected anthology of the playwright's work which was prepared as "an exclusive offering" for the distinctly un-avant-garde members of the "Fireside Theatre Book Club." The last laugh, however, was reserved for 2002, when Albee's status as a Broadway playwright, effectively destroyed by press responses to these uncompromisingly experimental plays of the early 1980s, was restored with the success (*de scandale*) of *The Goat, or Who is Sylvia?* – easily the most consciously controversial play he had written since *The Man Who*, and the most sexually "deviant" since *Lolita*.

NOTES

1. Hobe, review of *The Lady from Dubuque*, *Variety*, February 6, 1980, p. 132; Robert Brustein, "Self-Parody and Self-Murder," *New Republic*, March 8, 1980, p. 26; John Simon, "From Hunger, Not Dubuque," *New York*, February 11, 1980, p. 74.
2. Stanley Kauffmann, "*Lolita* Undone," *Saturday Review*, May 1981, p. 78; Howard Kissel, "Theater," *Women's Wear Daily*, March 20, 1981, p. 20; Douglas Watt, "Albee's *Lolita* a script tease," *New York Daily News*, March 20, 1981, p. 3.
3. Frank Rich, "Stage: Drama by Albee, *Man Who Had 3 Arms*," *New York Times*, April 6, 1983, p. C15; Humm, "*The Man Who Had Three Arms*," *Variety*, April 6, 1983, p. 86; John Simon, unheaded review, *New York*, April 25, 1983, p. 92.
4. Other adaptation work during the 1960s included Albee's libretto for a one-act opera by his friend William Flanagan, based on Melville's short story *Bartleby* (1961), and his book for a musical based on Truman Capote's novel *Breakfast at Tiffany's* (1966). He was happy with neither project, and the scripts remain unpublished.
5. Anne Paolucci, for example, in *From Tension to Tonic: The Plays of Edward Albee* (Carbondale: Southern Illinois University Press, 1972), notes simply that "because Albee's novelty can best be appreciated where the demands of original content and original form come together, I have excluded [his adaptations] from consideration in this book" (xiv).
6. Roland Barthes, *Image Music Text*, trans. Stephen Heath (London: Fontana, 1977), p. 146.

7. See Peter Egri, "American Variations on a British Theme: Giles Cooper and Edward Albee," in *Forked Tongues?: Comparing Twentieth Century British and American Literature*, ed. Ann Massa and Alistair Stead (London: Longman, 1994), pp. 135–151.
8. Philip C. Kolin, ed., *Conversations with Edward Albee* (Jackson and London: University Press of Mississippi, 1988), p. 6.
9. Ibid., pp. 33, 164.
10. Gilles Deleuze, *Bergsonism*, trans. Hugh Tomlinson and Barbara Habberjam (New York: Zone Books, 1988), p. 8.
11. Carson McCullers, *The Ballad of the Sad Café* (Harmondsworth: Penguin, 1963), p. 7. Further references are to this edition and will be cited parenthetically in the text.
12. Edward Albee, *The Ballad of the Sad Café* (New York: Dramatists Play Service, 1991), p. 25. Further references are to this edition and will be cited parenthetically in the text.
13. C. W. E. Bigsby, *Albee* (Edinburgh: Oliver and Boyd, 1969), p. 77.
14. Bigsby, *Edward Albee*, p. 80.
15. Edward Albee, *Malcolm* (London: Jonathan Cape, 1967), p. 129.
16. See James Purdy, *Malcolm* (New York: Farrar, Straus and Giroux, 1959).
17. See Stephen J. Bottoms, *Playing Underground: A Critical History of the 1960s Off-Off-Broadway Movement* (Ann Arbor: University of Michigan Press, 2004), Chapter 8.
18. Edward Albee, "Introduction" to *Selected Plays of Edward Albee* (New York: Nelson Doubleday, 1987), pp. viii–ix.
19. Edward Albee, *Lolita* (New York: Dramatists Play Service, 1984), p. 5. Further references are to this edition and will be cited parenthetically in the text.
20. See Thomas P. Adler, "Albee's Meta-*Lolita*: Love's Travail and the Artist's Travail," *Publications of the Mississippi Philological Association*, 1986, pp. 122–129.
21. J. Madison Davis, "*Lolita*: Albee's Struggle with Nabokov," *Publications of the Mississippi Philological Association*, 1986, p. 107.
22. Vladimir Nabokov, *The Annotated Lolita* (London: Penguin, 1995), p. 315.
23. Edward Albee, *The Lady from Dubuque* (New York: Dramatists Play Service, 1980), p. 67.
24. Douglas Watt, "Edward Albee's latest play," *New York Daily News*, April 6, 1983, p. 49.
25. Clive Barnes, "Two cheers for Albee's *Man With 3 Arms*," *New York Post*, April 6, 1983, p. 34
26. Edward Albee, *The Man Who Had Three Arms*, in *Selected Plays of Edward Albee*, p. 459. Further references are to this edition and will be cited parenthetically in the text.
27. See David Savran, *Breaking the Rules: The Wooster Group* (New York: Theatre Communications Group, 1988), pp. 39–41.

9

CHRISTOPHER BIGSBY

"Better alert than numb": Albee since the eighties

The American theatre can be an unfriendly place. Eugene O'Neill despaired of it producing his last works. Tennessee Williams went out of favor with critics and public alike from 1960 onward, while Arthur Miller found his plays of the 1970s, 1980s, and, to some degree, 1990s rejected. Edward Albee also visited the outer planets of the critical world for several decades, despite picking up a second Pulitzer Prize for *Seascape* (1975). American lives, it seemed, really did not have second lives, at least as far as American critics were concerned. Then came *Three Tall Women* (1991) and the sun shone again. Another Pulitzer burnished the gold of his reputation. But Albee had not been silent, merely working out of the limelight – content, if not happy, to continue to write and direct, whether in America or in Europe.

Finding the Sun, commisssioned by the University of Northern Colorado in 1983, played some of the same games with characters of different ages as *Three Tall Women* was to do, though without the central conceit which distinguishes that play. It was performed in Colorado and at the University of California at Irvine – where it was paired with another play, *Walking*, also set on a beach. (That play, unpublished and now withdrawn by Albee, had no actors, though there was an offstage voice, while natural objects were also allowed to speak.) In a note, Albee explains that he had withheld a subsequent New York production of *Finding the Sun* because of the similarity of setting to Tina Howe's *Coastal Disturbances* – written later but produced first. Both plays do, indeed, take place on a beach with what Albee suggests is "a not dissimilar group of characters and – inevitably – some of the same general preoccupations."[1] Quite what force the "inevitably" is supposed to have, though, is far from clear beyond references to the setting.

   Viewed naturalistically, the characters in *Finding the Sun* are altogether too obliging in their willingness to express inner truths, confess motivations, and reveal details of their lives which they have every reason to conceal. There is a precosity to Fergus, a sixteen-year-old boy, matched by a surprising generosity of information on the part of Henden, the seventy-year-old man who talks with him. This, however, is a convention of a play in which the characters walk to the front of the stage and confess their private thoughts and feelings, acknowledging, thereby, those who watch and listen and hence play their own role. Phrases are picked up and carried forward, memories recycled, relationships adumbrated and shuffled as affections are redirected or misdirected. The characters view one another with suspicion or irony. They range in age from sixteen, through the twenties and thirties to sixty and seventy, and these age gaps generate their own energies, ironies, counterpoints.

There is, in fact, very little naturalistic about the play. The sixteen-year-old hardly speaks like one when observing, at one point, that "I suspect I'm a little young for a sense of continuity. There's a theory afoot, though, that we young and old have things in common should bind us together against those in the middle" (11). Told that two of the men on the beach had once been lovers, Fergus observes that they "gave each other physical pleasure," but that since they have subsequently married and separated from one another, pleasure has passed into pain. This is not the language of a teenager, but verisimilitude is not Albee's objective. In some degree, indeed, the play's humor derives from the inappropriateness of the language, the gap between the characters and the language they use. The influence of T. S. Eliot, so strong in Albee's early plays, remains relevant as the characters address one another with a calculated archness which conceals underlying tensions.

The themes are familiar from Albee's other works: loss, love and its indirections, its waning, and dying. The play tracks the parabola of experience, from innocence through anxiety to a growing alarm as time runs out and the body runs down. And if a forty-five-year-old woman announces that there is "danger in consciousness" (28), the seventy-year-old Henden replies with a sentiment which lies at the heart of Albee's work: "We go through it only once . . . better alert than . . . numb, or not comprehending" (28). Daniel and Benjamin, once lovers and now married to Cordelia and Abigail, have "fallen between stools" and suspect they would have been "better perched on our specialness" (3). Denial, Albee suggests, is merely another form of anesthetic, another way of refusing to live in full consciousness. Nearly a quarter of a century earlier, the protagonist of *The Zoo Story* (1959) had done his best to provoke the placid Peter from his isolated bench, to force him to acknowledge his plight, to acknowledge that he is alive. As Edmee remarks in *Finding the Sun*, "We have so much to be thankful for, being alive. *Being alive!!*" (32). That remains Albee's concern here. His elliptical style is merely a reflection of his earlier expressed belief that seeming indirection might ultimately prove a path to truth.

There is something of the tableau vivant about *Finding the Sun*. The characters, largely static, are stripped to some degree of their protections, and reveal something of the starkness of their lives, the conventions behind which they have hidden their needs, their vulnerabilities. Albee's intention, though, is plainly not psychological realism: though the characters can come to tears, this is not a play which invites conventional empathy, even when one of them attempts suicide (offstage) and another dies (onstage). It is a chamber piece which ends on a reiterated note: "Fergus? (*Pause.*) Fergus? (*Pause; slow fade.*)" (39). *Finding the Sun*, a play in twenty-one scenes, one of which is no more than a few seconds long, is a series of variations on a theme. Like many of Albee's earlier plays, it is a play about dying which is also a play about the necessity of living. It is about love – imperfect, sometimes denied, but ultimately the key to escaping entrapment in a self in danger of a reflexive self-concern.

Marriage Play, which according to Mel Gussow was originally to have been called either *The Old One-Two* or *News From the Front*, had its world premiere at Vienna's English Theatre – which had commissioned it – in May 1987. (It was another five years before the play reached America, opening at the Alley Theatre in Houston in January 1992, and then in New York, at the Signature Theatre, in 1993.) It begins as Jack, a man in his midfifties, arrives at his suburban home, at 3.30p.m. on a weekday afternoon in late spring, and casually announces to his wife Gillian that he is leaving her. The season, location, and time seem to do no more than underscore the apparently unexceptional nature of the context. But as so often, what Albee wishes to do is drop a metaphysical coin in a seemingly placid pond, disrupting the assumed equanimity of the quotidian.

Gillian, who is reading, a glass and bottle nearby, at first takes the news impassively. What follows is a lively double act, an unlikely comic turn as they debate, correct one another's usages, fight (linguistically and physically), and reminisce. They are like George and Martha, from *Who's Afraid of Virginia Woolf?* (1962) – except for the fact that there are no Honey and Nick to watch. They admire one another's style, praise each other's resilience and even savagery. There is a certain truth in Gillian's observation that "I am talking so as not to scream," but their conversation is not devoid of meaning.[2] On one level, it is a kind of phatic communion, a reassurance as to their mutual presence; on another, it is what keeps them alive. It is in their language, and indeed in their physical battles, that they are most alive. They regenerate through such rituals. Even when they have a pummeling fistfight, she says to Jack, "You're pretty good," as he replies, "so are you." After a particularly affecting speech, Jack applauds and Gillian curtsies. This is the mutuality of George and Martha. This is life as theatre in which theatre nonetheless contains both an essential truth of human behavior and a means of sustaining an engaged life.

They are both in their fifties. Their "glow," they confess, has gone. These performances are what has replaced it. The game of life, of necessity, contains its own games. Loss, entropy, require a resistant strategy. Love has not died – "I dreamt you loved me"; "I *do*"; "Yes, I know" (31) – but it has to be renewed. An edge has to be kept on the knife. The spark has to be blown on. The wounds they inflict are both their means of staying alive and the evidence that they are.

Disturbingly, Gillian has kept a record of their lovemaking over the years, recording the circumstances, satisfactions or otherwise, conversations. She chooses to call it *The Book of Days*. He notes that it seems to be written in the style of a number of different writers, as if she were already processing experience, reshaping it as art. Yet though the passion has changed, it seems not wholly to have disappeared, merely to have changed its meaning. At the same time, decline, entropy, a loss of sharp focus seems structured into existence. The crisis is not, though, finally, to do with their marriage, even in a play which carries the name of marriage. It goes far beyond that. As Jack observes:

> it all goes. [. . .] no matter what, *or* where, *or* with whom, we come to the moment we understand that nothing has made any difference. We stare into the dark and know that nothing is enough, *has* been enough, *could* be enough, that there is *no way* not to have . . . wasted the light; that the failure is built into us, that the greatest awareness gives to the greatest dark. That I am going to lose you, for example – *have* lost you – no more, no less than fingers slipping from each other, that I'm going to lose *me*, *have* lost me – the light . . . losing the light. (38)

The fear which Albee addresses in so many of his plays is the fear that had obsessed Tennessee Williams and many of his characters: a fear of death. For Albee, as opposed to Williams, however, the greater fear is to have lived a life without full awareness. "Awareness is all," Jack remarks. Routine, habit, drift, illusion are the enemies. As Jack observes, "everything has a time when it goes on for the sake of going on" (39). The threat to leave his marriage is not in itself real, perhaps. But it is the ritual they enact as a reminder that they need to have a reason to continue. They do battle with one another not merely to demonstrate that they retain the energy to do so but because they need to sustain a sense of themselves within a conspiracy against the eclipse of meaning. As Gillian says, "I hope that what's-his-name was right, that [. . .] a good marriage, a useful marriage – makes individuals! That when two people choose to be together though they're strong enough to be alone, *then* you have a good marriage. [. . .] Clearly we've not become each other; we've become ourselves [. . .] With any luck we've not compensated, we've complemented" (39–40).

The play ends as they sit in silence, with no movement. They will continue. They will continue to look for reasons to continue. They are not wholly at peace because that might prove an echo of the peace of the grave. The ending is reminiscent of *Who's Afraid of Virginia Woolf?* The words speak of a dissolving relationship but there is a countercurrent to the language. The two sit together. They hardly speak. The game is over, at least for the moment. Gillian "*Leans toward*" Jack. Her tone is "*Gentle.*" There is a series of long silences. There is no movement. Unlike the earlier play, *Marriage Play* offers no comment on the political and social world, except, perhaps, by inference. Here, as in many of his later works, he is concerned less with social forms than with more fundamental issues. Though so many of his plays have seemingly been concerned with attrition, the dying of passion and, indeed, of the light, he has centrally been concerned with justifying life to itself.

Every year Jack sows seeds in his garden: "it's hopeless every year – everything: the garden, going on, everything. You put in a garden; you do it every year. It is . . . what you do. That is what you do" (40). In *Death of a Salesman*, the bewildered Willy Loman lets his seeds fall on stony ground, bemused by a world he can no longer fully comprehend, a world that has lost what he wrongly believes to have been its rural innocence. In the world of Samuel Beckett, such a gesture would be the root of a seemingly disabling irony – paradoxically only transcended by its expression – and there is something apparently Beckett-like in Jack's announcement that he is leaving Gillian, given his failure even to move. But Albee is not Beckett. For all the apocalyptic overtones of his work, for all its elegiac force, there is a resistant spirit. There is something celebratory in the sheer inventiveness of his characters, their refusal to be contained within the parameters of possibility. They are storytellers, alert to the function of story. They are Sheherazades, knowing story for what it is and keeping the game alive to keep themselves alive.

In *Who's Afraid of Virginia Woolf?*, Albee had issued a warning against evasions and pretences which, as in Ibsen, corrode the spirit. There is, however, a distinction to be made between self-deception and the games his characters play. Tennessee Williams insisted that there are no lies except those thrust down the throat by the hard-knuckled hand of need. This was a position which Albee had resisted in his first Broadway success, parodying both Williams and O'Neill with his seeming faith in "life lies." Yet George and

Martha had been doing something more than walk what was left of their wits. They had also been magnificent in their linguistic battles, the performances which they had invested with the full force of their human vitality. The danger lay in taking as real what had once been a conscious game. It lay in subverting a human connection too easily traded for habit, ambition, immunity from pain. Love, in Albee's work, is not a sentimentality, nor yet a consolation prize. It is flawed, betrayed, too easily accommodated to routine, drained of its defining ambivalence. Yet in *Marriage Play* (1987), as in *The Zoo Story*, *Who's Afraid of Virginia Woolf?*, and, indeed, a whole range of his plays, it is the source of a meaning not to be derived from social role, reason, religion, or any validating agency. In that sense, he does share something with Tennessee Williams.

For the most part, though, we are not dealing with realism here. The sometimes baroque prose, or at least the self-conscious deployment of an overprecise language by his characters, is an indicator of this, as is an increasing emphasis on performance, theatricality. There may be no audience to the verbal fencing match in *Marriage Play*, as there had been in *Who's Afraid of Virginia Woolf?*, but that audience is implied. It is us. Increasingly, indeed, Albee was to have his characters turn to that audience, deliver speeches to them, welcome them back from the intermission as though to remind them simultaneously of the artifice of what they see and their complicity in the drama being enacted.

In 1993 Albee wrote another play which advertised its theatricality and which, like *Finding the Sun* and *Three Tall Women*, presents characters of different ages and perceptions, generating thereby a series of ironies and misunderstandings. *Fragments* begins with a defensive Author's Note:

> While *Fragments* is a play – looks like a play, sounds like a play, acts like a play – an unnerving number of critics (not audiences, I hasten to add) have declared that it isn't a play as they understand the term. While the problem *is*, I think, theirs – the critics' – I have decided to call the piece a sit-around, and let the critics figure out what *that* means. Certainly, anyone who decides to mount *Fragments* will not be accused of not doing a "play." (While they may be criticized for mounting a "sit-around" there are only so many of the world's problems I can solve.)[3]

Unnerving, it is tempting to ask, for whom? The answer would seem to be Albee. After years of critical neglect or abuse, it seems he was, uncharacteristically, feeling the pressure. The usual irony and seeming wry detachment reveal rather than conceal a sense of vulnerability.

The play was commissioned by, and received its premiere at, the Ensemble Theatre of Cincinatti, in October 1993. A cast of eight (four men and four women, ranging from twenty-five to sixty-five), "sit around" on cubes and rectangular forms against a black backdrop. The characters do move from time to time, though casually, so that audiences should scarcely be aware of it. The actors are not so much choreographed by the director as allowed to find their own special relationships to one another. Directors (Albee directed his own premiere) are advised not to be specific about "'where we are' or who the characters 'are'; they are who they portray, and they are where they are" (4). The work is to be informal, building its own tensions and shape.

The play opens as the sixty-five-year-old man announces, "O. K. Let's begin, shall we? *(to the audience)* FRAGMENTS; ACT ONE" *(7)*. In other words, the theatricality of the piece and the circumstances of its production are made clear from the beginning. Indeed, within a few minutes the oldest man tells the story of a celebrity auction, one of whose participants is "Edward Albee, who wrote this play." Coy collusion or metatheatrical gesture? It is hard to tell at this stage, though later one of the characters offers a description of a dream in which he had attended an experimental play – reminiscent, perhaps, of the work of Richard Foreman – in which unnamed characters moved in ultraslow motion. Theatre, in other words, becomes a point of reference. At the midway point, the oldest man announces: "I think it's time for an intermission" (35), and the actors file off.

This is not a work which involves an empathic identification with the characters. It is not called *Fragments* for nothing. It lacks a conventional plot. It offers instead a kind of kaleidoscope, a series of conversations characterized by tonal differences as well as shifting subjects. It is a vaudeville – often, indeed, humorous – with the humor generated out of character, mismatched languages and experiences, the overself-conscious awareness of people who are simultaneously actors and characters in a play.

The sixty-five-year-old man and woman reminisce about a world that has gone, a world of knife grinders and organ grinders, baffling terms to those younger than themselves and, indeed, linguistically curious ("Who'd want to grind an organ?" asks the twenty-five-year-old). The characters occupy the same space but scarcely the same world, and in that sense they replicate the condition of the audience and the society they reflect. These are conversations which are never entirely transitive. The characters speak out of their own obsessions and needs and hear only what makes sense in terms of their own knowledge or perception. Language, too, is fragmented – as are lives, which are not the same at sixty-five as they had been four decades earlier. Where there appears to be continuity there is hiatus, cesura.

These are characters who scarcely ever settle on a subject. In Arthur Miller's *Mr. Peters' Connections* (1998), the protagonist is always asking, "What's the subject?" as the world seems to go out of phase, as certainties dissolve, people die, and the reassuring structures of thought begin to crumble. There is something of that here. The oldest of the four women observes that "You get to a point you miss things – once you get past the point you realize you're missing things but you don't know what they are" (21). The response from those younger than her is "Hunh." Loss, central to her, is marginal to them. Offered a glimpse of their future, they are baffled or bored. They have their own necessities, concerns, distractions. The future seems either bright with possibility or irrelevant, as though they will never inhabit it, never become old.

The play gets under way as the oldest man invites the company to "do some proverbs" (7), and, accordingly, they each contribute one, from the familiar to the gnomic. Albee invites the actors to add their own remarks. This is not, though, an improvised play. It is a series of conversations carried out across the genders and across the ages. It is a play for voices, though not solely that. It has something of the air of an encounter group, with the characters seemingly endeavoring to be supportive of one another. The characters are identified only as Man 1, Woman 2, and so on, but this does not mean they are undifferentiated. The actors are invited to wear whatever makes them feel comfortable, while the thirty-year-old man is to be African-American. Otherwise, our sense of distinctive characters slowly emerges from their language, their preoccupations, their differing perspectives – rather as, in *Three Tall Women*, three generations would address one another across a gap of age and experience.

Fragments offers a series of stories and anecdotes which have a meaning to those who tell them that does not necessarily communicate to those who hear. What seems an amusing story may conceal pain. Meaning, in other words, is more often implied than stated. Even apparent revelations conceal privacies which they hug to themselves or communicate only imperfectly. The man in his forties explains that, when he looks in the mirror, "I see that I'm not looking back at myself." What he sees is something detached from himself. The response by the twenty-year-old is to say, "Awww, come on" and then "you better work this out yourself" (31–32).

The same young man opens the second act (the words ACT TWO being projected) with an extended speech in which he confesses that "People want me; people have *always* wanted me" (36). He has, he explains, after the death of his father, and after "a couple of years" on the street, been taken care of by a man who "didn't want anything I couldn't give him with my eyes closed." The sexual connotation seems clear and, indeed, the story he now tells, of a man's incestuous desire for his daughter, offers further insight into the degree to which sexuality is a language, a mode of being for him. The others mock and parody him, no more willing to respond to him than he has been to others. For the black character, in particular, the self-regard seems objectionable. As he points out, for the most part, *he* is not wanted by people, except the police.

At the heart of the play, though, as at the heart of the later *Mr. Peters' Connections*, is an awareness of death and its power, either to dissolve or to consolidate meaning. As the play ends, the focus shifts to the man in his sixties (as was Albee, at the time of writing). As he remarks, "I used to think that middle age was something I'd get to one day, while young – or youngish – stretched on and on" (52). Now he has overheard someone calling him "old." Friends are beginning to die, and with them goes confirmation of his own existence, shared memories, a sense of not yet being at the leading edge of death. And although there is a hint that Aids is undoing even the young, the central question raised by this character – and indeed by the play itself – is what impact the fact of death has retrospectively on those still living.

As the man remarks, "I'm pretty sure – that there is a way to get through it – so long as you know there's doom right from the beginning; that there is a time, which is limited, and woe if you waste it" (55). In a sense, this has been Albee's central concern from the beginning, from *The Zoo Story* and *Who's Afraid of Virginia Woolf?* through virtually all his plays. An unexamined life is not worth living. The fact of death should inspire not a retreat into illusions, not a recoil from the real, but an engagement. The central truth is that adumbrated by this oldest male character: "there is no guarantee of anything – and that while we may not be responsible for everything that *does* happen to us, we certainly are for everything that *doesn't*; that since we're conscious, we have to be aware of both the awful futility of it and the amazing wonder. Participate" (55). There has probably never been a clearer statement of Albee's central belief.

There is an artifice to the language spoken by Albee's characters. Sometimes, and disturbingly, the linguistic overprecision, deepening toward pedantry or the self-consciously ironic, is shared between different characters in different plays. It is as though they all have a family relationship in the way that David Mamet's characters seem to operate in the same linguistic universe. They correct one another's usages, explore words as if they were objects to be turned in the hand to see how they reflect the light. They all seem privy to the joke which is largely at their expense, the joke of their lives – which in *Three Tall Women* offers us a vital but uninformed youth that leads, seemingly inevitably, to a worldly-wise but enervated old age. The same irony is evident in *The Play About the Baby*.

There is an archness to the exchanges of Albee's characters. They have a self-conscious appreciation of their dilemmas, an awareness of ironies, minor and major. This tone is often Albee's own characteristic mode in interviews. There is often something guarded, wry, calculated, overprecise about his replies – as if language were simultaneously exact, compacted with meaning provided it is respected, and a useful protection against intrusion. Language, it seems, is the site he has chosen for the kind of overprecise gavotte he dances. There are linguistic fencing matches in his plays just as in his encounters with eager questioners, who are often brought to heel by lessons in grammar.

Of course, language is an instrument of power, in his interviews and plays alike. Albee's ironies are designed to prevent intrusion, just as they are an insistence on the need for acute attention. And the detachment which is an aspect of precision and irony alike is a function of the overt theatricality he deploys and the honesty for which he implicitly, if ambiguously, calls. His characters do not so much feel emotions, it seems, as explain, explore, describe those feelings. They are performers, and in his more recent plays they seem fully conscious of this, addressing the audience as if they were confederates. His fascination with language – its sounds, overtones, inflexions, precisions and imprecisions, its harmonies and dissonances – sometimes takes precedence over character in any conventional sense. But then these are not characters in a conventional sense. It is not that they have no backstory: sometimes we are offered accounts of past relationships. It is that he deploys methods which resist an empathic response; that he is asking us to connect to them less through the emotional demands they make on us than through the rhetoric which the play itself develops and of which they are a part.

The apparent realism of the sets of some of his early plays and the baroque invention at the heart of *Tiny Alice* (1964) aside, Albee has a fondness for spare stages, with little more than a bench, a few chairs, some abstract shapes. The emphasis lies on the figures and, in a sense, still more their voices. Indeed, as time has gone on he has been ever more inclined to put his cards on the table and confess to the theatrical nature of what is presented, both because theatre is something more than a metaphor for social behavior and because there is fun to be had from moving back and forth between what are presumed to be separate spheres. There is, after all, an unavoidable irony in plays which seem to urge the necessity to acknowledge the reality of experience through the mechanism of artistic falsification. These are the lies which, he has explained, are designed to corrupt in the direction of truth. But, then, a part of that reality is itself performatic.

Albee is acutely conscious of the sound of his plays and of their inner architecture. They are as much composed as written. *Box* (1968) is a solo, *Counting the Ways* (1976) a duet, *Three Tall Women* a trio (or perhaps a quartet in which one instrument is silent), *The Play About the Baby* a quartet. Meaning is in part a product of the tonal quality of the plays. Certainly it is in *The Play About the Baby*, which opened in England, first in Malvern and then at the Almeida Theatre in London, in September 1998, before being staged in New York in February 2001.

Gussow reports that Albee had finished the first act by the end of November 1996 (having, reportedly, finished it in his head by June), and was seventeen minutes into the second. It was plainly not finished in his head, however, since at that stage he thought of adding an extra character, the baby whose problematic existence lies at the heart of the play. It hardly needed Gussow to underscore the biographical relevance of a play in which a child is suddenly acquired and then dismissed. It was territory Albee had visited before and which had its roots in his own role as a disaffected adopted child. Beyond that, though, it was a play that entered familiar territory of a different kind as he explored the nature of the real, the fact of loss, the process whereby youth gives way to age.

When he had written only part of the first act, Albee told Gussow that there "were four characters, a middle-aged couple, who are or are not related, and a young couple. The themes were identity, people as possessions, and sur- rogate parents" – themes, Gussow noted, that had persisted since *The Lady from Dubuque* (1980) and other plays where "reality is created by our need for it."[4] At one stage he thought to have "a smallish female inside a large rubber baby" – a notion that, thankfully, he abandoned. For Gussow, the play shown to him in March 1997 was "an absurdist comedy with farcical overtones about paternity, maternity, and how the imagination can act to control reality" (389). It had, he thought, echoes of *Who's Afraid of Virginia Woolf?* not merely in that there are two couples and a baby whose existence seems problematic, but because of this concern with the uncertain status of reality itself. In truth, the play contains echoes of a number of Albee's plays, perhaps most clearly *A Delicate Balance* (1966). Certainly that was the play he himself confessed to me to be the most relevant when we were waiting to go onstage to have a discussion about it on its British premiere. The connec- tion lies in the fact that a young couple suddenly find themselves menaced by another couple who threaten to dispossess them – on this occasion not of their home but of their child.

The play opens with a pregnant Girl (all the characters have generic names). She leaves the stage and the audience hears her protracted screams as she gives birth offstage. She immediately returns to announce, "There," while the Boy declares it to be "the miracle of life."⁵ After the offstage screams and the crying baby, their immediate reappearance has the air of a comic turn and, indeed, there is more than a touch of vaudeville about what follows as the characters, particularly the Man and Woman who shortly appear, mug to the audience.

The Girl seemingly cradles and nurses a baby as the Boy recalls a time when he, too, had suffered pain having his arm broken by a group of thugs. ("If you have no wounds how can you know you're alive?" the Man later asks (49) – just as Jerry, in *The Zoo Story*, had once spoken of pain as one root of education.) The Girl leaves the stage in the middle of the Boy's speech, seemingly uninterested, returning to console him. It is into this situation that the Man now comes, casually greeting the audience as he does so, soon to be joined by the Woman, equally conscious of the audience and the role she is seemingly to play. The Man and Woman seem in some way to be the future of the younger couple, older versions, perhaps, of the younger selves. Their ironies replace the passion of those they visit until the question becomes who intrudes on whom. Is it the older couple who bring news of loss and abandonment, or are the young couple conjured up as a memory which taunts, a reminder of what was and is no longer?

The Man's first observations to the audience concern the sense that, when you are driving somewhere you have never been to before, the journey there seems much longer than the return. Beyond an echo of Jerry's comment in *The Zoo Story* that sometimes it is necessary to go a very long distance out of your way in order to come back a short distance correctly, this refers, perhaps, to the time it takes for a life to unfold – as opposed to the speed of that life viewed in retrospect. The young couple are at the beginning of their journey, and the older, perhaps, at the end. Memory, meanwhile, has the power to bring past and present together.

But this is not a play which deals in certainties. The Man himself tries out, and for the moment seemingly rejects, two interpretations of his opening observation: "that which we *feel* we've experienced is the same as we have"; "Reality [is] determined by our experience of it" (8). Reality, in other words, is what we perceive it to be, whether that experience is projected or actual. It is an interpretation which the Man rejects, but what is the reality of a play if not experiential? The Albee who in *Who's Afraid of Virginia Woolf?* had proposed the necessity of confronting the real thereafter asked the more fundamental question of what might constitute the real. What is the reality of the three ages of women in *Three Tall Women* but their shifting needs, feelings, and interpretations of experience? What is the real in *The*

Play About the Baby, in which the real can range from an intense and satis-fying experience to irony and even regret, all passion apparently spent? Are memories real?

As the Man observes, "we *invent*, and then we *re*-invent." Who was it, he asks, who said that "our reality . . . is determined by our need?" (10). He now withdraws his earlier rejection of the idea that reality might be subjective. As he confesses, "Pay attention to this, what's true and what isn't is a tricky business . . . what's real and what isn't" (10). It is an injunction that could be applied to most of Albee's work, and the point is underscored now as the Woman enters and addresses the audience, breaking the frame and momentarily dissolving the barrier between the supposedly real and the apparently fictitious. She is, she explains, "not an actress . . . though why you'd think I *was* . . . I don't know" (12) – a line which always prompted laughter in production but a line which is by no means there simply to prompt a laugh. The Woman hints at a possible familiarity with the Boy as he develops an extended sexual metaphor, as though flirting with her as he had with the young woman. "Where there's a boy there's a girl," she observes to the audience, which can see that, apparently, where there is a Man there is a Woman.

The Play About the Baby features a series of arias, stories elaborated by each of the characters, sometimes only tangentially related to the unfolding action. The Man recalls a visit to a London museum. The Woman recounts her efforts to contact publishers. These are self-conscious turns – perfor-mances – and signalled as such: "Did you like our little performance?" The Boy describes a possibly fanciful account of his first encounter with the Girl, who in turn talks of her meeting with a gypsy fortune-teller. Behind all this, though, is a gathering sense of trepidation. As the Boy remarks, "I can take pain and loss and all the rest *later* [. . .] when it comes as natural as . . . sleep?" But for the moment, he pleads, "Give us some time" (23). They are to have no time, however, since the Man and Woman have come to take the baby – as babies are always taken in the sense of growing into children and then adults.

The first act ends with the announcement by the Man that he and the Woman have indeed come to take the baby. The second act begins with the former welcoming the audience back from the intermission, joking about the inadequacy of women's toilets. The cast, at his bidding, reassemble and he prompts the younger couple in their lines, which reprise those that had ended the first act. The Man and the Woman echo other lines which the younger couple had once addressed to each other in privacy, quite as if they were versions of them. Indeed, they are seemingly aware of everything that has passed between their young counterparts, now and in the past.

Finally, the Woman comes on, apparently with the baby wrapped in a blanket but there is, it seems, nothing there. The play ends as the young couple appear to deny its existence. Speaking of the play, Albee sought to clarify it. The baby, he insisted, was real: "We see its blanket. She [the Girl]'s not nursing a blanket. She's not crazy. And she has mother's milk, so obviously she's had a baby." It is, however, and echoing a line from the play, "made evident that reality is determined by our need" and that the younger characters "realize they cannot take the pain and loss of having a baby, so it ceases to be real" (Gussow 398). In *Who's Afraid of Virginia Woolf?*, George and Martha had created a baby out of need, out of fear of reality. The young couple in *The Play About the Baby* surrender their baby, or the idea of their baby, for much the same reason.

Looking back over a career that to date has lasted some forty-five years, it is clear that Albee's themes have remained constant, as has his commitment to language. His plays are, for the most part, not heavily plotted. His characters are storytellers but the plays themselves are seldom driven by narrative. At times character itself seems attenuated as he settles for seemingly generic figures, representatives of different stages of life, different interpretations of experience, different gender or familial roles. But this is to say no more than that he is not a realist with a realist's assumption about the nature of the real and how it is constituted. For him, it is born out of need of one kind or another, out of an urgency structured into experience.

There is also a fair amount of dying in Albee's work, real and symbolic. Lives wind down. In *Box*, *Three Tall Women*, and *Occupant*, a voice seems to come from beyond the grave. Albee, like Beckett, is certainly in no doubt that we are born astride the grave. The product of that knowledge, however, is something more than irony, something beyond the absurd. In his world it breeds urgency, the need to connect, an acute awareness of denial and evasion. It prompts, above all, a belief in the necessity to accept that pain may be the evidence of life but that life itself is to be embraced in its particularities.

A gay man, he was forced for many years to deny who he was, as later he was invited with equal disregard to define himself solely in terms of that identity. No wonder that in his early work he accused America of a dereliction of the real, of generating a fictive world which it invited its citizens and the rest of the world to inhabit. Later, he was content to allow others to project the social and political implications of plays seemingly focused on the personal, which explored the slow attrition of the ideal and an animating passion in private lives. That was not to say, however, that he had no interest in the public realm, as was evidenced by his work for PEN and his willingness to stand up for causes which seemed to him to press on the rights and needs of individuals and communities. Although he appears not to be an autobiographical writer, he is, if not identical to the author of his plays, at least close kin.

In 2002 Albee completed another play, *Occupant*, which tackles an artist's biography directly. However, owing to the ill-health of its intended star, Anne Bancroft, it has yet to be staged professionally. A work for two characters, it is presented as an interview between a man in his forties and the late sculptress (and friend of Albee) Louise Nevelson – born, we learn, Leah Berliawsky. She appears first encased in a costume "cage," silhouetted, as if this were the image to be deconstructed. When she is introduced to an invisible audience, against a background of canned applause, she disentangles herself from the costume and steps down onto one of two or three platforms which constitute the stage. There is, Albee comments, very little else, except, perhaps, a bench. In the course of the play, as she is led through her life, so the stage gradually fills with her sculptures.

Daughter of an immigrant Jewish family from Russia, Nevelson apparently struggled to sustain a sense of herself as an independent person and an artist. The child of an arranged marriage, she herself entered a marriage without love. The play is an account not merely of her life but, crucially, of her lives since, as she confesses, "I'm a lot of people . . . and I shift all the time."[6] The play is the story of the construction of a self. "Who am *I*?" she asks, echoing the central question of *The Lady from Dubuque*. The answer, as in *Three Tall Women*, is that she is everything she has been, everything she has done. She is all of these things and none of them, in so far as each one is taken to define her. Leah Berliawsky is not the same person as Louise Nevelson. She is a kaleidoscope shaken by life, but she is also a constructor of that life in the same way that she builds her sculptures from the given, transforming it.

As the play unfolds, it becomes apparent that some of the stories she tells are untrue, that she forgets, embellishes. Memory can be a weapon as well as a resource. A life is a sculpture, formed by a combination of instinct and conscious craft. There is also a space between this woman and her public reputation, as there is a space between Albee and his. The play raises the question of what constitutes a self – whether it is constructed by others or by the processes of living. In a sense, Albee's response as a writer must be what, in *Occupant*, Nevelson's is as a sculptor. As the stage fills with her work, the work which in the end defines her, "All of a sudden I had become *me* . . . if you finally know the space you . . . occupy . . . well, then . . . you go on." (2.38–39). And yet, of course, not so. When Nevelson is dying, she has her name taken down from the door of her hospital room and the word "Occupant" put in its place. She is not the famous sculptor; she is another person there until she is not. Yet at the play's end she returns to her carapace, the shell of her reputation. Who is she – the confused, ambiguous, vulnerable, talented individual or the famous artist? Who is Albee and where is he?

There comes a moment in *Occupant* when Louise is opened to life by looking at an exhibition of Noh robes: "I said, Oh, my God, life is worth living if a civilization can give us this . . . a little bit of *light*. Sometimes things *happen* and they change everything" (2.20). Albee is neither an absurdist confronting audiences with the cold facts of mortality, nor a salesman for American platitudes about a secure identity and deferred but imminent happiness. He is prepared to settle for "a little bit of light" generated by an acknowledgment of the truth of the human condition, an acceptance of pain as well as pleasure (this being part of the contract), and recognition that art is evidence of transcendence.

NOTES

First citations from each of the plays discussed are noted below. All further citations refer to these editions and will be cited parenthetically in the text.

1. Edward Albee, *Finding the Sun* (New York: Dramatists Play Service, 1994), p. 3.
2. Edward Albee, *Marriage Play* (New York: Dramatists Play Service, 1995), p. 20.
3. Edward Albee, *Fragments: A Sit-Around* (New York: Dramatists Play Service, 1995), p. 3.
4. Mel Gussow, *Edward Albee: A Singular Journey* (New York: Simon and Schuster, 1999), pp. 388–389.
5. Edward Albee, *The Play About the Baby* (New York: Dramatists Play Service, 2002), p. 5.
6. Edward Albee, *Occupant* (unpublished manuscript, 2002), p. 1.13.

10

RAKESH H. SOLOMON

Albee stages *Marriage Play*: Cascading action, audience taste, and dramatic paradox

For over four decades now, Edward Albee has closely supervised or directed professional productions of nearly all his own plays. Among his many directing credits, he was responsible for the Broadway premieres of *The American Dream* (1968), *Seascape* (1975), and *The Man Who Had Three Arms* (1983), and the Broadway revival of *Who's Afraid of Virginia Woolf?* (1976). He also staged the world premieres of *Listening* (1977) at the Hartford Stage Company, *Marriage Play* (1987) and *Three Tall Women* (1991) at the English Theatre in Vienna, and *Fragments: A Sit-Around* (1993) at the Ensemble Theatre of Cincinnati. In addition, he directed the American premieres of *Counting the Ways* (1977) at the Hartford Stage Company and *Marriage Play* at the Alley Theatre (1992) and the New York premiere of *Finding the Sun* (1993) at the Signature Theatre Company. For several seasons, moreover, he served as an associate director at the Tony award-winning Alley Theatre of Houston, where, in addition to staging several of his own plays, he directed Samuel Beckett's *Happy Days*, *Ohio Impromptu*, and *Krapp's Last Tape*. He has also directed plays by other fellow dramatists including Lanford Wilson, Sam Shepard, and David Mamet.

In view of this dual career – unprecedented among contemporary American dramatists – Albee's rehearsal deliberations compel attention, and in the following pages I would like to provide a brief overview of his influential staging of *Marriage Play* at the Alley Theatre in 1992. I will first highlight some of his main directorial concerns during this staging and then present his rationale – in his own words – for some of his key decisions during the four weeks of rehearsals and previews.[1]

Albee has put his directorial imprint on several of the most important productions of *Marriage Play*. He staged the first three productions of this taut two-hander – its world, American, and East Coast premieres – and he collaborated closely with the directors who staged the play's New York and London premieres. At Vienna's English Theatre he directed the play's first stage performance in 1987, with two veteran Albee actors, Kathleen Butler as Gillian and Tom Klunis as Jack. Then, in 1992, he directed both the first

164

American performance of the play at the Alley Theatre, with Shirley Knight as Gillian and Tom Klunis again as Jack, and the first East Coast performance at the McCarter Theatre in Princeton, New Jersey – where, using the same actors, he restaged the Alley Theatre's thrust-stage production for the McCarter's proscenium stage. Many theatre professionals from nearby New York City saw this Albee staging. Among them were members of the Signature Theatre Company and its artistic director, James Houghton, who devoted his company's entire 1993–94 season to Albee plays.

For that season's opening production, Houghton staged the first New York performance of *Marriage Play*. Albee wielded considerable influence on that production, too. Exercising his prerogative as the playwright, ensured him by the Dramatists Guild standard contract, he took an active part in all aspects of that production, serving as advisor, attending selected rehearsals and ruling on myriad details of the setting, furniture, props, costumes, and even publicity.[2] Furthermore, he was available to the director and cast for consultation much more than usual: not only was he being consulted on all the other plays being readied for the Albee season, he was also serving as a fellow director at the Signature Theatre Company staging his own newly titled work, *Sand* – a triple bill consisting of *Finding the Sun, Box*, and *The Sandbox*. Most crucially, Albee insisted that director Houghton cast Kathleen Butler, his Gillian from the Vienna production, and Tom Klunis, his Jack from the Vienna, Houston and Princeton productions, thus ensuring that his original molding of these actors' portrayals would continue or strongly color the New York staging. Similarly, during rehearsals for the London premiere of *Marriage Play* in 2001, on a double bill with *Finding the Sun*, Albee played an active backstage role, offering guidance and feedback to director Anthony Page and his cast of Sheila Gish and Bill Paterson at the Royal National Theatre.[3]

The two-character *Marriage Play* concentrates on Jack and Gillian's unblinking dissection of their thirty-year marriage. With several linguistic echoes from Beckett, the play is also a marital *Waiting for Godot*: it begins as it ends, with Jack's declaration to Gillian, "I'm leaving you," but with no indication of his actually doing so. Bracketed between those identical declarations, Jack and Gillian battle – in anger or in sorrow, verbally but on one occasion also in savage physical combat – over their years of affection and betrayals, attention and neglect, passion and distance. They recriminate and reminisce about not only their marriage but their entire lives, and their contemplation of despair resonates well beyond themselves, for they consider whether ultimately "nothing" is really enough.

Albee conducted his rehearsals for the Alley Theatre *Marriage Play* from December 3, 1991, to January 7, 1992.[4] When planning these rehearsals, he decided that since both actors have to be onstage all the time, he would not have them work more than four to five hours each rehearsal day. His schedule provided for a total of twenty-four days of rehearsals, including technical and dress rehearsals, and five days of previews. Uncharacteristically, he began by devoting two full rehearsals to reading the script; usually he spends only half a session on his initial readings. He spent another three days on blocking Act 1, and five days on blocking Act 2 while simultaneously running Act 1. The next eleven days were devoted to work on specific scenes and daily run-throughs, followed by three days of dress and technical rehearsals.

During the early sessions, Albee guided the actors toward the overall thrust of the play by telling them how he had considered some alternate titles for the play. He had first thought of naming it *The Old One-Two*, and later *News From the Front*, but he confessed, "I hate plays that are too neatly tied up," and thus preferred the more neutral and ambiguous *Marriage Play*. Albee also stressed his play's ambiguous ending and quipped that the title was not "Death of a Marriage" but could be "Illness of a Marriage." These humorous comments served to relieve tensions and anxieties common in early rehearsals, while simultaneously conveying his broad authorial intent to his actors. Prior to these rehearsals, the characters in the script were simply named He and She. Since neither character addresses the other by name in the play, Albee felt that giving them names was a "waste," but he reluctantly bowed to the actors' wishes and named them Jack and Gillian. In a conversation outside the rehearsals, he admitted that the names were also a private joke evoking the Jack and Jill of the nursery rhyme.

Receiving only its second production, the *Marriage Play* script underwent radical and substantial cutting during these rehearsals. In a conversation with him, reproduced below, I therefore probed him in some detail on his rehearsal-inspired revisions. Such was the extent of Albee's cuts that at one stage he assured the actors, "I promise you these are the last changes!" He carefully reconsidered almost every aspect of his text in order to translate it into effective performance. Thus, his explanations for his cuts and modifications, and for his few, rare additions to the dialogue and stage business, provide insights into his dramaturgy and his overall theatrical aesthetic. More starkly than did his rehearsal work on any of the older scripts I have observed in production, Albee's work on *Marriage Play* reveals how the demands of performance can alter an author's idealized vision, as contained in the original, literary version of a play. This conversation, conducted toward the end of the rehearsal process, is also unusual because here Albee uncharacteristically acknowledges the practical considerations for his textual revisions.

Albee provided extensive explanatory comments on character subtext, meaning, and authorial intent to coax out an accurate performance. Albee

also showed that he is an astute handler of actors of different tempera-
ments. Faced with his two actors' strong differences in personality and acting
approaches, Albee proved patient, deft, and diplomatic as a director. With
Tom Klunis anxious to set delivery, business, movement, and overall interpretation as early as possible, and Shirley Knight compulsively experimenting
until opening night (and beyond), Albee preempted several potential problems and smoothly and economically navigated unavoidable differences.

Beyond refinement of script, elucidation of characters and situations, and
handling of actors and myriad practical matters, Albee's crucial focus was
on fleshing out this domestic drama with an accumulation of business that
translated character psychology into credible stage behavior – what George
Bernard Shaw once described as "making the audience believe that real things
are happening to real people," and what he argued was "the beginning and
end of the business" of directing.[5]

Albee's conversation with me about his *Marriage Play* script and production was part of an ongoing dialogue that I have had with him over several
years. I have observed Albee direct professional productions of a dozen of
his own plays in New York and elsewhere. I have also seen Albee stage two
of Samuel Beckett's plays, *Ohio Impromptu* and *Krapp's Last Tape*, and in
1980 I observed Albee work with his long-time director, Alan Schneider,
when the latter staged the Broadway premiere of *The Lady from Dubuque*.
Typically, I attend every rehearsal for a production – from the first reading to
final preview – and document and critique each day's work, while carrying on
an intermittent conversation with Albee between rehearsal sessions, culminating in one or two extended tape-recorded interviews near opening night.
At that time I also usually tape-record interviews with some actors, scene
and lighting designers, and the stage manager. This exchange on *Marriage
Play* was taped at the Alley Theatre during the previews in the first week of
January 1992.

In the following discussion, Albee offers insights into the details of his
rehearsal process, from his special perspective as both playwright and director. Journalists and scholars have sought and received more interviews from
Albee than from most other contemporary American playwrights, both
because he continues to provoke interest and because his frequent lecturing,
teaching, and directing oblige him to grant interviews. My long professional
relationship with Albee and my thorough acquaintance with the particulars
of his rehearsals, however, allow me to press, persist, and probe further than
most. Albee comes well-armored against the interviewer's probes: he brings
deeply ingrained, almost reflexive interview habits of defense through deft
deflection, shrewd rationalization, the too-simple explanation, or the opaque
comment. His caution stems partly from his personality and partly from a

distrust of authorial or critical paraphrase as a substitute for the essence and experience of a work of art – a trait he shares with many writers in what Nathalie Sarraute terms the "age of suspicion." During our conversations over the years, however, Albee has become progressively less guarded, and I have had to nudge him less. It is still difficult, nonetheless, to elicit from him a candid, blunt, or spontaneous response, especially about matters of sub-text, allusion, and interpretation – subjects about which interviewers have found him adroitly evasive or uncooperative.

This conversation on *Marriage Play* is distinct from most other Albee interviews in its sustained attention to a single play and in its concentration on matters of rehearsal and performance. Albee ranges widely from broad topics such as the function of each scene in a play, to details of his many textual revisions and specifics of his set and lighting. He reveals his ratio-nale for crucial textual revisions made during rehearsals and distinguishes between a script's dramaturgic refinement during rehearsal versus revisions to cater to audience taste. Finally, Albee's assertions in the following pages merit attention not only because they are grounded in four decades of broad practical experience in the American theatre, but also because they reveal the thinking of an eminent playwright. The way Albee articulates his artistic concerns, moreover, offers a glimpse into his personal sensibility.

* * *

During these Marriage Play *rehearsals you have made several substantial cuts. Could you talk about one or two major deletions and your reasons for cutting them?*

In the "Why would I put in a fucking garden?" speech, that section was just a long thing, holding it up.

Now you always say, "That's holding it up."

It's the old rule. Any scene in the play has got to do two things: reveal character further and advance the action. The two things that I've cut: the south of France thing and the thing about the difference between men and women and courtship and all the rest weren't doing anything. They were interesting. They were nicely written. I liked them a lot. I'm not going to lose them, no. I can use them somewhere else. I probably will.[6] But they had nothing to do with moving the action of the play forward. They were static moments. The illusion of the static is O.K. But those were just really static; they were set pieces. So I cut them.

Well, some of the deleted passages did reveal character a little.

They must do *two* things, both of them. If they only do one of them, then you've got to look at them carefully, because maybe they can go.

Well, theoretically it sounds good, but in practical terms I think some lines do not necessarily . . .

Well, not lines, no. You can't apply that rule line to line. It's scene to scene. Beat to beat. The top of the play has to cascade downhill at that particular point to its ending. It started cascading, then there was this long plateau, and then it cascaded a little further. I was watching the audience for five nights, coughing and rustling, as this started to happen. Now that's my fault because I as director was not being as tough with me as writer. But I have to learn things, and I have to figure them out. I knew at the end of last night's performance. That's why I went and stood on stage and wrote to myself what went wrong. It came to me. I knew exactly what I had to do, and what the lines were, and no more fooling around.

You gave me two absolutely essential reasons for all those large cuts, i.e., for cutting of scenes. But there were several other line cuts, too, and some of them were significant ones, it seems to me. What other specific reasons compelled you to make those cuts?

Well, I have to relate to what interests me and to what bores me. If something's starting to bore me, who's the author and the director, I can assume that the audience has been bored too. At the same time, I'm *not* trying to suggest here that I am trying to accommodate to the audience's taste, the audience's lack of desire for complexity and unpleasantness. No. But I don't think that one should give the audience the opportunity to disengage. I think you've got to make the play as sturdy and as involving as it possibly can be. So that if they want to turn off, it's their fault rather than mine.

Both your major cuts were in the second act.

Because I had a first act about forty-two minutes long, and a second act about fifty-four minutes long. There was an imbalance – not only a time imbalance but a psychological imbalance. Two major sections I cut bring the second act down, I imagine, to about forty-two minutes. I bet I cut about twelve minutes all-together.

What's the rule of thumb? That the first act is a little longer?

Oh, I don't think there is a rule of thumb. First acts – in a three-act play, first acts tend to be the second in length. The second act tends to be the longest and the third act tends to be the shortest. In a two-act play, oh, some equivalency is usually nice. And if anything, the first act would usually be a little more. Here, they're just going to be about the same.

It's always, I would imagine, a little nice to surprise the audience with an earlier than anticipated ending.

But I didn't shorten the second act to make it shorter than the first act. If I was going to do that, I would have put those two scenes somewhere in the first act. The fact is that would have made the first act tedious.

When you directed Everything in the Garden *at the Ensemble Theatre of Cincinnati, I remember you changed your two-act play into a three-act work. Was that for similar kinds of reasons?*

It was better in three acts. In Cincinnati it just seemed better with two inter-missions.

So you obviously had just one intermission in the original New York production?

Yes, with only one intermission in New York, I felt the first act was too long.

Any other reasons why you change things? Were there things that you thought this particular actor or actress could not do?

I never do that.

Yes, you claim that. But sometimes you do cut and then you say, "I'll put it back in when I publish the play."

Well, I don't think I've done that here. You have to strip down to essentials without losing anything. But I would rather overwrite than underwrite. You can always cut. Some passages cut here were set pieces – they were not inherent to those two people. Maybe that's one of the reasons I could cut them so easily.

Yes, without trauma.

Because they're set pieces.

What about your short, one-or-two-line cuts here and there?

I'm sure they were cut for the same reasons, and for the rhythm. A scene goes on for thirty seconds too long; a speech goes on for five seconds too long or five seconds too short; you adjust it.

What about changes in movement and business? Obviously, that's what you do in rehearsal. You had Jack sit down earlier yesterday, stay on the bench. Why? Was it because it repeated Gillian's movement too much and was predictable, a bit like a set movement?

Yes, exactly. Because what I had done was very stagey. It was not good directing. It was bad blocking. You don't hold to something you have done just for the sake of holding to it. That's stubbornness and foolhardy.

At the end now you have them holding hands.

I like it.

Figure 6. *Marriage Play*, McCarter Theatre, Princeton, 1992. Directed by Edward Albee, with Tom Klunis as Jack and Shirley Knight as Gillian.

Does it mean they are closer now?

No. I like the paradox. It's the first time in the play that they are touching each other. Except in violence. And it's interesting to me that they're holding hands when he repeats the fact that he's going to leave her.

Could it be interpreted that now that he has made up his mind to leave her, his touching is out of pity for her, especially since there is a calmness in his voice?

No, I'd say it's a lonely decision that he's making. A terrifying decision.

Well, pity for her.

Mm . . . . No. Pity for himself. Two kids in the dark.

It works fine, but it really stresses the positive aspect of the relationship.

It doesn't do any damage. I think it's sort of a nice little touch.

Yes, and it also wakes people up to thinking that he may not be leaving. Those in the audience who have decided that Jack is leaving.

Makes it more ambiguous. Paradox does that sometimes.

Overall, how different is this production from the one you directed at Vienna's English Theatre?

Well, when you have a different actress, you have a different wife; and so you have a different production. I think this is probably a better production only because I've learned from the Vienna production. I added some things after the Vienna production. I wrote about a page and a half in the "Do you still care by the way?" area; "What are we going to do?" – that wasn't in the Vienna production. And also seeing it in Vienna – and seeing it in Stockholm, I suppose – both gave me the opportunity to make this a little richer. During rehearsals for Vienna, I cut out a lot of stuff. Just too much writing.

Any changes in staging?

There's no fundamental shift.

Did the Vienna production have just two chairs?

That's right. And a little side table. Small stage; that's all that it allowed for.

What about the Stockholm set?

It was a terrible set. A sofa, a footstool, and a rocking chair. I didn't care for the set.

What about the backdrop?

Just curtains. Inexpensive production. They did it in one act, which was their big mistake. And the play became much too long. Much too long.

[Editor's note: As a result of the various cuts he made to the text, Albee himself eventually decided to eliminate the intermission and had *Marriage Play* published as a one-act play, running for eighty or ninety minutes. It was in this form that it appeared, in double bill with *Finding the Sun*, in its 2001 British premiere.]

Did you originally write Marriage Play *as a long one-act play?*

No. I don't think so. I don't remember.

I can't imagine such a long play as a one-act.

It would be. I think I realized early on that there were going to be two acts and that Act 1 was going to have to end with the fight. The only difference is that originally I began Act 2 at the *beginning* of the fight [rather than at the *end* of the fight, as now]. But I realized that that was not a good idea – I couldn't have the actors duplicate the fight.

It's very nice when Act 2 shows the actors still fighting. It certainly surprises the audience.

The intention was to make it seem like they hadn't had an intermission.

In effect, to give an illusion of the continuous action of a one-act play.

The story thus far, so to speak.

What did you tell the actors about the implication of the "Don't you care" speech?

He still cares. It's a dreadful irony. "You used to care enough to pay attention to the fact that you were hurting me and now you just do it without even thinking about it."

Obviously you're interested in themes about people listening, communicating, not listening. Is that why in Marriage Play *quite often your actors look out when speaking to each other and often speak while behind their listener's line of vision?*

You don't have to look at somebody to talk to them.

Did the actors feel the need to look more towards each other?

Maybe a little bit more than I would like. You don't have to look at them to listen to them. Maybe a little bit more. Not as much as the awful problem I had in Los Angeles [during his directing of *Who's Afraid of Virginia Woolf?*].[7] Ah, what's her name? Glenda Jackson – who said, "I can't act unless I can see the eyes of the person to whom I am talking." So I had to restage a whole bunch of things. And then as soon as she got on stage in front of an audience, she never looked at anybody else. That was her attitude during rehearsal. She decided to do a solo performance.

With your actors in Marriage Play, *what areas needed particular attention during these rehearsals?*

Well, I don't want to get into things that you have to stop the performers from doing. Because the only things you stop the performer from doing are things that you've been critical about. No need to talk about that. But there are certain things that one tries to get out of a performance. Personal attributes or attitudes of an actor sometimes show – traits that you don't think belong to the character. I mean, just subtly work them out.

Did you suggest Jack's using the briefcase to threaten Gillian with?

Well, I originally issued no more than the slap, in spite of the "Oh, it's best to put blood on stage." So I thought that I would try the briefcase. I think it is going to work just as effectively as the slap.

In the script I think it was a slap.

It was. In a movie I could have a slap.

But you recently did use slaps in your production of Everything in the Garden. *Two of the actors slapped each other twice, but I think those did prove a bit problematic.*

Oh yes, yes.

I know it is daytime in the play, and I also know that you don't like any dramatic light changes. But is the lighting a bit too harsh and unchanging now?

Well, you have to be able to see the actors. It was harsher, and I brought the levels down a little bit. I might want to bring them down yet further. I prefer the light the way we rehearsed it this afternoon – a much gentler light. You have that in small theatres. But you can't have that here at the Alley; you have to have things brighter in a huge theatre.

Could the lighting on the glass windows be a little muted?

Well, yes, but I can't fuss about that now.

Did you select the set and costume designer, Derek McLane, or did you have to use whoever the Alley Theatre provided?

He was recommended to me. We had some talks, and then I said, "O.K."

Do you like the set?

It's very nice, but I want one more thing on it.

What is that?

I don't know. Some African piece somewhere.

Did you talk to the actors about it?

Maybe I mentioned it. I would like something on it. Something more. It's a little sparse overall.

Coming from you, I'm pleased to hear it because it allays some of my own concerns.

I insisted on having that big tree. That was mine. I insisted on that. And I insisted on the South-western rug. Now I need one more thing up there.

At least a sculpture.

A sculpture or a painting. An abstract painting. I have an abstract painting perhaps that could work.

With this experience of directing Marriage Play *here at the Alley in this particular set, what changes are you planning for your production of the play at the McCarter Theatre in Princeton?*

We have to use a different set. The McCarter Theatre, of course, is a proscenium theatre. This set was built specifically for the thrust stage here. I imagine if we go into a small theatre in New York City I'll try to accomplish a combination of the two sets.

In contrast to your wanting a bit more than what the designer has given you here, I remember that on the set of the Broadway production of The Lady from Dubuque *you kept wanting less and less while your director, Alan Schneider, wanted more and more. You dubbed him prop-happy for introducing so many props. He also wanted much more color and kept bringing in those color prints which you didn't think worked with that Bauhaus-style drawing-room set. In that context, and given your long working relationship, how would Alan have directed* Marriage Play?

I don't know. I don't know. It's a very hard question to answer. I think Alan would have had a problem only with the wit and sophistication of the characters. Perhaps a little bit.

What do you mean?

These people are upper-middle class. He would have had a little problem with them, but he would have done fine.

Most of your characters tend to be upper-middle class.

Yes. But that would have been where the problem was.

Many of your characters also are very self-conscious about language and often correct themselves and others. You know a lot of people like that?

Probably only me. Oh, some other people. Howard Moss [poetry editor of *The New Yorker*] is good that way when he has other close friends around.

You do that with your friends?

Probably.

But you're very precise yourself.

Also those people! That's the way these people behave.

I have got to know you a little more over the years. In this play, you seem to be drawing quite a bit on the traits of people you know and on who you are.

Maybe I'm beginning to become like some of my characters. Consider that possibility!

All the publicity material announces the title of your play as "Edward Albee's Marriage Play." When did you add "Edward Albee's" to the title?

That's the only way to guarantee at a regional theatre that you're going to get your name in the proper size and place it's supposed to be.

At first glance it seems somewhat redundant. I know that you are very self-aware, so I thought you were instead trying to make some point.

No, no. I'm getting tired of incorrect billing. Most regional theatres don't pay any attention. My contract has always said – all of my contracts from the very beginning have said – the author's name shall be 100 percent of [the size of] the title. But they just ignore it. And the only way that I found to get around that is to say that the title of the play is "Edward Albee's *Marriage Play*." That's the only way that they can't fuck up the billing.[8]

What size of letters do you ask for for the name of the director?

That has to be 50 percent. It's either 50 or 75 percent. I think 50 percent. It doesn't have to be very big. That's by contract also.

The program lists two casting agencies – what role did they play in your selection of the actors?

Everybody has casting directors these days. They make suggestions. I can turn them down.

I heard that you had considered Ben Gazzara for the role of Jack in this production.

I've heard all sorts of things.

You didn't consider him?

Well, one considers the possibility of everybody. I must confess, though, that I can't imagine anybody really doing it better than Tom Klunis. They wanted another name. They wanted a bigger name. So they kept throwing people at me. But I wasn't happy with any of them. Didn't seem right. And I had seen Tom do it, and I knew that he was right. Might make it more difficult for Broadway later. I don't know. But (a) you can't betray people; and (b) You go with the best performance you can get. There's too much compromise in the theatre as it is.

NOTES

1. I documented Albee's rehearsals from December 1, 1991 to January 4, 1992, and attended the first three evening previews on January 2, 3, and 4, 1992, at the Alley Theatre, Houston, Texas. The full account of this production, and of a dozen other Albee productions of his own plays since 1978, appears in Rakesh H. Solomon, *Albee in Performance: The Playwright as Director*, forthcoming from Indiana University Press.

2. For a humorous account of Albee's dictating the details of director James Houghton's production of *Marriage Play* at the Signature Theatre Company, especially the number of couches that Albee rejected for the set, see David Blum, "What's It All About, Albee?," *New York*, November 15, 1993, pp. 70–78.

3. Albee made several minor revisions for the London production to transform Jack and Gillian into a British couple living in Richmond, Surrey. See Charles Spencer, "Echoes From the Wilderness Years," *Daily Telegraph*, May 10, 2001, and Benedict Nightingale, "Unholy Deadlock," *The Times*, May 10, 2001.

4. All rehearsal information and quotations of directorial comments come from my personal records of these rehearsals.

5. George Bernard Shaw, *Shaw on Theatre*, ed. E. J. West (New York: Hill and Wang, 1959), p. 153.

6. In fact, Albee incorporated those speeches into his next play, *Fragments: A Sit-Around*, which premiered a year later under his direction at the Ensemble Theatre of Cincinnati.

7. For a detailed account of Albee's 1989 staging of *Who's Afraid of Virginia Woolf?*, see Rakesh H. Solomon, "Text, Subtext, and Performance: Edward Albee on Directing *Who's Afraid of Virginia Woolf?*," *Theatre Survey* 34.2, pp. 95–110.

8. Albee retained this version, with equal ratio of the lettering for his name and title, on the cover and title pages of the printed version of the play. See Edward Albee, *Marriage Play* (New York: Dramatists Play Service, 1995). This decision has misled most libraries into listing the title not as *Marriage Play* but as *Edward Albee's Marriage Play*.

II

LINDA BEN-ZVI

"Playing the cloud circuit": Albee's vaudeville show

Gags and bits without narrative continuity; absence of traditional exposition or plotline; surprise turns; unexpected entrances and exits; extended monologues, crossover dialogues, word games, ribald repartee and sexual innuendo; props used for shocking or humorous effects; simplification of stage settings; heterogeneity of material; snatches of song or musical routines; presentational acting style; rapid delivery and pacing to achieve affective immediacy and emotional impact; brief scenes with shifts in tone and subject matter; frequent climaxes at the end of discrete sections leading to the central climax, usually at the end of the penultimate scene; slippage from low to high art or the reverse and from comedy to tragedy. The items in this list are familiar to Albee scholars; examples can be found in varying degrees and forms throughout his dramatic canon. They also happen to be the significant features of vaudeville, that particularly American theatrical entertainment which the playwright's grandfather and namesake, Edward F. Albee II, is credited with developing and selling to the American public.[1]

The senior Albee, whose portrait bears an uncanny resemblance to his adopted grandson (fine, sculpted face, dark hair and eyes, arched brows, piercing stare[2]), shocked his solid Maine family, and may well have provided a model for the younger Albee, when he left home at nineteen, in his case to join the circus. There he met B. F. Keith and they soon became partners, establishing the most extensive, prestigious, and successful vaudeville circuit in the country. By the time Keith died in 1914 and Albee took sole control in 1918, the Keith-Albee chain numbered more than 1,500 theatres including its flagship, the New York Palace.[3] Thought to be the originator of the line, "There's a sucker born every day,"[4] Albee was known as a fierce competitor and uncompromising administrator. He broke the back of a nascent performers' union, consolidated his holdings, and enacted a program of reshaping and domesticating vaudeville to make it appeal to the growing number of women and middle-class customers who frequented his theatres. Yet, for all his considerable entrepreneurial talents, he could not withstand the onslaught of "the talkies." In 1928 – the same year in which he told his son Reed that he expected him to produce a male heir – Albee sold most of his shares to another famous patriarch, Joseph P. Kennedy, who established RKO (Radio/Keith-Albee/Orpheum).

Although his grandfather died two years later, on March 12,1930, Albee's second birthday, his vaudeville legacy continued throughout the playwright's childhood. Albee remembers Ed Wynn and Sophie Tucker visiting his home, and by the time he was seven, his father began sending him off to Broadway shows, accompanied by a nanny, in order to see former vaudevillians in musical comedy: Jimmy Durante in Billy Rose's *Jumbo*, Wynn in *Hooray for What!*, and Olsen and Johnson in *Hellzapoppin*.[5] The outings were Albee's "first experience with the Theater of the Absurd," he told his biographer Mel Gussow, and they had a lasting impact.[6] His close friend in later years, William Flanagan, described how "the cavortings of Bobby Clark or Bert Lahr" would send Albee into "helpless laughter." Flanagan assumed that the "henpecking female" in *The American Dream* was "kith and kin to the Eternal Harridan that so relentlessly dogged the exacerbated footsteps of W. C. Fields, Groucho Marx, and James Thurber's male animal."[7]

Whenever interviewers have asked him about his early years, Albee has stated repeatedly that his family's history is "something completely separate" and of no consequence to him, and that when he slammed the door at twenty and left his adoptive home, he cut his physical and emotional ties with the past.[8] His plays belie the claim. Critical studies have repeatedly focused on his use of the themes of the adopted son, the unwanted or fantasy child, the dysfunctional family, and the upper-class milieu and its moral and spiritual bankruptcy. However, one aspect of his life story that has not received scholarly attention in relation to the playwright's work is vaudeville, the Albee family business, source of its fortune and reputation, and a defining force during the playwright's formative years. In the same way that Eugene O'Neill, while creating a new American dramatic form, never totally escaped his early exposure to melodrama (deny it as he might, his father's performance in the title role in *The Count of Monte Cristo* hovered in the wings of more than one O'Neill play), it is possible to detect elements of vaudeville, both its forms and its content, embedded to a greater or lesser degree in numerous Albee plays throughout his career. Jerry's quick-paced dialogue and extended "stand-up" monologue in *The Zoo Story* and George and Martha's verbal routines, songs, and sight-gags in *Who's Afraid of Virginia Woolf?* come to mind immediately. However, since Albee tends to be thought of as an intellectual playwright – his bent "arcane," his tone "elegiac"[9] – the power and impact of such examples is not always apparent. Albee notes that actors, after performing his play for the first time in front of an audience, will often "grab me, look at me with wild eyes and say, 'Edward, this play is FUNNY!' And I have to say, well, I knew it all along."[10] What makes his vaudeville acts hard to identify and classify is the fact that they are usually performed in incongruous places by unexpected entertainers: on a quiet Sunday afternoon in Central Park by a seeming derelict, or at a late-night gathering in a living room in a university town by a middle-aged history professor and his somewhat older wife.

The effects of such routines are similar to what Henry Jenkins describes in *What Made Pistachio Nuts?* – one of a growing number of critical studies on the subject of vaudeville.[11] Jenkins's point of departure in his introductory discussion is an obscure musical film of the mid-1930s, *Stand Up and Cheer*, a typical amalgam of the time: there is a simple narrative line with actors playing defined roles, and famous performers, including Shirley Temple and Stepin Fetchit, doing routines only tangentially related to the plot. The groups are carefully delineated; actors and performers do not cross lines. However, in one scene, two "somber minded" United States senators begin to engage in a debate with other characters about funding for a new "Department of Amusements," one source of conflict in the film. When left alone, they suddenly drop the naturalistic style of acting that has marked their actions up to this point, and begin slapping each other, kicking, wrestling, engaging in fragmented strings of clichés, comic patter, quick-fire questions ("What makes pistachio nuts?"), culminating their performance by executing a pair of back flips. Once the others return, the elegantly clad senators stand, brush themselves off, and assume their sartorial airs and their parts. As Jenkins notes, "Their exit abruptly ends a major subplot, not through its resolution but through its explosion . . . the sketch was not simply a digression from the central narrative; rather, it challenged the further development of the causal event chain."[12] In other words, realism was sundered, the realistic comedic convention put into question or, rather, it became more elastic or porous than a simple definition of the form usually allows.

Albee has no back-flipping senators in his plays, but he does have knock-down fights, giant talking lizards, singing professors, dramatic divas, disappearing babies, parasol-sprouting guns, telegram and flower swallowers, and enough puns, plays on words, grammatical confusions, and jokes to supply a comic vaudevillian enough material to more than fill a "two-a-day" schedule. These physical and verbal acts, usually executed in realistic settings and performed by recognizable types, create the same unsettling, disorienting, and explosive effect that Jenkins describes as the vaudeville aesthetic: dissolving or calling into question the carefully delineated world of the play, rendering it strange and disturbing.

Of course, Albee is not unique in making use of vaudeville or comedy routines for theatrically explosive and deconstructive ends. "Highbrow writers have been enthusiastic about clown and vaudeville for decades," Eric Bentley observed, particularly "the great 50's vaudeville act: Beckett, Ionesco, and Genet," as Albee called those whom Martin Esslin labeled absurdist.[13] The first reviews of *Waiting for Godot* focused directly on its vaudeville-like origins. The French playwright Jean Anouilh described the play as "the music-hall sketch of Pascal's *Pensées* as played by the Fratellini clowns"; the Irish writer Denis Johnston likened it to "an Eggheads Harlequinade," and the American critic Walter Kerr, confusing actor with playwright, credited vaudeville clown Bert Lahr, the first American Estragon, with initiating "the rhythms of musical comedy, of revue, of tanbark entertainment."[14] However, because the characters in *Godot* were generally assumed to be clown avatars performing their philosophical pratfalls and verbal pirouettes, most critics did not "ask questions about their origin, social condition, or language," Geneviève Serreau rightly observed, just as "one does not ask these questions about the Fool of *Lear*, about Touchstone or Thersites."[15] In Albee's case, they do, and expect answers because his characters do not look or act like clowns. This is what differentiates them from Beckett's people or from those of American off-Broadway playwrights such as Maria Irene Fornes, who began writing when Albee did, around 1960, and sometimes employed vaudeville routines.[16] Like Jenkins's back-flipping senators, Albee's figures are often unsettling and riveting precisely because of the disparity between their expected modes of behavior and their shocking, annihilating routines that call into question the reality of the world in which they appear.

Antonin Artaud, in a note praising the Marx Brothers' films *Animal Crackers* and *Monkey Business*, made a similar observation about the subversive power of anarchistic comic acts in otherwise traditional settings. He argued that "these events comprise a kind of exercise of intellectual freedom in which the unconscious of each of the characters, repressed by conventions and habits, avenges itself and us at the same time." Such humor, he continued, can lead "toward a kind of boiling anarchy, an essential disintegration of the real by poetry," culminating in "the powerful anxiety which their total effect ultimately projects into the mind."[17] Some of the same observations might be made concerning Albee's writing, particularly when he reaches into his vaudeville bag of tricks and brings out those unexpected bits that he interjects into his otherwise recognizable family dramas, momentarily sundering the realism of the scenes and creating the type of "powerful anxiety" to which Artaud refers. "I don't like the audience as voyeur, the audience as passive spectator," Albee has said. "I want the audience as participant. In that sense, I agree with Artaud: that sometimes we should literally [*sic*] draw blood. I am very fond of doing that because voyeurism in the theater lets people off the hook."[18]

* * *

Albee's routines borrowed from vaudeville draw, if not blood, certainly immediate visceral responses from his audiences and from those observers or witnesses he often positions within the plays to act as surrogates for the spectators. *The Zoo Story* (1959), Albee's first produced play, reflects this technique. It is built on a classic two-person act: Jerry as comic agent and Peter as straight man. The latter is usually a passive figure – either naive or a bourgeois symbol of contemporary mores, an easy target for the active party to tease, prick, or expose. Jerry speaks, Peter listens; one directs the action, the other follows the cues. From the safe distance of the darkened auditorium, the audience can find subversive pleasure in the anarchistic potshots lobbed by the one who dares to step out of line. They laugh because of their sense of superiority to the victim, despite an often tacit recognition of themselves in the character. As the pace of the exchanges quickens, they also feel heightened emotion, excitement, and a sense of shared energy, even danger. *The Zoo Story* is carefully structured to follow this standard vaudeville form. The act begins without any exposition, *in medias res*, with Jerry's declaration, "I've been to the zoo."[19] Typical of many such routines, action is created almost completely through dialogue not physical movement, usually in a question and answer format, with the straight man or woman generally reluctant to participate, and the comic partner using various ploys to keep the action going.[20]

Embedded within this two-man act, Albee has another vaudeville borrowing that ordinarily would constitute a separate act on a bill, traditionally in the penultimate slot: the playlet or extended monologue performed by a leading figure from the legitimate stage, usually an actress, preferably with European credentials such as Sarah Bernhardt or Mrs. Patrick Campbell, a headliner who could provide the high-culture act that Albee's grandfather pioneered in vaudeville and paid handsomely to acquire.[21] The playlet or monologue structure tended to be built on traditional dramatic conventions of exposition, conflict, rising action, and climax, yet simplified to fit the vaudeville requirement of "compression and intensification."[22] Often, all roles were played by a single performer, with the delivery exaggerated and presentational, the focus a single dramatic conflict, the actor striving to hold and move the audience by the sheer force and power of personality and theatrical skill. Jerry's monologue, which he introduces as if he were reading from a vaudeville billboard – "THE STORY OF JERRY AND THE DOG!" (30) – conforms to this type of act. He plays all the parts: growling, snarling, and making the sounds of his mongrel antagonist; mimicking the benign hamburger seller as well as the grotesque landlady. He even provides his own explanatory parse on the presentation. The goal of his performance is exactly what the grand stage stars were paid to deliver: to startle, enthrall, and, as Leigh Woods puts it, "pitch their efforts directly at an audience known for its restlessness, impatience, and distractibility."[23]

Yet, for all Jerry's efforts and talent, Peter does not respond as planned: "I don't understand," he says twice, the second time with capital-lettered emphasis (36). Jerry must try another approach to keep his audience from deserting the theatre. Albee next has him resort to physical action, first tickling and then pushing, perhaps correlatives for the titillating dance acts or physical displays that were intended, despite the management's protestations to the contrary, to arouse customers and make them continue to occupy their seats. The ploy works. What Jerry could not produce with questions and a dramatic monologue he achieves with his physical attacks. Peter is no longer a voyeur to the performance. Depending on how one interprets the play, he either stops being straight man and becomes an active agent or continues to play the part Jerry designed for him, finally propeled to action not from understanding or from compassion but from animal instinct based on territorial imperative. The final tableau with its denouement after the climax of the knifing is also in keeping with the resolution of the completed bill, the final act providing a needed quietus after the emotional and frenetic moments that precede it.

Although Albee's one-acts *The Sandbox* (1960), *FAM and YAM* (1960), and *The American Dream* (1961) contain some material that can be traced to vaudeville, the early play that most closely approximates *The Zoo Story* in its successful adaptation of vaudeville forms for specific theatrical ends is *Who's Afraid of Virginia Woolf?* (1962) – perhaps the reason its most ardent early Broadway supporter was the producer Billy Rose, who first cut his own theatre teeth on vaudeville.[24] In certain respects, George and Martha can be likened to consummate old troupers, their act honed by long years of practice in front of a variety of guests and, most significantly, each other.[25] They even look like classic vaudevillians: she *"large, boisterous* [. . . .] *Ample, but not fleshy"* in the mode of Lily Langtry and Sophie Tucker; he physically slight as befitting the familiar straight man.[26] From their first entrance they assume these fixed roles, in keeping with vaudeville rules requiring immediate audience identification. She is dominant, the initiator of the action, speaking first, directing the dialogue; he is the reactive party, the unwilling audience for her Bette Davis imitation, the reluctant respondent to her rapid-fire questions and queries.

It is George, however, who first employs a technique that Albee uses repeatedly in this and subsequent plays and that has its roots in vaudeville: a joke predicated on a grammatical or rhetorical allusion. Martha's "she's married to Joseph Cotten or something . . ." (4) is followed without a beat by George's corrective ". . . Some*body* . . ." (5). Wordplay as Albee employs it is never merely for laughs. In this scene, it sets up the central question implicit in the marital relationship: is George a "something" or a "somebody"? Martha has already called him "a cluck!" and a "Dumbbell!" so the audience is aware of the subtext of the joke, and its complicity through laughter is similar to what spectators often feel in vaudeville routines, particularly the more outrageous and violent acts. Thus, in the first minute of the play, Albee skillfully establishes the themes and the tensions to follow, condensed and simplified for maximum effect, just as a well-written vaudeville act does. And just as in the best acts, his performers are able to hold the audience's attention, not through a clearly delineated plotline but through the sheer energy and the skill of their delivery.

George and Martha are clearly pros; their timing and responses to each other and to their guests are perfect. On cue, they can immediately launch into routines – Martha's "you just trot over to the barie-poo . . ." is picked up and completed by George's ". . . and make your little mommy a gweat big dwink" (48). Nick's "houseboy" denial triggers their "I'm nobody's houseboy now . . ." song (196). Yet, like any performers who have repeated their act too long, they appreciate change – up to a point. In Acts 1 and 2, whenever George seems to improvise or comes up with a new spin on old material, Martha shows surprise and delight. After his short-barreled shotgun, aimed at her head, brings forth a red and yellow Chinese parasol – a typical vaudeville sight-gag – the stage directions indicate that she reacts "*joyously*" and delivers what passes for a positive review: "Yeah . . . that was pretty good. (*Softer.*) C'mon . . . give me a kiss" (58). His later speech defending his paternity of "our . . . blond-eyed, blue-haired . . . son" is followed by her "You rose to the occasion . . . good. Real good" (72). George's "Flores; flores para los muertos" bow to Tennessee Williams elicits Martha's appreciative laugh and inspires a rapid-fire exchange climaxing with her own dramatic borrowing: "Pansies! Rosemary! Violence! My wedding bouquet!" (195–196). Such new "bits" provide, albeit for the moment, a sense of spontaneity for them in their overly determined act.

Additional vaudeville routines which keep the action going can be found in George's exchanges with the "second bananas" Nick and Honey. The repetitions and confusions in his conversation with Nick that opens Act 2 are patterned directly on common vaudeville dialogues built on pronoun juggling:

NICK: She's making coffee . . . in the kitchen. She . . . gets sick quite easily.
GEORGE (*Preoccupied.*): Martha? Oh no, Martha hasn't been sick a day in
her life, unless you count the time she spends in the rest home . . .

NICK (*He, too, quietly.*): No, no; *my* wife . . . *my* wife gets sick quite easily. Your wife is Martha.
GEORGE (*With some rue.*): Oh, yes . . . I know.   (89–90)

Their protracted apologies that soon follow are also familiar vaudeville turns:

NICK (*With some irritation.*): I'm sorry.
GEORGE: Hm? Oh. No, no . . . I'm sorry.
NICK: No . . . It's . . . it's all right.
GEORGE: No . . . you go ahead.
NICK: No . . . please.
GEORGE: I insist. . . . You're a guest. You go first.   (104)

The central "bit" of the evening, of course, concerns George and Martha's fictional son. "Just don't start in on the bit about the kid, that's all" (18), he warns her before the guests arrive, thus providing the clear and present danger the audience is told to expect. Her failure to heed the warning precipitates the climax: George's announcement of their son's death. Throughout Act 3, "The Exorcism," leading up to this point, there is a perceptible shift in the fixed roles and delivery established earlier. George slowly becomes the initiator of action, improvising as he goes along; and Martha is made to play catch-up, unsure of what is coming next. "All right, George; all right," she repeats, indicating her frustration and wariness. It is at this point that Albee shows his consummate skill in being able to turn vaudeville tricks and business into great theatrical moments. Once the illusion of their child is shattered and George tries one last vaudeville trick – claiming to have eaten the telegram bringing the news (a comic equivalent to killing the messenger) – the pair run out of routines and stand for the first time exposed to their audience and each other. The manic activities of the evening, the verbal bloodbath, the physical battles, have led inexorably to this moment of nakedness. The result is akin to what Artaud describes as the potential end of anarchistic comedy, embodying "something disquieting and tragic, a fatality (neither happy nor unhappy, difficult to formulate)."[27] Albee has said that for him this end holds out the possibility of some new relationship for his characters, since they have reached the point "where they've run out of diversions, and they now stand in the ruin of the illusions they have used to get by."[28]

Vaudeville acts often ended with the comic performers standing amid the rubble they had created or confusions they had caused by the "anarchy and social disruption" of their antics.[29] However, as Jenkins argues, even the Marx Brothers were finally scripted. Seeing them as purveyors of their own chaos is to blur the lines between content and form.[30] Groucho himself indicated his captivity to his vaudeville role when he referred to his old boss Edward F. Albee II as "the Ol' Massa," the one who finally called the shots.[31]

Albee presents a different sort of conclusion at the end of *Who's Afraid of Virginia Woolf?*. He allows George and Martha to actually step out of their defining and confining roles and consider the possibility of an anarchistic act far exceeding that of the Marx Brothers: to become the authors of their own actions.[32]

* * *

"The Exorcism" may have rid his characters of their illusions; it also seems to have rid the playwright of those elements of vaudeville that he had used as ballast in his early plays. There are some jokes and bits in his subsequent plays – for instance Claire's balancing drink act, accordion playing, and yodeling, and Julia's gun-toting defense of the family bar in *A Delicate Balance* (1966) – but few routines are directly traceable to traditions of vaudeville. Not until 1976, with *Counting the Ways*, did Albee return directly to the form. This short one-act was followed by three other plays, spread over a twenty-two-year period – *Finding the Sun* (1983), *Marriage Play* (1987), and *The Play About the Baby* (1998) – that also drew on vaudeville in both form and content.[33]

His return to vaudeville was concurrent with the beginning of that period which Gussow calls Albee's "Into the Woods" years, when, "somewhere in the middle, he got lost in a dark forest" or – in a shift of metaphors reminiscent of many Albee characters – he went "deeper and deeper into the quicksand."[34] *Everything in the Garden* (1967), *Box* and *Quotations from Chairman Mao Tse-Tung* (1968), *All Over* (1971), and *Seascape* (1975), despite its Pulitzer Prize, all had limited runs and were critical and box-office failures. *The Lady from Dubuque* (1980) and *Lolita* (1981) each closed after twelve performances, *The Man Who Had Three Arms* (1983) after sixteen. It would take another eleven years for a new Albee play to return to New York, and then only to a small, off-Broadway venue (*Three Tall Women*, in 1994). Albee, in the parlance of his paternal grandfather, was no longer considered a top act or bookable; when he opened a new play, he did so on the road, out of town. Perhaps with nothing to lose, he felt free to go back to basics and explore the bare-bones structures of the vaudeville form, creating illusion as truth that might be more real than what passes for reality. Ironically, whereas his earlier plays had been dismissed by critics such as Robert Brustein for being "hollow," "suffer[ing] from a borrowed style," or presenting "supernatural conversations in a 'House and Garden Setting'" (often because of what was seen as the inappropriate behavior of characters in a naturalistic drama), these more direct vaudeville plays were generally attacked for the same "hollowness," since they made use of what Christopher Bigsby calls "a redundant form, as exhausted as the naturalism which Albee has consistently shunned."[35] Bigsby's assessment might be true of English music hall; however, *The Zoo Story* and *Who's Afraid of Virginia Woolf?* illustrate that elements borrowed from vaudeville, in the hands of a fine playwright like Albee, are neither "redundant" nor "exhausted," and that Albee was able to avoid the naturalistic pitfalls in part because of those very subversive vaudeville routines he grafted onto his naturalistic dramas. If there are weaknesses in the following plays, they arise not because of but in spite of Albee's handling of the vaudeville form.

Counting the Ways is subtitled "A Vaudeville," an addition that Gussow claims Albee made to indicate the "briskness," "pace," and "'attack' speed" at which the text was to be acted. It also was to forestall repetition of what the playwright saw as the catastrophe of the 1976 National Theatre premiere in London, when the forty-minute chamber piece, slotted for evening performances in the cavernous Olivier Theatre after the four-hour matinees of *Tamberlaine*, was allowed to expand to seventy minutes, filled with what Albee called "slow-moving, leaden sentimentality, punctuated occasionally by slow-motion attempts at humor."[36] Even without the word appearing on the title page, there are enough clear references to vaudeville to make it impossible to overlook the borrowings. The set is minimal, containing the standard objects for two-person routines – a small table and two chairs. Signs introduce the play and, in some productions, announce the name of the playwright and director, just as they did in most vaudeville bills. Albee in his printed directions makes clear that they should drop from above, stay four seconds, and be raised again or, if impractical, should "*appear on signboard, far stage right, in the old vaudeville manner – placed there by a disembodied hand.*"[37] Total blackouts are to end the twenty-one scenes or, alternatively, a curtain should be "swiftly drawn and as swiftly opened" (6) – another standard vaudeville practice.

The characters themselves are modeled directly on typical vaudeville husband and wife teams.[38] Albee, typically, is chary with names, and here the couple are simply designated She and He, types not individuals, but instantly recognizable as they deliver their lines. She is practical and direct; he is tentative and demanding. Their movements are precise and spare, their exits and entrances frequent and timed for comic effect, their words often addressed to the other's retreating or absent figure, or thrown out directly to the audience. Typical of such acts, the dialogue focuses on one general topic, introduced immediately. The subject here is Love: What is it? How is it defined? How do you know you feel it? How can you be sure it is reciprocated? Albee parodically reformulates Mrs. Browning's eponymous poem and has his performers use different ways of "counting the ways" they love and are loved. They ask each other directly; resort to the old game of petal counting, "She loves me, she loves me not"; decipher newspaper ads promising "Love in the

Afternoon"; dredge up memories of earlier flower rituals, such as corsages at proms; revert to "protocol"; and quote and misquote poets. They do not seek love to "the ends of Being and ideal Grace" that Mrs. Browning's poem describes, but rather till, as She explains, "cease or corruption" (10), much more in the Albee mode.

She begins by asking with "objective curiosity": "Do you love me?" He responds with evasion and finally a perfunctory, "Yes." "Well . . . good" (9), she replies, but of course "well" enough is not left alone. More follows, and in a darker, more disturbing register. After reading the items on her food list, including bone marrow – the level Albee claims that George and Martha must reach – and eliciting from her hungry husband a more enthusiastic proclamation of love, She launches into a monologue, building on images of food and lovemaking, that call to mind Agnes's words in *A Delicate Balance*:

> Do you suppose stuffing it in me for you fat and flabby is something I enjoy? Do you? Putting it in me like a wad of dough . . . hoping it'll "rise" to the occasion? Do you think that fills me with a sense of . . . what? Fills me with anything but itself? . . . One day . . . one day stuffing it in me for you – fat and flabby, yes, fat and flabby – it will *not*, in its own good time, "rise" to the occasion, and nevermore, as the bird said. When *that* day comes . . . well, that day comes. (*Short pause.*) And knowing all that, what do you call it now!? (*Short pause.*) You call it love! (*Longer pause, more determined.*) You call it love! Remember it! (10)

While the short play has no conventional plotline, all the scenes that follow further the sense of alienation between the couple, delineate the nature of their personality and psychological differences, and point to the ways in which the very possibilities of love have been coopted by romantic notions (Mrs. Browning's poem), sex for sale ("Love in the Afternoon" advertisements), and the wearying, enervating facts of everyday life. The themes are familiar Albee topics found in other plays, but since here they are embedded in a vaudeville routine, the images are even more unsettling and disorienting because of the dissonance between form and content. In *Counting the Ways*, unlike *Who's Afraid of Virginia Woolf?*, there seems no escape from illusion. Behind the stock characters are actors playing the parts. At one point in the action, Albee calls for a sign to descend suddenly with the words "Entre Scene," and a disembodied voice demands, "IDENTIFY YOURSELVES." The stage directions indicate that the actors playing He and She are then to speak to the audience in their own persons, improvising stories about their personal lives. After the bit, they take up their roles once more, She explaining, "There's more there in the program; you can read it – after the play. I think the author would rather" (23). This unusual break with the fiction of the performance may serve to call attention to the double roles of popular vaudeville teams: familiar to the audience as themselves and as the personas they are identified with in their acts. It also indicates that what is being staged is an act, but one that is controlled not by the volition of the characters but by the rules of the vaudeville act in which they are appearing.

Seven years later, Albee once more borrowed from vaudeville to provide certain structuring elements for *Finding the Sun*, a play commissioned by the University of Northern Colorado and premiered there in 1983.[39] The action is set on a New England beach in August, where eight characters, whose names range alphabetically from A to H, have gathered to enjoy the rays of the sun. In the program notes for the first production, Albee called the work "pointillist in manner," and under his direction the staging resembled an animated version of Seurat's *Sunday Afternoon on the Island of la Grande Jatte*, with characters arranged in isolated groups of two or three, on a three-leveled raked stage, moving only to deliver their lines and then returning to their original places. The technique replicates vaudeville *tableaux vivants*: static pictures sometimes presented as curtain openers or part of playlets on the bill. Before the characters appear, the opening scene in this production, later omitted in the printed version, calls for the light on the empty stage to *"rise from black to full sun fairly quickly, hold four seconds, fade slowly to black."*[40] The next scene (now the opening) introduces the matched pairs: Abigail married to Benjamin; Cordelia married to Daniel, Benjamin's former lover; Edmee, a widow, mother of sixteen-year-old Fergus; and Gertrude, mother of Cordelia, second wife of Henden, who is the father of Daniel. They speak in alphabetical order offering some phrase about the sun, after which they heave a collective "Ahhhhhhhhhh!"[41] The introduction of the ensemble borrows a technique sometimes employed in vaudeville houses which offered a type of "coming attractions," by having all the performers on the bill appear together in front of the curtain. Albee originally used another vaudeville form in the play but later abandoned it; in the manuscript version, Scenes 1 through 11 ended in blackout. He did retain three monologues addressed to the audience: by Henden, Fergus, and Cordelia.

"Oh what a wangled teb we weave," Albee writes in *Marriage Play* and repeats twice in *The Play About the Baby*, indicating his pleasure in the phrase and/or the situation. In *Finding the Sun*, the "wangled teb" is presented but it has too many strands for Albee to weave into any coherent pattern. "Everything proceeds comparatively" says Edmee (perhaps a stand-in for the playwright), emphasizing the pointillist technique (7). To illustrate the principle, Albee has Henden, the oldest, die; Fergus, the youngest, disappear; and Daniel and Benjamin acknowledge their love for each other and their conflicted feelings for the women they have married. However, the balancing act is awkward, and it does not create the effect Albee describes in the program: "The author believes the play examines how we are startled by the inevitable." The characters, with the exception of Edmee, never appear startled, either by death or by attempted suicide; and the audience is given little to surprise or excite them. The only vitality comes from the ensemble presentation, and the monologue bits, particularly Fergus's long and funny speech on the obstacles he faced trying to find corrupting influences in a Grover's Corners childhood, a fine vaudevillian routine. From the excisions of the first scene and blackouts, it would appear that Albee may have started with a vaudeville model in mind, and then shifted, hoping that the "inevitability" of the events he describes would be enough to carry the day. It doesn't.

After the clutter of relationships and stories in *Finding the Sun, Marriage Play*, commissioned by the Vienna English Theatre, and presented there in 1987, returns to familiar Albee territory: husband and wife in a living room talking about their failed marriage. In its form, it also appears to return to a more directly naturalistic style. There are no descending cards, blackouts, voices from above, characters addressing the audience, or actors stepping out of roles. However, certain elements of vaudeville still remain, more successfully handled than in *Finding the Sun*; and they provide much of the power of the play. Again Albee begins in vaudeville fashion, without exposition. The husband, Jack, returns from his office unexpectedly in the middle of the afternoon and announces to his wife, Gillian, "I'm leaving you."[42] Rather than react to his words, she reacts to his language, a defensive strategy that Albee had employed sparingly in *Who's Afraid of Virginia Woolf?* and would use extensively in *The Goat, or Who is Sylvia?* (2002), another husband/wife duel. "Are you having a dalliance?" she asks. "A dalliance; another dalliance. Are you dallying . . . with someone?" (5–6). The repetition of the word renders it humorous, making the act it signifies seem absurd, and shifts the register from content to form. He responds in kind. "My dear woman, this is not to be dealt lightly with. (*Thinks about what he said.*) With *lightly*; dealt with lightly" (6). Ending a sentence with a preposition becomes, at least for the moment, the egregious act, not the ending of their marriage. But Albee is not content with verbal jokes; he also resorts to one of the oldest sight-gags in vaudeville: the rapid exit and reentrance of a character, who then repeats the same lines in hopes of being better understood or eliciting a different response from the addressee. When Jack fails to rouse Gillian, he goes out and comes back in again four times, replaying, with variation, the same opening scene. It doesn't help. His announcement, "I'm leaving you," is still greeted by her sarcasm: "Darn! Ya know, I knew it!? I had a feeling!" (10).

The ninety-minute play is not divided into scenes, as in the preceding two works discussed, nor are there signs demarcating shifts. However, tacit divisions, like those that abruptly change the direction of the action in a vaudeville bill, are present. The first scene might be called "The Revolving Door," the second "The Book of Days," a sequence in which Gillian informs her husband that the book she was reading when he entered was the one she has been writing throughout their marriage. It contains comments on, and facts about, each time they have made love in their thirty-year marriage, "nearly three thousand . . . events" (12), she explains. What follows is an extended act of sorts. He picks a number, she reads the entry, and he critiques the style: "That's nice – Hemingway, but nice" (13), he calls one; "Henry James; an attempt at Henry James" (17), he labels another. It is his turn to seek diversions by resorting to form in order to forestall the pain of content. After several such sequences, the action wears thin, and the subject of separation appears unavoidable. However, in response to Gillian's question, "Have I gotten too old for you? Too . . . ripe? Are you not up to me anymore? Do I *frighten* you?" (23), Jack responds, "Quite a performance," again deflecting the issue. But his ploy doesn't work. "You're not up to this. Rhetoric is beyond you" (24), she shouts at him, and as if to make the point, the action shifts from verbal to physical sparring in a third "scene."

Despite all the anger Albee's couples spew out at each other, this is the only marital fistfight scene in all of his plays, and it is a beauty. Albee carefully describes what he wants. It is to be long, violent, and graphic; "*Can there be blood from his nose, say?*" (25), he asks at the end of the stage directions. The fight comes approximately in the middle of the play, offering the characters and the audience that visceral moment of heightened excitement that physical acts provided on vaudeville bills. However, instead of following this miniclimax with an even stronger one in the last sections of the play, Albee has his husband and wife return to their bitter verbal dueling, many of the thrusts-and-parries sounding like warmed-over and not so funny or so brutal *Virginia Woolf* material. At the end of the play, though, there is the quietus that marks the most moving moment of *Virginia Woolf*. Jack comments, "It's time for the garden; it *would* be time for the garden," that is, were it not for the fact that "I'm leaving you." Gillian's response, which ends the play, is, "I know; I know you are." The stage directions, borrowing from *Godot*, indicate that "*They sit, silence; no movement*" (40). As the title implies, what has been staged may well be their "marriage play," or act, that someday will end, but not this season. "Sad husband, sad wife; Sad day; sad life" (9), Gillian says, echoing *Virginia Woolf*, but at the beginning of the play, not at the end. She knows from the beginning the direction of the action; she has played the part before.

* * *

The final play to date that directly employs vaudeville does so with a vengeance. *The Play About the Baby* is Albee's most extended, obvious, and successful vaudeville work. While still working on it, he admitted enjoying friends' confusion when they would ask its title and he would answer, "The Play about the Baby?" causing them to respond, "But what's the title?" – a variation of the Abbott and Costello routine, "Who's on first," itself a borrowing from earlier vaudeville routines.[43] The play opened at the Almeida Theatre in London in 1998 and was staged in New York in 2001, the first new Albee work to be presented in the city after his successful Signature Theatre season of 1993–94 (which included *Marriage Play, Counting the Ways*, and *Finding the Sun*), and the off-Broadway production of his widely acclaimed *Three Tall Women* (also 1994), which officially marked his "return from the woods" and reinstatement as a major American playwright.

The Play About the Baby is deceptively simple. The cast consists of four unnamed characters: Boy, Girl, Man, and Woman. The younger couple are recently married, deeply in love, sexually engrossed, and, as the play opens, about to have a baby. The older pair, their relationship unspecified, are entertainers. They tell jokes, spin tales, talk in character to the audience, sing, dance, and clown – all done, presumably, to divert attention from their stated aim: to steal the baby. The central structure and action of the play is borrowed from that most common of vaudeville routines, the disappearing act, in which a male magician and his comely female assistant continue a running dialogue with each other and the audience in order to win the spectators' confidence, divert their attention away from the preparations for the trick, and build expectation for some spectacular climax. The high-point of such performances is the disappearance itself, introduced with much flourish and theatricality. Albee follows this pattern closely, except that in his presentation Girl and Boy do not volunteer, and their response to the baby's disappearance is not wonder but anguish and, finally, resignation.

The play is carefully structured to lead up to the disappearance trick. Rapid vaudeville business begins the action. Girl announces, "I'm going to have the baby now."[44] She and Boy exit, sounds of labor and delivery are heard, then a baby's cry, followed by silence, and the couple's immediate reentry, Girl concluding "There" (5), a sign that they can resume their sexual play. From this point on the baby is heard but not seen, a blanket seeming to swaddle its body. Next, Man enters and addresses the audience – "Hello there! Boy, girl? Yes?" – and launches into a monologue about how it seems to take much longer to get to a new destination than it does to return. "Have you noticed that? Hm?" he throws out, the stage directions indicating that if he gets a reply, he is to improvise a response before going on – a common vaudeville occurrence (8). This engagement and questioning of the audience is a way of establishing familiarity, intimacy, and trust, a necessary prerequisite for what is to follow. However, his words are not random; they focus attention

Figure 7. *The Play About the Baby*, Century Center, New York, 2001. With Kathleen Early as Girl, David Burtka as Boy, Brian Murray as Man, and Marian Seldes as Woman.

on the central question Albee is exploring in the play: if "that which we *feel* we've experienced is the same as we have," or the contrary, is "reality determined by our experience of it?" (8).

After Man warms up the audience, Woman arrives, breathless, aware that the act has already begun. While he did not explain his presence, she feels the need to justify hers: "I'm with him. [. . .] To help . . . *him*; to . . . assist *him*," she tells the audience (12). The stage directions indicate that she is to be played broadly, continually winking at the audience and exaggerating her responses. In Marian Seldes's bravura performance in the New York production, she often literally kicked up her heels and curtsied after a verbal turn. At one point Albee even writes a one-word stage direction for Woman's line: "*Groucho.*" In fact, Groucho inflexions punctuate the entire text, marked by the repeated word "whatever," the verbal equivalent to the ironic raised eyebrows (and a punctuation Albee will use with abandon in *The Goat*). The entire play approximates a Marx Brothers' act: obfuscations, digressions, dead-end stories, rapid questioning, and an increasingly frenetic pacing, until the other characters collapse in confusion, exhaustion, and frustration, with Boy echoing Peter's comment to Jerry, "I don't know what you're talking about" (34).

To balance Man's diverting monologues about his failing memory (he is not able to recognize his own mother), and his feigning blindness (in order to experience a museum exhibition by touch), Woman launches into the longest story in the play, describing her search to uncover that well-guarded secret of a writer's "creative process": how you "move your words from your mind to the page" (14). Cleverly, Albee thus conflates the vaudeville magician with the playwright who is often accused of employing tricks or sleights-of-hand, and carefully guarding the secrets of his plays. "What's the matter with these people? Do they think we're trying to steal their tricks?" (13), Woman complains, when a writer she has called is unwilling to have her observe him at work. "I'd rather die," he tells her before hanging up. The implication is that writing and vaudeville acts may have something in common: they both resort to that old "truth and illusion" dichotomy introduced in *Who's Afraid of Virginia Woolf?* Having made the analogy, Albee moves to the main act itself. Aided by Woman, Man announces, "Ladies and gentlemen! See what we have here! The baby bundle! The old bundle of baby!" Then, as Boy and Girl look on in horror, he throws the bundle up in the air, catches it, and proclaims, "Now the really good part, the part we've all been waiting for! (*He takes the bundle, snaps it open, displays both sides; we see there is nothing there.*) Shazaam! You see? Nothing! No baby! Nothing!" (48).

This routine, however, is only a prelude to the final trick: making the young couple deny that they ever had a baby. Albee is once more interested in exploring how individuals adjust their memories to suit their needs and how they create illusions to keep themselves from facing truths too painful to endure. "First we *invent* and then we *reinvent*" Man explains (10), illustrating the point by repeatedly asking Girl and Boy, "You have a baby?" Slowly, their adamant "yeses" give way to ultimate "Nos." The baby disappearing is now complete. Denial as self-protection – an old trick of Albee characters – is played out here with a variation: the young seek not salvation but postponement of their pain until "we're older . . . when we can take . . . terrible things happening? Not now" (51). However, the last sounds they hear are those of the baby crying, indicating that it still exists, and, presumably, that they cannot finally escape the stigmata that, Man argues, come with living: "If you don't have the wound of a broken heart, how can you know you're alive?" (36).

Thirty-six years separate *The Play About the Baby* and *Who's Afraid of Virginia Woolf?* In both, vaudeville becomes a vehicle by which Albee illustrates the human tendency to seek refuge in illusion, when the pain of life becomes too much to bear. Vaudeville may be predicated on artifice, pretense, and trickery, but when performed skillfully it has the potential, through its anarchistic comedy, physicality, and immediacy, to explode the far more dangerous subterfuges that pass for everyday life. Albee may have been too young to recognize the subversive nature of the form when he first saw it; but his early exposure to vaudeville was certainly one of the catalysts that prompted him at seven to declare that he was going to be a writer. At the least, vaudeville was his first model of what theatre could be: immediate, shocking, funny, transformative, and dangerous. And while critics such as Walter Kerr and Robert Brustein rarely "got" Albee's plays, Edward F. Albee II, despite his recorded puritanical tastes, probably would have.[45] He knew the form and he knew it worked.

NOTES

1. See Henry Jenkins, *What Made Pistachio Nuts?: Early Sound Comedy and the Vaudeville Aesthetic* (New York: Columbia University Press, 1992). In Chapter 3, Jenkins argues that these elements constitute the vaudeville aesthetic.
2. For portraits of Edward F. Albee II, see M. Alison Kibler, *Rank Ladies: Gender and Cultural Hierarchy in American Vaudeville* (Chapel Hill: University of North Carolina Press, 1999), p. 16, and Robert W. Snyder, *The Voice of the City: Vaudeville and Popular Culture in New York* (Chicago: Ivan R. Dee, 1989), p. 108.
3. On the Keith-Albee chain, see Kibler's "Introduction," and the Keith-Albee Collection, University of Iowa: http://www.lib.uiowa.edu/spec-coll/MSC/To Msc400/MsC356/msc356.html.
4. Margaret Miner and Hugh Rawson (eds.), *New International Dictionary of Quotations*, 3rd ed. (New York: Signet, 2000), p. 155.

5. Mel Gussow, *Edward Albee: A Singular Journey* (New York: Applause, 2001), pp. 36–38; Philip C. Kolin (ed.), *Conversations with Edward Albee* (Jackson and London: University Press of Mississippi, 1988), p. 194.
6. Gussow, *Edward Albee*, p. 38.
7. Quoted in Richard E. Amacher, *Edward Albee* (New York: Twayne, 1969), p. 37.
8. Gussow, *Edward Albee*, p. 24.
9. Christopher Bigsby, *Modern American Drama: 1945–1990* (Cambridge: Cambridge University Press, 1992), p. 128.
10. Robert Berkvist, "Albee Returns to the Living Room Wars," *New York Times*, January 27, 1980, np.
11. See also Kibler, *Rank Ladies*, which focuses on race and gender depictions; Snyder, *The Voice of the City*, focusing on popular culture; Myron Matlaw (ed.), *American Popular Entertainment* (Westport: Greenwood Press, 1979), focusing on minstrel and ethnic comedy; Albert F. McLean, Jr., *American Vaudeville as Ritual* (Louisville: University of Kentucky Press, 1965), on ritual; and Leigh Woods focusing on American cultural imperialism in "American Vaudeville, American Empire," in *Performing America: Cultural Nationalism in American Theater*, eds. Jeffrey D. Mason and J. Ellen Gainor (Ann Arbor: University of Michigan Press, 1999), pp. 73–90. Any of these topics could be related to further studies of Albee and vaudeville. In this essay, I concentrate on the general vaudeville aesthetic, based on Jenkins.
12. Jenkins, *Pistachio Nuts*, pp. 2–3.
13. Bentley quoted in Ruby Cohn (ed.), *Casebook on Waiting for Godot* (New York: Grove, 1967), p. 61. Albee interviewed by Leslie Blake, "Everything is Albee: Edward Albee Talks about his Legendary Career and his Continued Popularity," TheaterMania website, March 21, 2002: http://www.theatermania. com/content/news.cfm?int_news_id=2026
14. Cohn, *Casebook*, pp. 13, 37, 60.
15. Ibid., p. 171.
16. See Maria Irene Fornes, *The Successful Life of 3* (1965), in her *Promenade and Other Plays* (Baltimore: PAJ Publications, 1987). Also see Stephen J. Bottoms's discussions of plays by Fornes, George Dennison, Tony Barsha, and others using vaudevillian approaches, in his *Playing Underground: A Critical History of the 1960s Off-Off-Broadway Movement* (Ann Arbor: University of Michigan Press, 2004).
17. Antonin Artaud, *The Theatre and Its Double*, trans. Mary C. Richards (New York: Grove, 1958), pp. 142–144.
18. Quoted in Matthew C. Roudané, *Understanding Edward Albee* (Columbia, SC: University of South Carolina Press, 1987) p. 12.
19. Edward Albee, *The Zoo Story* (New York: Signet, 1961), p. 12. Further references will be cited parenthetically in the text.
20. When the act consists of a man and a woman, there are a number of variations on this pattern. Either the woman is the naïve one, as in the case of Burns and Allen, or Jack Benny and Mary Livingston, or she is the brow-beating shrew tormenting her weaker spouse. For descriptions of husband and wife teams in vaudeville, see Jenkins, *Pistachio Nuts*, Chapter 9, and Snyder, *The Voice*, pp. 151–152.
21. On theatre and vaudeville, see Jenkins, *Pistachio Nuts*, pp. 81–85, and Woods, "American Vaudeville."
22. Jenkins, *Pistachio Nuts*, p. 83.

23. Woods, "American Vaudeville," p. 78.
24. On Rose as producer of *Who's Afraid of Virginia Woolf?*, see Gussow, *Edward Albee*, pp. 165–166, 175–176, and Stephen J. Bottoms, *Albee: Who's Afraid of Virginia Woolf?* (Cambridge: Cambridge University Press, 2000), pp. 23–25.
25. When Mike Nichols and Elaine May performed the parts in a short run at the Long Wharf Theatre in 1980, the theatre critic Frank Rich noted that "it's as if Mr. Albee had consciously set out to write the ultimate Nichols and May routine," though he argued that the last act never got "to the marrow." See Rich, "Nichols and May in *Virginia Woolf*, New Haven, May 4, 1980," in *Hot Seat: Theatre Criticism for the New York Times, 1980–1993* (New York, Random House, 1998), pp. 8–13.
26. Edward Albee, *Who's Afraid of Virginia Woolf?* (New York: Atheneum, 1962), np. Further references will be cited parenthetically in the text.
27. Artaud, *The Theatre and Its Double*, p. 142.
28. Video conference with Edward Albee, American Embassy, Tel Aviv Office of Public Affairs, May 13, 2002.
29. Jenkins, *Pistachio Nuts*, p. 8.
30. Ibid., pp. 6–10.
31. Quoted in Gussow, *Edward Albee*, p. 23.
32. Such a reading might also connect Albee to Pirandello, as Anne Paolucci has done in her studies, using different arguments. See, for example, Anne Paolucci and Henry Paolucci, *Hegelian Literary Perspectives* (Smyrna: Griffon House, 2002), Part 5.
33. *The Goat, or Who is Sylvia?* (2002) could be added to the list. Most of the techniques discussed in this chapter find their way – and most successfully – into this vaudeville-cum-tragedy.
34. Gussow, *Edward Albee*, pp. 298, 309.
35. Brustein quoted in ibid., p. 265; Bigsby, *Modern American Drama*, p. 147.
36. Quoted in Gussow, *Edward Albee*, p. 296. The only extended essay analyzing the play is Philip C. Kolin's "Edward Albee's *Counting the Ways*: The Ways of Losing Heart," in *Edward Albee: An Interview and Essays*, ed. Julian N. Wasserman (Houston: University of St. Thomas, 1983), pp. 121–140.
37. Edward Albee, *Counting the Ways and Listening* (New York: Dramatists Play Service, 1978), p. 6. Further references will be cited parenthetically in the text.
38. See the Burns and Allen routine that Snyder describes (*The Voice*, p. 152), which echoes routines in *Counting the Ways*.
39. I attended this opening and wrote a review. See Linda Ben-Zvi, "Review of *Finding the Sun*," *Theatre Journal* 36.1 (March 1984), pp. 102–103.
40. From the unpublished, unpaginated manuscript made available to me in 1983 by the author's agent.
41. Edward Albee, *Finding the Sun* (New York: Dramatists Play Service, 1994), p. 5. Further references will be cited parenthetically in the text.
42. Edward Albee, *Marriage Play* (New York: Dramatists Play Service, 1995), p. 5. Further references will be cited parenthetically in the text.
43. Gussow, *Edward Albee*, p. 388.
44. Edward Albee, *The Play about the Baby* (New York: Dramatists Play Service, 2002), p. 5. Further references will be cited parenthetically in the text.
45. See Edward F. Albee II, "Twenty Years of Vaudeville," *Variety* 72.3 (September 6, 1923).

Figure 8. *The Goat*, publicity image from 2002 Broadway production. With Bill Pullman as Martin, Mercedes Ruehl as Stevie, and Jeffrey Carlson as Billy.

12

J. ELLEN GAINOR

Albee's *The Goat*:
Rethinking tragedy for the 21st century

In the summer of 2000, the comic Ellen DeGeneres commenced a three-month tour of her new stand-up act, *The Beginning*, which was taped at the Beacon Theater in New York City on July 13th and broadcast on July 23rd as an HBO special. The tour was her first since creating a national sensation by coming out during the April 30, 1997 episode of her eponymous situation comedy, *Ellen*. *The Beginning* in part explores DeGeneres's experiences after that media event, humorously yet pointedly discussing the topic of sexual tolerance for consenting adults. In the monologue "Naked People," DeGeneres ponders the highly politicized issue of gay and lesbian marriage, parodying the ludicrous logic of those who oppose these unions:

> The people who are against it, some people say, "Marriage is a union between a man and a woman, and it's always been that way and it should always remain that way; if we change it, and it's between two people of the same sex, then what's next? Someone could marry an animal." That's where they go to right away. These people scare me, and they think we're weird. I don't want to marry a goat; I really don't. I can't imagine marrying a goat; I can't even imagine dating a goat. Getting to the point that you're that serious, to make that kind of commitment. Clearly, you'd live together for a little while, to figure it out and see if you're compatible. But I'm just picturing the apartment with you and the goat. Just photographs all over the place: you and the goat on the beach running, holding hands. You and the goat with the four-for-one photo strip [*DeGeneres mimes the photographic images in the booth*]. Sunday morning you're trying to read the paper; it's trying to eat it. "Don't you eat that section, don't, I haven't read that yet, don't you eat, don't you eat [*DeGeneres mimes chasing the goat and playfully fighting for the paper*]. Come here, I love you, you goat, you little goat [*DeGeneres mimes cuddling with the goat and tickling it under the chin*]." I would think that would be a tough day, even for the most liberal parents, the day you bring the goat home. "Mom, Dad, this is Billy. We are in love."[1]

Almost two years later, on March 10, 2002, Edward Albee's *The Goat, or Who is Sylvia?* opened on Broadway. Albee and the producers had already staged a publicity tease for the show. The campaign included print advertisements featuring a photo of stars Bill Pullman and Mercedes Ruehl (quite possibly designed to alert potential audiences to the involvement of these popular actors), as well as newcomer Jeffrey Carlson, in a seemingly perfect family portrait, except for the goat in their midst. Albee's own cryptic, published remark that the play features "four human beings and one goat . . . and it involves interrelationships" cemented his new work's titillation factor.[2] That sex plays a large part in the interrelationships should surprise no one, and Albee, like DeGeneres, uses the conceit of interspecies congress to both comic and political ends. Whether Albee knew of or saw DeGeneres's performance is less important, however, than the realization that both writers, seizing the *zeitgeist*, deploy strikingly similar logic and narratives to examine the highly charged struggle around sexuality in contemporary American culture.[3] Albee and DeGeneres calculatedly use bestiality as an aberration to make homosexuality appear normal by comparison. DeGeneres makes this argument subtly and humorously in *The Beginning* and then moves on to other issues. But for Albee, these personal predilections represent points along a spectrum of human sexuality that overlap with a larger range of social and private behaviors. *The Goat* tackles some of the most salient of these behavioral intersections to interrogate contemporary culture and humanity within a microcosm of privilege and success. Calculatedly setting his play in a world that closely mirrors that of his professionally accomplished and economically advantaged Broadway and, soon thereafter, regional theatre audiences, Albee refuses to allow a comfortable distance of denial from the environment he depicts or its connection with our lives.

The Goat, which ran for twenty-three previews and 309 performances and received the Tony award for Best Play of the 2002–03 season, depicts two days in the lives of the Gray family. Martin, a renowned architect, is celebrating his fiftieth birthday. Having just received the Pritzker Prize, the award equivalent to a Nobel for his profession, he has also recently been selected for a major design project in the Midwest. He appears to have a wonderful relationship with his wife Stevie, and both of them are handling fairly well the news that their teenage son Billy is gay. Martin's best friend Ross Tuttle, a noted television journalist, arrives to interview Martin on these latest achievements, only to find him distracted and uncommunicative. Ross persuades Martin to tell him what is going on; we learn that Martin has fallen in love and is having sex with a goat he has named Sylvia. Ross takes it upon himself to write to Stevie to tell her of Martin's affair. Confrontation scenes ensue within the family. Stevie ultimately storms out, leaving Martin to deal with his son and then with Ross, who returns after receiving an offstage call from Stevie. The play ends as Stevie reenters, dragging the corpse of the goat Sylvia whom she has slain.

Those who know the Albee canon will see from this brief description that *The Goat* incorporates familiar elements of a number of his plays. Albee grounds many of his dramas in marital relationships gone awry, including *Who's Afraid of Virginia Woolf?* (1962), *A Delicate Balance* (1966), and *Marriage Play* (1987). In terms of style, Albee has always called his plays naturalistic; *The Goat* may reflect our understanding of that tradition much more straightforwardly (some might say viscerally) than others of his works, including the recent *The Play About the Baby* (1998), which strongly resonates with the early Albee whom Martin Esslin famously, if not very exactly, categorized as absurdist. We find in *The Goat* Albee's perpetually razor-sharp wit and arch wordplay, along with the trope that shapes much of his writing, that of painful confession in the service of "the reconstruction of personal and social meaning," as Christopher Bigsby describes it.[4] Albee's prior depiction of an interspecies encounter, *Seascape* (1975), for which he received his second Pulitzer Prize, shares with *The Goat* an impetus toward significance that transcends the world of the play and the individual characters' lives, but he accomplishes this even more fully and explosively in the more recent work. We might return briefly to this earlier play, then, to compare Albee's deployment of a few of the works' shared themes and devices, in order to highlight the ongoing development of his dramaturgy.

Seascape opens on what had by 1975 already become familiar Albee territory – an extended dialogue between a married couple, Nancy and Charlie, who are picnicking on a beach. The pair, retirees who appear to be relatively content with each other, reflect on their life together and contemplate their future options. However, Charlie cannot seem to find the motivation to transcend a "decline," an "inertia" that has settled upon him, and Nancy tries valiantly to discover a way to reinvigorate her husband.[5] She reminds him of a compelling story he once told her of his boyhood desire "to live in the sea," which he clarifies as "under the water" (13). In an extended monologue, Charlie describes picking up heavy stones that would enable him to sink "twenty feet, fifteen" (16) to the ocean floor, where he would stay as long as possible to observe that environment. He explains that he could remain long enough to feel that he was no longer "an intruder" there, but rather "just one more object come to the bottom . . . part of the undulation and the silence. It was very good" (16–17). Through this speech, Charlie conveys a sense of vitality and belonging that we know he no longer feels. Equally important, however, is the relationship between this act of communion with another world and his sexuality. Almost in passing, Charlie recalls that at "twelve or thirteen" he would "strip off" and "learn about my body" when no one could see him, before his descent into the sea (16). Albee thus establishes an intimate connection between Charlie's primal, sexual self and nature; his sexual act appears to enable or lead directly to a (re)union with aquatic life (not to mention its status as a fantasy of regression to the womb). In response to Nancy's questions, "Did the fish talk to you? I mean, did they come up and stay close, and look at you, and maybe nibble at your toes?" (17), he acknowledges that some did.

Charlie admits that, as a child, he wanted to be "fishlike," with "gills," but also retain his human ability to "come home for lunch and bed and stories" (13) – in other words, to inhabit both his primordial and evolved selves with no sense of conflict or danger. He perceives that his attraction to the sea distinguished him from his peers, in that his friends "pined to have wings" – not ones "pasted on" like Icarus, but real ones that would not melt (13). This allusion to the mythic human quest for flight resonates in *Seascape* with the image of man's imperfect, mechanized solution – the airplanes that we repeatedly hear zooming overhead, prompting Charlie to remark, "They'll crash into the dunes one day. I don't know what good they do" (1). Charlie sees little value in an invention that appears to threaten the natural environment and an older way of life. He remarks that "progress is a set of assumptions" (124); he desires, yet also seems trapped in, a transitional state that can neither move forward nor regress. Playing in his title on the nostalgia inherent in the structure of landscape painting – the idea of freezing a moment of nature's time – Albee suggests, through Charlie, a comparable image of the sea.

Near the end of the first act, however, Albee disrupts this idealized perspective and gives Charlie the opportunity both to confront the literalization of his boyhood fantasies of communion with ocean life and to experience that world as he never envisioned it, when he and Nancy see two large sea lizards rising from the sea. The act closes on the humans' hilarious efforts to make sense of this discovery and to prepare for the encounter they are sure will follow. Act 2 opens with a shift in perspective to the anthropomorphized sea creatures, Leslie and Sarah, who are similarly at a loss as to how to respond to the two beings they have spotted. The couples tentatively engage each other, searching for a means of communication and trying to understand each other's lives. We soon perceive parallels between the lizards and the humans, most notably along gendered lines. Sarah shares with Nancy a sense of adventure and discovery; Leslie and Charlie alternate between vulnerability and bravado. Yet it also seems clear that we are to see the humans as the superior creatures – the ones with greater conceptual breadth and, especially, with a wider vocabulary with which to describe their physical and emotional worlds. Charlie's demonstration of the differences between "us" and the "brute beasts" (126) precipitates the inevitable confrontation between the couples; Nancy's subsequent offer of "help" (135) prompts the rapprochement that she and Charlie believe will lead to the necessary evolution of the lizards. But just how far are we to take the willing suspension of disbelief that must accompany our witnessing the interaction of these two couples, who both speak English and who share many common life experiences, despite their ostensible differences? One could argue that Nancy and Charlie's encounter with the Other has more troubling – perhaps even racist – connotations as a dramatization of metaphoric difference, replete with all the dominant culture's misguided assumptions that inhere in such meetings about the relative intelligence, morality, and value of the marginalized group.

Albee has called *Seascape* "a serious play which happens to be very funny," and he might well say the same of *The Goat*.[6] Yet the quarter-century that separates their composition appears to have prompted Albee to refine his concept of man's ambivalent relationship to his environment. In *The Goat*, he more thoroughly integrates this concern with the tensions among nature, civilization, and technology, giving the later piece a feeling of immediacy and urgency which the earlier drama lacks. While the two plays share the obvious plot device of contact with the Other, Albee eliminates the overtly fantastical – though perhaps maintaining, in a different register, the absurd – in order to force us to confront the reality of those tensions as they become more pressing on a global scale. Thus, the crisis morphs from one of existential dimensions to one with more overtly ecological significance, allowing the later drama to transcend the hermeticism of much of his previous writing. *The Goat* reflects Albee's perennial concern with the dysfunctional American family, but the issues his characters face take them (and us) beyond their individual lives and into a more politicized exploration of some profound and far-reaching questions for the Western dramatic tradition and modern civilization itself.

Given the calculated shock value of bestiality, however, it should not surprise us that the reviews of the Broadway production focused on this central act. These responses were mixed, as indeed has been the case throughout Albee's career, with opinions ranging from disgust to adulation. Elysa Gardner, in *USA Today*, pronounced *The Goat* a "self-indulgent mess, in which the cynical, disdainful view of family life that has informed some of Albee's more eloquent works reaches its nauseating nadir."[7] Clive Barnes, by contrast, called it "one of the wittiest and funniest plays Albee has ever

written," while London-based Michael Billington deemed it "a deeply serious and disquieting play about the vagaries of human passion."[8] Perhaps
equally expectedly, a number of reviewers could not resist the opportunity
to flaunt their own wit by crafting punning riffs on the title and plot. Clive
Barnes took the lead in the *New York Post* with his banner headline: "Well
Albee Darned – What's Dad Doing in the Field? It Isn't Kid Stuff." Meanwhile, Barbara Phillips concluded her analysis of "the love that dare not
bleat its name" by rhetorically asking her *Wall Street Journal* readers, "Does
Mr. Albee want to get our goats, or just PETA's? Don't ask me, kids; I'm
still chewing it over."[9] John Simon, in typically scathing fashion, entitled
his review "*Baa*, Humbug."[10] And the critic for the *Toronto Star*, ever conscious of Canada's bilingual citizenry, clearly savored the opportunity to
refer to Ross's letter as a "billy-doux."[11] These jokes and others like them
that shaped many reviewers' responses may reflect discomfort or even hostility toward the play's narrative, demonstrating how effectively Albee created a dramatic world whose actions and concerns could be neither easily
avoided nor dismissed. The critics' quips thus encapsulate Freud's notion
that such humor "will evade restrictions and open sources of pleasure that
have become inaccessible" and will "bribe the hearer into taking sides . . .
without very close investigation."[12] These reviewers valiantly, but ultimately
unsuccessfully, attempted to keep themselves and us at arm's length from
what Albee himself has called "one of the few remaining taboos" in our
culture.[13]

Other critics' resistance manifested itself interpretively, by taking the sexual transgression only as metaphor. Thus Ben Brantley announced in the
New York Times, "The subject is not bestiality but the irrational, confound-
ing and convention-thwarting nature of love."[14] Such readings may in part
stem from Albee's own remarks on the work. In an interview published in
Playbill at the time of the opening, the playwright revealed that *The Goat*
had a second subtitle in addition to *Who is Sylvia?*[15] This other heading,
"*Notes Toward a Definition of Tragedy*," which was not included in the
print publicity for the initial production but now appears in the published
version of the script, seemed to provide an explanation for how the play
could plummet from its sparkling comedic opening to an emotionally devastating conclusion.[16] Critics saw here, too, a connection with the animal at
the center of the conflict, for the original Greek meaning of tragedy is "goat-
song," and historians posit close connections between the themes, narratives,
and characters of tragedy and those of the satyr plays that accompanied,
and may have parodied, them in the ancient festivals. Anne Marie Welsh
of the *San Diego Union-Tribune* thus saw *The Goat* as a religious work,

explaining that its examination of "the longing for pure irrational ecstasy" is linked to the biblical revision of Dionysiac belief into the tale of "God the Father . . . separating the saved from the damned, the sheep from the bad, bad goats."[17]

Even if we take Ms. Welsh's and others' comments as tongue-in-cheek, we may still be forcefully struck by the number of writers reluctant to confront the awful – in the dual senses of inspiring dread and respect – truth of Martin's actions, their meaning, and their consequences. In an interview published around the time of the play's opening, Albee insists that Sylvia is not a "scapegoat":

> I chose the title . . . because I wanted the double goat. There's a real goat and also a person who becomes a scapegoat. It is a play that seems to be one thing at the beginning, but the chasm opens as we go further into it . . . With any luck, there will be people standing up, shaking their fists during the performance and throwing things at the stage.[18]

Albee clearly intends us to take his characters' deeds very literally, and we must grapple with that reality, as well as with the complex, related metaphorical significance of those behaviors that some of the critics also intuited. The heightened tension between reality and metaphor thus marks one of Albee's key dramaturgical developments between *Seascape* and *The Goat*.

Albee has also provided, through his three nested titles, clear indicators of greater engagement with the traditions of comedy, tragedy, and the pastoral, which resonate and overlap within the later play. Albee's third title might suggest that Aristotle's *Poetics* served as Albee's touchstone text, but I would argue that Albee is not as much concerned with the dramaturgical creation and structure of tragedy – in a rethinking of the "six constituent elements" outlined in the *Poetics* – as he is with tragedy's meaning. Thus, Nietzsche's speculations from *The Birth of Tragedy* seem more apt as a gloss on the significance of the tragic form for Albee. In the "Critical Backward Glance" of 1886 that serves as an introduction to the essay, Nietzsche poses some fundamental questions about the origins of tragedy:

> What is the significance, physiologically speaking, of that Dionysiac frenzy which gave rise to tragedy and comedy alike? . . . What does the union of god and goat, expressed in the figure of the satyr, really mean? What was it that prompted the Greeks to embody the Dionysiac reveler – primary man – in a shape like that? . . . Was it not precisely during their period of dissolution and weakness that the Greeks turned to optimism, frivolity, histrionics; that they began to be mad for logical and rational cosmology; that they grew at once "gayer" and "more scientific"? Why, is it possible to assume – in

the face of all the up-to-date notions on that subject, in defiance of all the known prejudices of our democratic age – that the great optimistic-rationalist-utilitarian victory, together with democracy, its political contemporary, was at bottom nothing other than a symptom of declining strength, approaching senility, somatic exhaustion?[19]

Nietzsche was, of course, writing about his own era within the nineteenth century's scientific and political revolutions as well as that of fifth century BCE Athens. Albee's third title suggests that he sees his play as participating in this ongoing theorization of tragedy. The union of man and goat that Albee graphically depicts differs from that envisioned by Nietzsche, just as the Grays' status as democrats (100) bears only the slightest resemblance to the Athenians' concept. Yet Albee's artist Martin – his "master builder" – nevertheless embodies the Nietzschean dualities of creativity and decadence inherent in these moments of astounding achievement at the brink of collapse. As Ross explains for his imagined audience during the interview taping, Martin will be the architect of the "dream city of the future," the $27 billion World City, "financed by U.S. electronics technology and set to rise in the wheatfields of our middle west" (24) – "the wheatfields of Kansas, or whatever," Martin echoes (26). Albee leaves dangling this description of a new Land of Oz, this jarring juxtaposition of nature and industry, this image both ludicrous and frighteningly possible, as Ross vents his frustration with Martin's inexplicable indifference to his recent accomplishments:

ROSS: Probably the most important week of your life . . .
MARTIN: (*Impressed, if uninvolved.*) Really!
ROSS: . . . and you act like you don't know whether you're coming or going, like you don't know where you are.
MARTIN: (*Self-absorbed, almost to himself.*) Maybe it's . . . love or something.

(30)

Ross suddenly realizes what's going on and smartly picks up his cue, saying, "So you're in love. [. . .] Ficky-fack! Humpty-doodle!" (32–33). But Martin resists a crassly sexual interpretation of his behavior, endeavoring instead to explain the circumstances through which he found this love.

Martin shares with his friend an Edenic reverie of the American pastoral ideal – a departure from his urban center toward a rural vista that his own professional vision soon thereafter fuses into the "dream city" design. Reminiscent of Charlie's narrative of escape by descent to the ocean floor and subsequent, life-changing contact with the fish in *Seascape*, Martin describes a trip "about sixty miles out" of town in search of "a real country place" (40) for himself and Stevie. He explains how he drove to the top of a hill, stopped, and the view was . . . well, not spectacular, but . . . wonderful. Fall, you know?, with leaves turning and the town below me and great scudding clouds and those country smells. [. . .] The roadside stands, with corn and other stuff piled high, and baskets full of other things – beans and tomatoes and those great white peaches you only get late summer [. . .] And I was getting back in the car, about to get back in the car, all my loot – vegetables and stuff . . . (*change of tone to quiet wonder*) and it was then that I saw her. (*Sees it.*) Just . . . just looking at me.   (41–42)

Ross asks Martin if he talked to her, and after "*considering*" this, he replies:

MARTIN: Hunh! Yes; yes, I did. I went up to her, to where she was, and I spoke to her, and she came toward me and . . . and those eyes, and I touched her face, and . . . (*Abrupt*) I don't want to talk about it; I can't *talk* about it.
ROSS: All right; let me help you. You're *seeing* her.
MARTIN: (*Sad laugh.*) Yes; oh, yes; I'm *seeing* her.
ROSS: You're having an affair with her.
MARTIN: (*Confused.*) A what? Having a *what*!?
ROSS: (*Hard.*) You're *screwing* her.
MARTIN: (*Sudden vision of it.*) Yes; yes; I'm *screwing* her. Oh, Jesus!   (43)

As Martin begins to see his actions from Ross's perspective, he breaks down, crying out Sylvia's name. Ross, respectfully, asks Martin, "Who is Sylvia?" (44). Martin withdraws a photo from his wallet and hands it to Ross, who guffaws and then realizes the awful truth: "THIS IS A GOAT! YOU'RE HAVING AN AFFAIR WITH A GOAT! YOU'RE FUCKING A GOAT!" To which Martin can only respond, "Yes" (46).

This scene is actually the second in which Martin makes his revelation. Before Ross had arrived, during some "*Cowardesque*" repartee with Stevie (16), Martin had already confessed to the affair, but Stevie takes the disclosure as a joke:

STEVIE: Something's going on, isn't it!?
MARTIN: Yes! I've fallen in love!
STEVIE: I knew it!
MARTIN: Hopelessly!
STEVIE: I knew it!
MARTIN: I fought against it!
STEVIE: Oh, you poor darling!
MARTIN: Fought hard!
STEVIE: I suppose you'd better tell me!
MARTIN: I can't! I can't!
STEVIE: Tell me! Tell me!

MARTIN: Her name is Sylvia!
STEVIE: Sylvia? Who is Sylvia?
MARTIN: She's a goat; Sylvia is a goat! ([. . .] *serious, flat.*) She's a goat. (17)

The dramatic irony of the second admission to Ross makes it all the more powerful; we have heard the answer to the key question – "Who is Sylvia?" – in two registers, parodic and serious. What is the relationship, then, between the two tones of Martin's response and the play's second and third titles, which, taken together, gesture toward both tragedy and pastoral comedy? We may find a connection in Albee's sense of place, in his opposition of the onstage and offstage locales intimately tied to the play's narrative of sex, love, and violence.

Stevie rhetorically muses on the origin of Martin's name for his inamorata midway through their confrontation scene, invoking, yet subtly revising, Shakespeare: "Who is Sylvia/Fair is she/that all our goats commend her" (63). Albee's second title, of course, derives from the song in Act 4 of *The Two Gentleman of Verona*: "Who is Silvia? What is she,/That all our swains commend her?"[20] Northrop Frye famously singled out this Shakespearean play as exemplifying the "green world" of romantic comedy whose "ritual theme" is the "triumph of life and love over the waste land." In Frye's schema, the action of comedy "begins in a world represented as a normal world, moves into the green world, goes into a metamorphosis there in which the comic resolution is achieved, and returns to the normal world."[21] Shakespeare's Silvia is both a specific character, reflecting generosity of spirit and faithful love, and a pastoral ideal, the "nymph" to Valentine's "swain." The goat Sylvia mirrors her both as a real object of love and desire and as part of a contemporary rural and agricultural idyll, a locale equally remote, fertile, and mythic. When Martin retells the story of meeting the goat to Stevie in the second scene, Albee underscores what this green world now signifies: "As I said to Ross, I'd gone to the country . . . to find the place we wanted, our . . . country *place.*" Referring to his search as a quest for "Utopia," Martin also tries to encapsulate their "country needs" – "Verdancy: flowers and green leaves against steel and stone" (64). It would appear that Stevie, whom we first see arranging a bouquet of ranunculus (8), and who eagerly looks forward to the year's first shipment of shad roe (55), shares with her husband a powerful attraction to, yet a deep alienation from, the natural world of farms and wheatfields that have a rarified but indescribably magnetic role in their lives.

While we might see here a continuation of the eighteenth-century dramatic opposition of town and country, we are also more pointedly in the modern dramatic world that, as Una Chaudhuri has noted, characterizes "place as problem" – the "geopathic."[22] In Chaudhuri's analysis, the trope of failed homecoming structures the modern theatre; by a perfect twist of fate, Stevie does not accompany Martin on the day he discovers another home, a different kind of relationship with nature than what they had idealized. He can barely articulate its sublimity:

> it was . . . an ecstacy and a purity, and a . . . love of a . . . (*dogmatic*) un-i-mag-in-able kind, and it relates to nothing *whatever*, to nothing that can be *related* to! Don't you see!? Don't you see the . . . don't you see the "thing" that happened to me? What nobody understands? Why I can't feel what I'm supposed to!? Because it relates to nothing? It can't have happened! It did but it *can't* have! (81)

Albee leaves us to make the eco-connection that Martin violates nature as much through his intimacy with Sylvia as by joining forces with the electronics industry to transform the American heartland, paving over the paradise of the nation's agricultural center to erect the World City of stone and steel that, to contemporary capitalist culture, signifies a utopic future. The line between the comic and the tragic in *The Goat* is intimately tied to place, to the geopathic, to the estranged and tenuous relationship we now have between nature and progress. Sylvia, who becomes an absurd and comic parody of the "kept woman" (61), simultaneously embodies what has gone tragically wrong in Martin's heartfelt longing for communion with nature, for the rediscovery of a natural self. In moving beyond the characters' tentative contact in *Seascape* and their groping toward interspecies understanding, Albee now asks us to imagine fully the consequences of our personal and environmental behavior and its implications for generations to come.

In *History and Class Consciousness*, Georg Lukacs analyzes the radical redefinition of the relationship of man and nature under capitalism:

> Nature . . . acquires the meaning of what has grown organically, what was not created by man, in contrast to the artificial structures of human civilisation. At the same time, it can be understood as that aspect of human inwardness which has remained natural, or at least tends or longs to become natural once more.[23]

And John Berger, in his essay "Why Look at Animals?" suggests that in Lukacs's schema, "the life of an . . . animal becomes an ideal, an ideal internalised as a feeling surrounding a repressed desire" (15). That Martin should act on that desire through bestiality literalizes his extremity of alienation and longing; yet it also evidences his violation of perhaps an even more profound cultural taboo through a graphic illustration of the processes of reification and commodity fetishization endemic to capitalism. Martin's transcendence of that repression, his acting on that desire, reflects the agony of this cultural division of man and nature, the ecstacy of the reunion, and yet also its impossibility for those who would simultaneously reside in the society that has fostered their separation.

As Berger observes, twentieth-century corporate capitalism has ruptured what had previously been, throughout history, the close proximity of man and animal, man and nature. He reminds us of the Descartean internalization, within man, of the "dualism implicit in the human relation to animals" (9), when Descartes theorized the separation of the mechanical, animal body from the human soul. Berger describes the "anguish" that may result from man's attempt to transcend the animal within himself (10). He explains that "animals offer man a companionship which is different from any offered by human exchange. Different because it is a companionship offered to the loneliness of man as a species" (4). And indeed, Martin cries out to us at the end of the play, "Why can't anyone understand this . . . that I am *alone* . . . all . . . *alone!*" (109).

This sense of isolation was conveyed compellingly by the Broadway production, though interestingly, the performances of Bill Pullman and his eventual replacement in the role, Bill Irwin, made this felt in very different ways.[24] Pullman, perhaps best known for his roles as a regular, straight-up, slightly bumbling guy who nevertheless saves the day or gets the girl in such films as *Independence Day* (1996) or *While You Were Sleeping* (1995), brought to Martin a bafflement and almost naive awe at his fate. Irwin, by contrast, capitalized on his extensive experience as a mime, letting his physical neutrality (as in neutral mask) convey a sense of precarious control over profound, conflicting feelings and desires.

Berger, like Martin, depicts the core of this interspecies relationship in vision. In Martin's memories of his initial encounter with Sylvia, he repeatedly references her gaze: "There she was, just looking at me, with those *eyes* of hers" (43). For Berger, the animal

does not reserve a special look for man. But by no other species except man will the animal's look be recognised as familiar. Other animals are held by the look. Man becomes aware of himself returning the look . . . His recognition of this is what makes the look of the animal familiar . . . A power is ascribed to the animal, comparable with human power but never coinciding with it. The animal has secrets which, unlike the secrets of caves, mountains, seas, are specifically addressed to man. (3)

Berger describes here what Albee makes essential in Martin's response to Sylvia. We must believe Martin's conviction that the looks they have exchanged signify a love so powerful as to overwhelm taboo. Albee does not quote beyond the first stanza, but Shakespeare's song from *The Two Gentlemen of Verona* and Albee's exploration of its meaning continue:

> Is she kind as she is fair?
> For beauty lives with kindness.
> Love doth to her eyes repair,
> To help him of his blindness;
> And, being help'd inhabits there.
>
> (IV.ii.44–48)

But we must also understand how others perceive Martin's act, and not just what it means for him privately. Ross Tuttle – ever so close to tattle – writes to Stevie that "because I love you both [. . .] I can't stay silent at a time of crisis for you both, for Martin's public image" (49). Ross, confidant and chorus, as well as the personification of the media, must carry the too-obvious dramaturgical weight of representing the *vox populi* and of setting the wheels of tragedy in motion. Ross emerges as more of a structural device than as a thoroughly developed character. Albee provides little evidence of the foundation for their supposedly long-standing and meaningful relationship, but rather renders Ross the embodiment of the superficiality and hypocrisy of a mediatized identity (an impression reinforced in the Broadway production by the slick, crass quality brought to the role by Stephen Rowe). Ross privileges the salvation of Martin's public self, brutally yet acutely aware that the sanctity of his friend's personal life rests on continued professional success:

> *Me* bring you down!? This isn't . . . embezzlement, honey; this isn't stealing from helpless widows; this isn't going to whores and coming down with the clap [. . .] This isn't the stuff that stops a career in its tracks for a little while – humiliation, public remorse, and then back up again. This is *beyond* that – *way* beyond it! You go on and you'll slip up one day. Somebody'll see you. Somebody'll surprise you one day, in whatever barn you put her in, no matter where you put her. Somebody'll see you, on your knees behind the damn animal; your pants around your ankles. Somebody will *catch* you at it. [. . .] Do you know what they'd *do* to you. The press? Everybody? Down it all comes – your career; your life . . . everything. (108)

Ross's distinction here between two types of "tragic" plots resonates with the astute observation by Michael Feingold in *Village Voice* that "between 1840 and 1920, nearly every working playwright in Paris, London, Vienna, Berlin, Budapest, and New York" wrote a version of the story of marital infidelity that Albee, in "our own transgressive time," has brilliantly extended.[25] Albee thus invites us to consider *The Goat* not only as a work stretching back to the classical era, but also as an extension of a modernist theatrical tradition built upon the foundation of the "problem play" and its attendant critique of the dominant social order. Yet its calculated references to dramatic icons (including Albee himself) and characterological self-consciousness simultaneously mark *The Goat* as postmodern; Martin and Stevie, for example, are exquisitely aware of their status as tragic characters – "MARTIN: What are you doing? / STEVIE: Being tragic" (81) – even as they continue to enact the inescapable fate now controlling their lives.

The Goat is, of course, every bit as much a tragedy for Stevie, whose world unexpectedly disintegrates around her, as for Martin. Stevie controls the center of the play in the tour-de-force confrontation scene with her husband that alternately reveals her humor, fragility, intelligence, and inner strength. In this second scene, Stevie echoes Martin's earlier and still evolving comprehension of acts and sensations he never imagined possible. She describes how "we prepare for things" life may toss our way: "death," "stroke," "emotional disengagement." "But if there's one thing you *don't* put on your plate," she realizes, it's "bestiality" (59). Stevie cannot fathom how Martin can claim to love both her and Sylvia: "But I'm a human being; I have only two breasts; I walk upright; I give milk only on special occasions; I use the toilet. (*Begins to cry.*) You love me? I don't understand" (52). Albee punctuates their agony with Stevie's periodic destruction of the *objets d'art* that grace their tasteful living room. In Mercedes Ruehl's performance, these acts appeared as the physical projections of an internal rage held in tension with the sardonic, barely controlled tone of her dialogue. For Sally Field, who replaced Ruehl in the role on Broadway, the violence of the smashings seemed to take her Stevie by surprise, as she discovered a new, powerful self through the unraveling of her seemingly perfect marriage.

As the *Houston Chronicle* critic Everett Evans observed, Stevie's physical destruction of her surroundings in this scene turns "their perfect living room into a visible manifestation of their shattered marriage."[26] We might see, then, in Billy's offer to help to put the room to rights in Scene 3, following Stevie's departure and his own battle scene with his father, a gesture of hope for the reconstruction of at least one of the family relationships:

> BILLY: Then there's no point in setting all this right.
> MARTIN: (*Sad chuckle.*) It does look pretty awful, *doesn't* it.
> BILLY: Let's do it anyway.   (97)

However, their new rapport must be built on a greater foundation of understanding. Billy thanks Martin for "letting me think you're putting up with me being gay far better than you probably really are" (100). Martin, in turn, must come to accept his son's desires with equanimity, applying his newly gained insights on dominant and marginal practices. Significantly, Billy's conflicted feelings of love for Martin are made manifest in the only moment of onstage sexual contact depicted in the play; Billy kisses his father passionately, and Martin first rebuffs, then holds him, realizing the complexity of his son's emotions, which, as he understands well, can "click over" from one kind of love to another (102). Ross's return just at this moment results in his predictable further disgust and revilement, a response some critics shared, while others felt that Albee had not gone far enough with this alternate taboo of gay incest. The reviewer John Simon was right, of course, in his connection of Sylvia and the "goatishly named" Billy, who, while nearing the legal age of maturity, is still treated by his parents throughout the play very much as a kid. Stevie has already hinted at this link in Scene 2, when she associates the "guileless, innocent, pure" quality that Martin describes in Sylvia's gaze with that of "Billy when he was a kid" (80). She sarcastically expresses relief that Martin is not having a relationship with a male goat (65). But her rage leads her to suggest that Martin will "be fucking Billy next," though he "icily" replies that his son is "not my type" (85). Martin's later anecdote about getting a hard-on when holding his baby, which he insists "wasn't sexual" and "meant nothing" nevertheless must prompt our questioning the lines we feel compelled to draw between acceptable and unacceptable sensations and desires (104–105).

As James Kincaid argues in his study *Child-Loving*, Western culture from the Victorian era onward has fostered an image of children as innocent, pure, and asexual, thereby simultaneously creating a subversive echo of experience, corruption, and eroticism. By "attributing to the child the central features of desirability in our culture . . . we have made absolutely essential figures who would enact this desire" – in other words, the pedophiles and predators on adolescents whom the media both trumpet and abhor. Kincaid exposes this process of Othering, this structure through which we insist violently that these deviants are not us.[27] Albee need not belabor the complexity of this moment of contact, or its ties to the literal and metaphorical significance of Martin's extramarital relationship, to have its impact register. Albee has made his point economically. He confronts the dominant, hetero-normative culture with its designation of gay sexuality as aberrant, and challenges it to rethink not only these categories, but also the impossibility of making clear-cut distinctions among the manifold, polymorphously perverse expressions of sexual desire. As Billy explains ruefully to Ross, "I get confused . . . sex and love; loving and . . . I probably *do* want to sleep with him. (*Rueful laugh.*) I want to sleep with everyone" (104).

Inevitably, Albee concludes his drama through the collision of Eros and Thanatos. Stevie commits an offstage act as passionate and transgressive as that of her husband: a ritualistic murder. When she returns at the end of the play, dripping with blood and dragging the goat's corpse, we see her as a woman ghosted by the spirit of classical tragedy. Her act of violence echoes those of Agave, Medea, and other women driven to extremes by those they loved. In contemporary Western culture, however, the act of butchering an animal holds much less shock value than bestiality. Nevertheless, the explanation Stevie gives for her act forces us to question our perceptions of culpability in the play and the distinctions we make between ourselves and other life forms. Stevie has not killed Sylvia because of Martin's love for her, but because Martin insists the love was reciprocal: "She loved you . . . you say. As much as *I* do" (110). Stevie ultimately cannot accept an equation of herself with another kind of animal, an idea that so radically upsets the traditional cosmic order, long depicted in the Western dramatic tradition by what E. M. W. Tillyard has called the Great Chain of Being.[28] This fundamental disjunction in the couple's understandings of their place in the natural world – this essential conflict between ideas of a hierarchy of life and of an equality of life – thereby alters the theoretical horizon for drama, which heretofore has posited the relationships among men as paramount.

In raising profound questions of what constitutes tragedy for the postindustrial, capitalist twenty-first century, Albee intentionally leaves unresolved whether the salvation of Martin's career and the accompanying destruction of the family's life together will be permanent – whether the protection of the precarious shell will lead to interior rebuilding or to total collapse. Billy's final questioning – "Dad? Mom?" (110) – suggests that all such roles are up for renegotiation, that the radical instability of the family, nature, and civilization that Albee presents can both encompass such acts and demand that we confront them.

> Then to Silvia let us sing,
> That Silvia is excelling;
> She excells each mortal thing
> Upon the dull earth dwelling.
> To her let us garlands bring.
> (IV.ii.49–53)

NOTES

1. Ellen DeGeneres, *The Beginning* (HBO, 2000). (Transcribed from performance recording.)
2. Jerry Tallmer, "Life in Suburbia" (interview with Edward Albee), *Playbill* 118.3 (March 2002), p. 12.

3. In an interview published around the time of the premiere of *The Goat*, Albee claims to have begun the play about three years earlier and finished it in about a year and a half, which would mean that he and DeGeneres were developing their stories of bestiality virtually simultaneously. See Steven Drukman, "The Writing Life," *Interview* 32.2 (March 2002), pp. 106, 110, 181.

4. C. W. E. Bigsby, "Introduction" to *Edward Albee: A Collection of Critical Essays*, ed. Bigsby. (Englewood Cliffs, NY: Prentice-Hall, 1975), p. 8.

5. Edward Albee, *Seascape*, in *The Plays, Volume 2* (New York: Atheneum, 1991), 21. Further references will be cited parenthetically in the text.

6. See Philip C. Kolin (ed.), *Conversations with Edward Albee* (Jackson and London: University Press of Mississippi, 1988), p. 116.

7. Elysa Gardner, "A Perverse Albee Gloats in 'Goat,'" *USA Today*, March 11, 2002, p. 3D.

8. Clive Barnes, "Well, Albee Darned – What's Dad Doing in the Field? It Isn't Kid Stuff," *New York Post*, March 11, 2002, p. 33; Michael Billington, "Bestiality on Broadway," *The Guardian*, April 9, 2002, p. 10.

9. Barbara D. Phillips, "Theater: Animal Passions," *Wall Street Journal*, March 13, 2002, p. A16. PETA is the acronym for the activist organization People for the Ethical Treatment of Animals.

10. John Simon, "*Baa*, Humbug," *New York Magazine*, March 25, 2002, p. 134.

11. "Albee's Goat is Hard to Get," *Toronto Star*, March 17, 2002, p. D2.

12. Sigmund Freud, *Jokes and Their Relation to the Unconscious*, trans. James Strachey (New York: W. W. Norton, 1960), p. 103.

13. Everett Evans, "The Ultimate Two-Fer," *Houston Chronicle*, January 12, 2003, p. 10.

14. Ben Brantley, "A Secret Paramour Who Nibbles Tin Cans," *New York Times*, March 11, 2002, p. E1.

15. Tallmer, "Life in Suburbia."

16. Edward Albee, *The Goat, or Who is Sylvia? (Notes Toward a Definition of Tragedy)* (Woodstock: Overlook, 2003). Further references will be cited parenthetically in the text.

17. Anne Marie Welsh, "'The Goat' Shatters Family's Life," *San Diego Union-Tribune*, May 10, 2002, p. E1.

18. Drukman, "The Writing Life," pp. 110, 181.

19. Friedrich Nietzsche, *The Birth of Tragedy*, trans. Francis Golffing (New York: Doubleday, 1956), pp. 8–9.

20. William Shakespeare, *The Two Gentlemen of Verona* IV.ii.39–40. *The Riverside Shakespeare* (Boston: Houghton Mifflin, 1974), p. 165. All line references are to this edition and will be cited parenthetically in the text.

21. Northrop Frye, *Anatomy of Criticism* (Princeton: Princeton University Press, 1957), p. 182.

22. Una Chaudhuri, *Staging Place: The Geography of Modern Drama* (Ann Arbor: University of Michigan Press, 1995), pp. xii–xiii.

23. Quoted in John Berger, "Why Look at Animals?," in *About Looking* (New York: Pantheon, 1980), p. 15. Further references to this essay will be cited parenthetically in the text.

24. Pullman starred in the original cast with Mercedes Ruehl as Stevie. Irwin and Sally Field replaced them in these roles in September 2002.

25. Michael Feingold, "Albee Contemplates Tragic Victims," *Village Voice*, March 19, 2002, p. 68.
26. Everett Evans, "Alley Stages a Remarkably Human 'Goat,'" *Houston Chronicle*, January 24, 2003, p. 1.
27. James R. Kincaid, *Child-Loving: The Erotic Child and Victorian Culture* (New York: Routledge, 1992), pp. 4–5.
28. See Tillyard's *The Elizabethan World Picture* (New York: Vintage, 1967) for an elucidation of this concept.

13

RUBY COHN

"Words; words . . . They're such a pleasure." (An Afterword)

My title is spoken by FAM in Albee's early short play *FAM and YAM* (1960), which terminates with that character's startled realization that he has just been interviewed. Albee himself has indulged in so many interviews that critics sift through his remarks for those that bolster the particular argument.[1] I will avoid that temptation, quoting only from Albee's drama, his significant domain. Despite the source of my title, I will examine Albee's words in his published full-length plays, considered chronologically. In those plays, the very words about words in the dialogue reflect the pleasure of Edward Albee, a famous American playwright.

Albee's early short plays already display his typical language structures and textures while they further the plot, reveal character, or enunciate theme. *The Zoo Story* (1959) notoriously contains Jerry's monologal dog story as a rhythmic variant on his verbal thrusts at Peter. Jerry's monologue exemplifies one of Albee's main rhetorical patterns, while the other pattern is heard in Jerry's slashes at Peter. Albee's following one-act plays retain these dialogue structures, but the texture can vary. *The Death of Bessie Smith* (1960) again sports only one character with colorful language, and again that character, the Nurse, intersperses her vitriolic taunts (against Father, Orderly, Intern) with short monologues of self-disgust.[2] Albee's satiric *The American Dream* (1961) and *The Sandbox* (1960) are awash with the clichés of middle-class America, and Grandma implies that the American family is mired in illusion.

It is, however, in Albee's most famous play, *Who's Afraid of Virginia Woolf?* (1962), that illusion thrives on a pungent idiom. Only gradually does Albee reveal that George and Martha have grounded their marriage on the illusion of a son. Outwardly conformist – as to the drinking, backbiting, and adulteries of college life – the couple also harbor an "impressive" sadomasochistic language in their "equal battle."

Act 1's "Fun and Games" plunges us at once into verbal warfare, rhythmed by soundplay, questions, exclamations, imitations, repetitions, and repartee. Martha opens and closes the act with the oath: "Jesus." Her insult to

217

George – "What a cluck!" – sonically triggers her Bette Davis imitation – "What a dump!"[3] When Nick and Honey arrive, George boasts about his wife: "Martha's a devil with language; she really is" (20). Martha's diabolic language includes diverse epithets for her husband – cluck, dumbbell, simp, pig, blank, cipher, zero – and she off-rhymes her first of many insults: "You make me puke." (By Act 2 she will call attention to her rhyme of "past" with "last.") Before Act 1 is over, Martha adds to her lexicon for George: sourpuss, muckmouth, prick, swampy, bog, and flop. Although George addresses Martha with the surface courtesies of "dear" and "love," he slyly links her to animals – braying, chewing ice cubes like a cocker spaniel, and yowling like a subhuman monster. Aware of his own verbal dexterity, George twice foists upon Nick his witty "declension:" "Good, better, best, bested" (26). George makes his points sharply, but he repeats phrases for rhythm and emphasis, as in his reference to their son as "the little bugger."

Despite the Act 2 title, "Walpurgisnacht," which connotes a witches' sabbath, it is George who dominates the action. He wittily deflates Nick, and the latter's request for "bourbon" sonically triggers George's "bergin and water" monologue about the boy who shot his mother, and then, when driving, swerved to avoid a porcupine but killed his father beside him in the car. By the time Martha summarizes the story of George's "novel," we are familiar with its events. In this middle act, George's repeated phrase for their son shifts to a "bean bag," which he and Martha indeed volley verbally. By mid-act George charges Martha with revealing his deepest vulnerabilities: "Book dropper! Child mentioner!" (85).

Once the acerbic language of the academic hosts flows freely, it seldom sparks comments in the dialogue itself. Nevertheless, George completes Nick's sentence and corrects his "gangle" to "gaggle" of geese, as he had earlier completed Martha's sentence and corrected her "abstruse" to "abstract" – a correction she rejected: "Don't you tell me words" (44). In turn, George rejects Martha's correction of his "got" to "gotten." Although Martha accuses George of uttering "convoluted" sentences, she is inaccurate; he wounds, not through laborious syntax, but through pace and point. In this drama that thrives on soundplay, George names the evening's games alliteratively: Humiliate the Host, Hump the Hostess, Get the Guests, and Bringing up Baby. George mock-repeats the tale of the courtship of Nick and Honey, which his needling has elicited from the biologist. Despite George's dominance of the Act 2 dialogue, the bedrock remains the thrust-and-parry of George and Martha – to such an extent that she accuses him, "YOU MARRIED ME FOR IT!" (92). As husband and wife threaten "total war" on one another, Martha snaps her fingers, and, suiting word to action, she repeats forms of the verb "snap" to designate the disintegration of their relationship. But the act closes on George's invention of their son's death, which he repeats four times in monosyllables.

The Act 3 "Exorcism" often deviates from the basic thrust-and-parry rhythm. Martha opens the act alone on stage, but she voices a loving duet with the absent George. When Nick enters, she inflicts on him a monologue about her "pointless infidelities." After Martha lies to George that Nick is not a houseboy, the host flourishes snapdragon flowers, while he shouts, "SNAP WENT THE DRAGONS!!!" (119). He throws the flowers at Martha and Nick, one at a time, also echoing her earlier "snaps" at him. George trumps Martha's verbal "snaps" by joining image to word in his exorcising of dragons of illusion.

The son's death scene is Albee's rhythmic triumph. As Martha begins a sentimental biography of their son, George begins to chant the Requiem Mass in Latin. The son then serves George and Martha as a weapon, in which the words "Lies" and "Liar" boomerang between them. For a long moment George again recites the Requiem Mass while Martha repetitively defends their son against "the mire of this vile, crushing marriage" (133). Albee's scenic direction stipulates that husband and wife *end together.* When George finally announces their son's death, it is by a familiar accident: "with his learner's permit in his pocket, he swerved, to avoid a porcupine, and drove straight into a [. . .] large tree" (135). At the departure of Nick and Honey, the hosts' dialogue strips down to monosyllables, for husband and wife abandon rhetoric along with illusion. When George sings the title refrain – "Who's afraid of Virginia Woolf?" – Martha admits that *she* is (140).

Albee's dialogue has repeated references to "True or False" and "Truth versus Illusion," but it is problematic whether truth can survive in the world of the play, and Albee leaves it problematic. Dawn breaks on Martha's fear, and our enduring impression is not that of exorcism but of skillful verbal exercise. In spite of thin motivation of the characters, Albee's drama rests on its brilliant repartee, bolstered by subtle sonic effects. From its first production on, I have yet to see it fail on the stage (or in film), as its actors rise to its diapason of rhythms.

Who's Afraid of Virginia Woolf? sets the register for Albee's subsequent plays – educated urban American speech laced with inventive gibes and colloquialisms, including obscenities. His next play, *Tiny Alice* (1964), places generically named characters in a castle in an undesignated country, but the speech remains unmistakably American. Albee's protagonist is Brother Julian, a lay brother and secretary to a cardinal. Yet the play opens on a Lawyer talking gibberish to two caged cardinal-birds, a harbinger of other puns in Albee's dialogue (lay, pray, organ, solicitor, common-law). Lawyer calls them to our attention in Scene 2: "Puns and chuckles?"[4] In Scene 1, Lawyer and Cardinal virulently express their reciprocal loathing. Although each of them speaks of himself in the plural, they also splinter into their separate "I"s – a point which Lawyer underlines. Scene 2 also toys with its own dialogue; Butler twice mentions metaphors, and he summarizes the period that is missing from Julian's dossier with the line, "Six years in the loony bin for semantics?" (36). Julian protests that his search for God was not mere semantics, but when he hazards a remark about "rather tiresome exchanges," Butler retorts: "None more than this" (29). When Lawyer informs Butler that there is no such word as "screep," courteous Julian expresses pleasure at its "onomatopoetic ring" (31).[5] Julian, Cardinal's emissary to receive Miss Alice's gift to the Church, again disdains semantics (as to whether the small castle is a model or a replica).

In each of Albee's three acts, Julian gives vent to monologues in which faith is imbued with sexuality. Julian's Act 1 monologue describes an experience with a woman who sometimes hallucinated that she was the Blessed Virgin Mary, and Miss Alice in counterpoint punctuates Julian's recital with short phrases of her own desirability. Julian's Act 2 monologue is another zoo story, with Julian-gladiator-martyr attacked by a lion. While Julian indulges in rhapsodic rhetoric, Miss Alice first proposes marriage to him, then spurs him to sacrifice himself to Alice, whom she invokes in the third person. Act 2 introduces another form of counterpoint when Butler and Lawyer play at being Lawyer and Cardinal; then both converge on an absent Julian. Counterpoint is also present when Miss Alice "alternat[es] between a kind of incantation-prayer and a natural tone" (61–62).

Although Miss Alice has provoked Julian to admit that "Articulate men often carry set paragraphs" (77), he begins Act 3 with a series of bewildered questions. After Julian's offstage wedding (with Cardinal officiating), the whole cast of five assembles for the first time – each to offer her or his own toast. Shot by Lawyer, Julian understands nothing and calls on God for help: Butler recognizes Julian's phrases from Psalm 13. Left alone to die, the bridegroom recalls other biblical phrases, and yet his paragraphs do not sound "set." Julian eclipses his gunshot wound with thoughts of a childhood injury, before growing aware that he is dying. When Julian sees a light move in the model castle, he prays to his God, whom he equates with the Alice that the four other characters have urged him to accept. His dying monologue lasts more than ten minutes in the theatre, and some counterpoint is sorely needed.

Indifferent to the malice of the other men, Julian's three monologues pivot on his confusion between illusion and reality: his sexual experience may have been a hallucination; his martyrdom experience trembles between gladiator and wild beast (his tenses tremble between present and past); and he dies in a crucifixion position, even as he couples God with Alice. Julian's last monologue borrows biblical phrases, to draw an unbiblical realization: "Ah God! Is that the humor? THE ABSTRACT? . . . REAL? THE REST? . . . FALSE?" (114). Earlier, Lawyer has colloquially prophesied the conclusion of the play: "How to come out on top, going under." Julian may come out on top, but Albee does not, in this sordid sale of a man's loquacious soul to a conspiratorial religion, abounding in overly self-aware dialogue.[6]

Thereafter, Albee returned to middle-class America and its comfortable, discomfiting families. Four family members people *A Delicate Balance* (1966) – the head of the household Tobias, his wife Agnes, her drunken sister Claire, and the couple's often-married daughter Julia. The drama's drinking and talking convey the impression of a diluted *Who's Afraid of Virginia Woolf?*, which also ends at dawn. Each of the middle-aged, middle-class sisters states the play's theme, Claire crisply ("We can't have changes – throws the balance off") and Agnes convolutedly: "There *is* a balance to be maintained, after all, though the rest of you teeter, unconcerned, or uncaring, *assuming* you're on level ground . . . by divine right, I gather, though that is hardly so."[7]

The play is never called "the Trial of Tobias," but that sums up the plot. In the Friday night Act 1, his terror-driven friends Harry and Edna seek refuge in his home. In the Saturday night Act 2, Tobias assures his friends of their welcome, but his daughter Julia reacts hysterically to their presence. In the Sunday morning Act 3, the friends leave, and the delicate family balance is preserved. In this flaccid society, forty years of friendship prove to count for nothing.

Abjuring the verbal pyrotechnics of *Who's Afraid of Virginia Woolf?* and *Tiny Alice*, respectively, Albee nevertheless calls attention to his language. Julia's word "ilk" and Claire's word "pudenda" elicit comment, but otherwise the characters use an everyday vocabulary – though Agnes and Tobias may differ on the meaning of epigram and aphorism. For all the simple lexicon, the four family members speak in different rhythms, and they are aware of lapsing into clichés, with their "as they say." Agnes varies this by misquoting Shakespeare with "as the saying has it," and by referring to the atomic bomb with "as those dirty boys put it." Agnes begins, ends, and tries to mediate the drama with intricate sentences, and before Edna's Act 3 departure, she adopts the convoluted style of her best friend. Since Agnes deploys her speech as artifice, she is most aware of language; thus, she corrects her own phrase "dropped upstairs," she apologizes for her articulacy, and she announces to Tobias that they become "allegorical" as they age; she underlines the accuracy of Claire's name in her sister's clarity of vision.

Early in Act 1, the self-declared drunk Claire mocks the speech of Tobias – "snappy phrase every time" – but it is she, rather than her brother-in-law, who erupts in snappy phrases, if not "every time." Hers are the wisest and wittiest lines of the play. Less snappy are her monologues in each of Act 1's two scenes – about her performance at AA and about shopping for a topless bathing-suit. Her brother-in-law (and former lover?) tops her with three monologues. His Act 1 cat story predicts his rejection of his friends. In Act 2, prompted by Agnes's distinction between Julia's situation and her actions, he explodes in a graphic (and interrupted) monologue on his daughter's hysterics. In Act 3 Tobias rises to what Albee in his scenic directions calls *"an aria,"* replete with *"genuine [feeling] and bravura at the same time"* (87).

Sparing of imagery, Albee plays upon the verb *want*, meaning both wish and lack, to dramatize the delicate family balance. Claire wishes Agnes to die but does not know whether she wants it. A hysterical Julia makes a chant of wanting. In Act 2 Agnes needles Edna: "What do you *really* . . . *want?*" (59). After a few minutes, Edna replies, "if all at once we . . . need . . . we come where we are wanted, where we know we are expected, not only where we want" (65). In Tobias's final aria, he tries to have it both ways: "I WANT YOU HERE!" and "I DON'T WANT YOU HERE! I DON'T LOVE YOU! BUT BY GOD . . . YOU STAY!" (88). However, his *illusion* of friendship is what stays with us.

Illusions disappear from Albee's next full-length play, *All Over* (1971), which should probably be paired with the one he wrote nine years later, *The Lady from Dubuque* (1980). (Between these two plays, in 1975, came the Pulitzer Prize-winning *Seascape*, whose language is as juvenile as its premise, and on which I therefore refrain from comment.) Both try to dramatize the process of dying, about which his Long-Winded Lady also speaks in the more experimental *Quotations from Chairman Mao Tse-Tung* (1968) – in which Albee seeks a fugal effect in excerpting from Mao's Red Book and from a Will Carleton poem, in order to play these fragments against his original words as spoken by the Long-Winded Lady. With little interaction between his characters, drama is sparse. By contrast, *All Over* lacks quotations, and it sports interaction between its characters; yet the dominant impression is again elegiac rather than dramatic.[8]

The title phrase – "all over" – closes the play's dialogue, and resounds punningly throughout. During the course of the play, a famous man dies; it is finally "all over" for him, but that man's impact has been felt everywhere on stage, or "all over." Anonymous, the characters are designated only by their relationship to the dying man – Wife, Mistress, Son, Daughter, Best Friend, Doctor, and Nurse. Each of these characters utters at least one monologue, usually in colorless educated sentences (which does not preclude slang), and sometimes the monologues are irrelevant to the main action of dying. Even though the speech of the characters is undistinguished, a few of them are self-conscious about it. Mistress, who has summoned the group, quotes the dying man's distaste for the phrase "to be dead."[9] She refers to her irregular situation as "what I believe is called my . . . status" (39). She charges Daughter with: "accus[ing] me before of being – what is that old-fashioned word? – a gold-digger" (69). In one of her several self-indulgent monologues, Mistress stipulates: "There is no allegory here" (70). Above all, she lectures Daughter on the poverty of *her* lexicon: "What words will you ever have left if you use them all to kill?" (64).

Like Mistress, Wife summons memories dominated by her husband of thirty years, and when Daughter wishes to speak of the dying man in the present tense, Wife attacks her grammar: "Semantics from a C minus?" (13). She seems unaware that semantics involves meaning, and not verb tense. In true Albee style, Wife loathes both Son and Daughter, but only the latter utters colloquialisms – usually sneering: "Mistress is a pretty generous term for what it's all about, isn't it? So is *kept*. Isn't that *another* euphemism?" (43). When Daughter resorts to an obscenity – "Fuck yourself" – Best Friend feels that he has to explain: "It's usually said to men, but even there it's a figure of speech" (65–66).

The problem with *All Over* is that there are too many speeches, and too few figures of speech. In *A Delicate Balance*, flaccid language reflected the flaccidity of the characters, but Claire and Agnes, antagonistic sisters, varied the rhythms of exchange. In *All Over*, Daughter alone bursts into colloquial barbs, but they are inadequate to leaven a moribund dialogue.

The Lady from Dubuque is complementary to *All Over*, but in the later play Jo, the dying wife, is volubly onstage. In contrast to the punning title of the earlier play, this title depends on the recondite knowledge that Harold Ross, the first editor of the *New Yorker*, declared that his magazine was not intended for the little old lady in Dubuque. However, Albee's lady from Dubuque is stylish and sophisticated, and she travels with an elegant black man. Before their entrance at the end of Act 1, three couples play a game of Twenty Questions or Who Am I?, while also indulging in offensive recriminations. After the departure of the guests, and the retreat upstairs of the husband Sam and his agonizing wife, the mysterious couple take command of the stage. This time Albee gives his allegorical figures names, Elizabeth and Oscar.

Act 2 takes place the next morning, when Sam in his nightshirt finds the strange couple and insists on knowing who they are. Sam's erstwhile friends arrive and accept Elizabeth's explanation that she is Jo's mother, come from Dubuque, but Sam disputes this. The "friendly" jibes continue from the previous night. When Jo makes her painful descent, the lady from Dubuque comforts her. When Oscar in Sam's nightshirt carries Jo upstairs (presumably to her death), it is with Sam's soothing words of Act 1. The two strangers can then depart, much like the emissaries of *Tiny Alice*.

In *The Lady from Dubuque*, the criss-cross insults and drunken colloquialisms of Act 1 seem *déjà entendu*. Jo, the dying woman, has a more virulent tongue than her guests, but Albee also gives her maudlin expressions of love for her husband, whom she calls Sambo. Vituperation and suffering do not fuse, and Albee also introduces a new verbal device that further dilutes emotional intensity. In the one-act *Counting the Ways* (1976), written four years earlier, Albee experimented with two characters, who sometimes addressed their audience directly. But in *The Lady from Dubuque*, all eight characters address the audience directly, and often this address consists of a mere repetition of what has already been said "in character."

The lady from Dubuque, who claims to be Jo's mother, does not speak like an Iowa farmwoman, yet she maintains that she learned on her farm that the only important question is "Who am I?" – the subject of the friends' Act 1 game. Compared to this significant question, the lady declares, "All the rest is semantics."[10] She does not seem to know that semantics means *meaning*. However, it is her companion Oscar whom Albee invests with (too much?) linguistic variety. He quotes Blake and awakens Sam with the French "Voilà!" He sports baby talk, fake Japanese, and minstrel-show dialect. He uses derogatory words for his race and mocks a breakfast of "corn pone and grits." He calls attention to his adjectives, mentions the old-fashioned quality of the words "swell" and "goose" (as a verb), and even questions his own word "spillage." When he puts Sam to sleep, he concocts an elaborate spoonerism – "to the dreap and deemless," for "dreamless sleep" (53). He often addresses the audience directly, and he is the only one to be "chummy" with them. For all Oscar's versatility, however, Albee's language never rises to the pain he renders too easily with howls and tears.

The next play Albee published was *The Man Who Had Three Arms* (1983); that man, called Himself, also has an extensive vocabulary, and the play itself takes the form of his lecture. Albee therefore features Himself's many remarks directly to the audience. Secondary characters, Man and Woman, briefly play several roles that Himself merely describes. Yet for all Himself's loquacity, he comments only once on his language: "I dare be articulate, coherent." He also dares to pun about his third arm – bearing arms, armed for anything, twist the arm, up in arms. Himself accepts the American Dream, and he profits famously from his third arm; are we to care when the arm disappears, to be replaced by a jokey substitute? Albee's scenic directions are so coy that it is hard to believe that he took *The Man Who* seriously. A titular "three" brought Albee luck, however, since his next major play was *Three Tall Women* (1991).

Like *All Over, Three Tall Women* is set in a wealthy American bedroom, where someone is dying. More importantly, A is reliving fragments of her long life. In Act 1 the characters B and C are a caregiver and a legal secretary, but in Act 2 they become younger selves of A. Although the A of Act 1 is weepy, fragmented, and forgetful, she is controlled and rational in Act 2; overall she is entirely consistent as to character – self-absorbed and imperious, yet dependent and pathetic.

Among Albee's accomplishments here is a language that rarely calls attention to itself, but I cite a few exceptions. The play opens on C correcting A as to her age, and B in turn corrects C's grammar, as well as explaining to her that A uses "person" as a figure of speech. B helps A to find the words "ornate" and "African," and she lingers over A's old-fashioned phrase "get fresh." Only in Act 2 does B underline her joke as a joke; A's husband has one glass eye, so it is literally true that he "had his eye on me."[11] In both acts it is usually B who utters the sentence: "And so it goes." Once she varies this with, "That's the way it goes." The very ordinariness of the cliché phrase enhances the pathos of time passing.

In this late play, Albee uses his practiced structures with a difference. Instead of the thrust-and-parry of earlier plays, only the A of Act 1 makes occasional thrusts at B and C, whom she pays, as she insists on reminding them. Rather than ad hominem insults, A mouths racial insults – little Jew, uppity nigger, wop – without an awareness that they *are* insults. A dominates the dialogue of Act 1, but she rarely speaks a monologue of any length until her climactic story of the diamond bracelet on her husband's "pee-pee." That monologue, nominally interrupted, develops credibly and rhythmically. The subtext is A's horror of fellatio. With understated irony, Albee has A boast about being tall and strong, just before she succumbs to the stroke that finally kills her.

Since a dummy of A lies in the bed throughout Act 2, that act presumably takes place in A's mind, and all three aspects of her self gradually break into monologue – B and C about their respective lovers, and A and B about their son. Just before the play's end, each of them soliloquizes about the happiest time of her life. As is fitting for someone twenty-six years old, C looks forward to the future; B from her mountain peak of middle age sports a few obscenities and colloquialisms. A's final, rambling monologue shows rare self-awareness: "None of that 'further shore' nonsense, but to the point where you *can* think about yourself in the third person without being crazy" (53). A proceeds to do just that, and she realizes that "There's a difference between knowing you're going to *die* and *knowing* you're going to die. The second is better; it moves away from the theoretical" (53). And the pretentious. Finally, A accepts death simply: "That's the happiest moment . . . When it's all done. When we stop. When we can stop" (53). Her energy has driven a play that lives almost entirely in its language. Both in and out of their few monologues in Act 2, A, B, and C address the audience directly, but redundancy is avoided as each of them muses to us, in strong, tall words.

Repetitions run rife in Albee's next play to be published, *The Play About the Baby* (1998). A generation separates Man and Woman from Boy and Girl, who are nevertheless old enough to have a baby – perhaps. As Girl mimes its birth, Boy breaks into an interrupted monologue involving his broken arm. Despite his pain, Boy is curiously pedantic in his account; about whether the arm was broken "for" him, about calling guards, not guard dogs. Once Man enters, he addresses the audience in completely disparate monologues about deceptive distances and about not remembering his mother at a party. He concludes by warning us that truth and reality are "tricky."

Woman's entrance and Boy's reentrance occur almost simultaneously, and though Boy "*wears a towel only*," he claims to be mountain climbing, in a sexually suggestive account. When Woman is alone on stage, she addresses a monologue directly to the audience, asking our forgiveness for her "seeming discontinuity," and discontinuity is exactly what we hear as she rambles on about how "creative types" create.[12] She even wheedled a novelist: "What I really want is to watch you . . . uh . . . move your words from your mind to the page" (14). And we imagine how Albee's words move from his mind to this woman, as she barely glances at Boy and Girl nakedly streaking, but concludes enigmatically: "Now you know who I am *not*, what I do *not* do. As for who I am and what I *do* do, stay tuned" (14). During most of Act 1 the two couples do not interact. Within their several monologues a few phrases are repeated, but the single word "hard" is pleasurably uttered in the short-sentenced exchanges of the young couple. They mean it sexually, but we can hear it as insensitive.

Although Man and Woman have appeared separately, he praises her "splendid yarn" and launches on one of his own, about pretending to be blind so that he could "see with [his] fingers," including the penis of a bronze boar (17). Abruptly, Man concludes his monologue with words about the baby: "How much [do] they need it? [. . .] As the lady said, Stay tuned"

(18). He is replaced by Boy and Girl exchanging endearments. They then refer to their respective pasts. Girl has evidently had her fortune told by a gypsy, and this triggers Boy's interrupted monologue about the gypsies' bag trick and their kidnapping of babies. Girl worries that they may "injure us beyond salvation" (23). When the young couple fall silent, Man and Woman exchange heated barbs, but soon Woman veers into another discontinuous monologue about being a model for a painter. Man not only interrupts her, but also contradicts almost all she says. At one point Woman sums up her tale with a spoonerism: "Oh, what a wangled teb we weave" (25), and Man labors the phrase. (So does Albee; he had already used that same spoonerism in *Finding the Sun*.) Man reacts to Woman's literary clichés: "Nobody talks like that!" (26). When Woman concludes her long monologue, Man applauds her but then turns his attention to the young couple and their baby, announcing, "We've come to take the baby." Man overrides their protests: "What is it you don't understand? The noun 'baby'? The verb 'take'?" (28). The act closes with the young couple in panic.

Act 2 begins with Man's joshing the audience about how they spent the interval, but then it segues into a recapitulation of the end of Act 1; the same words are now shaded with a more sinister meaning. The repetition serves as a prelude to Albee's most musical rendition of semantics. Boy lards his empty threats with obscenities while Woman corrects Man – "[Everybody wants] *her* baby" (32) – and explains that this is "generics" (rather than gender). Man banters again before abruptly boasting, "I've touched the golden dick. Have *you*?" (34). This becomes his signal for intertwining in new contexts fragments of the previous monologues – Boy's broken arm, hospital visit, gypsy thief, and mountain climbing; Man's pretended blindness and non-recognition of his mother; Woman's painter lover and her naive interview. Again and again, Man and Woman assail Boy and Girl with familiar phrases until Man announces that he is putting the baby "in quotes." As they all narrow down to monosyllables (except for the word "baby"), Girl and Boy in turn renounce the familial illusion of their baby. At the last as at first, Boy and Girl are alone on stage; though they have sacrificed the baby, they can still hear it cry. Perhaps they have answered a question that Man has asked in different forms throughout Act 2; its last avatar is, "Without wounds, what are you?" (50). Earlier, Boy and Girl had feared that they would be injured "beyond salvation," but finally their salvation lies in the verbal injury that Man and Woman have inflicted on them – with Albee's echoic mastery.

After the complex and varied rhythms of *The Play About the Baby*, both *Occupant* and *The Goat, or Who is Sylvia?* (of the same year, 2002) retrench. *The Goat* retreats to a realistic surface, for all its preposterous premise, and its verbal techniques are limited. *Occupant*, namely the American sculptor Louise Nevelson, is interviewed after her death, so the play has a link to the lecture format of *The Man Who Had Three Arms*. I have chosen to restrict my examination to Albee's published plays, but I indulge myself with one paragraph on the superb *Occupant*. When the actual Louise Nevelson was in hospital with lung cancer, she had her name removed from her door, substituting "Occupant." In Albee's two-hander, he puts the title to more telling use when Nevelson declares, "You're going to . . . *occupy* that *space* . . . if it kills you."[13] In the dramatization of that occupation, Albee is abstemious of verbal devices. We hear about Louise Nevelson, born near Kiev as Leah Berliawsky, who arrives in Rockland, Maine as a child. Albee makes her aware of the words she uses in what is essentially a long, interrupted monologue. Man's only function is to *elicit* that monologue in a post-death interview. Occasionally, Nevelson hesitates before a word; more often she asks specifically – "What's the word?" Usually she finds it herself, but she accepts Man's word "revelation" for the idea that her driftwood should be vertically glued and painted black, white, and gold. She does not accept Man's word "metastasized." Louise Nevelson, American sculptor, emerges as a fourth tall woman in Albee's drama, and this woman invented herself. Only when Man describes her memorial service at the Metropolitan Museum of Art do we appreciate her early resolution: "You don't fit in – so you make everything fit to you." Her sculpture and Albee's *Occupant* have endowed us with that "fit." Albee dramatizes his friend affectionately, without ever diminishing her monstrous ego, or her awareness that words are not her medium.

Nor are words the medium of the married, fifty-year-old architect who is the protagonist of *The Goat*. (Beckett's Molloy wrote, "I would have made love with a goat, to know what love was." Could this sentence have inspired Albee's play?) Devoted to his wife Stevie and his gay, teenage son Billy, the love-smitten architect Martin is absent-minded about the interview which will be conducted by his best friend Ross. Martin may be absent-minded, but he is very present-minded about words. Having taught Stevie that the plural of ranunculus is ranunculi, he imposes on Ross the plural of bimbo as bimbi. Martin demurs over Ross's claim that he is the architect's oldest friend, choosing to interpret the superlative as an age-designator. Martin appreciates Ross's word "dandled" for his infant son, and he responds to Ross's shock at his goat-love: "You say fuck a lot."[14] In Scene 2, when Stevie confronts Martin with Ross's letter about the goat, the accused husband reacts to its style: "Tidings? [. . .] Jesus! Of comfort and joy?" (51). To Stevie's rage at Ross's letter, Martin replies by mocking her imagery, so that she apologizes: "Women in deep woe often mix their metaphors" (77). Martin corrects her word about the goat "bleating": "That's sheep." So, too, he corrects her grammar – not goats, but *a* goat. For his communion with the goat, Martin finds the Joycean word "epiphany" (82). Later, Martin calls the attention of his son Billy to *his* mixed metaphors, and as Billy grows increasingly disturbed, Martin emphasizes that he is speaking English; "one of your courses." He virtually congratulates his son on his insult: "Semanticist!" (94). In Scene 3 Martin paraphrases Stevie's parting words so that Billy can grasp their meaning, which is not quite what a semanticist does.

It is not semantics that is at fault in *The Goat*. A Noël Coward parody in Scene 1 furthers the plot, but it is not sufficiently telling to bear repetition by Stevie in Scene 2. Most unworthy of the say-it-again technique is Ross's letter, which Stevie quotes twice. Near the end of the play, Ross in person castigates Martin, who retorts, "Do you have any other words? Sick and Jesus? Is that all you have?" (105). Albee has a few more in *The Goat*, but the words and the pretentiously tragic theme are ill-matched.

To sum up briefly, I hope I have shown that Edward Albee tailors his dramatic language to the specific play. Almost always he limits his register to educated, middle-class American English, with an awareness of slang and colloquialism. For all his musical analogies in interviews, Albee is most subtle when he remembers that words *mean*, as he displays the devices at his command – soundplay, witty barbs, associational monologues (whether interrupted or not), and direct address to the audience. His vocabulary may well be the most varied of any American playwright (how does one count the words?), but such variety is not necessarily dramatic. His linguistic pinnacles seem to me the sonically inflected verbal patterns of *Who's Afraid of Virginia Woolf?* and the discontinuous obliquities of *The Play About the Baby* – both eroding pernicious family pieties.

<h3 style="text-align:center">NOTES</h3>

1. See Lea Carol Owen, "An Annotated Bibliography of Albee Interviews," in *Critical Essays on Edward Albee*, ed. Philip C. Kolin and J. Madison Davis (Boston: G. K. Hall, 1986).
2. It is problematic as to how long a speech must be before it is defined as a monologue, but in the main I evade this problem by remembering a monologal feeling in performance. Another problem about monologues is the following: Can a monologue be interrupted by another person? I evade that problem by stipulating that only perfunctory remarks (not interactive dialogue) punctuate a monologue.
3. Edward Albee, *Who's Afraid of Virginia Woolf?* (Harmondsworth: Penguin, 1965), p. 11. Further references will be cited parenthetically in the text.
4. Edward Albee, *Tiny Alice, Box and Quotations from Chairman Mao Tse-Tung* (Harmondsworth: Penguin, 1971), p. 30. Further references will be cited parenthetically in the text.

5. Mel Gussow, in *Edward Albee: A Singular Journey* (New York: Simon and Schuster, 1999), traces the autobiographical origin of this neologism, though the word does not appear in his Index.

6. Anne Paolucci, in her book *From Tension to Tonic: The Plays of Edward Albee* (Carbondale: Southern Illinois University Press, 1972), expands on the language of the play, which she admires unreservedly. Albee evidently abridged Julian's monologues in a 2000 revival, but he did not revise the unbelievable religion of *Tiny Alice*.

7. Edward Albee, *A Delicate Balance* (New York: Samuel French, 1967), p. 48. Further references will be cited parenthetically in the text.

8. Thomas P. Adler is particularly discerning about *All Over* in *Edward Albee: Planned Wilderness*, ed. Patricia De La Fuente et al. (Edinburgh, TX: Pan American University, 1980).

9. Edward Albee, *All Over* (London: Jonathan Cape, 1972), p. 4. Further references will be cited parenthetically in the text.

10. Edward Albee, *The Lady from Dubuque* (New York: Dramatists Play Service, 1980), p. 64. Further references will be cited parenthetically in the text.

11. Edward Albee, *Three Tall Women*. Published in *American Theatre*, September 1994 (pp. 39–53), p. 49. Further references will be cited parenthetically in the text.

12. Edward Albee, *The Play About the Baby* (New York: Dramatists Play Service, 2002), pp. 12–13. Further references will be cited parenthetically in the text.

13. Edward Albee, *Occupant*. This and subsequent quotations taken from the unpublished manuscript kindly supplied by the author.

14. Edward Albee, *The Goat, or Who is Sylvia?* (New York: Overlook, 2003), p. 34. Further references will be cited parenthetically in the text.

14

STEPHEN BOTTOMS

Borrowed time:
An interview with Edward Albee

The place: Mr. Albee's loft apartment in Tribeca, New York City.

The time: 10a.m., Friday, November 14, 2003.

Let's begin with right now. Are you currently working on any new writing?

Yes, I am. Let's see, the last thing that was done in New York – of new work – was *The Goat*, which is going into rehearsal next month in London, at the Almeida. And I've accepted a commission from the Hartford Stage Company to write a play to go with my play *The Zoo Story*. It's normally an hour long, and I have to keep approving other people's plays, or another one of my own, to be done with it. And it occurred to me that even though I was fairly happy with *The Zoo Story* when I wrote it, I really didn't do a full job on the character of Peter. Jerry we know very well. So I'm writing a play about Peter, before he meets Jerry, called *Homelife*. Peter at home with his wife, Ann, and how this affects his reaction to Jerry – to the extent that it *does*.

So it's a kind of prequel?

Well, I hate the term prequel, but I suppose I'll be stuck with it. The whole evening I'd like to call *Peter and Jerry – Homelife* and *The Zoo Story*. Anyway, the interesting thing about it is that I wrote *The Zoo Story* about forty-five years ago, which is a long time. (How could I do anything forty-five years ago when I'm only thirty-two now?) But after all those years, I find I'm writing about the character Peter as if it was yesterday. I found I haven't lost contact with him, which is very interesting. At least I don't think I have.

Didn't you once do another piece to go with The Zoo Story, *called* Another Part of the Zoo?

No; not exactly. It was just written for a special occasion – "an occasional piece" – and you know how those are. Even Elgar's were very bad. It was for some friends, for a fundraiser, but it's not a complete play.

Does it concern you in writing this new piece that people will inevitably compare it with The Zoo Story?

I don't see how they could compare it, unless maybe the writing's gotten better. Some people will try to compare anything, whether they should be compared or not. But I'll be very interested to see how people react to the two of them together. I'll be very interested to see how *I* react! *Homelife* tells me a good deal more about Peter, and so the balance of what happens in *The Zoo Story* is now more complete.

And would you like them to be performed together in future?

If I like what happens, I shall *insist* that they be performed together. It becomes a "full evening," as they say. Although I've been to ten-minute Beckett plays that were "full evenings."

Could I ask you about the plays that were first produced last year, The Goat *and* Occupant?

Well, *Occupant* never opened, because our star got sick. It never opened and was never reviewed. It was Anne Bancroft, at the Signature Theatre on West 42nd Street. We got about a week into previews and she got pneumonia, so we never opened. That still has to be done, so I've got to find some time when we can do that.

Could you say a little about what motivated you to write about Louise Nevelson, the sculptor, in that play?

I don't remember. She was a good friend, and I thought she was an interesting dramatic subject.

I'm intrigued, though, by your obvious interest in sculpture. Here we are surrounded by sculptures in your loft.

Yes, a lot of African work, particularly. I keep telling my playwriting students that it's not enough to study literature, you also have to study the visual arts, and classical music, if you want to be a playwright. I started out doing drawings, when I was eight or something, long before I started writing, and I discovered classical music when I was ten or eleven. So I've been involved very deeply with all of those since I was a kid, and I think it's very helpful for a playwright to have a visual sense, and to know music also.

Would you point to any of your plays as being particularly "sculptural"?

Well, of course *Occupant* more than any other. Maybe *Tiny Alice* has some sculptural elements, and a lot of visual elements in it, that a lot of other plays don't have. The mansion with the lights going on and off. It's a very three-dimensional, *object-written* play.

I was reading in Mel Gussow's book that you now aren't sure about Tiny Alice *– that you don't feel you can defend it as you can your other plays.*

No, that's not what I said. It's that it's the one play that I can't recall the experience of having written. I can't recreate the state of mind that made me write it. It's the only one of my plays that I can't, and I don't know what that means. I still like it fine, it's just that I don't recall what I was up to! There was a very nice production of it off-Broadway about three years ago, with Richard Thomas being John Gielgud – in a very different way.

It does seem to be a play that's particularly theatrical in its . . .

Operatic is what you mean, yes. It's a very operatic play: you have to conduct the damn thing. I suspect that I had thoughts of grand opera when I was writing it. I wouldn't be surprised. It's a very baroque and operatic piece.

Especially with that final aria, I guess.

Which I cut, of course. Finally. Sensibly. To about two minutes, from the eleven minutes it was. In a play like that you can have an aria because it's a grand opera, but I also had to cut about half a page from the end of *The Zoo Story*, when Jerry's sitting on the bench with a knife in his gut. In the original version, when I didn't know any better, he had a long, long speech. You can't do that when you have a knife in your aorta! So I cut that, because it was unnecessary. Many years ago. And it made the play a lot better.

Are the plays still published in their original form?

I try to get them corrected whenever they're being republished, especially in acting editions. And there's going to be a new, three-volume edition of all of my plays, through *The Goat* I guess, which will be coming out in the next couple of years.[1] Those will be the revised versions. I've cut about five minutes out of *Who's Afraid of Virginia Woolf?* I learn a lot by directing and observing productions. I don't rewrite in the sense of rethinking a play, or contradicting any of the premises in the play. But you know, if I bore myself, I think I'll bore other people, so I cut.

Do you find, when you write, that the work still comes quite fully formed, quite spontaneously?

Yes. Well, that's the illusion we give ourselves. I am doing the writing. But we have to play those games with ourselves that the characters are really alive and talking to us. Because if we don't do that, we don't believe them.

But to what extent do you preconceive a play, what it's going to be about, before you . . .

As little as possible. I hate that term: "what is the play about?" It's about two hours, or thirty minutes, that's what it's about. I guess I must know pretty much what I'm going to do, but I really write them to find out why I'm writing them. It's a trick we play with ourselves. I mean there are some writers who plot everything out very carefully – every turn of phrase and turn of plot. I don't do that. I like to find out what I'm thinking about, and surprise myself! If there's no surprise, it's just typing.

I was able once to read the draft manuscripts for Who's Afraid of Virginia Woolf? *up in the Lincoln Center collection, and I was intrigued by just how little changed between the first draft and the final version.*

Yes, there were about six or seven pages at the beginning of Act 3 that I cut, that were unnecessary, and I ended up cutting the last five minutes of Act 2.

And is that fairly standard? That you'll make small changes like that, but nothing more substantial?

Yes, I think so. I won't rewrite a play, because I'm not the same person who wrote it. I won't let anybody else rewrite my plays, so why should I let me? But I will cut or alter a bit of it if I think that it's become anachronistic or unnecessary. And in *The Zoo Story* I've had to raise everybody's salary! When I wrote the play, Peter, a publisher, was turning thirty-seven thousand bucks a year. Now it's up to a quarter of a million. Stuff like that you have to change, because the play exists *now* just as well as it would have in 1958.

You don't feel it's tied to that time in any way?

No, that's the interesting thing. Most of my plays are not tied to time, particularly. I can't think of one of them that needs to be – well, *The Death of Bessie Smith*, of course. That's 1937 and set in Memphis. But beyond that I can't think of any of them that need to be tied to a time. *Virginia Woolf*, clearly, is taking place in the Sixties, because there's references to a number of events in the Thirties and Forties. But I don't even like there to be a note – "1962" – or anything like that. You should just let it float.

Is that because you see the plays as timeless, in some way?

I'm not going to use that phrase, but I don't think they are beholden to specific dates. They're not historical plays, they're not costume plays. I'm always deeply troubled when I'm talking to a costume designer who wants to figure out the way people dressed in 1962. It's ridiculous! And besides, these people are in college, and they always dress the same way. They're not fashion victims. They wear wool and cotton, rather than synthetic fabrics – that's the only thing I insist upon, for a very wise reason. On stage, synthetic fabrics take the stage lights differently, and they don't look real. Isn't that interesting?

Again, a kind of sculptural concern, in a way.

Yes. And it's a dance concern too, because you've got choreography going on. It's the only art form that's got all that stuff in it.

Coming back to that, I was intrigued by this catalogue from the "Idea to Matter" sculpture exhibit that you curated a few years ago, and by the statement that you have at the beginning of it: "The illusion versus the real" – which immediately seems a very Albee-esque heading – "this represents the fundamental difference between painting and sculpture. In painting, all is illusion: color, shape, perspective. Nothing is real beyond the illusion of reality created by the painter. It is, after all, all flat, all false, and, in the best hands, all wonderful, all real. In sculpture, everything is real: object, color, shape, perspective, and, in the best hands, all is wonderful and filled with illusion."[2] I think that's such a wonderful paradox. Do you have a sense of where theatre would fit into that scheme?

Theatre is absolute artifice. Total artifice. I mean, the curtain rises and there are a bunch of painted sets, and people – actors – pretending to be characters. And we must have our complete "suspension of disbelief." It is *all* artifice, absolute artifice. But if it works, it becomes more real than anything.

You seem to have been emphasizing that sense of almost self-conscious theatricality more and more over recent plays . . .

Well, once you've experienced Pirandello, a lot of stuff opens up to you. You become aware of a lot more. I think half of my plays – what have I got, twenty-seven plays now? – in around half of them, the fourth-wall concept is broken, and the characters talk to the audience. So I've been doing that for a long time, ever since *The American Dream*. You see, I don't think that it's enough for the audience to be "at the peephole," so to speak – you know, "the spy in the house of love" (or hate). I think the audience needs to be *involved*. And I've learned this from a lot of playwrights – you know, Pirandello, and Brecht – over a lot of years.

When did you first encounter Pirandello?

Many years ago. Reading, I think, because he doesn't get a lot of productions in this country. Is he done a lot in Britain? I don't think so. But he's one of those playwrights who – the plays aren't as *good*, or as important, as his theoretical ideas.

And they don't translate very well.

No, they don't. But then again, they tell us Ibsen doesn't either. They even tell us that Ibsen had a sense of humor. Can you imagine that! I haven't found it in *any* English adaptation of him. But most people who translate him into English don't speak Norwegian.

Maybe the Norwegians have a particular sense of irony that doesn't translate.

They have a sense of irony. But have you been to Norway? I don't see a great deal of laughter echoing off the cliffs.

It does seem, though, that in the past couple of decades, it's almost become the norm rather than the exception that your characters will address the audience.

Well, in *The Goat* they don't. In *Homelife* they don't. But it happened in *The Play About the Baby*, it happened in *Three Tall Women*. I won't go back into the dark ages before that. So maybe it's happening every other time, but it always has. I think in half the plays, the fourth wall is broken.

My own contribution to this book is on Lolita *and* The Man Who Had Three Arms, *which I find fascinating plays, in the way they . . .*

I do too. I think we're going to get a production of *The Man Who Had Three Arms* again some time soon. Which version of *Lolita* did you read, the published one?

The Dramatists Play Service version.

OK, that's basically the version of the atrocity that was produced on Broadway. I wrote a two-evening version, which has never been done, which is the proper version. I admire that book so much, I admire Nabokov so much, and I was shocked by what happened to my play. I'll get sued if I get into it, but it was a combination of a producer that I thought was criminal, a director who was scared to death of the star, and an actor who to my mind thought he was a much better actor than he was – kept making cuts and changes without my permission. It was an awful experience. I don't know why I didn't just close the whole thing down. Maybe I didn't want to throw everybody out of a job.

But you haven't done any adaptations since then . . .

No, that was the last one. That sort of finished me for a while.

How do you feel about that process of adaptation? Is it something you do to push yourself in different directions?

Well, one of them is not really an adaptation. *Everything in the Garden* is a translation really, from English to American. The nicest part of that for me was taking the character, Mrs. Toothe in the American version, and making her British. In Giles Cooper's version she's a rather unpleasant Jewish refugee, which seems part of that particularly British form of antisemitism that I've always disliked – so I thought it would be very proper to have the whore mistress being a very elegant British lady. And that was the major part of the adaptation. Of the others, *The Ballad of the Sad Café* struck me as a highly visual experience, and it worked very well onstage. Only James Purdy and I seem to like my adaptation of *Malcolm*, but I've seen very good productions of that in colleges and other places. And *Lolita* was a disaster, but eventually it will probably be done in my two-evening version, and I think it will be all right then – if we ever get it onstage. I've seen a couple of productions of *The Man Who Had Three Arms*, which was *loved* in Chicago, before it came to New York. And the audience had a wonderful time during the two weeks of previews in New York: they were standing up cheering, and laughing all through it, and then these motherfuckers got at it . . . I rewrote the ending just a little bit, in time for the New York production, but they wouldn't put it in, even though I was directing it. You know, the part where he grows the foot out of his back at the end, which is much funnier.

What happened originally?

That didn't happen. He was just railing against fate. But I don't understand how anybody thought – how critics decided – that that play was about my career. Because I say, right in the middle of the play, "I didn't write fifteen string quartets, for Christ's sake, I didn't split the atom. I grew a fucking third arm. Where's the talent in that?" How they would pretend it was about me, and that I'd lost my writing ability, is just *gratuitous.*

And why would anybody think that about themselves? And then write about it!

Of course. Totally gratuitous and mean-spirited. But then you learn, very early in your career, that not only is life not fair, life is a lot fairer than theatre.

Himself seems to be as much an American Everyman figure as anything.

Yes. And the play is as much as anything an examination of how we construct false idols. And then when we don't like them anymore, we knock them down, and blame them, rather than us.

In that sense, then, maybe it did find its right audience – if it upset people that much, maybe that's what it was for!

Yes, but the audience it found seemed capable of closing it. Which is not a good thing. But we'll get it on.

Was part of the problem there because it played on Broadway, rather than in an off-Broadway house? Does that set up particular problems?

Well, there is the double-standard of criticism between Broadway and the serious theatre. And some things are more tolerated if they're not going to rock the boat. They're going to be seen by fewer people off-Broadway, and are not going to be considered as important – even though the best plays are done there, usually. So there's a double standard, but no, it should have been done right where it was. Liz McCann, my producer since Richard Barr died, she was told, "shouldn't you do *The Goat* off-Broadway?" She said "no, these people deserve it!"

It's great that The Goat *put you back on Broadway with a new play, after all this time. You do seem to have felt, throughout your career, that for all its flaws Broadway is the place that should be aimed for.*

The only thing that's important about Broadway is that that's where people take their cues as to what's important in the theatre. It has to be *on Broadway*. "If it isn't happening in New York, and it isn't happening on Broadway, then it doesn't matter." It's a preposterous notion. Actually I'm much happier off-Broadway, because all our Broadway theatres are too big, and the pressures are preposterous and other than they should be. I'd much rather have my plays done in a three-hundred-seat theatre. But you need to challenge things every once in a while.

Were you at all concerned at how The Goat *would be received? It seems to have gone down very well.*

Well, yes. A lot of critics came back to see it a second time, when we changed the cast, and they seemed to think it was a much better play. Maybe they should have seen it twice before they reviewed it!

Did you think it changed at all with the second cast?

No, not really. Both casts were splendid. They both did the play slightly differently, but same lines, same intention, same result. No, no cast was better than the other. And I always knew the play was funny and outrageous – and sad, of course – all at the same time. All actors of mine when they're in a play of mine are startled when they first go onstage, in front of an audience, and discover that the play is fairly funny. I remember when Jessica Tandy came backstage after the first act of the first performance of *A Delicate Balance* – the original production – and she was *quivering*. She said, "Edward, they're laughing out there!" I said, "Yes, because it's funny. Get back onstage."

And yet A Delicate Balance *is never talked about as a funny play. Most of the criticism treats it as this very somber piece.*

Well, it is, but it's also funny. I hate any play that's humorless. Which is why – poor Ibsen – I prefer Chekhov to Ibsen.

The Goat really does seem to run the gamut back and forth between total hilarity and quite gut-churning dramatic moments.

I like to catch people like that. I like catching people in the middle of a laugh, and them realizing that it's not funny – or catching them in the middle of something awful, and realizing that you can laugh at it. I like doing that, I guess – since I do it so much.

I was intrigued by your subtitle for The Goat, *"Notes Toward a Definition of Tragedy."*

A definition. Not *the* definition, or a redefinition. "Notes Toward a Definition of Tragedy." This is a paraphrase of somebody's famous book – "Notes Toward a Something Something" – I can't remember who wrote it. Some turn-of-the-century philosopher or scholar.[3]

And is there a particular logic behind it being there, or is it more of a provocation?

Well, it's a fact. So that's why it's there. It's not part of the title – it's a parenthetical comment, which is why it's in parentheses. The title is *The Goat, or Who is Sylvia?*

But there is that sense in the play – and it's true of The Play About the Baby *too to some extent – that there's this almost Greek-tragic sense of unavoidable harm that's going to happen, and there's nothing you can do to avoid it. Is that part of the thinking there?*

Maybe. See, I don't think about my plays very much. I don't think about me in the third person at all, and I don't think about my plays after I finish them, except making sure that everything happens the way I want it to. But I don't think about what they *mean*, or the implications or anything.

As you said, you don't like to talk about what they're "about." Let me ask you instead about Our Town, *which is not one of your plays at all, but which I'm directing right now, back home in Glasgow, and which I understand you're very fond of.*

Well, it's one of my favorite plays, because it is *not* the Christmas card that everybody thinks it is. It's a real tough play – tough and bitter and deeply moving, but everybody performs it like it was a fucking Christmas card. It's disgusting, most productions you see of it. A friend of mine has been commissioned to make an opera of it, and I wrote him a letter saying that this *does not need* to be an opera. And if you're going to do this opera version of it, pay close attention to what they tell doctors all the time: *do no harm.* It's a beautiful and sad, deeply cold play. Don't you think?

Yes – and very funny as well.

Of course it is.

And I was struck, in working on Wilder, and at the same time rereading all your plays for this book, by a certain shared sense of the need for people to wake up to the world, to live every moment more consciously, *I guess. We talked about Pirandello, but is Wilder a particular inspiration for you too?*

Well, he has two very good plays – *The Skin of Our Teeth* less so than *Our Town* – but every now and then Wilder has a moment in a play of his that just knocks me out. In *The Skin of Our Teeth*, the one moment where I just burst into tears, almost as soon as I start to think about it, is during the great storm, when Mrs. Antrobus can't find her son, and for the first time we hear his name, as she calls out: "Cain!" That is *so* chilling and so wonderful. And there's a moment in *Our Town* when Emily comes back from the dead, and she hears her father offstage coming down the stairs, saying "Where's my girl? Where's my birthday girl?" . . . I'm practically breaking up now . . . It is so moving, and so beautiful. And it takes a particular kind of genius to be able to do that sort of thing. Yet Wilder himself was a kind of cold guy. Did you know that he spent the last ten years of his life writing a book about *Finnegan's Wake*? And he never finished it, but he used to send me chapters of it to read, and I could never confess to him that I hadn't read *Finnegan's Wake*! But I think those moments, in those plays – well, they obviously had a profound effect on me. And you try to attain that particular kind of magic.

And those moments both revolve around parent-child relationships, which is a recurring thing in your work as well, of course.

Yes, that does seem to turn up, but I don't think that's the reason. I think it has to do more with *loss,* or to do with lost opportunity. But it all ties together. Did you notice, Mel Gussow finishes his book talking about Samuel Barber's setting of the James Agee thing, *Knoxville: Summer 1915*? Have you ever heard that?

This is the thing about "One is my mother who is good to me. One is my father who is good to me"?

You should listen to the recording some time – beautiful piece. And so, yes, it all ties together, probably. But I don't think about it very much.

It intrigues me, in that book, that Mel Gussow seems determined to read your work through your biography, and yet at the same time he acknowledges that you have a problem with that.

Well, it does tend to suggest that writers don't have any creative imagination. That we're limited to what has happened to us. You see, I don't think I've ever written about me. I'm not a character in any of my plays, except that boy, that silent boy that turns up in *Three Tall Women*. But that can't be me, since I talk all the time. No, I don't write about me. Of course, I write through my own experiences, and what I write is limited by my ability to . . . *perceive* things. But all biographers do this. They feel it's their responsibility to find the connective tissue, which may be valid, but if the work doesn't transcend the experience that produced it, then it's not worth the trouble in the first place.

How does that relate to something like Three Tall Women, *which is so clearly based on your mother. Is that also trying to transcend those particulars, in a way?*

Well, I had the strange experience when I was writing that play, that I wasn't writing about my adoptive mother – that I was inventing a character. And though there's a lot of fact in there, I did feel I was inventing her. People tell me I made her somewhat nicer than she was. Of course, that wasn't my intention, but it wasn't a revenge piece either. I tried to be very, very objective.

It is very frank, in that she's so obviously so cantankerous and bigoted, and yet it does seem to be a very loving portrait as well.

I had a rather grudging admiration for her survivability. We never got along, ever, and I used to think it was all her fault. But I think I was probably not a very easy kid, and I don't think it was any willfulness on her part to be awful. I just don't think she knew how to be a parent.

Mel Gussow describes how you once stood in for the actor playing the boy during a rehearsal for Three Tall Women.

Yes, and I got so interested in the other people onstage that I forgot my cue. It was only a visual cue, but I forgot it completely. I used to act when I was at school and college – I loved being onstage, but I don't think I forgot my cues back then. It was a very odd experience, playing somebody who's supposed to be you . . . Never mind.

Can I ask you about another of the recurring things in your plays, which is married couples – particularly couples who've been together for a very long time. On one level, they always seem to be at each other's throats, and yet on another level, there seem to be reasons why these couples are still together.

Well, you know, I can't imagine anybody writing a play that would be very interesting about a couple of people getting along terribly well. That would be pretty boring. It's called television. Plays are meant to have dramatic conflict, and if people aren't in conflict, what's the point of writing them? But you do write them hoping that people will stop behaving that way. And in *Who's Afraid of Virginia Woolf?*, George and Martha do love each other very much – they're trying to fix a greatly damaged marriage, yes.

What about Marriage Play *– which seems even harder, in a sense, and yet is very playful too?*

I like that play a lot. It's about that awful thing that – eventually you realize – no matter how good something is, it's not enough. That you're going to miss out on something. Terrible feeling, and a very important one. It's that feeling that you're going to be settling in, that you've had all the experiences that you're going to have. You know, you have a relationship going on for many years, and you're very happy, but there's a nagging feeling – have I missed the boat somewhere? Is there not something else that would have been . . . better? And that whole play's about that.

So that's about loss as well, in a way.

Well, can you have lost something that you never had? Yes. I guess you can. So it's about that, basically – but they're perfectly happy together, they enjoy each other. She knows what he's going through, and she's probably going through it herself, but he feels he has to act on it, which is the dramatic problem of the play.

I get the sense that they go through this whole routine quite often.

Oh, I think it's the first time they've been through that one. I don't think it's happened before.

But there is that very Waiting for Godot *ending, where he says he's leaving, and then he doesn't.*

A homage to Beckett? Not necessarily. It is quite true, but it's not the same thing. "I can't go on; I'll go on." "I'm leaving; I *am*." Yes, but she knows he's not.

These plays that deal with marriage, are they about marriage in the hetero-sexual sense – or rather the institutional sense – or are they about long-term relationships of any sort?

I don't notice very much difference. I mean, I've been in a relationship for thirty-three years myself, and that strikes me as being as valid, as three-dimensional, as intense as any heterosexual relationship would be.

Have you ever been tempted to write about a same-sex relationship?
Is that a dramatic subject?

Why not?
Maybe I will some day. After the bombing of the World Trade Center, we were all asked to write about our reactions to that – they wanted some kind of knee-jerk response. I was here, I saw the plane hit the second building . . . people falling out. I saw the whole thing, so maybe it'll turn up in a play some day. But no, I don't see that much difference between heterosexual and homosexual relationships, if they are two people really involved with each other, trying to make a life together. I don't see that much difference, except that the homosexual couple have to fight a lot of prejudices, and illegalities.

It does seem that The Goat *is a play that takes on questions of sexuality very directly – not in some simple straight or gay way, but in asking people to acknowledge that sexuality is much more complex than people give it credit for.*
Sure. That play isn't about goat-fucking. What I wanted people to do is not just sit there being judges of the characters. I wanted people to go to that play, and imagine themselves in the situation, and really think hard about how they would respond if it was happening to them. That's really what I'm after. Put yourself there. "How the fuck would I react? Why am I making this judgment about those people? Because I probably wouldn't make it if it was happening to me."

And yet it's a fairly extreme thing to ask people to imagine themselves into.
Really? I know people in this country . . . even Republicans! I mean that's a far more preposterous concept.

Republicans?
Yes.

Well, OK, let's talk about Republicans. I mean, you mentioned 9/11 – can I ask you how you feel about the situation right now, here in the States, and with the violence continuing in Iraq? It's off the subject of your plays, but I wonder if it does link up.
I find the erosions of our civil liberties deeply disturbing. I find that the lies that our government tells us are more naked than ever. I find that the

attempts on the part of the administration to move us way, way back and away from all the important socio-economic changes we've made over the past forty years are dangerous and disgraceful. And what's more dangerous is the fact that most people don't seem to give a fuck. I find that desperately threatening, so I shoot my mouth off all the time about it. Which it's my responsibility to do. How much faith have you lost in Mr. Blair?

Just about all of it.

I would think so. I think he's lying too, about so many things. I mean, there was no excuse – maybe there was a *reason* for going into that war, but all of the *excuses* we were given were clearly fallacious. They were just lying through their teeth and knowing it. And that's greatly troubling to me.

You've always had this activist streak, in terms of your work with PEN, and your tendency to get up and make speeches about these things. Do you think these political concerns come through in your playwriting?

I just have the feeling that the more we are in contact with ourselves, and *think* – spend some time thinking, rather than just in knee-jerk reactions to things – the more we'll vote intelligently. And so all plays are political, way deep down underneath.

Your plays always seem to involve lies or power games on one level or another . . .

And also, to a large extent, a number of them – like A Delicate Balance – are about people who have retreated from activism of any kind, and are living the rest of their lives on the surface. And I'm deeply opposed to that too.

So there's a level of affirmation that's going on, in terms of wanting to push people back out there?

That's right, yes.

I'm reminded of Peter Brook's comment about Samuel Beckett – that his "no" was so insistent that it became a kind of a "yes."

Well, you know what Sam said when somebody asked him why he kept on writing all these pessimistic plays? "If I were a pessimist, I wouldn't write plays." He made the assumption that there was communication possible. We all make that assumption when we write something. A whole set of assumptions: (a) that we have something to say, (b) that we have the ability to say it, and (c) that somebody will listen. Now, it could break down anywhere, but we make the assumption, because we are trying to change people's perceptions. That's what art is about – all art.

You seem to share with Beckett a very bleak streak – yet there's also this more positive, affirmative side to your writing.

The way we are, and the way we could be. They're two different things.

And do you have faith in people's ability to change?

The ability, yes. The willingness, no.

I like, for example, the end of Seascape, *with that line: "Begin."*

It's a threat. It's really a threat. So many productions of *Seascape* make the lizards cute, but right at the end there, they're going back under the water and destroying evolution – which amused me a lot. They're going back under the water because it's too awful up here, and they're learning things like loss and crying and death, which they'd never known. So they're wanting to go back home, even though they can't. And Charlie and Nancy say, "no, please wait, we can help you." And Leslie turns around and says, "OK buddy, begin." Meaning, "and if you don't succeed, I'll rip you to pieces." That's the whole intention of that last line. If you misunderstand that, then it's a misunderstanding of the play as profound as many misunderstandings of *Our Town*.

So is Seascape *comparable with* A Delicate Balance *in that sense? That the threat to go back under the sea is like the threat to withdraw into yourself and away from the world?*

Well no, it's different, because they *can't* go back under. Evolution cannot be denied – except by the religious right in this country. It can't be denied: they want to, but they can't, so they *are* going to have to evolve. And they *are* going to have to put up with the self-awareness of death and loss and all the rest of it. So it's not the same thing.

I suppose also that one is a more realistic play than the other.

Oh, I think that *Seascape*'s absolutely realistic. I directed the first production of that, and I remember I had to tell my actors who played the lizards, "You are not metaphorical, you are real creatures!"

Who happen to speak perfect English.

Because we're doing the play in America. It occurred to me it would have been funny – and I almost did it – to have them coming up speaking French. They thought they'd landed on the French coast. It seemed too private a joke to do, but if they come up on the French coast, then obviously they're speaking French. These are things we take for granted.

Seascape also seems to me to typify your use of a certain sense of wit and charm. Maybe this is just my perception, but that seems to have become more and more a part of your work over the past twenty years or so.

It was there in *Virginia Woolf*, except that everybody thought the play was so shocking that they didn't see it. I don't think the work has changed very much. I mean, there was an awful lot of funny stuff there in *The Zoo Story*. The ending's not very happy, but a good production of that will see the humor in it . . . *"charm"*?!

Do you have a problem with that?

No I don't, but I don't know quite what you mean.

A certain twinkle in the eye, perhaps.

I've become Father Christmas have I? I see.

No, but in things like Finding the Sun, *or* Fragments, *people seem to be sitting back a little bit more, and reflecting with a certain . . . dry . . .*

I think it's always been there. But perhaps, as I have evolved, I take myself less seriously. You may be right.

You also seem to have taken to giving some of your plays generic titles – Marriage Play *and* The Play About the Baby, *and* Fragments *sort of tells you what it is too.*

Isn't that helpful?

It is. But is that a way of saying, "Untitled", or . .?

No. A title is a title. That's the thing with *Marriage Play*: when people are going to do it, they always make the mistake of calling it *The Marriage Play*, but it is both a play about marriage, and it's a play about the play that takes place in marriage. It's a double title. Same way I don't waste names with characters.

I guess The Play About the Baby *works that way too. It happens around this thing that turns out to be an absence.*

A reality first, and then an absence. A real baby that is taken away. That troubled me, that some critics thought it was tied to *Virginia Woolf*. They're totally opposite things. Eventually the young couple realize that they *cannot have* the baby, and therefore it must disappear. For George and Martha it's the opposite.

Certainly the London critics seemed preoccupied with that link. But it was interesting that The Play About the Baby *didn't go down so well in London, and then did very well here in New York.*

Yes, I don't know why. The play was very much the same. There were no textual changes.

Do you think that the way a play is directed can substantially change the way it is perceived, given that the text is more or less fixed? When you chose to direct Virginia Woolf *in 1976, you said then that you were trying to amend certain misunderstandings about the play.*

Well, I thought the play was a lot funnier than it was in the original production. I didn't change anything, merely *revealed* a few things . . . I didn't think the production of *The Play About the Baby* in London was all that bad. There were a couple of problems, but I don't know quite what went wrong. Lord knows, the actors were fine. Anything Frankie de la Tour is in is good. Axiomatically.

Is she one of your favorite actors?

Yes, I love her. But there are a lot of actors and actresses that I seem to have worked with with some frequency over the years. I was very happy in London working with Peggy Ashcroft, and I like working with Frankie; I've worked with Maggie [Smith] well. Here, you know, there was Colleen Dewhurst, and Irene Worth, people like that I've had good relationships with. And [Elaine] Stritch, who actually played Martha in *Virginia Woolf* when she was thirty-something. Yes, some actors I seem to work very conveniently with.

Do you find there's a particular reason for that? Are they not imposing certain things, or bringing certain things to bear?

Well, classical training I find very important in an actor. Someone who really keeps working on stage, and doesn't just come in every now and then from a TV show, and *deign* to do a play. And there's intelligence – real intelligence, as well as an actor's intelligence – and the ability to handle language. Some of my plays are fairly baroque in language. Those are all important things.

And yet John Gielgud, in retrospect, was perhaps not the ideal person for Tiny Alice, *despite his ability with language.*

No, he wasn't. The sexual fires weren't quite right. I mean, his ability with language was extraordinary, but I've seen younger people do it better. He was a little too old for it. But I was grateful to have him.

Do you find that the Method approach to acting can be a hindrance at all – if people are wanting to know why they're doing things, when there may not be a simple, logical motivation?

Well, I don't find that good British actors, for example, have no interest in why they're doing things. I find that the two acting methods, of the very best actors, are quite similar. They know *why* they're doing it. John Gielgud kept saying, all the way through *Tiny Alice*, that he didn't understand what he was doing, but that was bullshit. He understood perfectly well: he was a bright man. And Ralph Richardson, for example, always knew what he was doing. He was as crazy as they come, and his reasons for doing things may have been bizarre, but his three-dimensionality and believability were never in question. It's only with second-rate actors that you can make the joke about the difference between British and American actors. Any actor who's really any good is a three-dimensional actor, and what happened at the [Actors'] Studio wasn't really any different from what was going on with actors who weren't catalogued in that way. I'm not going to believe any actor unless I believe what the character is doing, so I expect the actor to get there by whatever method. Whenever I'm directing a play – mine or Beckett's or anybody else's – I always tell the actors, "I want you to do whatever you want, with the exception that I want you to do the lines, every word that the author wrote, in the sequence that he wrote them. You can do whatever you want, as long as you end up with exactly what the author intended."

Do you still maintain an interest in directing?

I haven't directed in five or six years now, but yes, I'm still interested. But it's a lot of work, and for some odd reason I keep getting busier all the time.

You're certainly showing no signs of retiring. I notice in two or three of your plays that you cite seventy-five years old as the average male life span. Am I right that you're seventy-five now?

Yes. I think I should up that. How about ninety? But one lives on borrowed time anyway. All of us.

We've talked a little bit about some of your predecessors – Beckett, Wilder, Pirandello . . .

And Chekhov. I think the three most important playwrights of the twentieth century are Chekhov, Pirandello, and Beckett. They've had a really profound influence on us. And Irving Berlin, of course.

How about the people who've come after – your protégés, as it were? People like Adrienne Kennedy, John Guare . . .

Well, I don't like to talk about other playwrights besides Samuel Beckett and Chekhov. There are some very good ones, and you've mentioned a couple who I think are very provocative and interesting, but with people who are working in the theatre, I don't think one should have much of an opinion about "their work." One should have an opinion about individual pieces, yes. This play works, that play does not work. But with the possible exception of me, I can't think of any playwright, all of whose work I have some admiration for. And I know that I'm wrong about me. But I don't think that judgments can be fairly made until fifty, seventy-five years later.

My point is that you seem to have maintained – ever since the Playwrights' Unit in the Sixties, and right through to the work you still do in Houston – a certain concern with mentoring young writers.

I think there's a responsibility for somebody who knows their way around the craft to try to help people that you think are talented. There are two big boxes right there in the front hall with a hundred scripts that I'm supposed to read, in case I go back down to Houston and teach this year. I'm supposed to choose my own students, and I choose the ones that I think are provocative, and can be helped, and haven't made up their own minds about what theatre's all about yet. That's a responsibility, to push people in the direction of writing like themselves, and not being *employees*. I tell them to avoid all formulas, to stop imitating, stop copying, because there's enough commercial crap around. And I also try to warn them about the pitfalls of theatre – the commercial pitfalls. If you know something, you should share it, right?

I guess they're the new YAMs now, and you're the FAM?

Well, I've turned into one. I rewrote that play a little bit. I changed some of the references to who the young playwrights were. I took myself out of that category. This was a few years ago. But that play is really just a magazine article. I didn't even think about it as being performed.

Yet it was quite a provocative piece when it was first published. You were seen as off-Broadway's "enfant terrible," or "angry young man," or whatever.

Slogans. We're all supposed to represent something. Being is not enough. We have to be metaphorical.

And what do you represent now?

I don't know. A survivor of some sort.

I guess I'm asking if you're still interested in provoking people, in prodding them a bit.

Well, as I say, if a play is not provocative, in the best sense of the term . . . I mean one shouldn't be aggressive. I don't sit down at my desk and say, "I must now provoke." But it seems to be that it's my determination to shake people up, and make them change in some way. And that's fine. It's called playwriting.

NOTES

1. Edward Albee, *The Collected Plays of Edward Albee, Volume 1* (New York: Overlook, 2004).
2. Edward Albee, "From Idea to Matter: Some Thoughts on Sculpture," "Introduction" to the catalogue for an exhibition curated by Albee at the Anderson Gallery, Richmond, Virginia, in fall 2000. *From Idea to Matter: Nine Sculptors* (Seattle: University of Washington Press, 2000), p. 7.
3. Albee is perhaps referring here to T. S. Eliot's "Notes Toward a Definition of Culture" (1948).

NOTES ON FURTHER READING

A great deal of published material is available on the works of Edward Albee. Scott Giantvalley's *Edward Albee: A Reference Guide* (1987), the most exhaustive bibliographic guide to date, is almost as thick as a Russian novel, and with almost twenty years having now passed since he compiled it, it could be at least half as thick again. The bibliography that follows in this volume is necessarily select, but first-time students of Albee may also appreciate some guidance to circumscribe their research further.

Aside from Albee's plays themselves, there are a handful of indispensable books for anyone interested in reading around them. The importance of Mel Gussow's 1999 biography *Edward Albee: A Singular Journey* (published in paperback in 2001), written with Albee's full cooperation, should be apparent from the number of times it is cited by contributors to this book. It is listed here, in the bibliography, under "critical studies," for it is that too. Equally important is Philip C. Kolin's collection of *Conversations with Edward Albee* (1988), which collects all the most useful interviews given by Albee between the 1960s and 1980s. Kolin's other major contribution is *Critical Essays on Edward Albee,* edited with J. Madison Davis (1986), which selects not only key scholarly texts from the previous two decades, but also a judicious range of review material written in response to each of Albee's major premieres.

Among book-length critical studies of Albee, Matthew Roudané's *Understanding Albee* (1987) is probably the most accessible short introduction to Albee, but I would also recommend Gerry McCarthy's *Edward Albee* (also 1987), which manages to combine concision and clarity with some genuinely insightful critical twists, especially with regards to the plays' lives on stage. Somewhat more complex, but equally recommended, are Ruby Cohn's *Edward Albee* and Christopher Bigsby's *Albee,* both from 1969, though of course they deal only with Albee's earlier work. Bigsby's is distinctive in being one of the few books to look at Albee's adaptations in any detail, and he has subsequently updated his lucid overview of Albee's career in both his *A Critical Introduction to Twentieth Century American Drama, Volume 2*

(1984) and his *Modern American Drama: 1945–2000* (the second edition, published in 2000, of a volume originally dated *1945–1990*, when published in 1992). Another very useful study from earlier in Albee's career is Anne Paolucci's *From Tension to Tonic* (1972), which dares to make great claims for Albee's importance, and backs those claims up with some fascinating close readings of the plays (especially *Tiny Alice*). Her subsequent work on Albee and his Pirandellian concerns (see elsewhere in the bibliography) is also thoroughly recommended.

There are several very good anthologies of critical essays on Albee: in the bibliography, those edited by Bigsby, Bloom, and Kolin select from work previously published in a variety of sources, while De La Fuente, Jenckes, Mann, and Wasserman contain original work unpublished elsewhere. Given the range and quality of the essays in these collections, I have limited my own listing of individual, uncollected essays to more recent work, from the past decade or so. (Much the same goes for the listing of interviews with Albee, given that Kolin collects most of the key interviews up to the mid-1980s in *Conversations*.)

For those with particular interest in exploring Albee's work in performance, I recommend Rakesh Solomon's work on Albee as director: his useful essay in the Jenckes collection is soon to be complemented by his forthcoming book from Indiana University Press, *Albee in Performance: The Playwright as Director*. There is also my own, book-length study of the production and performance history of the playwright's most famous play, *Albee: Who's Afraid of Virginia Woolf?* And for a first-hand perspective on the premieres of many of Albee's key works, see the autobiography of his long-time director, Alan Schneider: *Entrances: An American Director's Journey* (New York: Viking, 1986).

SELECT BIBLIOGRAPHY

Primary works

Plays

First U.S. and U.K. editions, in chronological order.

The Zoo Story, The Death of Bessie Smith, The Sandbox. New York: Coward McCann, 1960.
The American Dream. New York: Coward McCann, 1961.
Who's Afraid of Virginia Woolf? New York: Atheneum, 1962; London: Jonathan Cape, 1964.
The Ballad of the Sad Café. New York: Atheneum, 1963; London: Jonathan Cape, 1965.
Tiny Alice. New York: Atheneum, 1965; London: Jonathan Cape, 1966.
Malcolm. New York: Atheneum, 1966; London: Jonathan Cape, 1967.
A Delicate Balance. New York: Atheneum, 1966; London: Jonathan Cape, 1968.
Everything in the Garden. New York: Atheneum, 1968; London: Jonathan Cape, 1968.
Box and Quotations from Chairman Mao Tse-Tung. New York: Atheneum, 1969; London: Jonathan Cape, 1970.
All Over. New York: Atheneum, 1971; London: Jonathan Cape, 1972.
Seascape. New York: Atheneum, 1975; Jonathan Cape, 1976.
Counting the Ways and Listening. New York: Atheneum, 1977.
The Lady from Dubuque. New York: Atheneum, 1980.
Lolita. New York: Dramatists Play Service, 1984.
Finding the Sun. New York: Dramatists Play Service, 1994.
Fragments: A Sit-Around. New York: Dramatists Play Service, 1995.
Marriage Play. New York: Dramatists Play Service, 1995.
Three Tall Women. New York: Dutton, 1994; London: Penguin, 1995.
The Play About the Baby. New York: Overlook, 2003; London: Methuen, 2003.
The Goat, or Who is Sylvia? (Notes Toward a Definition of Tragedy). New York: Overlook, 2003; London: Methuen, 2004.

Collected editions

The Zoo Story and Other Plays. London: Jonathan Cape, 1962. (Also includes *The American Dream, The Death of Bessie Smith, The Sandbox*.)
Edward Albee: The Plays, Volume 1. New York: Coward, McCann, and Geohegan, 1981. Includes *The Zoo Story, The Death of Bessie Smith, The Sandbox, The American Dream*.
Edward Albee: The Plays, Volume 2. New York: Atheneum, 1981. Includes *Tiny Alice, A Delicate Balance, Box and Quotations from Chairman Mao Tse-Tung*.
Edward Albee: The Plays, Volume 3. New York: Atheneum, 1982. Includes *All Over, Seascape, Counting the Ways, Listening*.
Edward Albee: The Plays, Volume 4. New York: Atheneum, 1982. Includes *The Ballad of the Sad Café, Malcolm, Everything in the Garden*.
Selected Plays of Edward Albee. New York: Nelson Doubleday, 1987. Includes *The Zoo Story, The American Dream, Who's Afraid of Virginia Woolf?, A Delicate Balance, Box and Quotations from Chairman Mao Tse-Tung, All Over, Seascape, The Man Who Had Three Arms*.
The Collected Plays of Edward Albee, Volume 1. New York: Overlook, 2004. Includes *The Zoo Story, The Death of Bessie Smith, The Sandbox, The American Dream, Who's Afraid of Virginia Woolf?, The Ballad of the Sad Cafe, Tiny Alice, Malcolm*.

Essays and articles

"Which Theatre is the Absurd One." *New York Times Magazine*, February 25, 1962. Reprinted in Horst Frenz (ed.), *American Playwrights on Drama* (New York: Hill and Wang, 1965), pp. 168–174.
"Some Notes on Non-Conformity." *Harper's Bazaar*, August 1962, p. 104.
"Carson McCullers: The Case of the Curious Magician." *Harper's Bazaar*, January 1963, p. 98.
"Who's Afraid of the Truth?" *New York Times*, August 18, 1963, Arts, p. 1.
"Who is James Purdy?" *New York Times*, January 9, 1966, Arts, pp. 1, 3.
"Apartheid in the Theatre." *New York Times*, July 30, 1967, Arts, pp. 1, 6.
"The Future Belongs to Youth." *New York Times*, November 26, 1967, Arts, p. 1.
"Albeit." In Howard Greenberger (ed.), *The Off-Broadway Experience*. Englewood Cliffs, NJ: Prentice-Hall, 1971, pp. 52–62.
"Foreword" to James Purdy's *Malcolm*. Harmondsworth: Penguin, 1980, pp. vii–ix.
"Louise Nevelson: The Sum and the Parts." In *Louise Nevelson: Atmospheres and Environments* (exhibition catalogue). New York: Clarkson N. Potter & Whitney Museum, 1980, pp. 12–30.
The Wounding: An Essay on Education. Charleston, WV: Mountain State Press, 1981. (12 pp.)
"On Lee Krasner." In John Cheim (ed.), *Lee Krasner Paintings, 1965 to 1970*. New York: Robert Miller Gallery, 1990. (Unpaginated exhibition catalogue.)
"On Alan Schneider and Playwriting." *American Drama* 1.2 (1992), pp. 77–84.
"Who's Afraid of Genius?" *The Guardian*, October 21, 1997, p. 11.
"From Idea to Matter: Some Thoughts on Sculpture." Introduction to Albee-curated exhibition catalogue: *From Idea to Matter: Nine Sculptors*. Seattle: University of Washington Press, 2000, p. 7.

Interviews and articles based on interviews

Bhasin, Kamil. "Women, Identity, and Sexuality." *Journal of American Drama and Theatre* 7.2 (1995), pp. 18–40.

Cuomo, Joe. "A Conversation with Edward Albee." *Dramatist* 3.6 (2001), pp. 4–15.

Goldman, Jeffrey. "An Interview with Edward Albee." *Studies in American Drama, 1945 – Present* 6.1 (1991), pp. 59–69. Reprinted in Philip C. Kolin and Colby H. Kullman (eds.), *Speaking on Stage: Interviews with Contemporary American Playwrights*. Tuscaloosa: University of Alabama Press, 1996, pp. 89–97.

Gussow, Mel. "Albee All Over, Or a Wealth of One." *New York Times*, February 17, 2002. Arts, pp. 5, 43.

Kolin, Philip C. (ed.). *Conversations with Edward Albee*. Jackson and London: University Press of Mississippi, 1988.

Maslon, Laurence. "Edward Albee." In Jackson R. Bryer (ed.), *The Playwright's Art: Conversations with Contemporary American Dramatists*. New Brunswick, NJ: Rutgers University Press, 1995, pp. 1–23.

Ramsey, Dale. "Albee, Weller, Blessing on the Playwright's Craft." *Dramatists Guild Quarterly* 30.2/3 (1993), pp. 6–14.

Rand, Harry. "Context is All." In Albee et al., *From Idea to Matter: Nine Sculptors*. Seattle: University of Washington Press, 2000, pp. 9–29.

Rosen, Carol. "Writers and their Work: Edward Albee." *Dramatists Guild Quarterly* 33.3 (1996), pp. 27–39.

Roudané, Matthew. "An Interview with Edward Albee." *Southern Humanities Review* 16 (1982), pp. 29–44.

Samuels, Steven. "Yes is Better Than No." *American Theatre*, September 1994, p. 38.

Solomon, Rakesh. "Text, Subtext and Performance: Edward Albee on Directing *Who's Afraid of Virginia Woolf?*" *Theatre Survey* 34.2 (1993), pp. 95–110.

Strong, Lester. "Aggression Against the Status Quo." *Harvard Gay and Lesbian Review* 4.1 (1997), pp. 7–9.

Secondary works

Bibliographies and checklists

Amacher, Richard E. and Margaret Rule. *Edward Albee at Home and Abroad: A Bibliography*. New York: AMS Press, 1973.

Bigsby, C. W. E. *Edward Albee: Bibliography, Biography, Playography* (*Theatre Checklist* 22). London: TQ Publications, 1980.

Giantvalley, Scott. *Edward Albee: A Reference Guide*. Boston: G. K. Hall, 1987.

Green, Charles Lee. *Edward Albee: An Annotated Bibliography, 1968–1977*. New York: AMS Press, 1980.

Tyce, Richard. *Edward Albee: A Bibliography*. Metuchen, NJ: Scarecrow, 1986.

Critical studies: books

Amacher, Richard E. *Edward Albee*. New York: Twayne, 1969.

Bigsby, C. W. E. *Albee*. Edinburgh: Oliver and Boyd, 1969.

Bottoms, Stephen J. *Albee: Who's Afraid of Virginia Woolf?* Cambridge: Cambridge University Press, 2000.
Cohn, Ruby. *Edward Albee*. Minneapolis: University of Minnesota Press, 1969.
Debusscher, Gilbert. *Edward Albee: Tradition and Renewal*. Brussels: Center for American Studies, 1969.
Gussow, Mel. *Edward Albee: A Singular Journey*. New York: Simon and Schuster, 1999.
Hayman, Ronald. *Edward Albee*. London: Heinemann, 1971.
Hirsch, Foster. *Who's Afraid of Edward Albee?* Berkeley: Creative Arts Books, 1978.
McCarthy, Gerry. *Edward Albee*. New York: St. Martin's Press, 1987; London: Macmillan, 1987.
Paolucci, Anne. *From Tension to Tonic: The Plays of Edward Albee*. Carbondale: Southern Illinois University Press, 1972.
Roudané, Matthew C. *Understanding Edward Albee*. Columbia, SC: University of South Carolina Press, 1987.
—. *Who's Afraid of Virginia Woolf?: Necessary Fictions, Terrifying Realities*. Boston: Twayne, 1990.
Rutenberg, Michael E. *Edward Albee: Playwright in Protest*. New York: Avon Books, 1970.
Stenz, Anita Maria. *Edward Albee: The Poet of Loss*. The Hague: Mouton, 1978.

Essay collections

Bigsby, C. W. E. (ed.). *Edward Albee: A Collection of Critical Essays*. Englewood Cliffs, NJ: Prentice-Hall, 1975.
Bloom, Harold (ed.). *Edward Albee: Modern Critical Views*. New York: Chelsea House, 1987.
De La Fuente, Patricia, et al. (eds.). *Edward Albee: Planned Wilderness: Interview, Essays, and Bibliography*. Edinburgh, TX: Pan American University, 1980.
Debusscher, Gilbert, et al. (eds.). *New Essays on American Drama*. Amsterdam: Rodopi, 1989.
Jenckes, Norma (ed.). *American Drama* 2.2 (Spring 1993). Special edition of journal dedicated to essays on Albee.
Kolin, Philip C. and J. Madison Davis (eds.). *Critical Essays on Edward Albee*. Boston: G. K. Hall, 1986.
Mann, Bruce J. (ed.). *Edward Albee: A Casebook*. New York: Routledge, 2003.
Paolucci, Anne (ed.). *PSA: The Official Publication of the Pirandello Society of America* 8 (1992). Special edition of journal dedicated to essays linking Albee and Pirandello.
Wasserman, Julian N., et al. (eds.). *Edward Albee: An Interview and Essays*. Houston: University of St. Thomas, 1983.
See also the following journal editions, which both collect several essays on Albee: *Educational Theatre Journal* 25 (1973) and *Publications of the Mississippi Philological Association* (1986).

Critical studies: book sections

Berkowitz, Gerald M. *American Drama of the Twentieth Century*. London: Longman, 1992.

Bigsby, C. W. E. *Confrontation and Commitment: A Study of Contemporary Drama.* Columbia: University of Missouri Press, 1968.

—. *A Critical Introduction to Twentieth Century American Drama, Volume 2: Williams, Miller, Albee.* Cambridge: Cambridge University Press, 1984.

Bigsby, Christopher. *Modern American Drama: 1945–2000.* Cambridge: Cambridge University Press, 2000.

Clum, John M. *Still Acting Gay: Male Homosexuality in Modern Drama.* New York: Palgrave, 2000.

Cohn, Ruby. *Dialogue in American Drama.* Bloomington: Indiana University Press, 1971.

Esslin, Martin. *The Theatre of the Absurd.* New York: Doubleday, 1961.

Kernan, Alvin B. (ed.) *The Modern American Theatre: A Collection of Critical Essays.* Englewood Cliffs, NJ: Prentice-Hall, 1967.

Mayberry, Bob. *Theatre of Discord: Dissonance in Beckett, Albee and Pinter.* Rutherford, NJ: Farleigh Dickinson University Press, 1989.

Paolucci, Anne, with Henry Paolucci. *Hegelian Literary Perspectives.* Smyrna: Griffon House, 2002.

Parker, Dorothy (ed.). *Essays on Modern American Drama.* Toronto and London, University of Toronto Press.

Scanlan, Tom. *Family, Drama and American Dreams.* Westport, CT: Greenwood Press, 1978.

Schlueter, June (ed.). *Feminist Readings of Modern American Drama.* London and Toronto: Associated University Presses, 1989.

Selected recent essays

Adler, Thomas P. "A's Last Memory: Contextualizing Albee's *Three Tall Women.*" In Joan Herrington (ed.), *The Playwright's Muse* (New York: Routledge, 2002), pp. 159–174.

Deans, Jill R. "Albee's Substitute Children: Reading Adoption as a Performative." *Journal of Dramatic Theory and Criticism* 13. 2 (Spring 1999), pp. 57–79.

Ditsky, John. "Steinbeck and Albee: Affection, Admiration, Affinity." *Steinbeck Quarterly* 26.1/2 (1993), pp. 13–23.

Drukman, Steven. "Won't You Come Home, Edward Albee." *American Theatre,* December 1998, pp. 16–20.

Egri, Peter. "American Variations on a British Theme: Giles Cooper and Edward Albee." In Ann Massa and Alistair Stead (eds.), *Forked Tongues?: Comparing Twentieth Century British and American Literature* (London: Longman, 1994), pp. 135–151.

Konkle, Lincoln. "American Jeremiah: Edward Albee as Judgment Day Prophet in *The Lady from Dubuque.*" *American Drama* 7 (Fall 1997), pp. 30–49.

Kundert-Gibbs, John. "Barren Ground: Female Strength and Male Impotence in *Who's Afraid of Virginia Woolf?* and *Cat on a Hot Tin Roof.*" In Katherine Burkman (ed.), *Staging the Rage: The Web of Misogyny.* Madison, NJ: Farleigh Dickinson University Press, 1998, pp. 230–247.

Leonard, Garry. "The Immaculate Deception: Adoption in Albee's Plays." In Marianne Novy (ed.), *Imagining Adoption: Essays on Literature and Culture.* Ann Arbor: University of Michigan Press, 2001, pp. 111–132.

Luere, Jeane. "Objectivity in the Growth of a Pulitzer: Edward Albee's *Three Tall Women.*" *Journal of American Drama and Theatre* 7.2 (1995), pp. 1–17.

—. "An Elegy for Thwarted Vision: Edward Albee's *The Lorca Story*: Scenes from a Life." *Journal of Dramatic Theory and Criticism* 9.2 (1995), pp. 142–147.

Paolucci, Anne. "Albee and the Restructuring of the Modern Stage." *Studies in American Drama, 1945 – Present* 1 (1986), pp. 3–23.

—. "Albee on Precipitous Heights (Two Arms are Not Enough)." In Matthew C. Roudané (ed.), *Public Issues, Private Tensions: Contemporary American Drama.* New York: AMS Press, 1993.

August W. Staub. "Public and Private Thought: The Enthymeme of Death in Edward Albee's *Three Tall Women.*" *Journal of Dramatic Theory and Criticism* 12.1 (Fall 1997), pp. 149–158.

INDEX

absurdism 3, 4, 10, 16, 17, 27, 30, 41, 140,
    163, 179, 181, 201
adaptation 4, 5, 10, 128–140, 236–237
Adler, Thomas P. 6, 9, 136
Agee, James 240
Albee, Edward
    autobiographical resonances in plays of 8,
        19, 24, 26, 28, 86–87, 101–102, 103,
        105–106, 143, 158, 162, 179, 241
    as director 6, 7, 11, 17, 117, 142, 154,
        164–177, 233, 247, 248
    early career of 2–3, 16
    as experimentalist 4–5, 49, 87–88,
        108–109
    as interviewee 11, 167–168, 217
    as playwriting teacher/mentor 4, 7, 125
        n.2, 249
    reputation of 1, 5, 6–8, 127, 148
    writing process of 166, 168–170, 233–234
Albee, Edward F. II (adoptive
    grandfather) 11, 178–179, 182, 185,
    195
Albee, Frances Cotter (adoptive mother) 2,
    8, 26, 86, 101–102, 103, 105–106, 241
Albee, Reed (adoptive father) 26, 101, 179
All Over 5, 6, 10, 27, 76, 91–92, 94–96,
    101, 105, 186, 222–223
Alley Theatre, Houston 150, 164–165, 174,
    175
Almeida Theatre, London 8, 158, 192, 231
American Dream, The 16, 24, 26, 27–33, 34,
    35, 43, 44, 60, 66, 88, 101, 118–119,
    131, 138, 164, 179, 183, 217, 235
animals 21–22, 77–78, 199–200, 202–205,
    207–211, 214
Another Part of the Zoo 231
Aristotle 205
Artaud, Antonin 12, 50–51, 181, 185

Ashcroft, Peggy 247
Auden, W. H. 120–121

Baldwin, James 33
Ballad of the Sad Café, The 4, 10, 128,
    129–133, 136, 137, 144, 237
Bancroft, Anne 162, 232
Baraka, Amiri 4
Barber, Samuel 240
Barnes, Clive 142–143, 145, 203–204
Barr, Richard 4, 7, 41, 238
Barthes, Roland 128
Bartleby 146 n.4
Baudrillard, Jean 13
Beat generation 3, 19–20, 25
Beck, Julian 50
Beckett, Samuel 3, 17, 27, 37 n.21, 39, 49,
    58 n.21, 83, 84, 94, 104, 108, 112, 118,
    124, 140, 152, 161, 164, 165, 167, 181,
    191, 228, 232, 242, 244–245, 248
Bennett, Robert 24
Bentley, Eric 181
Ben-Zvi, Linda 11
Berger, John 209–210
Bigsby, Christopher 10–11, 17, 69, 92, 131,
    186, 201
Billington, Michael 204
Billy Rose Theatre 41
Bloom, Harold 44
Bogosian, Eric 145
Bottoms, Stephen 10, 48
Box 5, 10, 16, 21, 47, 87–88, 91, 92, 101,
    108–109, 112, 114–115, 123, 124, 158,
    161, 165, 186
Brantley, Ben 204
Braun, Pinkas 35
Breakfast at Tiffany's 146 n.4
Brecht, Bertolt 235

259

INDEX

CAMBRIDGE COMPANIONS TO LITERATURE

The Cambridge Companion to Tom Stoppard
edited by Katherine E. Kelly

The Cambridge Companion to
Herman Melville
edited by Robert S. Levine

The Cambridge Companion to Nathaniel
Hawthorne
edited by Richard Millington

The Cambridge Companion to Harriet
Beecher Stowe
edited by Cindy Weinstein

The Cambridge Companion to
Theodore Dreiser
edited by Leonard Cassuto and Claire
Virginia Eby

The Cambridge Companion to Willa Cather
edited by Marilee Lindemann

The Cambridge Companion to
Edith Wharton
edited by Millicent Bell

The Cambridge Companion to Henry James
edited by Jonathan Freedman

The Cambridge Companion to
Walt Whitman
edited by Ezra Greenspan

The Cambridge Companion to
Ralph Waldo Emerson
edited by Joel Porte and Saundra Morris

The Cambridge Companion to
Henry David Thoreau
edited by Joel Myerson

The Cambridge Companion to Mark Twain
edited by Forrest G. Robinson

The Cambridge Companion to
Edgar Allan Poe
edited by Kevin J. Hayes

The Cambridge Companion to Emily
Dickinson
edited by Wendy Martin

The Cambridge Companion to
William Faulkner
edited by Philip M. Weinstein

The Cambridge Companion to Ernest
Hemingway
edited by Scott Donaldson

The Cambridge Companion to
F. Scott Fitzgerald
edited by Ruth Prigozy

The Cambridge Companion to
Robert Frost
edited by Robert Faggen

The Cambridge Companion to
Ralph Ellison
edited by Ross Posnock

The Cambridge Companion to
Eugene O'Neill
edited by Michael Manheim

The Cambridge Companion to
Tennessee Williams
edited by Matthew C. Roudané

The Cambridge Companion to
Arthur Miller
edited by Christopher Bigsby

The Cambridge Companion to
David Mamet
edited by Christopher Bigsby

The Cambridge Companion to
Sam Shepard
edited by Matthew C. Roudané

The Cambridge Companion to
Edward Albee
edited by Stephen Bottoms

CAMBRIDGE COMPANIONS TO CULTURE

The Cambridge Companion to Modern
German Culture
edited by Eva Kolinsky and
Wilfried van der Will

The Cambridge Companion to Modern
Russian Culture
edited by Nicholas Rzhevsky

The Cambridge Companion to Modern
Spanish Culture
edited by David T. Gies

The Cambridge Companion to Modern
Italian Culture

edited by Zygmunt G. Barański
and Rebecca J. West

The Cambridge Companion to Modern
French Culture
edited by Nicholas Hewitt

The Cambridge Companion to Modern
Latin American Culture
edited by John King

The Cambridge Companion to
Modern Irish Culture
edited by Joe Cleary and Claire Connolly